"WRITES WITH AUTHORITY.
AND WELL HE MIGHT . . .
HE WAS THERE."

—*Houston Chronicle*

"Arch Whitehouse contends that air combat of World War I was a much more highly skilled and individualistic affair than it came to be in subsequent wars. He gives tables showing the strength of the various forces and the number of planes destroyed and even by later standards they are impressive."

—*Library Journal*

"It is the injection of the personal narratives of the Sky Kings that makes the reader feel that he is firing the Hotchkiss, Lewis, and Vickers machine guns from the open cockpits. You live the pilot's life in the air."

—*Chicago Sunday Tribune*

THE
YEARS
OF THE
SKY
KINGS

BY ARCH WHITEHOUSE

CURTIS
BOOKS

NEW YORK, N.Y.

DEDICATED TO

*The thousands of unsung heroes of the
Allied air services who never saw their names in the
honours and awards lists.*

CONTENTS

Introduction by
   Maj. George Fielding Eliot   7

Foreword   11

1. How Air Fighting Began—1914   13

2. The Machine Gun Takes Wings—
   1915   41

3. The Zeppelin Killers—1915   69

4. The Year of Indecision—1916   105

5. The Year of the Sky Gods—1917   147

6. The Year of Tactical Aviation—
   1918   197

7. America's Great Contribution—
   1918   251

List of Allied and Enemy Aces—
   World War I   291

Conclusion   299

Glossary   305

Index   311

INTRODUCTION

☐ Since the days when Homer wrote of the heroes of the Trojan War, the battle-tales which have captured the imagination and held the interest of countless generations of readers and listeners have been those which were woven from the deeds of individual warriors—their courage, their address at arms, their unquenchable determination to excel.

These are the war stories that never grow old. Homer takes us back nearly 3,000 years, yet hardly a generation passes that some new romance is not woven round the martial strivings of Ajax, Hector, Achilles and the rest. The Knights of King Arthur's "Table Round" have been dust and their good swords rust for perhaps 1,400 or 1,500 years—yet it was barely yesterday that they lived again in an unusually successful Broadway production.

Of this same deathless breed were the "Sky Kings" of a mere fifty years or so ago of whom Arch Whitehouse—who was one of their gallant company—writes in these action-filled pages. We of the P.B.I.—("Poor Bloody Infantry") of that day used to look up enviously from our trench mud at the flicker of wings in the sky, and someone was sure to growl: "There he goes—on his way back to his snug billet, a hot dinner and a bed with sheets on it!" But for all our grousing, we were grateful just the same—for it was the fighter pilots who kept the Halberstadts and the Fokkers off our necks, who torched the balloons from which German artillery fire was directed on our trench lines, and who escorted the observation planes that brought us timely warning of enemy movements and directed the fire of our own guns. These and many other vital tasks they accomplished with an infinite variety of individual techniques. Many, it is true, became good team-fighters, but others—as our author tells us—were "lone wolves, with whom personal sky-prowling became instinctive." In this category the names of McCudden, Ball, Guynemer and Rickenbacker stand out in these pages, as in the ranks of the German airmen do those of Richthofen and Immelmann; and also the name of Werner Voss, son of a Jewish dyer of Krefeld, whom our author singles out as perhaps the most gallant of all the German aces. (We cannot help wondering whether that fact was ever brought to the attention of Adolf Hitler!)

Some pilots acquired a specialty—as did Frank Luke, the headstrong, undisciplined young Arizonian whose passion was setting fire to German observation balloons: a most dangerous business, since every such balloon was heavily protected by anti-aircraft weapons. Luke died as he had lived, fighting it out to the last beside his crashed plane—with one pistol against a platoon of German riflemen. He didn't know how to quit.

For all these young airmen of World War I, air war was the great challenge—the great unknown. They used their own methods at first, because there were no lessons of experience from which they could be taught: when the war began, perhaps 2,500 airplanes existed throughout the world, and not one of them was designed specifically for military purposes. The air warriors of 1914-18 had to create their own experience and learn its lessons as they went along—if they survived long enough. Many did survive, like our own Rickenbacker and the leading French ace, Captain René Fonck, who went through the whole war without taking a scratch while downing 75 enemy aircraft. Others—many others on both sides—died high in the wild blue yonder, or in flaming crashes. A few of the most noted died under circumstances which remain mysterious to this day.

The most useful of the "Sky Kings" were those who contributed something more than raw courage to the infant art of air warfare—men such as Billy Mitchell and Britain's "Boom" Trenchard. Our author shows us graphically how war in the air developed during these four years, laying the foundations for the next generation of air fighters who would have far more technology and far less hoop-la and hurrah in their battle experiences. Yet the pioneers who went aloft to war in planes with bamboo frames fastened together with piano wire left behind them a deathless tradition: the urge to excel, leading to the establishment of the title of "ace" as the ultimate reward of the fighter pilot. All through World War II and on into the Korean War, pilots who were becoming increasingly the servants of little black boxes rather than rugged individualists still strove to gain the five victories that admitted them to the ranks of the aces. In Korea, indeed, a new category arose—that of "jet ace," and we find pilots contriving to avoid relief and stick around a little longer when they had four victories to their credit and wanted just one more, exactly as their predecessors of World War I were wont to do.

This old doughboy, for one, is happy that his fellow veteran of that long-ago war of 1914-18 has brought together between two covers the stories of the men who fought the first air war of history and left to those who came after them a tradition which will not perish. "Their like," says our author, "we shall never know again." In a sense, that is true, for the conditions that they had to meet—all unprepared—we shall not know again. But there will be other conditions, other challenges of the unknown, which the young men of our generation and of future generations will face with equal courage and will overcome. Our astronauts are doing that today, and the challenge of the vast new frontier of interplanetary space has not yet even begun to be brought within the limits of human comprehension. That is what men were saying about the challenge of air warfare fifty years ago!

—Maj. George Fielding Eliot

FOREWORD

☐ Eleven short years after Orville Wright lifted his 12-horsepower biplane off the dunes of Kitty Hawk and gave the world its first aeroplane, a few men confirmed H. G. Wells' fantastic predictions by staging a war in the air over Flanders. This early conflict first employed flying machines of 50-70 h.p. Some were capable of speeds of 70 m.p.h. Such velocities seemed contrary to the accepted laws of physics, but, suitably stressed with piano wire and three-ply stiffening, these aircraft of bamboo and Irish linen held together long enough to establish this new method of warfare.

A few French Nieuports were armed with 37-mm. air cannon, and others went into action against observation kite balloons with strut pods of explosive rockets. Giant German dirigibles were bombing London and Paris. A British cruiser —H.M.S. *Furious*—had adopted a flight deck to accommodate naval aircraft already equipped with folding wings. The *Argus,* another cruiser, had been converted to a seaplane tender because giant flying boats (made in U.S.A.) and seaplanes were carrying out long-distance anti-submarine patrols.

The aeroplanes of World War I were capable of performing a very intricate pattern of manoeuvres and were armed with one or more machine guns that had an effective range of about 350 yards. The weapon fitted the flight pattern of the aircraft. Only such a machine armed with such weapons was capable of the true air duel or could battle effectively within the limited arena of the dogfight. As a matter of fact there were only three actual dogfights during the First World War and, while the term has been loosely used, there have been none since. The true dogfight is an air action in which 60 to 100 fighter aircraft are engaged within a very limited area.

Each side knew the other's weakness, blind spots and most efficient manoeuvres. Formations went into action with planned methods of attack and used prearranged tactics.

There were, of course, the individual stars, the lone wolves. In practically all cases their tactics were based on their personalities and the characteristics of their machines. Jimmy McCudden concentrated on two-seaters while flying at 20,000 feet—without oxygen. The Sunday-school boy and amateur violinist, Albert Ball, was a master stalker and generally attacked from below with a semi-flexible gun. America's Eddie Rickenbacker was a conservative but deadly strategist. Aflame with tuberculosis, Georges Guynemer was an unreasoning rocket who blindly attacked until the day he died, leaving the war's most fantastic legend. Baron Manfred von Richthofen killed with cold precision from the security of a well-drilled formation. Werner Voss, the son of a Jewish Krefeld dyer, was probably the most gallant of them all. Whatever their background or ambitions, the fighter pilots of World War I were distinctive personalities, and their like we shall never know again.

——Arch Whitehouse

1

HOW AIR FIGHTING BEGAN—

1914

☐ On the morning of October 27, 1918, the epic air battle of World War I was staged when Major William G. Barker, a British-Canadian fighter pilot, took on about sixty enemy aircraft and brought his score up to fifty-three victories before he himself was shot out of action. It was the most dramatic air contest of the war, for it pitted the finest fighter plane of the Allied services against a complete German *Jagdgeschwader* of the latest Fokker triplanes and D.7's. With the Armistice only two weeks away, it was a display of gallantry that marked the peak of Allied courage and military aircraft design.

Major Barker had served for many months on many fronts and, with his seven decorations, was finally rewarded with a supervisory post at a British air-fighting school. Previous to this he had spent considerable time on the Italian front and before assuming his new post he decided to find out what conditions and enemy tactics his pupils would be likely to encounter in France and Belgium.

To gain this experience he had himself posted temporarily to No. 201 Squadron of the Royal Air Force, which had just been equipped with the new Sopwith Snipe. This machine was the ultimate development of the rotary-powered fighter-scout peculiar to the period; it had a speed of 121 m.p.h., climbed to 10,000 feet in nine minutes, and fought with two fixed Vickers guns. The engine was the Bentley B.R.I., which had a maximum power output of 242 h.p. at sea level. As a fighting machine it was far superior to anything previously produced by the Allied or German aircraft manufacturers—as Major Barker was to prove.

On this particular morning Barker was scheduled to fly back to England to take up his Home Establishment duties. He had already delayed his departure in order to get in one more day's flying, but on the morning of the twenty-seventh he took off for Hounslow. The route home took him along the hottest sector of the whole front, where the German Flying Circus was still valiantly trying to stem the Allied tide, and it was in this area that Barker decided to stage his last offensive patrol.

As he flew parallel to the battle front he spotted a German two-seater well over on its own side of the line, flying at a very high altitude. German two-seaters of 1918 were particularly efficient at these thin-air levels, but Barker crossed over and attacked. The enemy gunner gave a good account of himself, but within a few minutes the two-seater was falling and throwing away its wings. At the same instant a Fokker triplane, one of the most successful German scouts of the day, attacked Barker. The first enemy burst smashed the Canadian pilot's right thigh, but Major Billy immediately put the Snipe into a tight attack turn and shot down the triplane in flames.

By the time this action was over a complete German circus composed of well over fifty triplanes and new D.7 biplanes had surrounded the wounded Snipe pilot. Barker probably knew he was on his last patrol, but he huddled down in his seat and decided to fight it out. His stand turned out to be a classic of air fighting.

Pencil lines of tracer bullets converged on him from all directions. Again and again the Snipe was spattered with lead, but the amazing aircraft continued to fly, and Barker fought on. A Fokker D.7 exploded before his guns and twisted earthward. Another followed it in short order. Meanwhile the Canadian pilot was whipping in and out of the enemy mass formation like an enraged hornet.

A new burst of Spandau fire shattered his other leg, but still Barker maintained control. Once, after a wild circuit, he fainted and, lacking human control, the Snipe went into a spin. The resultant rush of air revived him and he pulled out of the spiral to find another Fokker in front of him. He pressed the double triggers, and the enemy biplane went into the ground.

Then an explosive bullet shattered Barker's left elbow and he passed out again, but the sturdy Snipe continued to fly on its own until the pilot recovered once more and with a last supreme effort charged his assailants. A Fokker D.7 burst into flames, but a score of enemy bullets closed the Snipe's fighting career and it began to fall in a series of helpless sideslips and flutters. Eventually it piled up just inside British territory, where the unconscious pilot was rescued by a party of Scottish troops.

For this gallant fight in which he destroyed at least six enemy planes—and somehow survived—Major Billy Barker was awarded the Victoria Cross, the highest honour the Empire can bestow.

This particular air fight was the high point of the last few weeks of the war. It presented the skill and daring of a well-trained and experienced pilot who had an efficient military aircraft at his command. It was not typical of the whole war. It was a display that could be fought only after four years of aeronautical advance.

Air fighting was totally unlike this at the outbreak of the war on August 1, 1914. Many strange and wondrous events happened in the First Great War. It produced the greatest naval battle fought up to that time. Artillery advanced from the pop of light fieldpieces to a monster weapon that hurled shells 75 miles. It saw a front-line stalemate that took a war machine, cryptically known as a "tank," to pierce. Infantrymen wearing masks fought hand to hand in clouds of poison gas. Regiments that had gone to the front in 1914-15 with four machine guns as support equipment were eventually armed with thirty-six. Paradoxically, the entrenching tool became as vital a weapon as the hand grenade or the trench mortar.

Squadrons of proud cavalry were denied a vital part in this campaign. Their role was limited to prisoner escort, pioneer battalion grubbing, or odd assignments of ceremonial duty for the big brass in the safety of the rear areas. The flash of the sabre was no more.

But most important the First World War established the art of air fighting. It gave us the first war in the air. It took the aeroplane from the world's fair grounds and race tracks, where breathless thousands paid extravagant admissions to see "intrepid birdmen" loop the loop, fly simple circuits, or complete inter-city air races. There was a barnstorming period prior to World War I that often outraged international amity. Every time some headline-hunting fool took off to leap some new stretch of water or land mass, the newspapers loaded their galley forms with prepared charges and countercharges of international intrigue, sabotage, and unsportsmanlike conduct that often reached the attention of the Department of State or the Foreign Office.

Nevertheless, these contests resulted in some improvement of the breed. Bicycle undercarriages were replaced by equipment designed expressly for heavier-than-air craft. Engines graduated from the "adapted" motor-car plant, and guy wires were flattened to offer less resistance. A French aviator named Bonnier had bolted together an all-steel Voisin that had hand brakes on the wheels. Sporting-type airmen engaged in speed, distance, and duration contests, while more militant types were offering newspaper editors fuzzy prints they swore were aerial photographs taken in the air at 1,000 feet! A few devilish wags simulated bomb dropping with oranges or paper bags of flour. One American birdman had his photograph taken holding a Lewis gun between his legs while seated on the lower wing of a Wright biplane.

During 1912 aeroplanes and airships took part in the Tripoli campaign of the Balkan war, but mainly for the interest of war correspondents and newsreel photographers. Dusty records also claim that a Wright biplane was used for scouting along the Mexican border early in 1914. Its reconnaissance value and active-service efficiency were deplorable—according to official Signal Corps records.

By the time the German cavalry invaded the territory of Belgium the aeronautical designers had produced approximately 2,500 aeroplanes not one of which had been created purely for military purposes. The only feature that concerned the military mind was that most of them could be dismantled and loaded aboard a general-service wagon in one hour.

The planes and licensed pilots of that day were as follows:

Country	Planes	Pilots
France	1000	1273
Germany	840	680
Great Britain	450	750
Russia	?	875
United States	100	252
Italy	?	600
Belgium	?	250
Austria	?	400

Only France boasted of a separate air force. Great Britain's Royal Flying Corps had just recently escaped from the control of the Royal Engineers. Its Naval Wing was "naval" only in that it flew aircraft that floated on the water, for the Royal Navy studiously ignored all this ridiculous flying business. In April 1918 these two orphan services fused and became the Royal Air Force.

The Imperial German Air Force was organized on paper in 1912. After the Wright brothers staged their historic flight in 1903, German military officials were probably the first to appreciate the aeroplane as a potential war machine. To encourage home designers, a very large sum was offered as prize money and to finance the building of aircraft and engines. Strangely enough, little came of this since most Germans were concentrating on lighter-than-air gasbags and were gazing in wonder at Count Zeppelin's famous dirigibles which were establishing new and amazing records all over Europe.

It was not until 1911 that an Austrian, Igo Etrich, produced a satisfactory design. Etrich had tried to sell his first models to his own government, but he suffered the same treatment that the Wrights experienced in their homeland. Later a German Secret Service operator got in touch with the Austrian, with the result that his "Taube" or Dove design was purchased outright by the Rumpler factory at Berlin-Lichtenberg. The government ordered Rumpler's to turn out twenty Taubes at once. Etrich took his money and was never heard of again.

These machines were the first of this popular Dove design —so called because of the wing form and their resemblance to a bird in flight. Eventually twenty factories produced various Taube types powered by either Arugs or Mercedes engines with speeds varying between 56 and 70 m.p.h. according to where they were made. The Rumpler model surpassed all others. On July 9, 1913, Linnekogel, chief pilot of the Rumpler factory, made an attack on the altitude record with a 100-h.p. Benz-engined Taube. He took off from Templehof Field in Berlin and landed later with a barograph showing a height of nearly 20,000 feet, an effort that played a great part in Rumpler's future plans, for the company designers aimed for height and a rapid rate of climb rather than forward speed. This decision was to make their photography and reconnaissance machines some of the most successful in the war.

In the spring of 1913 the German High Command placed orders for additional aircraft, half of which were to be biplanes, half monoplanes. The latter were practically all Taube types, while the biplanes were manufactured by Rumpler, A.E.G. (Allgemeine Elektricitats Gesellschaft of Henningsdorf, Berlin), Euler, L.V.G. (Luft Verhers Gesellschaft, Johannistal), A.G.O. (Aerowerke Gustav Otto, Johonnistal), and the D.F.W. (Deutsche Flugzeug Werke of Lindenthal). Twelve months later, when Germany was making active preparations for undeclared war, an army bill was passed granting

what was left of the original design prize and a further large
sum to the Imperial Air Service. More aircraft were ordered
and all old types replaced. A rider in all contracts stated that
all new machines were to have seats for a pilot and a passenger. They had to be entirely of German manufacture and
were to include bomb racks and fittings for an aerial camera.
No engines of less than 100 h.p. would be accepted, and a
minimum top speed of 65 m.p.h. and a flight duration of at
least four hours were mandatory.

Thus when the drums rolled, Germany's Air Force was far
ahead of any other belligerent nation. They had thirty-eight
Zeppelins or Schutte-Lanz dirigibles and more than eighty pilots. In heavier-than-air hangars they had eight hundred aeroplanes, thirty-six seaplanes, and a personnel of 2,600
mechanics.

The flying equipment was catalogued as follows:

WARPLANES OF GERMANY—1914

Make	Engines	Speed m.p.h.	Purpose
Albatros	Mercedes 100 h.p.	56	General
D.F.W.	Mercedes 100 h.p.	62	General
Gotha	Benz 100 h.p.	60	General
Goodekker	Mercedes 100 h.p.	60	General
Halberstadt	Mercedes 100 h.p.	68	General
Etrich	Argus 100 h.p.	56	General
Jeannin	Argus 100 h.p.	55	General
Rumpler	Mercedes 100 h.p.	70	General
Stahalz	Argus 100 h.p.	65	General
L.V.G. B2	Mercedes 100 h.p.	60	General
D.F.W. C	Mercedes 100 h.p.	80	General
Friedrichshafen FF.17	N.A.G. 135 h.p.	62	General
Friedrichshafen FF.27	N.A.G. 135 h.p.	60	General
Sommer	Gnome 80 h.p.	70	General

The Friedrichshafen FF. 17 was a tractor seaplane.
The Friedrichshafen FF. 27 was a pusher seaplane.

There was no segregation of aircraft for specified work,
and pilots flew any mission they were assigned, aboard any
machine available. In the beginning pilots were considered
mere chauffeurs and graded as N.C.O.s. The passengers or
observers were commissioned ranks, but later, when some
military prestige rubbed off, the N.C.O. pilots were elevated
to Leutnants (second lieutenants). Also officers from the first-

class cavalry regiments were transferring to the flying services in droves.

On August 14, 1914, the Imperial German Air Force struck its first blow when Leutnant Franz von Hiddeson flew to within a mile of Paris, dropped two 4-pound bombs on the suburbs of the city, and scurried home. Von Hiddeson became a "first" of sorts, for two weeks later he was shot down by a battery of anti-aircraft guns near the Bois de Vincennes, the first raiding airman to fall in the war.

Von Hiddeson was not the first German airman to go down, however. On August 24, while carrying out a scouting flight aboard an Aviatik, Pilot Unteroffizier (sergeant) Kausen was shot down by the British near Quesnoy. Another German airman, unnamed, was forced down in a 90-h.p. Mercedes Rumpler-Taube in British territory by Lieutenant H. D. Harvey-Kelley and his gunner, Sergeant Major Street. The machine was captured, but the crew somehow escaped.

It is generally agreed that throughout that war the pilots and observers of the German Air Force fought their British counterparts with a more or less friendly rivalry, but they attacked the French with something akin to animal hatred. For years these two nations had snarled and glared at each other, and the end of the feud is not yet in sight.

French military aeronautics can be traced back to 1870 when balloons were used during the Prussian siege of Paris to fly out important personages, for observation, bomb dropping, dispatch carrying, and even ammunition airlift. Ironically enough, it was against these balloons that the first true anti-aircraft guns were used. The Krupp factory designed and produced on demand the first high-angle gun which became the basic weapon for all anti-aircraft defences.

Early in 1910 the Aero Club of France advised the War Cabinet that the aeroplane had great possibilities in warfare. Three weeks later the French Air Service was formed, its first flying officer being a Lieutenant Cameron, who took his brevet on March 9, 1910. Again acting on the Aero Club's suggestion, the French Cabinet set up their first aerial manoeuvres in Picardy, and throughout 1911 flight exercises were held and experiments carried out with radio and artillery co-operation. In March 1913 a Naval Air Service was formed and some 160 aircraft, mainly Nieuport F.3A and Caudron types, were provided. The pilots were generally N.C.O. ex-sportsmen, who gave the service a tremendous boost.

France also showed the way in the development of flying

fields and before the war had laid out St. Cyr, Villacoublay, Pau, Juvisy-sur-Orge, Issy-les-Moulineaux, Le Bourget, Buc, and a naval station at Juan-les-Pins. St. Cyr was the principal testing and training station and it held that responsibility throughout the war simply because it was rough, difficult, and surrounded with hazards. The explanation was: "In case of war, pilots will have to use practically any open piece of ground; therefore they should be trained under circumstances as closely approaching war conditions as possible." In fact, St. Cyr was a pilot's nightmare, being entirely covered with tree stumps, small bushes, and hillocks. No one can accuse the French of not being thorough in their training plans. Each field had a fleet of motor trucks, two breakdown cars, and a steam traction engine for service and transport. The personnel were trained to dismantle the sheds and hangars and load them for moving within two hours.

When the great god Mars unloosed his bolts, French *Aviation Militaire* was as complete and ready an arm as any among the combatants. They had 830 aircraft in actual flying condition with 850 *military* pilots to fly them. The lighter-than-air arm had twenty-eight airships of various values and crews to maintain and man them.

Their aeroplanes were drawn from the twelve following types:

WARPLANES OF FRANCE—1914

Make	Engines	Speed m.p.h.	Purpose
Astra C.M.	Renault 70 h.p.	56	General
Blériot 11	Mono-Gnome 80 h.p.	75	General
Blériot 39	Le Rhone 60 h.p.	68	General
Blériot 43	Mono-Gnome 80 h.p.	78	General
Caudron G.2	Mono-Gnome 80 h.p.	76	General
Farman Longhorn	Renault 70 h.p.	85	General
Farman Shorthorn	Renault 70 h.p.	95	General
Morane-Saulnier	Mono-Gnome 80 h.p.	78	General
Morane-Saulnier	Mono-Gnome 80 h.p.	87	General
Nieuport Mono	Le Rhone 60 h.p.	85	General
R.E.P.	Le Rhone 60 h.p.	70	General
Voisin	Canton-Unne 140 h.p.	68	General

In comparison with the aviation equipment and training of France and Germany, the British Royal Flying Corps had no right in the war. On paper they claimed 450 planes and 750 pilots, but when war broke out early in August the best they could do was to assemble four skeletal squadrons. They had less than fifty machines that would fly. Under the command of Brigadier General Sir David Henderson, who had learned to fly at the age of forty-nine, the R.F.C. actually started for France on August 13—nine days after war was declared. Henderson's chief of staff was Acting Colonel F. Sykes, a Boer War veteran who had been floating about in free balloons since 1904. In 1911 he took his ticket on a Bristol biplane—presumably the early Bristol Bullet.

Some pre-war emergency plans had been drawn up and these stated that each squadron would be allowed three days to mobilize. On the fourth they were to proceed to Dover and over the next forty-eight hours were to "do a Blériot" and fly across the Channel to France. Their motor transport was to go by ship.

At this point history becomes very confused. Those who took part have stated that few planes actually made the over-water flight, but professional historians claim that practically all but one made the trans-Channel flutter safely. One plane crashed on taking off, killing Lieutenant R. R. Skene and Air Mechanic R. K. Barlow. Each pilot carried a revolver, field glasses, spare goggles, a water bottle, a small stove, biscuits, cold meat, a piece of chocolate, and some soup cubes. It was just as well as most of them spent the next few days and nights huddling against French haystacks awaiting the arrival of their transport and spare parts. Nos. 2, 3, 4, and 5 squadrons and a variegated outfit called an aircraft park went over first.

It was a real musical-comedy effort. No one had any idea where the war was or what uniforms the German soldiers would be wearing. They had no military maps of France or Belgium until M. Michelin, the famous tyre manufacturer, provided them with a few automobile road guides. These profusely illustrated charts were most interesting to auto tourists but of little use to aviators. Still they had to suffice for weeks and weeks. Later a London newspaper obliged with a few sheets of gaily coloured "war maps" which were being given away to subscribers as premiums.

The equipment assembly provided some burlesque situations. Blériot tails were bolted on Avro fuselages. Undercarriages designed for Morane Parasols were "bent a bit" and affixed to a B.E.8 aircraft. Engines intended for Farmans were blandly attached to R.E.2's—but everything seemed to fly. What didn't was hauled over by Channel packet steamer, unloaded, and towed through French streets to the nearest cow pasture and flown to the battle areas.

Nos. 2 and 4 Squadrons were equipped with B.E.2's. These machines were said to be Blériot-inspired—a real slur on M.

21

Blériot—and were registered as Blériot Experimental. They were manufactured at the Royal Aircraft factory at Farnborough. No. 3 squadron had a mixed bag of B.E.2's and Henri Farmans. Avros, Maurice Farmans, and B.E.8's, affectionately known as "Bloaters," were the mounts of No. 5 Squadron.

This heterogeneous collection took off at two-minute intervals and eventually arrived in France. One plane even got as far as the final destination—Amiens—the first night, and its pilot, Lieutenant H. D. Harvey-Kelley, got a severe reprimand for taking a short cut and arriving on French soil before his commander, Major J. C. Burke, formerly of the Royal Irish Regiment. Lieutenant R. M. Vaughn was forced down by engine trouble at Boulogne and was arrested by the French authorities and kept in confinement for a week. At any rate by August 16, Nos. 2, 3, and 4 squadrons left Amiens for Maubeuge, and four more casualties were suffered en route. Two Bloaters crashed.

Transport was composed mainly of borrowed furniture vans, commercial delivery vehicles, and one odorous tumbrel that had been used in the collection of garbage. A bright red truck was commandeered from a renowned provision firm and was used by No. 2 Squadron as its mobile service unit. During the retreat from Mons this gaudy vehicle was better than any electronic guidance system—for both sides! After all, it could be easily seen and it could travel almost as fast as the military aircraft it was serving.

The flying equipment was particularly prehistoric, much of it consisting of Maurice Farman Shorthorns and Longhorns, B.E.2 biplanes, a parasol-type Blériot only a few bolts removed from the contraption that had mastered the English Channel five years before, and some nebulous R.E. (Reconnaissance Experimental) aeroplanes of doubtful parentage and performance. The Farman Longhorn was a pusher biplane encumbered with a Wright elevator mounting which projected out in front on a pair of ski-like landing skids. In the rear was a tail assembly large enough to be employed as a billboard. The Shorthorn was equally ungraceful, but came minus the frontal grape-arbor equipment and had a simple monoplane tail.

The Farman brothers, who were responsible for these aeronautical creations, were the sons of a Mr. Richard Farman, British correspondent for the London *Daily Telegram* in Paris. Henri, Maurice, and Dick were all of English descent but were born in France and acquired French nationality.

Henri studied painting and was exceptionally good. Along with his brother Maurice he was also a champion tandem cyclist. Dick was an automobile nut and as early as 1896 had written a book about motorcars. Maurice devoted himself to astronomy, meteorology, and ballooning, but Henri was the first to take up aeroplane flying. In 1907 he bought a Voisin biplane and learned to fly at Issy-les-Moulineaux. He was still flying antiquated biplanes in 1937, doing wild cross-country flights with a tomboy daughter.

In 1908 Henri built a pusher biplane that captured some lucrative prizes for covering a few hundred kilometres under the watchful eye of the French Aero Club officials. In fact Henri is credited with several respectable records.

For a short time Maurice and Henri were induced to set up a shop in Bradford, England, to supply the British Army with equipment that would fly. Maurice did the drawing-board work, Henri built the machines, and Dick took over the business end of the project. At Bradford and at another factory they set up at Billancourt in France they turned out 1,084 of their bathtub pushers for the Royal Flying Corps. These aerial dreadnoughts stayed in the service until well into 1916. The Shorthorn biplanes of No. 4 Squadron, which arrived in France early in September of 1914, were the first active-service aircraft definitely armed for aerial combat. They were, indeed, armed with a Lewis gun, but unfortunately the machine would not leave the ground if a gunner was included in the pay load.

One of these old war birds turned up and actually flew again in the Old Crocks Parade of the 1936 R.A.F. display at Hendon, England. The effect was terrifying.

The engines available for R.F.C. airframes were mostly 50-, 70-, and 80-h.p. Gnome rotaries. There were a few 70-h.p. Renaults and a government factory product known as an R.A.F. (Royal Aircraft Factory) air-cooled engine. This monster had eight cylinders which "blew off in the order of firing"—according to one irrepressible gunner who served with me—and what was probably the world's most elaborate exhaust-pipe system.

The following is the inventory of the flying equipment taken to France by the R.F.C. in 1914:

WARPLANES OF GREAT BRITAIN—1914

Make	Engine	Speed m.p.h.	Purpose
Avro	Gnome 80 h.p.	70	General
B.E.2	R.A.F. 90 h.p.	62	General

B.E.8	R.A.F. 90 h.p.	65	General
Farman Shorthorn	Renault 75 h.p.	88	Reconnaissance
Farman Longhorn	Renault 75 h.p.	75	Reconnaissance
Blériot XI	Gnome 80 h.p.	66	Reconnaissance
Sopwith Tabloid	Gnome 80 h.p.	84	Scouting
R.E.5	R.A.F. 90 h.p.	62	Reconnaissance
R.E.7	R.A.F. 90 h.p.	68	Reconnaissance
Bristol Scout	Gnome 80 h.p.	89	Escort
Short Seaplane	Sunbeam 275 h.p.	90	Bombing

Most of the flying personnel were sportsmen fliers who had worked out some fraternal association with this new aviation arm, and when the call came they simply donned a double-breasted uniform, borrowed a motor-cycle, and rode around until they found a covey of aircraft. Many of the airmen were boisterous types who had been deprived of their motor-car licences because of frequent speed infringements, so they had taken to flying to avoid the frowns of the highway bobbies. Lieutenant W. B. Rhodes-Moorhouse, the first Britisher to win the Victoria Cross in the air, was such a culprit.

The observers and gunners were at first blindly selected from the ranks of mechanics or orderly-room officers if they were not otherwise engaged that day. None had had any air or gunnery training, their chief qualifications being the ability to load and fire a cavalry carbine, drop *fléchettes* (metal darts), and have jacket pockets that would accommodate two half bricks for dropping on unsuspecting enemy aircraft. One of Britain's finest war airmen, Major James McCudden, began his career in this way. It seems he knew how to load and fire a Parker shotgun.

While a few rollicking characters had considered the possibility of "having a go" at enemy aircraft with small arms of some sort, nothing deliberate or premeditated had been thought of. A Maurice Farman biplane of No. 3 Squadron had allegedly taken to the air carrying a Hotchkiss machine gun—but not for shooting purposes! It was simply an experiment in weight carrying.

There was nothing offensive in the way of aerial armament until scouting pilots noticed the air was becoming crowded. Everyone went about his business, checking the movement of troops, photographing the real estate, and wondering what the devil was burning down there.

Of course these idyllic conditions couldn't last forever. There is always some uncouth oaf who has to bespoil the sanctity of harmless routine patrols. As stated above, half bricks *were* tossed; lengths of rusty chain were flung; large lead weights dangled from lengths of wire with the idea of fouling some Rumpler's propeller. Another ill-mannered type amused himself firing a Webley pistol at passing Aviatiks. The Parker shotgun idea finally broke down the *entente cordiale* completely.

The Germans retaliated with rifle fire, and during the first week of the war a Lieutenant Waterfell was shot down and killed over Ath in Belgium. He was the first such casualty of the 7,589 who died in the British flying services during the more than four years of air action.

Then within a few days special clips to mount army rifles were fitted to all available aircraft. Air fights of varying decision were being reported from all fronts. In most cases the gunners or observers who manned these weapons sat in the front seats of the biplane types and as a result were somewhat handicapped in having to aim and fire through a network of struts, stays, flying wires, a whirling propeller, and fluttering wing tips. On several occasions over-anxious gunners shot their own struts away and returned to enjoy the concern of their squadron mates until the details of the self-inflicted escapade were revealed.

Towards the end of September two Bristol Scouts were delivered, one to No. 3 and one to No. 5 Squadron, both armed with a rifle on each side of the pilot's cockpit and set to shoot at an angle of 45 degrees to avoid hitting the propeller tips. Whether they ever went into action with any success has not been related.

Rifles, shotguns, and carbines gave the air crews some small measure of satisfaction, but the German aircraft were so superior in gaining and maintaining height that it was impossible for British or French planes to get at them. German Rumplers would be buzzing over the Allied areas while their observers drew maps, took photographs, or wrote out detailed reports, completely undisturbed. Frustrated British airmen floundered about 3,000 feet below, vainly shooting off carbines at the nosy jerries.

Since they couldn't vent their wrath on the enemy airmen above, the Britishers took it out on the ground troops below. Cardboard boxes of steel darts were poured over the side, and it was claimed that these missiles could drill a man from his skull to his crotch. Multipointed variations of these darts were dropped along roads to cripple enemy cavalry or transport horses. I never met anyone who ever admitted taking part in this kind of warfare, but I have seen boxes of the frightful devices.

There were several variations of aerial bombs during those early days. The first was a streamlined canister of gasoline

25

which was presumed to ignite on impact with the ground and was often used against German hangars and airship sheds. Another incendiary bomb was a simple can of explosive which was wrapped with sticky tarred rope. Burning rope was supposed to fly in all directions and do the arson job. Then there was a treacherous melinite shrapnel bomb, actually a converted French shell fitted with an unpredictable nose-striker. These would sometimes explode while being hung in the racks and eventually had to be discarded. Later parachute-braked bombs were tried, the parachute to delay the fall and give the airman a chance to escape from the explosion and debris. Some shell bombs were tied to the upper *longérons* with wrapping cord, and when the airman wished to release them over the target he used his pocket-knife.

The first real bomb raid was carried out against Brussels early in the war. All available R.F.C. aircraft took part, with each plane carrying six 20-pound bombs which were dumped over the occupied city. Several of the planes were damaged and had to land in Holland, but instead of being interned for the duration, the air crews signed on as ships' firemen in Rotterdam and worked their way back to England.

The former Naval Wing, now the Royal Naval Air Service, had something of an edge over the Royal Flying Corps. In the first place, what planes they had were of greater power and all were equipped with wireless sets. Furthermore, they began operations from their home bases. On the outbreak of the war R.N.A.S. squadrons took over many patrol duties along the coasts and escorted transports across the Channel. Once this routine work was well under way, the General Staff suggested they look into what they could do against hostile airfields and airship sheds. Britain was already anticipating the Zeppelin menace.

Around the middle of September, Wing Commander C. R. Samson, who boasted of being a "pirate," took his command over to Ostend to assist in the defence of Antwerp. While that city was being evacuated Flight Lieutenant Marix and Squadron Commander Spenser Grey, flying Sopwith Tabloids, set out to bomb the Zeppelin sheds at Düsseldorf. Grey ran into bad weather, so he dropped his bombs on the railroad station at Cologne. Marix, however, had a few 20-pound bombs and found Düsseldorf with ease. Going down to 600 feet, he let the lot go and scored a direct hit; the shed went up in flames and with it the brand-new Zeppelin Z-IX.

But the defence fire was heavy and Marix's Tabloid took a real beating, and he had to go down and land about 20 miles

26

from his base. Knowing the general situation, he sensed he had to move fast and, being a persuasive man, he swapped the shot-up Tabloid for a Belgian peasant's bicycle and rode home. Twenty-seven years later, almost to the day, Air Vice-Marshal Marix bombed and sank a German vessel in the Norwegian harbour of Aalesund.

When he wasn't flying, Wing Commander Samson bolted slabs of boiler plate on his Daimler touring car and drove around the occupied areas amusing himself as an armoured-car driver. The Germans immediately put a price on his head—dead or alive. Samson's antics gave an Admiralty official named Winston Spencer Churchill the first idea of the armoured tank.

After the evacuation of Antwerp the Royal Naval Air Service settled down at Ostend, but it still had militant ideas concerning the Zeppelin sheds. The main hangars at Friedrichshafen were practically in Switzerland, so they gained permission to use the French field at Belfort and from there four Avro planes of Samson's mob took off to blow up the dirigible hangars on Lake Constance. The actual attack was carried out on November 21. One Avro broke its tail off taxiing out and had to withdraw. The other three, led by a Commander Briggs, got away safely, and to avoid Swiss neutrality had to fly a crooked course that took them first to Mülhausen and then over the Black Forest to Schaffhausen. Here they turned southward to reach Lake Constance, a flight of about 125 miles, which was a real effort in those days. They flew over the lake at a height of 10 feet and went up to 1,200 feet on reaching the shed area. Anti-aircraft guns went into action, but all three, Commander Briggs, Flight Commander Babbington, and Flight Lieutenant Sipps, scored direct hits, and severe damage was done.

Briggs was shot down and badly mauled by German civilians and had to be rescued in a fainting condition by the military. Babbington and Sipps returned safely.

The fourth and last raid of 1914 was carried out against the Zeppelin sheds at Cuxhaven on Christmas Day, and this time the attacking force consisted of both land and seaplanes with naval destroyer and submarine support. The object of this raid was not only to bomb the airship hangars but to gain information on the strength of the German Navy at Wilhelmshaven and in the Schilling Roads. By 6 a.m. on Christmas morning the force had reached a position 12 miles north of Heligoland. An hour later seven of the nine seaplanes were put over the side and took off. By 10 a.m. three of the British seaplanes had returned safely; the other four had been shot down, but three crews were rescued by the submarine E.11 while close to Norderney Gat. These proceedings were watched by a Zeppelin which manoeuvered to drop bombs where they would do the most good. They fell a few seconds after the last airman had been hauled aboard and the sub crash-dived to 40 feet. The fourth crew was picked up by a Dutch trawler and was interned for some time in Holland.

The sheds at Cuxhaven were not found, but the raid was not entirely wasted as the R.N.A.S. observers came back with a very comprehensive picture of the German harbours and roadsteads. Seven battleships, three cruisers, and a number of other warships were identified.

Meanwhile on the continent the R.F.C. and the German Air Force were developing the rivalry and competition that were to mark their activities over the next four years. Musketry was exchanged whenever possible, and each day provided new variations of war in the air. Among the first of the British casualties was a Sergeant Major Jillings, who was flying as an observer with Lieutenant Noel. Jillings was credited with actually downing a German two-seater Albatros with a single rifle bullet, but on the way home from his success someone on the ground took a shot at Jillings and hit him "where he sat down." According to official reports, the sergeant major had to be assisted out of the machine, but later he went on to glory, became a squadron leader, and was awarded the Military Cross.

During this time the German army under von Kluck was storming across eastern Belgium and north-east France practically unopposed. The French army had consumed two weeks getting mobilized and only the heroic delaying actions of the Belgians held the Germans in check. During August the field-grey hordes had practically encircled Paris, and Britain's little army had been shoved to the area around Meaux. It looked like a walkover for the Germans.

Britain's air squadrons were scattered about between Amiens and Compiègne. The toughest battles they fought whenever they landed on any stretch of open farmland were with outraged French peasants. The rustics mistook them for the enemy and usually made gallant pitchfork attacks before asking questions. The result was the British decided to identify their aircraft by painting Union Jacks on the wing tips. Later this insignia was simplified by daubing on a design of red, white, and blue roundels. The French reversed the British sequence of colours, making the outer circle red and the inner spot blue. Out of that simple precautionary measure came the first military aeroplane insignia. Before 1914 was ended the Germans selected their Iron Cross design—each airman hoping he would one day be awarded the coveted honour.

During the opening period of the campaign the R.F.C. often found themselves further ahead than their infantry. On several occasions No. 3 Squadron had to stand by with loaded rifles resting against the undercarriages while they made routine repairs. Once a patrol of Uhlans was driven off just as the last of the squadron's motor transport was being cranked up to move out.

Late in August the Germans began using kite balloons, and the first report on these captive sausages resulted in some understandable amusement.

"Several Zeppelins seen zooming over Maubeuge," one young mechanic-acting-observer scribbled on his patrol report.

Later he amended the statement and explained, "Well, after all, they looked as though they were zooming. They had their noses stuck up in the air. How was I to know?"

Anti-aircraft gunnery—particularly from the German side —was not to be taken lightly. The Krupp factory had produced a very good high-angle weapon, and with targets of limited altitude they kept the British and French airmen busy darting in and out of sheltering cloud layers.

Americans have long been puzzled by the British term "Archie" which was applied to enemy anti-aircraft fire. This is how Archie came into being. Back in London the famous comedian George Robey had been singing a rather risqué ballad in a musical comedy which was being whistled and sung by all the playboys haunting London's theatre district. The various choruses always ended with the words, "Archibald, certainly *not!*"

Many of those playboys were now in action with the R.F.C., and whenever a jerry shell burst uncomfortably close the British pilot would raise one hand in remonstrance, assume the George Robey leer, and exclaim, "Archibald, certainly *not!*" This soon became "Archibald!" and with the weeks the catch phrase was eventually whittled down to the single word "Archie." During World War II the more ominous term "flak" replaced it—but that was a more ominous war.

Regardless of the apparent ragtime behaviour of Britain's air arm, they were doing an amazing job of observation and reconnaissance. So well, in fact, that on August 22 Sir John French held a conference at Le Cateau with General Lanrezac, commander of the 5th French army, and decided to fight a defensive action and hold on for at least twenty-four hours. R.F.C. reports had given a reliable hint that von Bülow was massing across the Sambre River and that an enveloping movement was expected from Grammont. The next day the Battle of Mons was fought along a twenty-five-mile front. Allied artillery was on hand—but they had no shells—so all available planes of the Royal Flying Corps flew unceasingly, marking enemy movements and locating enemy batteries. That night the retreat began, and for the next nine days R.F.C. pilots and observers were in the air almost continuously, writing a gallant chapter to the history of that glorious military movement that was to save Paris and the French Army.

The outstanding hero of this "Eyes of the Army" air service was second Lieutenant William Bernard Rhodes-Moorhouse of No. 2 Squadron. He was the first of nineteen British airmen to win the Victoria Cross. Prior to the outbreak of the war Rhodes-Moorhouse had been a devil-may-care young man and his driver's licence carried many red-ink citations because of his disregard for his neck on the public highways. Since moody officialdom frowned on such motoring, this slim athletic character with the toothbrush moustache turned to civilian flying at Brooklands. Being the experimental type, he had often speculated on what would happen if one zoomed an aeroplane steeply and then shut off the engine.

Would it come back and do a sort of tail slide? he wondered.

He tried it, and the plane slid back on its tail, driving his onlookers into nearby cellars. However, William Bernard managed to recover in time and another stunt was added to the primitive book of aerobatics.

He had been flying for two years before he bothered about applying for an official certificate, his theory being that if you consorted with officialdom you were likely to come under its ridiculous jurisdiction. He simply wanted to fly and damn the red tape. However, he took his pilot's certificate in October 1911 and by then was considered a first-class cross-country pilot. In 1912 he finished third in Britain's Aerial Derby and afterward established a record by carrying two passengers across the English Channel in an ancient Bréguet. He enlisted in the Royal Flying Corps when war was declared and was posted to Farnborough, where he fretted and stewed until March 1915. He then joined No. 2 Squadron at Merville and immediately began active-service patrols.

During the Second Battle of Ypres on April 26—a few

days after the first poison-gas attack—a message was received from Air Headquarters that the Courtrai railroad junction and station were to be bombed at all costs. German reinforcements were said to be pouring through the station. With a hole 2 miles wide in front of Ypres, where the Allies had been driven out by chlorine gas, the situation was most precarious.

Four aircraft—presumably B.E.2's—were assigned the job, but only Rhodes-Moorhouse succeeded in getting to the target. He was carrying a 100-pound bomb slung between his wheels and before take-off was told to use his own discretion as to how low he would go in for the attack. He went in at 300 feet, bombed the station, and scored a direct hit on the all-important signal box. He could have zoomed into the smoke and cleared off, but instead he circled and circled the area, picking up all the information possible. What he saw convinced him that Ypres was in for a rough time.

(It is a historical fact that Germany's failure to get reserves into the poison-gassed area in time completely sacrificed what initial surprise the gas attack had established.)

During the minutes that Rhodes-Moorhouse was over the Courtrai area he came under heavy rifle and machine-gun fire, but he continued to "spot" the enemy. Then a bullet went through the fingers of his left hand, so he decided to head home. Flying low over the city, he roared past the belfry of a Courtrai church. The Germans had set up a machine gun in that tower, and as Rhodes-Moorhouse buzzed past, a savage burst caught him cold. One bullet smashed his thigh and another tore through his stomach. His base was 30 miles away, and below were many suitable landing areas where he might have dropped down and requested medical assistance, even though he was well inside enemy territory. But he thought only of the hordes of Germans moving toward the Courtrai station that might make the difference between hanging on or losing the war at Ypres. The General Staff should know of this concentration—and the fact that he had damaged the signal box.

No one knows what Rhodes-Moorhouse suffered over those 30 dreadful miles. Once he was inside his own lines, he did not land but flew on to the rear area and dropped down near the British headquarters. There he huddled in his bullet-torn plane and dictated his report to an infantry officer and then added before he fainted: "I didn't want them to get my machine. It's not too badly bashed about, is it?" He died in the hospital twenty-four hours later without ever knowing he had been recommended for the Victoria Cross. In his citation someone had written, "The bomb he dropped perhaps did more definite service on a great scale than any bombs released during the war, but his last act set a standard of courage which others may hope to equal but can never excel."

Throughout the late months of 1914 both sides had come to realise the value of aerial reconnaissance. It was obvious that some means and methods of defence would have to be established. If there were a pilot and observer in the air, the way to eliminate them was to destroy the aircraft. So far anti-aircraft had assumed the brunt of aerial defence, but more direct action was necessary. Young airmen with warlike instincts were still vainly attempting to destroy enemy aircraft by gunfire and other missiles. As previously stated, they tried everything from pocket pistols to duck guns, but, after all, such popgun efforts were only outlets for personal frustration. But if a machine gun with its rapid rate and cone of fire could be hauled aloft, something productive might be established.

A Lieutenant Louis A. Strange deserves the accolade for first taking a machine gun into action aboard an aeroplane. Strange was an English lad of Dorset parentage, schooled at Oxford, and, to keep out of mischief, had served some Saturday-afternoon Territorial time with the Dorsetshire Yeomanry.

In the piping times of peace, yeomanry were fresh-air mounted infantry organisations held in readiness in case another Boer War broke out. Their ranks were made up of country gentlemen who served as officers, providing their own horses, and a slew of urban types who groomed all the nags and swanked about the country pubs wearing bandoleers, breeches, and spurs. It was harmless fun prior to 1914, but when the drums rolled that summer, the yeomanry turned out to be a deadfall for those who had hoped "to serve."

Louis Strange had teethed on H. G. Wells and the flaming editorials of Charles G. Grey, editor of Britain's famous aeronautical journal, *The Aeroplane*. As a result he was not entirely sold on the old cavalry concept and during their bosky-dell exercises he often denounced the ridiculous antics his weekend troopers were asked to perform.

"These are Boer War manoeuvres," he argued. "What the devil good is all this? If we ever get into a flare-up with the Germans, cavalry will be about as useful as a platoon of Girl Guides!"

How right he was. I myself had worked my way over to Britain on a cattle boat in 1914 and had fallen for the yeomanry. Those bandoleers and spurs mouse-trapped me, and I was months wangling my way out in order to become a gunner on an old pusher biplane.

In time Lieutenant Strange talked himself clean out of the yeomanry and started buying lessons at so much an hour at Hendon. After two more copies of *The Aeroplane* he obtained a transfer into the Royal Flying Corps and was sent to their Central Flying School. By the time the Germans were roaring through Belgium, Strange was one of that small number who flew across the Channel and headed for Amiens.

But so what? The aeroplane was just a winged cavalry mount. For ten days or so Lieutenant Strange fluttered about looking for German troops and German ground activity. The war-in-the-air theory was only in books. No one did any fighting in the air. They were just looking.

Strange's observer, Lieutenant Penn Gaskell, was another warlike lad. They flew in a Farman, one of those pusher machines with a nacelle or cockpit wired in between the upper and lower wings. In the back was a 75-h.p. Renault engine that twirled a wooden propeller, and the seating arrangements were such that the pilot sat in the front and his observer huddled in what space was left between Mr. Strange and the engine.

"Now a machine gun——" Penn Gaskell remarked early one morning.

"My view completely," Strange agreed, and they poked around among odd boxes in the Squadron Stores. They told no one of their plan and had to smuggle the Lewis gun covered in burlap to their battleplane and hide it in Gaskell's rear office.

All this took place on August 22, 1914, and a German Rumpler obliged by appearing over Maubeuge. Strange and Penn Gaskell exchanged winks and began a nonchalant saunter toward their line-up of planes. They'd show this German blighter on which side his bread was buttered.

Unfortunately Messrs. Strange and Gaskell had not made a careful computation of their load, and in spite of Strange's best efforts and their combined programme of profanity, the old Farman could not be persuaded to fly any higher than 3,500 feet. Unaware of the fate that had been planned for them, the German airmen simply buzzed about at 5,000 feet, probably wondering what that horrid contraption was doing 1,500 feet below. They were perfectly satisfied with their lot. They were booking a few more air hours in their log—and how they hoarded their air time in those days!

We should add that Penn Gaskell *did* fire a short burst at

the Rumpler, but the roar and vibration of the weapon so startled Pilot Strange that he yanked the gasping Farman into a steep zoom and almost flipped Penn Gaskell out of the nacelle. With that he decided to return to earth, breathing a silent prayer of thanks that they were still intact.

"The thing went off like a bloody Jack Johnson," Strange admitted later.

When their commanding officer learned of this noisy experiment he ordered Penn Gaskell to return the weapon to Stores. "If you two must stir up strife in the air, please use a rifle. Machine guns are for the infantry, not aeroplanes!" he expounded.

Very little was heard of Penn Gaskell after that, but Strange, apparently made of sterner stuff, carried on and finished the war with a double row of decorations and a lieutenant-colonelcy.

While flying a Martinsyde scout with No. 6 Squadron in May of 1915, Strange inadvertently provided the front line with a hair-raising performance. He was cruising around at 8,500 feet when he spotted an Aviatik from a German Staffel located outside Lille. As usual, the German outclimbed him, and the enemy observer peppered Strange with his Parabellum gun. He decided to retaliate with the Lewis gun bolted to his top plane, but nothing much happened even though he had sprayed the sky with a full drum.

The next problem was to replace the ammunition pan, and to do this the British pilot had to loosen his seat belt, try to hold the stick between his knees, and reach up high to get at the drum's release latch. The Martinsyde went up into a stall as he struggled to remove the drum. Before he could drop back into his seat, the British scout went over on its back and Strange went out of the cockpit.

"I felt like a fool," he explained later. "I had been swearing because I couldn't get the damn drum off and now I was praying that it would stay on!"

The scout was on its back, Strange was hanging free of his cockpit and was clinging to the machine gun's ammunition pan. Its sharp edge was cutting his fingers badly, and he tried to wriggle so he could grab a rear centre-section strut. All this time the Martinsyde was in a flat upside-down spin and circling over the German trenches. Exactly where the aeroplane was in relation to himself was something of a puzzle. His chin was practically resting against the gun drum and his legs were somewhere outside.

"I finally grabbed a centre-section strut and felt more comfortable. Below I could see Menin twirling around and naturally wondered where I would crash, but I kept kicking upward until at last I got one foot hooked inside the cockpit. I took a second or two to get my breath and finally got the other foot anchored."

Getting most of his body inside, Strange kicked the aileron over, which eventually righted the machine. He then dropped down with a plop and went straight through his wicker seat and found himself practically sitting on the floor of the aircraft. While he had been dangling outside the plane he had lost his seat cushion and everything else not nailed down. The engine, which had stopped when the machine was on its back, suddenly caught again and the Martinsyde was diving like a banshee for Menin Wood. When he tried to pull the stick back to level off, he found that the broken seat frame had jammed it completely and so spent a few anxious seconds clearing out the debris. Once he had zoomed over the tree tops and levelled off, he discovered he had kicked all the instruments out of his panel. However, he was so delighted to discover himself alive, he didn't bother about the niceties of flight and found his field at Abeele with no trouble at all.

Some years later, while on a friendly tour of Germany, Strange became acquainted with a former German Staffel leader named von Leutzer, who remembered this amazing incident.

"We reported that fight, but no one would believe us when we explained that the pilot had gone down, hanging from his wing gun while the plane was flying on its back," von Leutzer laughed.

"What about me? I don't think I ever really convinced my C.O. how I had kicked all my instruments out," Strange ruefully remarked.

The humorous incident which involved Penn Gaskell did not end machine-gun experiments. Gun "racks" were fitted to British Moranes in February 1915, and the gunners, who sat in the front sea, were expected to fire through a maze of flying wires and struts. It was somewhat like fighting from inside a bird cage.

We know now that military aircraft had to grow up before machine guns could be included in their load. Practically all 1914 airplanes were two-seaters, designed to carry a pilot and an observer. This was generally the limit of their capacity, and if a bomb was carried the observer was left behind. By the same token, machine guns with their drums, spare parts, and mounts could total something like 75-90 pounds, so unless the observers were ex-jockeys or flyweight boxers, mounting machine guns was out of the question.

The idea of a single-seater fighter had not yet been seriously considered. In the first place, no one had dared to presume that one man could fly anything so intricate as an airplane *and* fire a machine gun. It was assumed, of course, that the gun would be flexible and aimed in any general direction. Only two men in the whole aviation world were studying the possibility of a machine gun becoming a fixed feature of an aircraft. The weapon would have to be set within reach of the pilot—somewhere beside or in front of him. Thus mounted, it would be firing straight ahead and the pilot *could* direct his whole machine at the enemy target.

But how would the bullets get past the whirling blades of the propeller?

The British gave it a try by sticking a stripped-down Lewis gun on a Goldbergian bracket high on the plane top so the bullets would pass over the whirling propeller tips. It worked after a fashion, but, like Lieutenant Strange, the pilot couldn't remedy stoppages or change the ammunition drums. The gun was out of reach.

Next they tried mounting the gun beside the pilot where it was handy for stoppages or reloading, but the weapon had to be mounted at an angle in order to clear the propeller blades. To attack an enemy target the pilot had to go into action flying crabwise!

Since most early two-seaters had been designed for the pilot to use the rear seat, the observer or gunner was cramped under the centre section. It was some time before the B.E. and R.E. types were revamped to place the observer in the back seat. Then he was provided with a couple of metal pegs on which to swivel a gun and at least protect his own tail. Air action under these conditions were all broadside engagements, and deflector sights had to be designed to "lead" the target before passing aircraft could be shot at.

In the beginning, then, because opposing airmen seldom encountered each other during observation patrols, there was very little justification for the employment of machine guns. When 1915 dawned, the revolver and carbine were still general armament on both sides. Nevertheless, a surprising number of aircraft were shot down during those early days. In February 1915 a Morane Parasol—a monoplane with the wing mounted high on a bracket above the fuselage—flown by Second Lieutenant V. H. N. Wadham with Lieutenant A. E. Borton as his observer, fought an air duel with an Aviatik biplane near Merville.

The German gunner opened rifle fire at long range and the pilot used a pistol, but the Britons conserved their ammunition until they were within 100 yards of the Aviatik. Borton then went into his "fifteen rounds rapid," and they could see his bullets splintering the German fuselage. Suddenly it dived and was seen to force-land 2 miles from its field outside Lille. When the Morane returned it was discovered it had a bullet through its propeller and two more through its wings.

Meanwhile haphazard engagements were reported. On August 29, 1914, a German Aviatik dropped three bombs on the R.F.C. field at Compiègne and managed to elude several British machines that set out to overtake it. In October the Germans began their bombing in earnest. A special squadron was formed at Ghistelles as Battle Squadron No. 1, but became known more familiarly as the Ostend Carrier Pigeons. Its first mass raid was carried out against Dunkirk, probably the first formation flight of the war. One machine from this squadron made a raid on Dover on December 21 but for some unknown reason dropped its load of bombs into the sea. Still another appeared over Sheerness on Christmas Day but was forced to flee from a patrol of R.N.A.S. planes that chased it out to sea.

During the first five months of the war the German airmen claimed the destruction of ten enemy planes and an additional seventeen claimed as "out of control."

In those same five months German manufacturers had produced some 1,350 service aircraft—a remarkable achievement for that period.

The early aviation records of the French Air Service are very meagre. France had the only independent air force and a very respectable amount of aircraft and pilots, but she failed to compete in the matter of mobilization. Nothing much happened with the French Air Force for several weeks except that, like the British, they had to fight their own people (farmers and infantrymen) more than they did the Germans. Anyone with a gun took pot shots at *anything* that flew.

Adolph Pegoud, the flying Frenchman who has always been credited with originating the loop-the-loop, was the outstanding performer along the French front. Actually it was a Russian named Nestoff who managed the loop feat in an early Nieuport, but it was Pegoud who made a general habit of it. He had transferred from the artillery some time before the beginning of the war because he believed that someone ought to design more efficient aircraft for the military. He did the best he could, but war soon hauled him out of the mock-up sheds and sent him roaring out over the heads of the German

37

invaders. For weeks he was a veritable hellion, pouring darts on moving troops, bombing horse transport, and actually going as far as the Rhine to drop impudent handbills.

He became the idol of France with cocktails and cigars named in his honour and soon sported the Legion of Honour and the *Médaille Militaire*.

However, in August 1915, Pegoud took on a great formation of German planes and fought until he ran out of fuel. Weeks later the French sought his grave when the Germans had been pushed back. Villagers who had remembered where Pegoud fell pointed out a crude wooden cross, but when the grave was opened to remove the French hero's body to Paris it was discovered that the occupant wore a British uniform. Pegoud's resting place was never found.

Another French air hero of this early period was Georges Madon, who scored forty-one official victories. He was born at Bizerte, Tunis, and sent to Paris to finish his schooling. Instead he joined *L'Aviation Militaire* and lived to see the war to its conclusion. He enlisted in 1911 and learned to fly an old Blériot 39. When war began Corporal Pilot Madon was posted to Escadrille Blériot, stationed at Soissons, and after the trial-and-error programme of the early weeks had his first great adventure. While he was flying an observation mission his machine was hit by an artillery shell which lodged in his fuselage. Fortunately it failed to explode and Madon just managed a landing before the tail booms buckled, collapsing the whole machine.

Next he was transferred to a Farman Shorthorn squadron and soon stirred up more trouble for himself. While on a reconnaissance patrol he became hopelessly lost, and when the tank went dry he landed, but unfortunately he had selected neutral territory near Berne, Switzerland, and Madon and his observer, Sergeant Chattelain, were soon interned. The two Frenchmen made half a dozen attempts to escape and on one occasion were actually crossing the Italian frontier when they were caught. Nine months later they were contacted by a French agent and new plans were made for freedom. Late one night the agent chloroformed the guard and led them to a waiting motorboat, and they were rushed to safety. Their return to France was not rewarded with a hero's welcome, however. Instead they were court-martialled for the violation of neutral territory and the loss of a French machine. Madon was sentenced to sixty days of solitary confinement while his observer received sixty days' ordinary imprisonment.

By May of 1916 Madon was back in good graces again and

joined Morane-Saulnier Squadron No. 218 and went on to fame.

Another Frenchman they couldn't kill was the famous Armand Pinsard. He had joined the French cavalry in 1905 and and won the *Médaille Militaire* in 1913 for his daring flights year was out. He transferred to the aviation service in 1912 and won the *Medaille Militaire* in 1913 for his daring flights made during the Picardy exercises of that year.

Three days after the war started Pinsard was assigned to a Morane squadron and was awarded eight citations for exceptional courage and devotion to duty. Once he flew home 40 miles with a shattered wing. On October 22 he was forced to land behind the German lines with oiled-up spark plugs. He calmly spent the next hour cleaning the plugs and then, swinging his own propeller, he just managed to get off as a troop of Death's Head Hussars came charging through a hedge. He was given the *Croix de guerre* for that.

Then in February 1915 while on a long-distance mission he was shot down by rifle fire. He crash-landed in German territory, shattered two ribs, and received a severe concussion. Any sane observer would have figured that Pinsard's war career was over. He was in a hospital for five weeks and was then moved into a prisoner-of-war camp. Within three weeks after that he had made two attempts to escape but was recaptured and put in solitary confinement. Undaunted, he made twelve more attempts, once getting to within 2 miles of the Dutch border when he was caught by a party of farmers. For this he was sent to the "escape-proof" Prinz Karl Fortress at Ingolstadt late in 1915. Three more months went by before another opportunity presented itself. On March 26, 1916, Pinsard and a Captain Meynard dug their way through a wall 12 feet thick and had a six-hour start before an alarm was raised. The experiences they went through over the next three weeks were an escape classic of the time, and in April two half-starved airmen presented themselves at the French Mission in Switzerland—and asked to be reassigned to active service.

The air war had progressed considerably since Pinsard had been shot down and he had to undergo refresher training. By the middle of that summer he was well on his way again and finally headed the famous Stork Squadron and racked up twenty-seven confirmed victories.

Pinsard lived to enjoy the celebration of Armistice Day and stayed on with the French Air Service for many years after.

All this is a compilation of the first few months of the first war in the air. Four more long years were to pass before the battle-planes were to make their last patrol. So far they had at best flown only as the "Eyes of the Army." They had accomplished a great deal with what they had, but within a few weeks a very simple device was to revolutionise all air action. A small wedge of metal was to make the observant dove a killer bird of prey.

2

THE MACHINE GUN
TAKES WINGS—

1915

☐ The morning of April 1, 1915, brought in the dawn of a new day in military history. A new weapon and a new breed of man were conceived. The day also provided a most tragic April Fool joke.

In spite of the calendar the day was cold and raw. In the barnyards of the French countryside steam rose from the manure piles. The Soissons rustics clumped about in heavy *sabots* and blew on their work-gnarled knuckles. A biting south-east wind off the Graian Alps knifed through woollen jerkins and froze men to the marrow.

A dished-wheeled monoplane scurried down a deserted meadow take-off track and hissed into the sky. A typical or routine flight, but it was to become one of the most memorable in history. Few realised it at the time, of course—least of all the pilot. Inventors have little idea of the real significance of their creations or what they have wrought.

This was a rickety, underpowered monoplane with a savage temperament. It snarled through the hydro nostrils of an 80-h.p. Le Rhone rotary engine, primitive airplane of spruce, linen, piano wire, and some cockpit stiffening originally intended for the sides of orange crates. The Morane Bullet was already an outmoded type and had been stowed away in a spare-parts hangar awaiting final disposal when it was resurrected for this grim experiment. It was too treacherous for newly trained men to fly, too bedevilled for routine war scouting patrols.

The militant pilot had for years believed the aeroplane

could be used as a fighting machine—not simply a platform for aerial observation. That is, it could if one apparently insolvable problem could be overcome. If one mechanical block could be by-passed. The man flying the Morane Bullet that morning was convinced he had solved it.

That same day two young German aeronauts, as they were then listed, took off aboard an Albatros two-seater with orders to check on French military activity behind Epernay. It was a routine patrol, one they had accepted and carried out a dozen times before.

The minute they crossed into Allied territory the French 75's, mounted as high-angle guns, opened up and dabbed white splotches of smoke all around them. The white smoke markers caught the eye of the French pilot in the masquerading Morane and he noted the German two-seater about 500 metres above him. He was glad he had no dead-weight observer with him. He spent the next ten minutes stalking and climbing up to the level of the observation machine.

The two Germans watched him with only nominal interest as they continued their reconnaissance work. When the Bullet curled to a position behind their tail and gained the last few feet of necessary height the German pilot simply presumed the Frenchman was out on an observation mission too. He had no observer waving a rifle or loading a machine gun. What was there to worry about? This mid-air activity had to be carried out by both sides. So long as the Morane Bullet didn't get in the way, he could have his share of the sky, and welcome.

And just so long as the Frenchman didn't start crabbing up sideways, it was only another observation patrol.

April Fool!

A few seconds later a burst of fifteen rounds of Hotchkiss machine-gun fire tore through his shoulder blades. The burst had come *straight* from the Morane Bullet directly behind. Only Observer Fritz Dietrichs saw that the slugs were apparently coming through the sheen of the propeller—from a stripped-down gun mounted over the engine cowling.

Firing through the whirling blades of the propeller? How could that be?

Dietrichs never lived to find out. He knew nothing about piloting an Albatros and he went down, utterly helpless to aid himself. In his last breath he screamed his outrage that a French monoplane could shoot at him with a gun set behind the spinning blades of a wooden propeller! The Albatros plunged to its end with a dead man hunched over its controls.

But it was true. A Frenchman named Roland Garros had

given the machine gun wings. His fantastic device gave birth to a new and most deadly weapon, providing the military forces with a lethal piece of armament. It made the aeroplane as important a war machine as the naval dreadnought. It turned a collection of rickety flying machines into an air service, and overnight the aeroplane became the platform for sky-high gunnery, not simply an airy-fairy vehicle of observation.

The man who turned the fragile World War I aeroplane into a deadly bird of prey had started out as a very unobtrusive music student who gave little promise beyond the salons of Paris. He was born at St. Denis on the island of Réunion in October 1888. His father was a well-known lawyer who provided a luxurious home and a first-class education for the young man.

Roland Garros was quick at almost everything. He had good hands and could draw, paint, and play musical instruments as well as manipulate most mechanical devices of that day. His parents had decided he should become a professional musician, and by the time he was of voting age they shipped him off to Paris to finish his piano technique.

In Paris he saw his first aeroplane and became entranced with the idea of flying. Through family connections he obtained an interview with the famed Alberto Santos-Dumont. In 1909 Santos-Dumont was better known than either of the Wright brothers—he was a better publicist and as early as 1898 had thrilled Parisians with almost daily displays with various forms of the dirigible airship and topped that by being the first man in 1906 to make an aeroplane flight over Europe.

This Brazilian coffee millionaire even produced a hybrid dirigible-aeroplane by using the gasbag to get the contrivance into the air and then skimming madly about the Paris chimney pots with the aeroplane. He also created an alarming machine known as the 14-Bis, a garish biplane, fitted with a balloon basket for a cockpit, which flew tail-first! Nevertheless, it flew, covering 200 feet at 25 m.p.h., and won 3,000 francs for this Brazilian Coffee Cooler. A short time later he picked up another 1,500 francs by flying his improbable device about 700 feet in twenty-one seconds.

Santos-Dumont performed all these epic flights standing erect in the wicker basket while wearing a neat business suit and a floppy-brimmed Panama hat. How could the staid Wright brothers compete with that?

Somewhat later Santos-Dumont developed something he

called a Demoiselle monoplane, which without its engine weighed but 59 pounds. Actually it was nothing more than a bicycle-wheel landing gear carrying a monoplane wing and a tail assembly held on by three bamboo booms. The engine was a tiny 12-h.p. plant bolted on top of the wing and gave it a speed of 55 m.p.h. Snide bystanders dubbed it "The Infuriated Grasshopper," but it certainly flew as early as 1909, flipping from St. Cyr to Buc, a distance of four and a half miles, in less than five minutes. Today it can still be seen by the incredulous in the Aeronautical Museum at Chalis-Meudon near Paris.

"So you want to become an aeronaut?" the dapper Santos-Dumont is said to have queried. "And who doesn't these days?"

"But I can afford to pay for my lessons," explained Garros, who intended to do a quick switch with his musical education funds.

"Money is not important. Let me see your hands."

Somewhat puzzled, Garros held out his long delicate fingers. Santos-Dumont took them, turned them over, and studied them carefully. They were exact replicas of his own.

"You are lucky. I take it you are a musician. With such hands you will make a splendid airman. I will take you on."

Santos-Dumont had no idea how right he was. Within a year the quiet, unassuming music student had become one of the most skilled aeronauts in the world. It was fantastic what this delicate-fingered man could do with any contraption of bamboo, linen, and bicycle wheels. In October 1910 Garros came to America with a French aviation team and competed in the famed Statue of Liberty race. It was eventually won, after considerable controversy, by Count Jacques de Lesseps, who flew a Blériot monoplane. Garros flew a Paulhan biplane which was not manoeuvrable enough to make a tight turn around the goddess and he had to be content with third place. Later in 1911 Garros won the $100,000 Paris-to-Rome race, was first in the Paris-to-Madrid race, and led the pack in the Grand Prix d'Anjou event the same year.

He was one of the few men who early appreciated the value of the aeroplane as a military weapon, and on his various exhibitions he pointed out its fitness with displays of bombardment tactics. In a demonstration over Mexico City he peppered a Mexican artillery battery with oranges and forced the juice-spattered gunners to take cover.

In the summer of the eventful year of 1914 Garros was in Germany giving a series of exhibitions with an early Morane monoplane. Quite possibly it was a Morane Bullet. He held

44

large audiences spellbound with his acrobatic displays. At night he was the honoured guest at many banquets, where he enthusiastically publicized the military value of the heavier-than-air machine. Every word was digested and the German newspapers gave columns of space to his fascinating theories. He couldn't have selected a better subject for the militaristic Germans of those days.

Garros's name was on every German tongue, but he was a most modest although popular hero. Not only could he give an amazing exhibition of flying, but on returning to the ground he would delight music-salon groups with his skill at the piano. Garros had never enjoyed such dual acclaim before, and we can only imagine his amazement when late one afternoon he slowly interpreted the newspaper headlines and the screechings of the newsboys at the street corners and learned that the Kaiser's troops had invaded his beloved France.

War?

War had been declared!

But how ridiculous! How unfair. He had been all over Germany pointing out the military value of the aeroplane, had even showed them how to use it for observation and bombardment. Now these people who posed as his friends had decided to make war on his country.

And that was not all. The situation automatically produced several tricky problems. According to the international rules of war, he was now virtually a prisoner and could be interned for the duration of the hostilities. Even worse, the Germans could unquestionably confiscate his exhibition machine. They might even fly it and use it against his own people!

Shocked and frightened, he crept back to his hotel and packed his bags. Leaving by a rear exit, he moved in a very circuitous route, hat pulled down over his eyes to avoid being identified and arrested, and went down quiet back streets and skulked across the exhibition grounds. Fortunately the excitement of the war had drawn all guards to the nearby *Gasthaus*, and Garros had little trouble dragging his monoplane from a shed and checking the Le Rhone engine and fuel supply. He stowed his bags, swung his own propeller, and climbed aboard.

At that time few men had flown at night, but Roland Garros took off boldly and made for the nearest border. He landed safely in Switzerland and several days later managed to get across another border and continued on to Paris. A great furor went up in Germany and Garros's name was again in all their headlines. Now he was on the Fatherland's

"Wanted" list, being called everything from a habitual thief to the scurviest of international spies. That Garros! He is a tricky one. Exhibition flights, indeed. That criminal Garros must have photographed every fortress in Germany!

Garros immediately reported for military service and, along with Armand Pinsard who is mentioned previously, was sent to St. Cyr, where he was put into uniform, taught parade-ground drill and something that went for aviation tactics at that time. This dreary formula was soon fulfilled and Garros and Pinsard were sent off on a simple reconnaissance flight as their graduation effort. Completing this successfully, they were then sent to Paris for reassignment.

The Morane-Saulnier Escadrille No. 23 was being formed at Buc, and Garros and Pinsard were ordered to report there. To their delight they joined several other experienced exhibition pilots, including Pegoud, the Frenchman who made looping-the-loop an aviation exhibition feature. There was also Vedrines, a noted aeroplane designer, Eugene Gilbert, and Marc Pourpe.

With Pourpe was a Wallingford, Connecticut, young man called Raoul Lufbery, who had been with Pourpe for four years, acting as his mechanic after they had somehow gotten together out in Indo-China. When war broke out, Pourpe and Lufbery were in Paris to pick up a new machine and both of them wangled their way into the French Air Service.

Late in September, when the German infantry was only twenty-five miles from Paris, this M-S. 23 Squadron was rushed to the front-line area at Breteuil. The French Army was in retreat and the gay capital was in imminent danger of capture. Every available plane and airman was urgently needed, for if France was short of anything, it was reliable information. The Eyes of the Army were sent out to determine the strength and movements of the German war machine.

Along the Marne, Allied pilots in the flimsy craft of the time vied with the bamboo-and-baling-wire machines from the Rumpler, Fokker, and Albatros plants. They made scouting and observation flights. They checked the roads and railroads. They calculated the strength of enemy troops and in many instances enabled the French artillery to shell enemy concentrations.

Garros, Vedrines, Pinsard, and the rest did their full share in turning the German advance along the Marne into a crushing defeat.

But there was a sameness to all these flights. Anyone who could fly and had some primary military training could undertake these patrols. A pilot and an observer received an order

46

and they simply carried it out. Their only dread was engine failure, bad weather, or the possibility of a million-to-one-shot hit by anti-aircraft fire. It was the same on both sides of the line. Men went into the air, performed an observation or a primary bombing patrol, and returned to write out a report. It was little removed from delivering a load of rations in a general service wagon.

War in the air was still something fictional in a book. Because of the scouting successes, in September 1914 the aeroplane was fully catalogued as an observation machine. It had proved itself in that service and, as such, it was typed for that role for a long while.

In October military intelligence showed that the German High Command had established headquarters at Thielt. Remembering his theories of using the aeroplane as a weapon of offence, Garros suggested that the German nerve centre be raided—with bombs!

"It is wasteful," he is known to have argued, "to put the machines into the air for simple observation reports. After all, captive balloons can do that and do it better. Balloons can be sent up at night. They work in silence and can hardly be detected. Most of the reports our observers bring back are not worth the *essence* they burn."

Garros, as usual, had been somewhat carried away by his militant enthusiasms, but Armand Pinsard was equally enthusiastic. "The enemy airmen have no respect for us. They come over here and do the same thing. If we could bombard their headquarters, they would appreciate the menace of our service."

Then there was Eugene Gilbert, another deep thinker who didn't talk as much but was quietly working on another theory that would make the airplane more of a war bird.

Pinsard and Garros kept broaching their suggestion until responsible officials—more to be rid of them than to display any agreement with their plans—said that they might try a few hand-dropped bombs. They had little hope of any success, but perhaps it would quiet down these two insistent airmen.

Garros selected the day and Pinsard agreed to accompany him. "Oh, what fun this will be," the gay Armand cheered.

It might have been more amusing had they known that Garros's date coincided with Kaiser Wilhelm's first visit to the new German headquarters. They were not aware of this until sometime later.

Two "converted" Parasol monoplanes carrying simple artillery shells trailing linen streamers for tails, their nose caps set for impact detonation, swept out of the clouds over Thielt.

Their "bombs" rained down, and the Kaiser, without waiting for his swanky entourage, made a dash for his Mercedes limousine and cleared out of the area. He never again went up close to the front line.

The German Emperor nurtured a bitter hate for all French pilots after that. What damage was actually done to the German G.H.Q. was never fully explained, but it had been successful enough to make the French aviation staff consider the aeroplane from a new tactical angle. Both airmen were promoted for their exploit.

On February 8, 1915, Armand Pinsard had engine trouble over the enemy lines and had to land in occupied territory. He was taken prisoner, and Garros was desolate as he and Pinsard had formed a warm friendship during their many reconnaissance forays together. More important, they had deep respect for each other.

So far as Garros was concerned, the sun rose and fell on his companion and he was unable to put the old Moroccan campaign veteran out of his mind. At first he secretly considered a rescue flight into Germany with the idea of personally springing him from some Boche prison. How he would have found him is a mystery, for Pinsard was soon taking matters into his own hands and over the next twelve months was either on the loose trying to slip across some border or was in solitary confinement for having made still another attempt. By February 1916 he did manage to sneak back into unoccupied France and argue his way back into the service. Before the war was over, Armand Pinsard had run up no less than twenty-seven victories as a fighter pilot.

He had Roland Garros to thank for that.

While gnawing his heart out about Pinsard, Garros eventually sensed he could do nothing with an unarmed aeroplane. He might as well go over in a country-fair balloon. Getting deep into the German area was one thing, but to land there, rescue his pal, and fight his way out through the swarm of enemy aircraft sent up to intercept him would be something else.

At the same time Eugene Gilbert must have been reading Garros's mind. He too pondered on how the aeroplane could be armed. Properly armed, that is. All sorts of rumours were afield concerning how some Englishman or some German had actually taken a machine gun into the air, but there was no specific instances or reliable information. Gilbert was one of the first to sense that to make an aeroplane earn its keep it had to be flown fast, handled with smart manoeuvrability, and be able to strike—or thrust, exactly like a good swordsman.

48

There was the secret in a nutshell! The aeroplane had to be able to fire in the direction in which it was flying. Such a machine could be a single-seater. It must be small and fast. It could be designed to be most manoeuvrable—like the wrist of a duellist.

But that meant that a gun had to be so fixed that it would fire directly forward. All this had been talked over before, but it was just as true in the early spring of 1915 as it was in the autumn of 1914. The gun had to be available to the pilot for reloading and the clearance of stoppages. There was the rub. Any gun mounted so conveniently would be *somewhere* behind the 9-foot propeller.

Apparently Eugene Gilbert said, "Let's face it. We *have* to mount any gun behind the prop. A percentage of the bullets would hit the whirling blades and pierce them. It would take only a few to weaken them . . . and . . . boom, no prop!"

At this point rumour, legend, and hearsay take over. It has been stated by several armament experts writing in the European press that Eugene Gilbert decided that steel-tape wrapping on each propeller blade at the point where the bullets might strike would, because of the curved shape of the butt, deflect such rounds. Gilbert had such a propeller prepared and tested a gun mounted on the engine cowling.

This historic event was made at Luxeuil aerodrome as early as December 1914. Gilbert employed a Morane Bullet, as Garros was to do, and mounted a light Hotchkiss gun. It is also stated that in January of 1915 Gilbert actually shot down a German Aviatik using such a fixed weapon.

The reader will naturally ask, "Then why was not the device more widely used, as crude as the idea was? Why didn't Garros and the other men at M-S. 23 know of it?"

The story goes something like this. After his success against the Aviatik, Gilbert decided on some deflector-sleeve improvement and next had a V-shaped wedge of armour plate bolted to the back of each blade, sensing that the propeller could be better balanced in that way. During a gun-butt test he asked a couple of fellow officers to help him put the Morane up in flying position, steady the wing tips, and make the plane generally secure while he ran the engine and fired a test burst at a pile of sandbags.

Something went wrong with the new deflector plate and two French officers were killed by ricocheting bullets. Gilbert was so distressed by this accident, he immediately gave up any further experimentation and from all accounts never mentioned or considered his project again.

Strangely enough, Garros conceived exactly the same plan

of protecting the butt end of the propeller blade with some sort of deflector device. He spent long hours in the armourer's shed figuring out weights, recoil, loading procedures, and the rate of fire. Once he touched on this latter point, he was on the right track. Knowing that the hotchkiss gun—the lightest available and the simplest to reload—fired at the rate of 300 rounds per minute, he checked on the speed of the propeller.

With the armourer he pondered on the idea of bolting a Hotchkiss gun along the engine cowling so it would fire along the actual line of flight. There was some question whether Garros's theory would work, but he argued that by his figuring, less than seven per cent of the rounds fired would strike the propeller; that if the propeller could be protected at this bullet area, he could go into the air and simply aim his nose at any enemy plane—and shoot it down.

The armourer brought up the fact that Eugene Gilbert had tried the same thing with most tragic results.

But Garros still argued for his fixed-gun plan, pointing out that putting a gun high on the top plane as the Nieuport designers were doing was not the answer. It was too far away; it could not be reloaded, nor could any stoppage be cleared. The more he thought about it, the more he was certain that Gilbert had selected a deflector that was curved at a dangerous angle.

However, Roland Garros investigated further and eventually got a Parisian machinist to turn out a collar of armour plate which could be bolted around the base of the propeller blade. This was designed with a sharp angle so that any bullets deflected would continue on in a narrow V to the line of the undeflected rounds. He wanted to avoid any accidents and sacrificed some propeller efficiency to get it.

During this period Garros evolved an even better idea, but it couldn't be put into play until he could find an aero engine with a hollow crankshaft.

When the collars were finished and delivered Garros bolted them to the butt ends of the propeller blades and had the protesting armourer bolt a Hotchkiss gun along the engine and cockpit cowling. Next he had him carry a trigger cable down to the joystick. The Hotchkiss gun (originally an American automatic rifle) was fed by straight metal clips, each carrying twenty-five rounds. The gun could be loaded easily and the weapon itself was much lighter than the old Maxim or Lewis guns. All this was mounted on a discarded Morane Bullet, and Garros was ready for his experiment.

Once again legend scrawls some bewildering inserts. One is that an unidentified pilot had a Hotchkiss gun mounted outside his cockpit and went into the air without providing any protection for his propeller. He, of course, shot himself down when he fired at a Fokker monoplane. Another is that a young hothead stole Garros's plane and went over the line to engage the enemy. In this fable he hammered the propeller clean off the shaft and went down out of control.

None of these tales can be substantiated. Most of them were conceived after Garros made such a success of his front-firing gun. Everyone wanted to get into the act.

The truth is that after learning of Eugene Gilbert's experience Garros left no stone unturned to make certain his device would work perfectly. Clip after clip of Hotchkiss ammunition was fired into a test buttress while the Bullet was jacked up in flying position with the engine running at various speeds. What few shots struck the collar were deflected off harmlessly.

Roland Garros was ready to revolutionize aerial operations.

All this began during February of 1915, but Garros was not ready to try his device against the enemy until April 1 of that year.

In the meantime a lad, First Class Air Mechanic James Byford McCudden, was flying with No. 3 Squadron, R.F.C., as a gunner on a Morane Parasol from an advanced landing ground at Annequin.

A young Uhlan officer named Lieutenant Baron von Richthofen was doing lowly infantry duty on the Verdun front.

A certain Lieutenant William A. Bishop was slopping around in the mud of horse lines in England, wondering why he had left Canada.

One Edward V. Rickenbacker was taking a correspondence course in engineering and working as a test driver for an automobile manufacturer in Indianapolis.

A semi-invalid, Georges Guynemer, was holding down a light-duty sweeper-up job on a French training field outside Paris. Two Americans, Norman Prince and Elliott Cowdin, had arrived in France to volunteer to fly in the Aviation Service. The U.S. Marine Aviation Service was being organized within the U.S. Navy establishment.

Albert Heurteaux, a Hussar officer, was transferring to *L'Aviation Militaire,* where he was to be wounded twelve times and score twenty-one victories before his twenty-fifth birthday.

Andrew McKeever, who was to become the world's leading

two-seater ace, was in the trenches with the First Canadian Division. Albert Ball was a subaltern in the Sherwood Foresters and buying flying lessons which he took before breakfast at an airfield sixty miles away from his battalion training ground. Another English youth, mild-mannered Reggie Warneford, was flipping about the French and Belgian coasts looking for Zeppelins. He finally caught up with one over Ghent.

A young Prussian, Ernst Udet, was a dispatch rider for a reserve Württemburg division, who apparently busted up motor cycles faster than the manufacturers turned them out. His superiors gladly let him transfer to the German Aviation Service.

Willy Coppens, a young Belgian, was transferring from the 2nd Regiment of Grenadiers to train in England (at his own expense) at the Ruffy-Baumann Flying School. He eventually became an ace balloon-buster and was credited with thirty-six victories. His government made him a Chevalier of Honour as a reward.

A fine soldier named George Lanoe Hawker was bombing Zeppelin sheds all over Belgium and was to become Britain's premier ace until his death in 1916. Hawker never flew a plane with a fixed machine gun.

Oberleutnant Hermann Goering, who headed a scouting cyclist regiment, was in the hospital with rheumatism where he met one of Germany's premier airmen, Bruno Loerzer, who persuaded him to transfer to the air service.

An arrogant, self-assured man, Max Immelmann, had just cracked up an old L.V.G. belonging to Flying Section No. 10 at Vizry. He had been credited previously with bombarding Paris with warning handbills shortly after the outbreak of the war. The truth is, Immelmann had never been in the air even as a passenger until November 12, 1914. He was to be shot down by a British air gunner, Corporal Waller.

A German schoolteacher named Oswald Boelcke, a nondescript Fokker pilot, had just been transferred to No. 62 Squadron at Dessau, where he was to be something of an equipment inspector. Nothing much was expected of him, but he turned out to be the man who put the German Air Service on a real operational basis.

The author was doing servitude with the Northamptonshire Yeomanry, taking courses in maching gun, sniping, the lance, the sabre, and seriously considering outright desertion. He had seen a military aeroplane.

After Garros's first victory against an early Albatros, which has been described, he was in the air again on April 11 in his

52

deadly Morane Bullet. This time he came upon two unsuspecting Aviatik two-seaters and again employed the same strategy of moving to their rear and making the most of the belief that he could offer no opposition from that angle. The first Aviatik went down under a hail of Hotchkiss lead; the second stood and fought, the German observer vainly trying to hold off Garros with a revolver! It was a game stand, but the effort was hopeless. The second Aviatik soon followed the first to a fiery finish.

The following afternoon while returning from a visit to another escadrille, Garros caught an L.V.G., also a two-seater, and battered it into the ground near Dunkirk. Again a German was trapped by the Morane Bullet's approach.

Two days later one of the newer Aviatiks, equipped with a Parabellum machine gun in the observer's rear seat, was spotted flying toward the French lines. The German pilot hurriedly dumped his bomb load to gain more manoeuvrability. The German observer's first burst caught the Morane Bullet's wing root and punctured Garros's reserve fuel tank. Trailing a long cloud of petrol vapour, he disregarded the possibility of fire in the air and closed in.

The German observer died with five bullets in his chest. The next five of that first clip tore through the pilot's head and slammed through the instrument panel and ignited the fuel line. The Aviatik went down and burned to a cinder in a marsh.

On the morning of April 16 Garros was attacked by four Albatros two-seaters which were returning from a bombing raid. A number of rifle bullets penetrated his machine—one of them hit the engine cowling and fell back into his lap. The moment the Frenchman's fixed gun began to sparkle behind the sheen of the propeller, all four two-seater pilots remembered important engagements elsewhere.

However one Albatros appeared to be slower than the others and soon lagged behind. Garros darted in fast to get within range. The others, noting their companions' danger, turned about and tried to head off the impudent Morane, but Garros was "on" and his bullets gradually tore away the left wing of the laggard Albatros and the unfortunate crew went down in a fuselage that rejected the other wing before they spun in.

Five victories in sixteen days! That was the initial harvest of Roland Garros's front-firing gun.

That night Garros was cited for the Legion of Honour and every newspaper in Europe carried the news of his five victories. The gay *boulevardiers* toasted the newest hero and cried: "Oh, that Garros! That Roland Garros! Five enemy machines he has destroyed. That Garros is an ace!"

The word "ace" was a popular catchword of the day in Paris. Any newsworthy person who had performed anything unusual was an "ace" to the Parisians. The latest winning cyclist racer was an "ace." The newest popular jockey was an "ace." It was natural then that the phrase should be applied to Roland Garros.

The enthusiasm was overheard by an American newspaperman, who interpreted it to refer to any pilot who had downed five enemy planes. In his next dispatch back to New York he applied the word to the name of Roland Garros and it became the journalistic standard by which a fighter pilot in any air service was rated.

Later the Germans doubled the requirements and any airman who had scored ten victories was publicized as a *Kanone*. The British ignored the "ace" standard for over two years and until well into 1915 no official record of "enemy machines destroyed" was kept or compiled. They did not publish the names and the day-by-day scores of their aces, and it was only upon the occasion of the decoration of these heroes that the number of their victories was made public.

However, the term "ace" has lasted to this day.

So Roland Garros became the world's first ace as well as the man who revolutionised aerial warfare. He was invited to appear before the Directorate of Military Aeronautics to give his views on this new art of aerial combat. The date was set for April 25, but unfortunately Roland Garros was unable to keep the appointment.

On the afternoon of April 19, 1915, Garros took off to bomb the railroad sidings at Courtrai. Why he was given such a mission with his single-seater fighter is something of a mystery. Although he was now the world's premier air fighter, he apparently still carried out routine bombing raids.

That day the pilots of Escadrille M-S. 23 fully expected him to return with another addition to his score. But that was not to be. Garros flew all the way to Courtrai without encountering an enemy aircraft of any kind. He presumed he would be more fortunate on the way back. He cut his Le Rhone engine, went into an attack glide, swept over the freight yard, and dropped his bombs.

He had no idea what he hit or whether he had missed the target entirely. He was too concerned with getting the impact-fused bombs overboard without blowing himself to bits. When he went to switch on his rotary engine again, the Le Rhone refused to pick up. Nothing happened! The propeller simply windmilled in the slipstream. Garros knew immediately what was wrong and cursed himself for his imbecility. In the long sure glide for the Courtrai freight yard the spark plugs had oiled up. He had forgotten to "burn" them off with intermittent blipping of the ignition switch and so had no alternative but to stretch his glide until he found a suitable spot to land.

He came down near Ingelmunster, about 40 miles from the Dutch frontier. His first thought was to destroy his plane and the details of the propeller's protective collar, which metal device was the secret of his front-firing gun. He did his best to set fire to the Morane, but the wing fabric and the spruce framework were damp and refused to burn. How ironic! Had an enemy bullet flicked a spark off a metal fitting near a punctured petrol tank, the whole machine would have gone up like a pan of gunpowder. On the ground, with no slipstream draught, nothing that Garros could do would set up so much as a smoke smudge.

Soon a party of German soldiers turned up and Garros made one last desperate bid for liberty. Running across the field, he slid into a ditch for cover where the depression was full of muddy water, weeds, and half-frozen sedge. He stayed there until darkness fell and then clambered out with the idea of reaching the Dutch border, but by sheer bad luck he wandered straight into a group of soldiers who were out gathering firewood. The game was up.

The Germans had examined the undamaged Morane and were of course interested in the strange steel wedges bolted around the propeller-blade butts. Blued bullet markings soon disclosed the purpose of the deflection plates, and in a flash the secret of the gun that could fire bullets through the whirling blades of a propeller was revealed.

The Germans moved fast. The French *cocardes* were quickly daubed out and the Morane Bullet was flown to Berlin. A young Dutch engineer, Anthony Fokker, was called in to examine it.

The story of Anthony Fokker is fairly well known, although it has often been distorted in the telling. Those with a flair for the dramatic have awarded him full credit for the development of the interrupter gear that allowed a machine gun to fire between the whirling blades of the propeller. In addition, since the gun and gear were first incorporated with some success in Fokker's E.1 monoplane, the alliterative phrase "Fokker fodder" was thoughtlessly applied to any Allied airman who was shot down by *any* German aircraft of the late 1915 period. I have met few British or French wartime flyers who ever felt they had been sent out against insuperable odds or sensed any especial dread at the appearance of that particular Fokker aeroplane. The phrase, I feel quite sure, was conceived sometime *after* 1915 and klieglighted to a grim connotation by the Hollywood air epics of the 1920s. One seldom finds it in air-war material that was actually written at the time.

Anthony Fokker was a self-taught engineer who had designed several worthy aircraft types that had gained some local renown during the military competition and air-race days prior to the outbreak of World War I. He immediately offered his designs and services to France, Great Britain, and Italy. He had no trust in any Russian business operations.

France had a wealth of first-class aircraft designers. Britain had little or no faith in the monoplane, which was Fokker's favourite mount. He was uncomfortably in debt to his father and a few close friends who had financed him. Thus, when the German Naval Air Arm made an offer for a number of his E.1 (Eindekker) monoplanes and spread the money on the counter, Fokker naturally accepted.

In all fairness to the young Dutchman, he made the deal after the Allies had ignored him. Actually he had very little to offer beyond a youthful zest for experiment and an open-minded approach to any new problem. His E.1 monopolane lasted less than a year, after which he had to yield to the demand for tougher biplanes. He honestly believed his aeronautical future was in the light sports types and since the war "couldn't last past the first Christmas" he held onto his Dutch citizenship, took over a small factory at Schwerin, and concentrated on his contracted order for twenty-four Fokkers a day.

As an independent Dutch manufacturer, Anthony enjoyed operational freedom denied most German manufacturers. He was not hampered by stodgy thinking and was always ready to take on any new problem. For this reason Garros's Morane Bullet was next flown to Schwerin, and the fixed gun and deflector device was explained to him.

"We want you to duplicate this armed-propeller idea and incorporate it into a few of your Fokker Eindekkers," the German aviation brass demanded.

They gave Fokker a German Parabellum gun, an infantry weapon that employed 100-round ammunition belts. Fokker had never had a machine gun in his hands before, but within an hour he had decided that the deflector plate was not the answer to the front-firing gun. Like Garros, he compared the rate of fire to the r.p.m. of the Oberursel rotary engine that powered his monoplane.

(The Oberursel was an exact copy of the French Le Rhone rotary—copied without benefit of manufacturing licence, of course.)

Fokker did not trust the deflector-plate idea. He was convinced that eventually one bullet would strike with such force that the propeller would either shatter from the impact or the deflected bullet might ricochet into a vital section of the aircraft engine.

He placed the gun on the engine cowling and in some dreamy fashion conceived the idea of pressing the trigger only when there was no blade in front of the gun barrel. In that vague thought he had the basic idea for an interrupter gear. The gun had to be interrupted in its rate of fire whenever there was a propeller blade in line with the gun barrel.

The rest was easy to an enthusiast such as Fokker. He simply fitted a light cam ring to the back of the propeller. This cam depressed a lever which, operating through a series of cranks and rods, either pressed or released the trigger. In theory the idea worked beautifully. In practice a few bugs had to be ironed out to accommodate the irregularity of fire caused by faulty ammunition or friction lags in the gun mechanism.

At any rate, Fokker had his device mounted on an E.1 monoplane within five days and had the top aviation brass on hand to see it work. He set the machine up against a test butt, started the engine, and fired three 10-round bursts. When the paunchy aviation officials inspected the propeller and found no damage they felt that Fokker was playing some trick. Fokker obliged again—with a 100-round burst.

After some lengthy huddle the military spokesman came up with: "We are most satisfied with your device, Herr Fokker, but would it work in the air? Would you be willing to give such an exhibition?"

By now Fokker was seething at all this pigheadedness. He ordered some of his help to take a couple of discarded monoplane wings and lay them out on his airfield. He then took off, and the suspicious-minded military men crowded up close to the wing target. Fokker tilted over at 900 feet and roared at the ground. He ignored the examiners completely and let a burst of 100 rounds pour at the monoplane wings. Naturally some of the slugs ricocheted in all directions. So did the German military officials. Later, when Fokker had landed, they timidly crept out of the hangar and inspected the bullet-riddled wings.

But Fokker had not convinced them yet!

"Would you mind, Herr Fokker," they inquired, "making one final test for us?"

"Not at all."

"We realize your device works—under these—er—factory conditions; but we feel that before we would be justified in awarding recognition and—a suitable contract for its manufacture and application to your monoplane, it should be demonstrated under active-service conditions."

"You want me to go to the front and shoot down a French or a British airman?"

They all bowed in agreement.

"But I am a Dutch subject. I am neutral in this war."

"You also have several German contracts, eh? You have a very remarkable invention here, Herr Fokker. You wouldn't want to lose the financial reward, would you?"

Fokker was trapped. There was no way out. In a day or so he and his Fokker monoplane were hustled to the front and he was introduced to the liaison headquarters of General von Heeringen. The gun was demonstrated again the next day before the German Crown Prince. Little Willie was delighted with the whole idea but somehow became confused as to who young Herr Fokker was.

"Did your father devise this gun and its interrupter gear?" the Crown Prince inquired.

Anthony explained that his father was in Holland and that it was *he*—young Tony—who had invented the device.

But while Little Willie was very pleased with the Fokker gun gear the big brass never gave up the idea of Fokker's trying it out against the enemy. They even fixed him up with a German Aviation Service uniform, a couple of decorations, and an identification card explaining he was Leutnant Anthony Herman Gerard Fokker of the German Air Force. For two days he went aloft seeking out French or British aircraft, but apparently there was very little activity in the area. Moving up to the Douai front, he finally caught up with a French Farman two-seater 2,000 feet below him. The rest could have been a repetition of Garros's fixed-gun attack, but Fokker always claimed that he decided then and there to abandon the whole idea and returned to the flying field at Douai.

"I am sorry, sir," he explained, "but I cannot in all conscience take such an active part in this war. I am ready to sacrifice my contracts and return to Amsterdam."

So his plane was turned over to a young German airman, Leutnant Oswald Boelcke, who was given several days of instruction on the gun and its mechanism. Fokker returned his uniform and went back to Berlin. On his arrival he was informed that Leutnant Boelcke had destroyed an enemy aircraft on his third flight, and this success convinced the German Air Service that Fokker's synchronized gun was most efficient, and their original scepticism billowed up into the wildest enthusiasm for the new weapon.

One or two favoured German airmen were given extra models of the Fokker Eindekker to work out the bugs, strategy, and general practice with the new weapon. Boelcke, Max Immelmann and others were running up their scores, but full production on these fixed-gun Fokkers did not begin until the late summer of 1915. The new weapon was noticed, of course, and French and British planes were for a time at a serious disadvantage, but their designers were not idle or simply wringing their hands.

Within a short time a young and very impetuous German pilot flying a new Fokker monoplane became lost in a fog and generously handed the French an undamaged fixed-gun monoplane. There had been a very strict rule to the effect that no one flying the new Fokker was to risk capture by crossing the front line. However, this was poetic justice for the undamaged Morane Bullet Garros had presented to the Germans.

Fokker always claimed that this capture gave the Allies the secret of his interrupter gear, but the fact of the matter is that Great Britain was already working on the device and while it was being perfected had designed several new pusher-type planes that were flown as single-seaters and thus required no fixed-gun interrupter gear.

Shortly after the first rumours of Garros's fixed-gun plane began to trickle along the front, the British sensed the value of the device and put their engineers to work on an interrupter-gear project. It was then discovered that as early as 1910 a German engineer named Euler had actually patented the idea of mounting a gun on an aircraft and firing it along the line of flight.

While a handful of Fokker E.1's were enjoying themselves in front of Douai, a British armament sergeant by the name of Kauper devised a gun-timing gear similar to that being employed by the Germans. He was immediately assigned to the Sopwith Aviation Company for further experiment, and his gear became known as the Sopwith-Kauper gear.

This was first adapted to the Sopwith two-seater known as the one and one-half Strutter. The name emanated from the splayed centre-section struts, which appeared to be composed of "one and a half" struts, the inner short, the outer long.

Also, this very efficient biplane actually had a set of wing flaps or air brakes.

The Sopwith company tried out the Kauper gear aboard this machine, and since it had also the new Scarff mounting for the rear-seat gunner, it was the leading Allied two-seater fighter of its day. The first batch of these one and one-half Strutters went to the Royal Naval Air Service during the autumn of 1915. For some strange reason the Royal Flying Corps would not accept it until an adjustable tailplane had been included, and thus lost a lot of valuable time in getting a front-gun fighter into the air against the Fokkers.

The Kauper gear was next installed on the Sopwith Pup, a most manoeuvrable single-seater. This machine was allotted to Squadrons Nos. 46, 54, and 66 on the Western Front. Nos. 3, 4, 8, 9, and 13 Naval Squadrons of the R.N.A.S. also used them. A special flight fitted with deck skis operated from the Royal Navy's H.M.S. *Furious*. With these two fixed-gun mounts the British began their uphill climb to outshoot the Fokkers.

The Germans enjoyed fixed-gun supremacy for but a few months. Most historians have been under the impression that the British did not counter with a fixed front gun until late in 1916. Such was not the case.

During 1915 Great Britain had three additional interrupter-gear devices in the works. One was being tested by the Vickers company. There was the Scarff-Dibovsky gun gear and another listed as the Arsiad. All three employed the common feature of a depressed cam and rod and bell-crank principle. The delay encountered could be laid to the fact that the British were trying to synchronise their light Lewis gun until it was discovered that the heavier Vickers was more adaptable to a synchronisation mechanism.

Nevertheless, a French mechanic, Sergeant Alkan, devised an interrupter gear for the Lewis gun, which was being tested by the Royal Flying Corps. It produced some promising results and might have been adopted had it not been rendered obsolete by the successful conversion of the Vickers gun which could be fed by belts of 250 rounds. At that time the Lewis was using a 47-round ammunition drum.

The Arsiad gear was designed in the field by a Major A. V. Bettington of the No. 1 Aircraft Depot. It was fairly successful and was actually fitted to a number of R.F.C. machines in the autumn of 1915. The Scarff-Dibovsky gear was the joint invention of Lieutenant Commander V. V. Dibovsky of the Imperial Russian Navy and Mr. F. W. Scarff of the British Admiralty Air Department. This was used for some time by the Vickers Aircraft Company and to some extent adopted by the R.F.C.

The most important step in synchronised armament was also made by the British; a new and improved form of hydraulic synchronisation, so superior to any mechanical gear that it quickly replaced the latter. This gear is in use in most air services even to this day.

This device was the invention of George Constantinesco, a Rumanian inventor of wave transmission who was connected with the Vickers company. Instead of Fokker's complicated system of gears, rods, and other moving parts, Constantinesco's device synchronised the firing of the gun by means of impulses transmitted through a length of copper tubing and a small reservoir containing a mixture of oil and paraffin under pressure. Furthermore it had the advantage of adaptability to any type of aero engine or aircraft.

The first R.F.C. squadron to arrive in France equipped with the Constantinesco gear was No. 55 (D.H.4's) on March 6, 1917. No. 48 (Bristol Fighters) and No. 56 (S.E.5's) went over within a month. Later an improved version, specially adapted to accommodate two guns aboard Sopwith Camels and other single-seater fighters, was put into production.

It should be pointed out that by early 1916 practically all Royal Flying Corps machines were appearing on the front carrying synchronised guns of some kind, and the Fokker menace was fairly well under control. At the same time a refinement of the Lewis gun gave pusher-plane observers a smart weapon for engaging enemy aircraft. Most important was a fitted collector bag which took in the ejected shell cartridges. Previously these empty shells had been hurtling back through the pusher propeller. The ammunition pan was also doubled in depth so that it carried 97 rounds instead of the original 47.

Next the British also concentrated on the Vickers gun. The water jacket had been dispensed with and used only as a support for the recoiling-barrel packing gland. It was speeded up to 600 rounds per minute and its weight cut considerably. Later a muzzle cup and conversion set raised the rate of fire to nearly 1,000 rounds per minute.

At first the ammunition was fed into the breech block by means of the standard canvas belt. This was suitable for ground action but ungainly for use in the air. Stormy weather conditions also tightened the "bind" of the loops, and in many cases it was impossible to withdraw the live rounds from the belt.

By 1917 an ingenious metal-link belt in which the cartridges themselves became the pins in the links was introduced. As each cartridge was fed into the breech, the link automatically fell away. At first the links were allowed to drop overboard, but when a shortage of aluminium became acute, special scoops were fitted to the side of the gun to catch and hold the disintegrating links. Electrical breech heaters were introduced to prevent the lubricant in the gun mechanism from becoming so viscous at high altitudes as to impede proper working speeds.

The improvement of the ammunition developed along with that of the aerial guns. Until the autumn of 1915 ordinary ball cartridges were in general use, although a form of "tracer" had been devised sometime before the war. The idea of a "tracer" round was just that. It was believed that gunnery might be improved if a tracer round marked the general direction of a machine-gun burst. A wad of a mixture of one part magnesium to eight parts of barium peroxide was plugged into the end of the bullet casing. When the round was fired the wad was ignited and the bullet dragged a short but brilliant tail of white fire.

Officially known as the S.P.K. Mark VII T., but more generally referred to as the "Sparklet", this bullet was approved for issue in July of 1916 and thereafter was almost invariably used in proportion of one tracer to every three rounds of regular ammunition. By early 1917 an armour-piercing round was added to this formula so that Lewis-gun drums and Vickers belts were loaded—one armour-piercing, one regular, one tracer, and one regular. The armour-piercing slug was adopted when it was discovered that the Germans were bolting on odd slabs of Krupp plate to protect the pilot, fuel tanks, and vital parts of the engine.

The writer, who fired many thousands of rounds as a gunner, was never impressed with the intent of the tracer bullet, and soon learned not to employ it as a guide, for shortly after it left the gun barrel it usually took on a very erratic flight, simply because the bullet burned itself out of true missile form as the phorphorus was consumed. Thus, the bullet did not actually follow the path of the more stable armour-piercing and regular rounds. At short distances it gave some temporary satisfaction when it was seen entering the fuselage or wings of an enemy machine, but it is questionable whether a tracer ever torched an enemy fuel tank or even burned an enemy balloon. These flamers were usually caused when a regular round struck a frictional spark off other metal or balloon grommets which in turn ignited the petrol or hydrogen gas.

Three other special bullets, primarily intended for anti-airship or kite-balloon use, were the Buckingham, Brock, and Pomeroy rounds. The Buckingham, which was the invention of a Coventry engineer, employed phosphorus as the basis of its incendiary composition and was first adopted by the Royal Naval Air Service in December 1915 and by the Royal Flying Corps the following April.

In June 1916 the Buckingham firm improved this bullet and its incendiary content and redesigned the round with a flatter nose. In tests it was discovered that the more pointed type made only a small perforation in the balloon fabric and did not allow enough gas to escape to ensure ignition. The flat-nosed bullet punched a large circular hole and gave free escape of gas, but—as so often happens with good intentions —the flat-nosed bullet was not as accurate and its jacket often collapsed before leaving the barrel of the gun. Further improvements were made and were continued until the war ended, but generally speaking the Buckingham bullet was much overrated. Fiction writers had a field day with Buckingham ammunition and shot down thousands of balloons with it. There was a story going the rounds that if a pilot was assigned to destroy an enemy balloon and he took Buckingham ammunition to do it, he was "covered" in employing this very inhuman projectile by carrying a blue card in his flying jacket. Thus, if he was shot down and taken prisoner during this frightful mission, he would be saved from immediate court-martial and execution by showing his blue (Buckingham) card. He was not, of course, supposed to fire Buckingham at an enemy aircraft.

I never actually saw a round of Buckingham and I have never met an ex-war pilot who had ever seen a blue card. There may have been such credentials. But after all, no war is without its legends.

The Brock bullet was invented because of a misapprehension during 1915 that the exhaust gases from a Zeppelin's engines were led between the outer and inner fabrics of the envelope to produce a layer of inert gas as a protection against incendiary ammunition.

Now, there was a dilly for you! A layer of red-hot, carbon-pitted gas to protect several thousand cubic feet of very explosive hydrogen.

However, apparently to go along with the gag, Commander F. A. Brock—in civilian life a fireworks manufacturer—produced a special bullet designed to explode between the first and second layers of fabric in such a way that the hydrogen would contact the outside air and so facilitate ignition. Half a million of these Brock bullets were ordered and delivered, but there is no record of one having destroyed a Zeppelin. They were, however, used by the Royal Naval Air Service throughout the war for anti-Zeppelin work over the North Sea.

The Pomeroy, or P.S.A., was yet another form of the explosive bullet and was first produced in quantity in early 1916. It had qualities similar to those of the Brock and was so sensitive it would explode even on striking loose fabric. But even this was not enough to ensure setting a Zeppelin on fire, and after much experiment the Pomeroy was so perfected that it would pierce the outer cover of an airship *without* exploding and then explode on the surface of the inner gas ballonets. Its use was confined almost exclusively to Home Defence units of the R.F.C., whose guns on anti-airship patrol duty were usually loaded with a mixture of the three types of bullets.

A new missile known as the R.T.S. round, which was a combined incendiary and explosive bullet of great sensitivity, was in great demand late in 1917. During 1918 a delivery of 200,000 rounds weekly was made to air squadrons in the field. For a time it was restricted to use against enemy bombers raiding England, but it proved so effective that its use overseas was sanctioned by September 1918.

In addition to the aircraft weapons already described, various types of heavier calibre guns were experimented with and in many cases became standard equipment. It has been erroneously stated that only the French used what were called air cannon in World War I. Actually the British used a 1-pound "pom-pom", or what they called a cow gun, aboard nightflying F.E.2b pushers in their attacks on troop concentrations and transports behind the German lines. A heavier type of pom-pom was the Coventry Ordnance one and one-half pounder quick-firer, an automatic gun designed to fire a maximum of five rounds at one loading. This formidable weapon had a bore of 37 mm. and a muzzle velocity of 1,950 feet per second, but its weight of 200 pounds restricted its use to flying boats and an occasional, specially strengthened D.H.4 of the Royal Naval Air Service.

The German Air Service devoted much time to the standardisation of their available machine guns. The basic weapon was their Parabellum, probably the first air-cooled infantry gun, which had been introduced into the German Army in 1913. It was not gas-operated as was the Lewis but employed the "short recoil" principle, a purely mechanical system whereby the bolt, locked to the barrel for a certain length of recoil, was unlocked and withdrawn about 3 inches from the barrel after the latter had completed its recoil. The barrel was chambered to take a German service cartridge of .311 calibre and was rifled with four grooves in a right-hand twist. It weighed 22 pounds and was fed by a 100-round cartridge belt led into the right-hand side of the breech. This was the accepted movable weapon for the rest of the war. Mounted on a cockpit ring-mount, it was fitted with a shoulder stock, and the ammunition belt was run over a heavy circular drum which must have been very ungainly to handle in the air. It was certainly not as convenient as the Lewis gun with its simple quick-release drum.

The Spandau, also a .311-calibre weapon, was actually a converted form of the old Maxim, so it was as simple to fit into a fixed-gun interrupter-gear system as was the Vickers to the Sopwith-Kauper and Constantinesco hydraulic gear. The Vickers was a much lightened and simplified form of the Maxim. When air-war conditions necessitated the use of two fixed guns on most single-seater fighters, German armament men devised a remote operating lever by which the pilot could reload his Spandaus or take what was known as immediate action to remedy stoppages or ammunition failures. They also set up a counter system which indicated how many shots he had fired so the pilot would not inadvertently go into another fight with an almost empty gun belt.

When Baron von Richthofen zoomed to the heights as the leader of the Boelcke Circus, he claimed it was more natural for a man to fire a gun with his trigger finger rather than with his thumb. He argued that firing would be more instinctive and therefore more efficient if the trigger operated like that of a rifle. The Red Baron's every wish was law, and this resulted in a complete block of armament production while several thousands of the new triggers and spade grips were made and fitted to all fighter aircraft then in service.

Although Garros employed the Hotchkiss automatic rifle as his original fixed gun, the weapon was seldom used again in the air. As a matter of fact, no one else even tried his deflector-plate idea. It was believed that it had in some way betrayed him when he did not return that eventful day, so the device was held in some disrepute.

From that point on the French adopted the British Vickers gun as their fixed weapon and the stripped-down Lewis for their movable weapon. They did, however, contribute one unusual feature to the armament programme when in 1916 they introduced an anti-balloon missile.

This was known as the Le Prieur rocket and was designed for attacks against kite balloons. These missiles were mounted

65

in hollow tubes bolted to the V-struts of the Nieuport Scout and were ignited electrically from the pilot's cockpit. There were four rocket tubes on each interplane strut, and the pilot simply charged at the balloon, snapped the igniter switch, and hopefully watched his fireworks streak out at the gasbag.

There are no available records which disclose how effective these missiles were, but during the heavy Zeppelin attacks in 1916 the British employed them from their old B.E.2c Home Defence biplanes.

After his capture Garros experienced a series of adventures that were as thrilling as any he had in becoming the world's first ace. When he was dragged before the officers of the German Intelligence his name was of course well remembered and he was treated as a dangerous captive.

First they planted him in a fortress of Magdeburg, where he made two attempts to escape during the first week. For this he was sentenced to fifty days of solitary confinement and forced to sign a register every hour. That kept the Frenchman well occupied for a time, but he never gave up planning to escape. In 1916 he was transferred to Cologne, mainly to break up any well-devised plans he had been working on. At Cologne he met Pierre Antoine Marchal, hero of a "bombless" raid on Berlin. Marchal had actually flown over Berlin, dropped a wad of propaganda leaflets, and continued on, hoping to land safely in Russia. His fuel supply ran short and he was taken prisoner.

The Germans made a big mistake planting these two men together. Once they were caught trying to dig a tunnel under the Cologne *Lager* and were almost in the clear. Garros was tossed back into solitary. He tried a starvation diet, hoping he could slim down enough to squeeze through the restraining bars. The Germans only doubled the guard.

But nothing could hold Garros and Marchal very long and their eventual escape was extraordinary.

Armand Pinsard, it will be remembered, had gone down early in 1915, but he too kept trying to escape and eventually wormed his way into Switzerland and safety. When he turned up again in France he naturally inquired for Garros.

"You have not heard? Garros was lost last April!"

"Roland is a prisoner too?"

"Very much so. We hear all sorts of stories of how the Boche keep him in irons and behind difficult stockades. When we last heard, he was in the Cologne area."

"Cologne? Oh, ho!" Pinsard laughed. "Then it will be easy. I know all about Cologne."

What Pinsard meant was that he knew a certain turncoat German N.C.O. who could be bought.

"Just give me a few days—and someone who can fly a Farman two-seater. We will get Garros out."

The details of this famous breakout were kept secret for years and, of course, with the telling were probably touched up here and there for dramatic effect. We do know that a certain German N.C.O. conveniently left a stockade door unlocked on the evening of January 23, 1918. A Sergeant Quette, an expert instructor who could do amazing things with the old Horace Farman biplane, conveniently managed to be in a certain field well inside the German lines at midnight. Pinsard flew a Spad fighter to provide cover while both Garros and Marchal were flown out.

The only questionable point to this story is whether the old Farman could have actually hauled a pilot and two prisoners out of a meadow under such circumstances, but men did amazing things in those glorious days, and until a better version comes along this one will have to be accepted.

What probably happened is that a number of people were financially involved and some such legendary escape was contrived to cover the conspirators concerned.

Of course Garros soon returned to action. Nothing could keep him from tackling his bitter enemy, although as an escaped prisoner of war he had every right to refuse to risk action on the front again.

Aviation had made tremendous advances during his months of captivity. The new Spads and Nieuports were machines from another world, but he resolutely took primary training all over again until he could fly as well as the next pilot.

But the advance in gunnery amazed him. The new high-speed Vickers and the lightened Lewis which had been adapted for air-gunner cockpits fascinated him. He *was* disappointed, however, to learn that nothing much had been done with the Hispano-Suiza 1-pounder, which had been available as far back as 1915.

As an armourer pointed out to him: "We tried to use it. Poor Georges Guynemer had one mounted to fire through the hollow crankshaft of the new Hispano-Suiza engine, but it was not a great success."

"Why not?" Garros argued, for he had left some crude drawings of such an engine-weapon arrangement and was positive it would be of great value if properly employed.

"It was too long. When it recoiled the breech shot back under the pilot's seat. Then, too, the fumes from the spent

67

cartridges collected in the cockpit and nauseated the pilot. It just won't fit into today's aeroplanes."

"Too bad. But you mark my word. We shall come to it. What good are mere rifle-calibre weapons against today's aircraft?" complained Garros.

He was soon to find out.

On October 5, 1918, only a month before the Armistice, Roland Garros was shot down and killed near Vouziers—by a rifle-calibre machine gun mounted on a German Fokker D.7.

So passed Roland Garros, pioneer pilot, inventor, and the first of the great French aces. His niche in the aviation world was already established, but Fate makes no distinction and takes its pick where it will.

3

THE ZEPPELIN KILLERS—
1915

☐ The eventful history of the Royal Naval Air Service, Britain's naval air arm, was inaugurated with a more definite programme than that of the Royal Flying Corps. From the opening week of the war, R.N.A.S. airmen were at the enemy hammer and tongs, their duties being entirely different from those of the R.F.C., since they had first a responsibility to the Home Fleet and many problems of home defence to assume.

While the military arm was aimlessly floundering about in France and Belgium, trying to make themselves useful to the Army, the R.N.A.S. was immediately active with definite missions. They undertook bombing assignments, did air-defence operations, and, with the threat of the Zeppelins, carried out nightly airship stalking. In addition, they performed daily routine patrols of great importance to the surface navy.

Since the military situation on the continent was "very fluid", the R.N.A.S. did not take over any permanent base along the European coast until early in 1915. They had used a few temporary landing strips along the beach at Dunkirk, but it wasn't until February that No. 1 Naval Squadron flew across The Streak—the airmen's phrase for the English Channel—to take up some fixed abode.

Their first real mission joined up a fleet of thirty-four naval aeroplanes and seaplanes in a mass attack on enemy bases between Zeebrugge and Ostend. This operation turned out to be a memorable one, for after encountering fog above the Channel the raiders ran into a violent snowstorm over the Belgian coast and very few reached their objectives. One of No. 1

Squadron's pilots, however, succeeded in finding a coastal battery at Slype and bombed it in the face of heavy ground fire.

The rest of the R.N.A.S. fleet was obliged to make for a temporary strip below Dunkirk, to which they had been told to return if bad weather set in. Obviously weather predictions were not very reliable and several pilots reported hair-raising experiences in this storm: one completely turned over in the air, and Flight Lieutenant H. Rosher of No. 1 Squadron, who became lost in the clouds, plunged 6,000 feet out of control before recovering. That famous pioneer airman, Flight Commander Claude Grahame-White, came down in the sea off Nieuport and was rescued in the nick of time by a French destroyer.

More raids were carried out on the Ostend and Zeebrugge areas during the next few days. Bombs were dropped on the Ostend and Blankenberge railroad stations, on gun positions at Middelkerke, and on the defensive works and locks of the Bruges-Zeebrugge Canal. Bruges also came in for some attention when it was learned that the Germans planned to use the industrial plants there to assemble their U-boats. During this raid a French scout squadron raided the Ghistelles airfield and completely grounded the German defence forces. No. 1 Naval suffered its first casualty when Flight Lieutenant Gordon Riggall failed to return from one of these forays.

Toward the end of February, No. 1 Naval was moved to Saint-Pol, from where they put on a sustained attack against enemy positions along the coast. At this time the R.N.A.S. equipment consisted of a miscellaneous collection of aircraft including Avros, Vickers Fighters, three American Curtisses, and a Bristol two-seater. The Avros were used for the "long-distance" raids, the main objectives being the airship sheds which the Germans had hurriedly erected in Belgium and from which their Zeppelins were raiding the French and English coasts.

The German submarine bases in occupied Belgium were also frequent targets for the R.N.A.S. during March and April, and one of their most successful raids was carried out on March 24 against the submarine depot at Hoboken near Antwerp. This raid, in which No. 1 Squadron's five Avros took part, was led by Squadron Commander I. T. Courtney, who was accompanied by Flight Lieutenants B. C. Meates, H. L. Rosher, B. L. Huskinson, and F. G. Andreae. The five pilots cut cards for the order of starting and, though they had planned to keep in sight of one another, they were soon scattered in low cloud and mist. Visibility was so bad that Andreae and Huskinson were soon lost and had to return before their fuel ran out. The others, however, succeeded in getting through to within 500 feet of the ground, where they ran into a murderous curtain of shrapnel and machine-gun fire. All three hit the submarine dock, and an official French communiqué issued that night confirmed that a shipyard had been set afire, two submarines completely destroyed, forty German workmen killed and sixty-two wounded.

On the return flight Meates was forced down by engine trouble and interned in Holland, but Courtney and Rosher both reached home, having covered 250 miles in a nonstop flight of more than four hours. A few days later, determined to make up for his previous misfortune, Flight Lieutenant Andreae set off alone by moonlight and delivered a telling surprise attack on the same dockyard.

The year of 1915 was marked by the heavy attacks on London and other British cities by raiding German Zeppelins. It was the first time in history that this type of warfare on helpless civilians was perpetrated, and there was little to be done about these giant gasbags, since practically nothing had been accomplished toward developing a high-angle anti-aircraft gun, and the existing aeroplanes were not capable of rapid climb. There was no radar, and all the Germans had to do was to take off from their sheds in occupied Belgium, climb to a favourable wind level late in the afternoon, and cut their engines. The wind would carry them in silence over the North Sea, so they generally arrived over Britain in the early darkness. Once they had released their racks of high explosives, they simply soared to a greater height and turned their noses for home.

As may be surmised, the prospects were not cheerful. For months the Allies had suffered reverse after reverse. The British still remembered Mons, as they were to remember Dunkirk a quarter of a century later. They had won at Neuve-Chappelle, but at what a cost! The Germans had staged their first poison-gas attack, and the British were still searching for a reliable gas mask.

This new atrocity, only tersely announced, aroused fresh suspicions. At home they had experienced the general blackout for the first time. Raiding Zeppelins, blackouts, and censorship? What next? The Germans must be at the Channel ports! What could be believed? If the gas attack at Ypres was censored, how much could be credited concerning the reported damage inflicted by the Zeppelin raids? What was to stop the Germans from bombing London clean off the map or drenching the chief cities with their poison gas?

By June of that year the British were as near morale disintegration as they have ever been. Fortunately confidence was restored by a schoolboyish youngster, Reginald Alexander John Warneford. The searching finger of Fate could not have selected a more British candidate for the hero's role of this early war drama.

Reg Warneford was a lively composite of the Commonwealth of Nations. His parents were cheery Yorkshire types who rattled about the Empire on various missions and pretexts, and Reg was born in India, educated at the English College in Simla, at Stratford on Avon Grammar School in England, and at an unnamed lyceum in Canada. Although his formal education was devoted to the arts and classics, Reg appears to have shown a marked preference for motor cycles, odorous chemical experiments, and mountain climbing.

When the news of the war reached him in Canada he broke out of the lyceum and raced for England. First he joined the much-publicized Sportsmen's Battalion, an infantry unit made up of well-known sporting and athletic figures, but the Sportsmen's Battalion was slack in unfurling its battle flags, and Reggie discovered that headlined athletes are usually physically attuned only to sport—not war. Fearing the conflict would end before the athletes were whipped into combat condition, he put in for an immediate transfer to the Royal Naval Air Service. He made a good selection, for by June 1915, less than eleven months after the opening of hostilities, he was a Flight Sub-Lieutenant with No. 1 Squadron at Dunkirk. Half a dozen solo flights on a Morane Parasol, and young Warneford was tabbed for honour and glory.

It must be admitted that World War I seemed to be designed for men who wanted fast action. Like Warneford, most flyers were afraid it would peter out any minute—and they'd all have to go back to school or work again.

On the evening of May 21, 1915, Hauptmann Karl Linnarz, a noted Zeppelin commander, carried out the first successful raid on London. He had taken off from an airship base located at Evère just north of Brussels, gained operating altitude over his field, and then allowed a friendly breeze to drift him in silence over the British Capital.

London watched the inadequate defences go into action. The searchlights lanced the skies but were unable to pick up the raider. The ineffective pom-poms grunted and growled but only showered the suburbs with jagged shrapnel. A few Home Defence flyers took off to do battle, but as usual nothing happened. The warning sirens shrieked and died down. The pungent smoke pall seeped across the Thames, and hurriedly organized rescue teams clambered through the wreckage, cursing a government that had failed to anticipate this form of warfare.

However, at a secluded airstrip across the Channel something new had been added. The British had set up a special anti-airship flight from No. 1 (Naval) R.N.A.S. Squadron at Dunkirk. A hundred feet below the homeward-bound Zeppelin—dramatically high-lighted by the yellow-blue exhausts of its four Maybach engines—cruised a tiny high-wing monoplane flaunting the new red, white, and blue of the British service. A series of smudged flame flicks spat out from the oval cockpit below the centre-section cutout. Gunfire! They were single shots of desperation from a cumbersome shoulder weapon, but alarming and disconcerting, nevertheless. After all, LZ.38's ballonets were filled with hydrogen, and it took only a single bullet to produce a spark.

Hauptmann Linnarz rushed to his control board and bellowed for emergency measures. As soon as his gasbag had lifted to safety he became the militant Prussian once more. He took a neatly engraved calling card from his wallet and on it scrawled: "You English! We have come and we will come again soon to kill or cure! Linnarz." He snatched a weighted message streamer from a flag locker and inserted the card and message in the stitched pocket. "See that this is dropped as near the Dunkirk aerodrome as possible. We will fly over it on crossing the coast line."

Four thousand feet below, Lieutenant R. H. Mulock of No. 1 Naval cut his gasping Le Rhone engine and eased into a gentle glide. He'd given it a try, but the little Morane Parasol was unequal to the task.

"There's no use trying to swat one wasp with a wisp of straw," Mulock later reported to his C.O., Commander Spenser Grey. "A wise man would pour a kettle of hot water down the hole and scuttle the lot. That's what we've got to do. Blast them out of their bloody sheds!"

From that night on, No. 1 Naval planned a new strategy and, to add a dash of personal competition and squadron animosity to the proceedings, a wandering navy artificer beachcombing along the Dunkirk dunes the next day came across Hauptmann Linnarz's insulting message. He turned it over to Commander Grey, and the boys at No. 1 Naval accepted the challenge.

When the Royal Naval Air Service first took over its base at Dunkirk, Spenser Grey decided to disperse the few machines allotted to him. Dunkirk was too obvious a target, but

Furnes, just across the French-Belgian border, was less conspicuous.

One three-ship flight under Lieutenant J. P. Wilson was therefore accommodated in three single canvas hangars set on the edge of a lush meadow, and there Wilson and Sub-Lieutenants Mills and Reg Warneford made up the duty roster. Their mounts were stripped-down versions of the French Morane-Saulnier observation planes. The high wing was given a sharper angle of attack for climbing, one seat was covered over, and a primitive form of bomb rack was bolted beneath the fuselage. Because of its weird wing arrangement, the British pilots had long dubbed it the Parasol.

This Morane machine was as flighty as its name, tricky on the controls and devilish to land. It was relatively fast as a single-seater and powered with an 80-h.p. Rhone engine. Other than the six so-called fire bombs and a light carbine borrowed from the Belgian Army, she carried no offensive armament.

On the afternoon of June 6 Wilson's Furnes flight reported to Dunkirk, where Spenser Grey had set up a council of war. The C.O. explained Mulock's abortive brush with the Zeppelin that had bombed London and impressed his flight leaders with the obvious impossibility of engaging Zeps in the air. Then Grey fluttered Linnarz's message streamer and belligerent calling card.

"The man who dropped this challenge played merry hell over London less than a week ago. Mulock did his best, but this Hun Linnarz returned to his shed at Evère unscathed."

"You are sure this calling-card bloke and his gasbag are located at Evère?" Wilson broke in.

"That, we know. Keep thinking along those lines, Wilson. Just one night attack might be very useful." It was pretty obvious what Spenser Grey and J. P. Wilson were considering.

On the way back to Furnes young Warneford explained to Wilson that he had never been off the ground at night, but Wilson insisted they were taking off as soon after midnight as possible.

True to his word, Lieutenant Wilson had his flight ready and waiting on the oil-stained turf by midnight, the racks were glutted with fire bombs, and the Belgian carbines rested in the brass prongs beside the cockpits.

Warneford was flagged off first, and before he realized what he had signed up for his Morane was well off the ground. He stared wide-eyed and then peered, trying to find the small grouping of instruments. A length of scarlet worsted knotted to a centre-section strut was flicking insistently at his nose, and he quickly realized this very primitive indicator was warning him that he was already in a dangerous sideslip. Gradually his eyes became accustomed to the yellow-grey nothingness below his Triplex windscreen, and he fixed his gaze on the white needle of the altimeter. He was already at 3,000 feet!

He looked around for some evidence of Wilson and Mills. There was nothing anywhere but the exaggerated roar of the Le Rhone and the drip-drip-drip of condensation off the centre-section that needled his cheeks like a fretsaw blade. Below hissed a poisonous glow that he had never encountered before—it was the blue-yellow flame of his exhaust. His indistinct compass float, dancing in a small window placed in the bulge of the centre-section, showed something that looked like the letter W. Encouraged by this, he risked a turn, hoping to pick up his flight mates.

He circled and circled for some minutes, but no sign of Wilson or Mills rewarded his patient patrol. Meanwhile he was becoming adjusted to his strange experience and as the area remained fairly clear he wondered whether, regardless of his failure to contact his flight leader and companion, he might make himself useful.

He had about decided to search for the Berchem-Sainte-Agathe airship shed, which he remembered was located just west of Brussels, when something caught his eye a few miles to the north. He blinked and looked again. That something was emitting the same blue-yellow flame as his Le Rhone. If that was Wilson and Mills, what the devil were they doing up there toward Ostend? And what in heaven's name was that long black mass floating above them?

Wilson and Mills had made immediate contact with each other and soon cleared the fog around Furnes to head east for Brussels, 75 miles away. On finding clear skies, Wilson decided to fly direct for Evère on the north side of the old Flemish city, and together they hit their objective on the nose. Circling the shed area once, Wilson went in first, mainly to start a fire and give Mills a pathfinder target. He released three of his bombs but only created a billowing smoke pall. By then the German defence gunners woke up and began plastering the sky with high-angle gun explosive, at which point Wilson discovered his last three bombs had become hung up in the primitive rack. Young Mills finally went in, Parasol wings fluttering, to dare the ground fire and pulled his bomb plug. All six of his 20-pounders slid clear, and he was rewarded with a gigantic explosion that illuminated the sky for miles around. Wilson, who had conceived and planned the raid, had to return with little to show for his effort.

Two weeks later British Intelligence, working out of Antwerp, reported that Hauptmann Linnarz's LZ.38—the same airship that had first bombed London—had gone up in flames during the raid on Evère. Thus the R.N.A.S. scored revenge for that caustic calling card.

That same night the LZ.37, commanded by Oberleutnant von de Haegen, had been ordered to carry out a routine patrol stretching from Ghent to Le Havre. There was nothing particularly offensive about the flight, for it was originated mainly to give a number of airship designers, specialists, and technicians from the Zeppelin factory first-hand knowledge of the various problems experienced by the crews on active service.

The LZ.37 was 521 feet in length and her eighteen main gas ballonets carried 953,000 cubic feet of hydrogen. She was powered by four new 210-h.p. Maybach engines and manned by a select crew of twenty-eight highly skilled airshipmen. For defence her designers had provided four machine-gun posts built into the outboard engine gondolas. These positions provided good visibility, a fairly wide arc of fire, and complete defence along both sides of the airship.

After Warneford had been flying north for a few minutes he stared in amazement at what he had stumbled onto—a Zeppelin that seemed half a mile long! He had to twist his head from west to east to take in its leviathan proportions. From its underside were hung several glistening observation cars, and the gleam from fantail exhausts indicated that the rubberized covering was daubed a yellow-ochre colour. Warneford wondered what the devil kept a thing that big in the air at all. But there was no time for reflection as the Zeppelin's machine guns opened up and the slugs clattered through the frail wings of Morane Parasol No. 3253.

Warneford wisely heeled over and cleared off out of range. He glanced around and saw that the fog was breaking up below and he could see the Ostend-Bruges Canal. The big gasbag was apparently headed for Ghent. The observation cars seemed twice as large as his Parasol fuselage.

Then, to his amazement, the big snub-nosed gasbag shifted course and came roaring on toward him. Two more streams of tracer-flickering machine-gun fire snapped from the forward gondolas and converged only a few yards from the Parasol. He gave the Le Rhone all she could gulp and tried to climb, but the crisscrossing tracers pencilled in a definite warning, and he had to peel off and dive. He sat and studied the situation and wondered what his carbine would do if he could hit something particularly touchy. After all, hydrogen . . .

He flailed the little Morane back and took the carbine from its prongs. Manoeuvring to a point under the mighty elevator and rudder framework, he gripped the control stick between his knees, and then, sublimely confident that he had not been seen, he began triggering off a few .303 shells at the massive target above and ahead. The first clip of cartridges was soon spent and nothing untoward had happened.

For the next few minutes he stalked the LZ.37 and popped away with his carbine, but it was like aiming at a cyclone-propelled haystack with an air rifle. Whenever he came within range or within view, the German gunners sprayed the sky about him with generous bursts of Parabellum fire, and time after time the impudent young Englishman was driven off.

Von de Haegen then played it safe and dumped some water ballast over Assebroek and left Warneford still potting away impotently at 7,000 feet. From there the Zep commander upped his speed and roared away for Ghent.

Warneford realized what had happened but refused to admit defeat. Instead he settled back to keep the Zeppelin within view and gain some valuable height.

It was a race for safety for the LZ.37, and while von de Haegen maintained his altitude Warneford was helpless; but this was not an ordinary mission. The German commander began to worry about his V.I.P. passengers when he should have concentrated on maintaining his safe tactical precedure.

By 2.25 a.m. the Morane Parasol pilot, still stalking and trying to get above the Zeppelin, was delighted to see the big airship suddenly nose down and apparently head for a break in the 7,000-foot cloud layer that spread toward Ghent. He had browbeaten his plane up to 11,000 feet, hoping he might get into a position where he could use his fire bombs, since he had expended all his carbine ammunition. Now the LZ.37 was actually below him and for the first time he realized that the upper cover was painted what seemed to be a dark green and that there was nothing resembling a gun turret on the top that could harass him. The other guns were in the underside gondolas and he was shielded from them by the bulging sides of the main framework.

She looked so big as he moved into position for his run-in, he felt he could make a landing on her topside.

The ground smear that was Ghent lay below and slightly to the east when the gnat-like Morane nosed down for the 500-foot top panel of the LZ.37. He must have chuckled to himself as his wheels passed over the high elevator and rudder structure.

One . . . two . . . three! he counted as the Morane jerked with the release of each bomb.

He said later that he had fully expected the Zeppelin to explode immediately when his first bomb pierced the envelope.

Four . . . five! He continued to count, and then a gigantic explosion ripped through the upper panel covering, baring the indistinct details of the framework.

Completely spellbound, he continued his run-in until the little Morane was swept up on a savage belch of flaming concussion. It whipped over with a violence that would have catapulted Warneford out of his cockpit had it not been for his safety belt. He gasped in astonishment, rammed the stick forward, and tried to get her into a dive. Chunks of burning framework hurtled by as he gradually floundered out of the aerial convulsion and streaked down through a great pall of choking smoke. The next few minutes were devoted to skimming clear of the debris, getting back on even keel, and frantically adjusting his air and gas mixture to overcome a series of warning pops from his Le Rhone.

A few seconds later the doomed airship fell on the convent of Saint Elizabeth in the Mont-Saint-Amand suburb of Ghent. One nun was killed outright and several women were badly burned, but the helmsman of the Zeppelin had a most remarkable escape. According to eye-witnesses, he actually jumped clear of the tumbling wreckage at about 200 feet, landed on the roof of the convent, crashed through it as though it had been made of matchwood, and landed in an unoccupied bed. He suffered only minor injuries and was the only crew member or passenger of the ill-fated LZ.37 to live.

At 7,000 feet above this widespread carnage Warneford sat waiting for his wings to part company with the fuselage. The Le Rhone snorted its wrath and contempt—and quit cold! The gleaming wooden prop wig-wagged to a halt as he calculated that he was at least 35 miles inside the German lines. There was nothing else to do but accept the bitter inevitable and go down. In spite of the darkness and the lack of ground flares, the young flyer landed the battered machine safely in an open field that was shielded on one side by a long patch of woods. There was a darkened farmhouse nearby, but no one appeared to question his unscheduled arrival.

His first impulse was to destroy the plane but an investigation of the tank disclosed there was ample fuel to get him back across the line to Furnes, and further probing indicated that his violent acrobatics had broken the fuel line. He figured

78

there was still a chance to escape. A quick search through his pockets produced a cigarette holder. The outer end was just what he needed, so he broke it off, fitted it to form a journal at the original break, and bound it secure with strips of a linen handkerchief. An experimental tug on the prop assured him that sufficient fuel was reaching the carburetor, so he decided to start the engine himself. The Le Rhone, of course, was still warm, and after two complete revolutions of the prop to suck in petrol he cut in the switch and snapped her over. The engine caught immediately and it was something of a scramble to get into the cockpit, but he managed it and roared away.

Approaching the coast again, he encountered more fog, so he tooled up and down until he found a hole and dropped through. At 3.30 a.m. he checked in at Cap Gris-Nez, 10 miles below Calais, where he picked up more fuel and called his squadron headquarters at Dunkirk.

He sat out the bad weather and finally returned to Furnes at 10.30 a.m. By that time the jubilant news was widely known and within hours his name was ringing from one end of the Empire to the other. All that week his photograph was flashed on hundreds of theatre screens to the delight of cheering audiences.

That afternoon, in keeping with the traditions of the Silent Service, Commanding Officer Spenser Grey of No. 1 Naval Squadron posted a notice which read:

Though weather has been extremely unsettled, our pilots have been active and busy

The next day King George V recognized Warneford's victory by awarding him the Victoria Cross, and the French government followed that decoration with their Cross of the Legion of Honour.

England tightened its belt from that day on and took a brighter view of the Zeppelin menace. Many more raiders would come and more devastation would be wrought, but now there was assurance that some young Britisher would mount the sky and take them on. Many more Zeppelins were destroyed before the Kaiser capitulated, and many other young men—Leffe-Robinson, Tempest, Cadbury, Sowrey, Leckie and Pyott—came along to take up Warneford's torch. All of them were great names in those days.

But Flight Lieutenant R. A. J. Warneford lived only ten more days to enjoy the laurels of his victory. He went to Paris on June 17 to receive his Legion of Honour and after the ceremony was ordered to pick up a new Farman biplane at the Buc aerodrome outside the French capital. The machine was brand new—so new in fact that much of its standard equipment had not been fitted—but most important, there were no safety belts in either seat.

An enthusiastic American newspaperman named Needham had asked to go along to Furnes, where he planned to write a story about Warneford and his Zeppelin victory. Warneford cheerfully agreed and they climbed in the biplane and took off. Almost immediately, for some unknown reason, the Farman pitched and bucked and both Warneford and Needham were thrown out in midair and killed. And so ended the brief but illustrious record of the first British airman to destroy a German zeppelin in the air.

Following the Warneford Zeppelin triumph, there were dozens of fabulous reports of other gasbag conquests. One of the most fantastic that persisted for weeks was that Roland Garros, the French ace, had tried to down a Zeppelin over Paris with his new gun, but when he failed with ordinary gunfire he boldly rammed the raider, flying his Morane Bullet straight through the massive framework and coming out the other side, leaving a jagged outline of his machine. After that, the Zeppelin folded in the middle and dropped in a French cornfield. There was, of course, nothing to the report, but faked photographs of this astounding adventure were on sale all over France for several weeks.

The myth of the Allied pilot who flew through a Zeppelin persisted for some time, but no more Zeppelins were downed for more than a year when a B.E.2c pilot of No. 39 Squadron, Royal Flying Corps, Lieutenant W. Leefe-Robinson, repeated Warneford's performance. In this case, however, he scored his victory on the evening of September 2-3, 1916, in sight of a million pairs of British eyes, and piled up the wreckage for all to see near the little village of Cuffley in Middlesex, whereas Warneford's action took place over the other side of the North Sea. Strictly speaking, the airship brought down was not a Zeppelin. It was a dirigible of the old Schutte-Lanz type. It had a maximum speed of about 60 miles an hour, but for purposes of fuel conservation this speed was seldom used; the cruising speed of 40 miles per hour was more usual. Its maximum altitude, by jettisoning its war load, was about 15,000 feet.

Leefe-Robinson was also born in India of British parents, in 1895, and when the family returned to Britain he was educated at St. Bee's School in Cumberland, a small academy that produced three Victoria Cross winners. After considerable travelling in France and Russia he entered Sandhurst military college in August 1914. The following December he was gazetted to the Worcester Regiment, but by March 1915 had transferred to the Royal Flying Corps where he served as an observer. On May 9 he was wounded in the right arm on a patrol near Lille, and when he had recovered he was posted to a flight training school at Farnborough, England, and took his ticket the following September. He was eventually assigned to No. 39 Squadron, a Home Defence unit located at Sutton's Farm.

By this time, while no longer in dread of the Zeppelins, the people of Britain were looking askance at the anti-aircraft defences the politicians and War Office martinets were bragging about. The Zeppelins were again raiding Britain almost nightly, and the civilian casualty roll mounted. Month after month passed and no one had emulated Reg Warneford's feat. In truth, the gasbag invaders were enjoying some immunity, but by the same token they were not scoring on important military points. As in World War II these raids, although spectacular and damaging from the point of view of the general population, were not seriously hindering the over-all war effort. The population was suffering mainly from too many sleepless nights.

Then on September 3, 1916, in full view of the Metropolis a giant raider fell in a roaring mass of flame. It struck the ground at Cuffley, Middlesex, and the entire crew of sixteen died as millions of Londoners cheered the unknown hero who had sent it to its fate. In an hour all roads leading to Cuffley were thronged with the curious who rushed to see the remains of the first raider shot down on English soil.

Shortly after eleven o'clock on September 2 the Maybach engines of these dirigibles were first heard over the sleeping countryside. It was a beautifully clear night with few clouds floating across the sky. The stars looked down with cool aloofness. Gradually the higher-pitched notes of the Home Defence B.E.2c's screeched across the skies in search of the raiders. Just after one o'clock a probing searchlight picked out a long, glowing pencil of light as it approached Woolwich Arsenal. There was no mistaking it, and other searchlights swept across the war-stricken sky and joined the first. Lieutenant Leefe-Robinson saw the dirigible held aloft on a tripod of blinding silver, and, although he was in danger of being hit by his own shells, he raced in to the attack.

81

This is his story as he scrawled it on a sheet of patrol report paper:

From: Lieutenant Leefe-Robinson,
Sutton's Farm.

To: The Officer Commanding
No. 39 H. D. Squadron.

Sir:

I have the honour to make the following report on night patrol made by me on the night of the 2-3 instant. I went up at about 11.08 p.m. on the night of the second with instructions to patrol between Sutton's Farm and Joyce Green.

I climbed to 10,000 feet in fifty-three minutes. I counted what I thought were ten sets of flares—there were a few clouds below me, but on the whole it was a beautifully clear night. I saw nothing until 1.10 a.m., when two searchlights picked up a Zeppelin S.E. of Woolwich. The clouds had collected in this quarter and the searchlights had some difficulty in keeping on the airship. By this time I had managed to climb to 12,000 feet and I made in the direction of the Zeppelin—which was being fired on by a few anti-aircraft guns—hoping to cut it off on its way eastward. I very slowly gained on it for about ten minutes. I judged it to be about 800 feet below me and I sacrificed some speed in order to keep the height. It went behind some clouds, avoiding the searchlight, and I lost sight of it. After fifteen minutes of fruitless search I returned to my patrol.

I managed to pick up and distinguish my flares again. At about 1.50 a.m. I noticed a red glow in the N.E. of London. Taking it to be an outbreak of fire, I went in that direction. At 205 a Zeppelin was picked up by the searchlights over N.N.E. London (as far as I could judge).

Remembering my last failure, I sacrificed height (I was at about 12,900 feet) for speed and nosed down in the direction of the Zeppelin. I saw shells bursting and night tracers flying around it. When I drew closer I noticed that the anti-aircraft aim was too high or too low; also a good many shells burst about 800 feet behind—a few tracers went right over. I could hear the bursts when about 3,000 feet from the Zeppelin. I flew about 800 feet below it from bow to stern and distributed one drum among it (alternate New Brock and Pomeroy). It seemed to have no effect; I therefore moved to one side and gave them another drum along the side—also without

82

effect. I then got behind it and by this time I was very close—500 feet or less below, and concentrated one drum on one part (underneath rear). I was then at a height of 11,500 feet when attacking the Zeppelin.

I had hardly finished the drum before I saw the part fired at, glow. In a few seconds the whole rear part was blazing. When the third drum was fired, there were no searchlights on the Zeppelin, and no anti-aircraft was firing. I quickly got out of the way of the falling, blazing Zeppelin and, being very excited, fired off a few red Very lights and dropped a parachute flare.

Having little oil or petrol left, I returned to Sutton's Farm, landing at 2.45 a.m. On landing, I found the Zeppelin gunners had shot away the machine-gun wire guard, the rear part of my centre section, and had pierced the main spar several times.

I have the honour to be, sir,
Your obedient servant,
(Signed) W. Leefe-Robinson, Lieutenant
No. 39 Squadron, R.F.C.

Once again the hero of the hour did not long survive his victory. On April 5, 1917, Leefe-Robinson was posted to No. 48 Squadron, the first R.F.C. outfit to fly the new Bristol Fighter. Flying as a flight commander (captain), he saw his six-plane flight attacked by a Fokker circus. Instead of breaking up and flying as fighter scouts, Leefe-Robinson's flight tried to fly the old two-seater Lufbery circle (nose to tail) formation and were badly cut up. It was the first and last time that the Bristol Fighter was so misused. Leefe-Robinson's engine was damaged and he had to land in enemy territory, where he was taken prisoner, spending most of the war in various German prisons including the infamous Holzminden, where for a time he was kept in solitary confinement. His health became undermined—he was hardly the rugged physical type—and shortly after being returned to his home in England fell a victim to one of the influenza epidemics. This courageous young man who gave London its most dramatic war spectacle made no spectacular exit himself. He died in bed on January 31, 1918.

London was the principal objective of the First World War Zeppelin raids, and between 1915 and 1918 no less than 208 airship sorties were carried out against Britain, a total of 5,907 bombs were dropped, 528 people were killed (mostly civilians), and more than 1,000 were wounded. The peak of the Zeppelin's threat was during 1915 and 1916, for during those two years 168 sorties were carried out against Great Britain, killing 115 people and wounding 324 in London. In the rest of England, 361 were killed and 692 wounded. In 1917 and 1918 the airship threat practically came to an end; only thirty sorties were made in 1917, and ten in the last year of the war.

The explanation is that Great Britain greatly improved her anti-aircraft gunnery, searchlights, and her warning system. A seldom-published item of interest is that many of the ground observers employed along the British east coast to detect the oncoming airships and aircraft were blind people, selected because of their acute hearing. It was probably the most rewarding task any such afflicted person has undertaken.

After Leefe-Robinson's success against S.L.11 the Home Defence squadrons seemed to be inspired. On September 23, 1916, eleven airships, including three new super-Zeppelins, left their sheds in Belgium and headed for the Essex coast. About midnight L.33 was over East London and had dropped twenty bombs. This time, however, the defence reacted fast and almost immediately L.33 was caught on a cone of searchlights and was riddled by the ground guns. One of her engines was damaged and she began to fly a very erratic course, and to add to her miseries a Lieutenant A. G. Brandon of the R.F.C. hove out of the night and for twenty minutes slugged her with machine-gun fire. As she laboured her way back to the North Sea the crew jettisoned everything that could be tossed overboard, but she never reached the Belgian coast line and was lost in the sea.

The famous Commander Mathy, aboard L.31 in company with L.32, crossed the English Channel and cruised over toward Kent, flying boldly on to the centre of London. Mathy dumped bombs on northern London and escaped. The L.32, however, was not so bold and spent some time circling the Romney marshes and finally crossed the Thames at Dartford, where it was picked up by searchlights. At this point Lieutenant Frederick Sowrey attacked with a machine gun and sent it down in flames near the village of Billericay. He had to be content with the Distinguished Service Order.

The bold Captain Mathy lived a charmed life. He seemed bullet-proof, and night after night, weather permitting, he would invade Britain from one direction of the other. He did not always float over to drop bombs; sometimes he would simply drift about making an important reconnaissance. One never knew whether he would come to London from the industrial north or appear suddenly over the Isle of Wight and fly inland from the English Channel.

On board the L.31 on the night of October 1, 1916, Mathy led a formation of eleven dirigibles and this time he first appeared over Lowestoft on the east coast at about eight o'clock and as usual steered a deliberate course for London. Soon after passing Chelmsford, he discovered that the outer London defences were ready for him, so he turned north-east until the furor died down. Then with a quick decision he turned south-west with the idea of getting into position for another dash across London. After drifting quietly in the vicinity of Ware, he started his engines again and headed for the northern fringes of the capital.

The ground defences had been just as wary, and the minute his engines opened up, the guns below responded and Mathy had to turn away, but unfortunately for him Second Lieutenant W. J. Tempest had struggled up to 12,700 feet while stalking the Mathy airship. He attacked resolutely in the face of heavy gondola machine-gun fire, and the L.31 went down in flames, piling up on the outskirts of Potters Bar. This was the last time a German dirigible attempted to attack London. After that the Germans gave their attention to the industrial areas in the north.

Then on the evening of November 27, 1916, eight dirigibles reached the British coast line, one being immediately destroyed on the coast near Hartlepool by Captain J. V. Pyott of the R.F.C. Another raider, L.21, was caught by anti-aircraft fire as she was leaving the coast of Yarmouth. This airship broke up at 8,000 feet and fell into the sea and sank at once.

The next year, 1917, on September 24 Captain Peter Strasser led a ten-airship raid against northern England, and Hull was successfully bombed. On October 19-20 of the same year a true "silent raid" was carried out when eleven airships rendezvoused over the Yorkshire coast for an attack on the industrial centres of the Midlands. It turned out to be the most disastrous experience of the airship war. While over Britain the Zeppelins flew at well over 16,000 feet and at this level the efficiency of the crews was apparently impaired by altitude sickness and intense cold, and the weather conspired to outwit them. Near the ground the air was misty and there was little wind, but at 16,000 feet a strong gale was blowing in from the north and the Zeppelins drifted blindly south. One airship passed over London without recognising the city, but somehow dropped a 50-kg. bomb which fell in Piccadilly and caused some casualties.

The London ground-defense officials played a cat-and-mouse game with Captain Strasser's dirigibles. Realising their searchlights could not pierce the low mist, they kept them doused, and the raiders floundered helplessly, unable to find the British metropolis. The raid ended in almost total disaster. Only one airship managed to get back to Germany over the usual route. Six had to risk the neutrality of Holland or cross the Allied battle-lines in France. The remaining four were destroyed the next day by gunfire as they floated about France.

This tragic climax provided one of the heart-rending incidents of World War I. As these four doomed aircraft drifted for hours over hostile territory, French and British observers listened to wireless appeals to their bases begging for advice, air protection, and for some reliable information as to their whereabouts. These messages and appeals were monitored and later transcribed and printed for general distribution. Several years later a Hollywood studio wrote much of them into a war film based on the Zeppelin raids.

Airship raiding was not resumed until the night of March 12-13, 1918, but the attack was ill-planned and made from such a height that the damage was negligible. The end of the Zeppelin as a raider occurred on August 5-6 when five dirigibles flew up the coast of Norfolk. No bombs were dropped on any land target, but the L.70, the latest in airship construction, was destroyed by the ground forces.

Britain was also raided by aeroplanes, but this method of attack did not begin until November 1916.

Below is a list of the aircraft that were added to the forces of the Royal Flying Corps and the Royal Naval Air Service during the year 1915.

BRITISH WARPLANES OF 1915

Make	Engine	Speed m.p.h.	Purpose
Avro 530	Hispano 200 h.p.	114	Bomber
B.E.2c	R.A.F. 90 h.p.	93	Reconnaissance
B.E.2g	R.A.F. 90 h.p.	95	Reconnaissance
Blackburn Triplane	Clerget 130 h.p.	115	Fighter
Blackburn L	Salmson 130 h.p.	81	Coast Patrol
Blackburn T.B.	Gnome (2) 100 h.p.	82	Zeppelin Fighter
Bréguet 5	Le Rhone 110 h.p.	75	Bomber

Caudron	Gnome 80 h.p.	71	General
Curtiss	Curtiss 90 h.p.	70	Trainer
D.H.1	Renault 80 h.p.	78	Fighter
D.H.1a	Beardmore 120 h.p.	90	Fighter
D.H.2	Gnome 100 h.p.	86	Fighter
D.H.3	Beardmore (2) 130 h.p.	90	Bomber
Farman Henri	Salmson 140 h.p.	90	General
F.E.2b	Beardmore 120 h.p.	75	Fighter
F.E.2d	Rolls 250 h.p.	93	Fighter
F.E.8	Gnome 100 h.p.	95	Fighter
F.2A	Rolls (2) 345 h.p.	90	Flying Boat
Handley-Page 0/100	Rolls (2) 250 h.p.	95	Bomber
Martinsyde S	Beardmore 120 h.p.	92	Fighter
Morane-Saulnier P	Le Rhone 110 h.p.	96	Fighter
Morane-Saulnier R	Le Rhone 110 h.p.	90	Bomber
Morane-Monoplane	Le Rhone 110 h.p.	102	Fighter
R.E.5	Beardmore 120 h.p.	78	Bomber
R.E.7	R.A.F. 150 h.p.	88	Bomber
Sage 1	Rolls (2) 190 h.p.	103	Bomber
Sopwith 1½ Strutter	Clerget 110 h.p.	98	Fighter
Sopwith Schneider	Gnome 100 h.p.	98	Sea Scout
Sopwith Baby	Clerget 110 h.p.	107	Sea Scout
Supermarine P.S.	Smith 130 h.p.	90	Sea Scout
Vickers F.B.9	Gnome 100 h.p.	84	Fighter

The year 1915 provided the primary training and early experience for many gallant airmen who were to become star-turn aces on both sides of the line. The new Fokker gun gave the Germans a certain advantage, and the few select pilots who were favoured with these mounts made the most of their chances. Airmen of France and Britain, however, had to be content with the best of extemporaneous gun mountings until an interrupter gear could be perfected. Several scout pilots of this era went on to the pinnacle of glory. A few began with a rocketlike surge and then petered out, but practically all had vivid personalities—a dramatic something that made compelling reading in the years that followed.

But strangely enough, Oswald Boelcke, who contributed most to Germany's power in the air, the man who created the flying circus, who devised the most successful combat tactics used by the aces of the Iron Cross, is today a shadowy and dim figure.

His story, when studied with care, is one of the more engrossing of war biographies. His modest personality, his orderly mind, and his sincere patriotism have left a sharp impression, and yet, because he was of this era—a period before the classics of air fighting were front-page news—Boelcke never won his rightful place in the international hall of honour.

Oswald Boelcke was the third son of a colourless German schoolteacher who spent many years in Argentina, where he taught at the German Protestant School in Buenos Aires before returning home to take the post of assistant master at the high school in Halle. Later he accepted a call to the Antoinette School in Dessau, where he subsequently became a professor.

Oswald's older brothers, Wilhelm and Frederick, were born in South America, but he first saw the light of day at Giebichstein, near Halle. Thus, he was the first of the Boelckes born on German soil. Later another brother and a sister were added to the family.

It was decided early that young Oswald would become a teacher, whereas the two older brothers were to take up more masculine professions. Oswald was a croupy, studious, retiring stripling who liked books. In truth, he showed little promise, for he was usually convalescing from some childhood ailment. He was never considered for any team sport and detested all forms of rough personal contact. Many writers in later years noticed this factor in so many young men who became ranking aces. They were the true individualists, horsemen, oarsmen, riflemen, and men who had a touch for the tiller.

Left to himself, Oswald took to floating about in his grammer-school swimming pool and when no one was looking he smoothed his stroke and kick. In a year or so he had improved his stature and gained much vitality, but Professor Boelcke still considered him as schoolteacher material. He was a good scholar and particularly proficient in mathematics and physics. Nevertheless, the martial music of the times, the uniforms, and the general talk of Germany's place in the sun generated a consuming desire to become a soldier.

Unlike his brothers, who also hoped for military glory, young Oswald did something about it. He bypassed all the regular channels and wrote to Kaiser Wilhelm direct. After all, his father couldn't afford to send him to a military academy, but he had heard of some simple method of palace appointment, so he wrote to the Kaiser and put in his request. At the time he was thirteen years old.

No one in the Boelcke family had any idea Oswald wanted to be a soldier, but one day a very impressive envelope was slipped under the door and they discovered that the Kaiser, evidently touched by the boy's sincerity, had enclosed an appointment to a nearby cadet school.

"You will of course complete your grammar-school subjects," the Kaiser warned in a friendly tone, "before you report to Leutnant General von Schwartzkoppen at Coblenz."

Wilhelm and Frederick were naturally envious and his father was astonished; but there was no ignoring a cadet appointment awarded by Kaiser Wilhelm! So Oswald, the student, no longer frail or asthmatic, first saw military service as a colour guard in a cadet telegraphic battalion. Later he was moved on to Darmstadt, where he first came in contact with the aviation branch of the military service. He devoted much time to becoming a trained telegrapher, hoping to be selected for aerial observation, but instead, because of his enthusiasm and science background, he was transferred to the Air Force and sent to a training school at Halberstadt, where he required but seven weeks to qualify as an N.C.O. pilot.

However, his brother Wilhelm, who had previously enlisted in the aviation service but did not have Oswald's cadet training, became an N.C.O. observer. When the war began both of them were sent down to the Champagne front early in September. This created an unusual situation, for Wilhelm immediately assumed the role of the elder brother. Reports have it that he bossed and bullied Oswald and so arranged matters that he would fly as his observer. This association did little for Oswald's standing in his squadron as the other pilots had small respect for a man who allowed himself to be ordered around by a brother who wore only one wing.

Throughout early September Oswald and Wilhelm, both N.C.O. fliers, carried out a number of routine observation patrols together. Later when bad weather set in they were grounded much of the time. One day a lieutenant observer requested that Oswald fly him out to do a special mission, and since he was only an N.C.O., he had to obey. When he returned Wilhelm was on the tarmac sweating and fuming because Oswald had taken an officer as his observer, and a marked coolness developed between them. Then on October 12 Oswald was awarded the Iron Cross for his determination and devotion to duty while flying many routine observation patrols. A week or so later Wilhelm was awarded the Iron Cross First Class for having flown more miles of observation than any German observer on the front.

There followed a dreary period of observation patrols, organisation, and the mud and slush of that dreadful first winter. On the ground both sides were digging in and hoping to bring up their reserves. The airmen went on patrol, made their reports, and then went back to their quarters where they played "Skat", whist, poker, or scrawled out dull pointless letters.

Early in 1915 Oswald's bronchial troubles returned and he was sent for a rest at a convalescent hospital in Rethel. When he had recovered he was posted to the German Aviation Service's inspectorate division, where he served two weeks in some routine ground assignment. Then he was sent to Döberitz, where Section 62 was being reorganised. This unit later turned up at Douai, where we first meet Oswald Boelcke being taught how to use a synchronised gun fitted to a Fokker E.1 monoplane.

Boelcke became acquainted with Max Immelmann at Douai and a remarkable friendship was fused. The story of Immelmann, who became a ranking German ace, has never been fully documented. A dozen legends have come out of war history about the man who was called the Eagle of Lille.

Max Immelmann was born at Dresden on September 21, 1890, and when fourteen years old was entered in the Dresden Cadet Corps and rose to ensign's rank in an engineer regiment. Unlike Boelcke, he was not the ideal soldier; but he was a brilliant mathematician and a first-class mechanic. His first flare-up with officialdom came in the summer of 1912 when he resigned his commission with the engineers because he was certain the army held no technical future for him.

Within a few days of the outbreak of war Immelmann received his mobilization orders and was told to report to his old regiment, but before leaving home he put in for a transfer to the Aviation Service. The mechanical features of aeroplanes appealed to him at first, and he had no idea of becoming a pilot; but when in November his papers finally came through to report to the Aldershof Flying School, he was overjoyed. This point again confounds the old story that Immelmann had "bombed" Paris in September 1914 with a warning note. There is such a note in the Paris Museum, but who wrote and signed it is a mystery, for Immelmann had never been in the air until late in November of that year.

Max survived the usual history of training-school crashes and was finally sent to Section 10, located at Vizry, on April 12, 1915. There he soon found himself in hot water, for on his first frontline flight he cracked up an L.V.G. as the result of a very bad landing. Two days later, after collecting a brand-new machine from an aircraft park, he repeated the performance. Thus, it is not surprising to note that Section 10 heaved a sigh of relief when two weeks later their crash expert was sent to Döberitz and assigned to the newly reformed Section 62. Here Immelmann finally recovered his touch and by the time the squadron was ready for active service at Douai on May 19, 1915, he had corrected most of his faults.

The theory that opposites attract was confirmed at Douai. Boelcke had seen his brother Wilhelm off to another section and had wished him good riddance. On the rebound he took to this arrogant, self-assured, and typical lone-wolf fighter who ignored all ideas of teamwork, formation flying, or any of the niceties of social behaviour.

Immelmann started his war-flying career by being shot down by an old Henri Farman. While flying a photography patrol on June 3, he suddenly found himself without power; the unknown enemy had shot his ignition away, and he had to land in a nearby field. Probably because he brought the aircraft down safely, Immelmann was awarded his first decoration—the Iron Cross Second Class—although the citation did make some reference to his coolness under fire.

Shortly after this incident Anthony Fokker arrived at Douai with two of his new Eindekkers carrying his synchronized gun. Immelmann and Boelcke were instructed to take a short one-hour course in the handling of the machine and its mechanism.

Early the next morning Section 62 was aroused by the roar of engines and the crash of exploding bombs. Ten B.E.2c's were plastering the airfield; but by the time the German pilots had reached the hangars to retaliate the British planes were on their way home. Both Immelmann and Boelcke took to the air with their new Fokkers and roared in wild pursuit, Boelcke not even waiting to dress but going aloft in a pair of flying boots, a helmet, and—his nightshirt!

Near Vitry Immelmann overtook the rearmost B.E.2c and triggered off 500 rounds from his new gun. He had moved in to very close range, but nothing happened until the fixed Parabellum jammed, and then for some reason the British biplane went into a spin, pulled out, and made a hurried landing. Immelmann followed him down and discovered that the only occupant had been wounded in the arm and about forty rounds had passed through the unoccupied cockpit.

Boelcke never got close enough to fire a shot. Some historians disagree on this point and credit Boelcke with scoring first with Fokker's weapon, but his official log discloses that he did not destroy an Allied plane until July 6, 1915, when he downed a French Morane over Vouziers.

Immelmann received the Iron Cross First Class and he ran up two more victories on September 9 and 21, a fact that confounds the general impression that both Boelcke and Immelmann went on a killing spree from the day Anthony Fokker delivered his first two fixed-gun monoplanes.

However, on September 23 Immelmann was caught napping again by a Farman two-seater. The observer shot away his undercarriage, plastered the engine, and drilled nine slugs through the fuel tank. How he survived that hail of lead is one of the many mysteries of the air war, but he was a doughty type and was soon back in action and downed another B.E.2c near Lille. Then while flying over Arras he caught a British biplane as he swept out of a thin cloud bank and shot it down before the gunner-observer could fire a shot. Another B.E.2c was downed on November 7 and a Morane torched on December 15, bringing his score to seven as the year ended.

Boelcke's logbook shows that he downed only five enemy planes between the time of the first Fokker delivery and the opening of the new year. He was, however, giving considerable thought to a more efficient manner of handling the weapon and was to become the guiding light of the Imperial German Air Force.

Sometime during the month of September 1915 a young man named Walter von Bulow joined the Imperial Air Force and established an amazing record. Today he is unknown, but he outscored Immelmann by thirteen victories. The scion of a famous house, von Bulow was born in 1894 and was educated at Heidelberg University. He won high honours as a student and was his class leader in the Cadet Corps when war brought mobilization. He immediately joined the famous 17th (Death Head) Hussars and distinguished himself against British and French cavalry patrols during the early advances. In January 1915 he was awarded the Iron Cross Second Class for his daring on the Lorraine front and in April was promoted to an oberleutnant. Within a few days of his promotion he transferred to the Imperial Air Service and after obtaining his pilot's certificate at the Hannover Flying School was posted to a flying section on the Champagne front in September 1915.

This fledgling was a killer from the beginning; within three weeks' time he had won the Iron Cross First Class for destroying two enemy aircraft on consecutive days. Early on the morning of October 10 while flying over Metz in a two-seater Fokker which had been fitted with a fixed gun, he spotted a pusher Voisin and dived on it. Before the observer had time to take action the Voisin was plunging earthward in flames. His second kill, which happened on the following afternoon, was not so easy. This time he was attacked by a Farman and two Voisins, and his machine and observer were well shot up before he was able to escape into a handy cloud. Although his engine was knocking badly, von Bulow did not give up. He babied his ailing Oberursel for half an hour until at last the Farman appeared to lag behind its companions. Suddenly the young German struck and before the Voisins had time to turn to give assistance, he poured a long burst into the Farman's tail and it went down out of control and crashed inside the German lines.

Before the year was out a third French machine fell to von Bulow's guns, and then early in February 1916 he was transferred to the newly formed Abteilung 300 and rushed off to Palestine, where Germany was contesting the Allied right of way to the Suez Canal. While stationed at El Arish the squadron patrolled the Canal, but since they had but two antiquated two-seaters, there was very little flying for some weeks. Eventually six Rumpler two-seaters and a pair of Fokker scouts were delivered, and von Bulow was soon engaged in the monotonous round of bombing and photographic flights.

Later on, with a Leutnant von Hesler as his gunner, von Bulow tackled three British raiders, a Short, and two Sopwith "Baby" seaplanes that were bombing El Arish. The German flyer moved in fast and outclassed the Britons, two bursts from a fixed gun sending a Sopwith down in flames. The other hung on, but von Hesler drilled it with his movable Parabellum, and it went down and made a sloppy landing in the sea. Then, turning on the Short, von Bulow fired a long burst and damaged the seaplane's radiator, and it made off, trailing a long cloud of steam, and landed beside its parent ship the H.M.S. *Ben-My-Chree*.

Soon after this affray von Bulow was flying a single-seater scout when he was attacked by four B.E.2c's, and, although he managed to shoot one down, he was hit in the shoulder and crashed in the Turkish reserve lines. The wound put him in the hospital at Jerusalem for a month, and he did not return to action until late in November. He requested a transfer back to a sphere of greater activity—the Western Front—where we shall pick him up later, flying Albatros scouts on the Champagne front.

Make	Engine	Speed m.p.h.	Purpose
Albatros	Mercedes 130 h.p.	85	Reconnaissance-bomber
A.G.O. C.1	Benz 150 h.p.	95	Bomber
Aviatik	Mercedes 130 h.p.	70	Reconnaissance
Fokker E.1	Le Rhone 80 h.p.	80	Scout
Fokker E.2	Oberursel 100 h.p.	85	Scout
Fokker E.3	Oberursel 100 h.p.	95	Scout
L.V.G. C.1	Mercedes 130 h.p.	97	Reconnaissance-bomber
Rumpler C.1	Mercedes 130 h.p.	87	Bomber-fighter
Halberstadt D.2	Argus 120 h.p.	90	Scout

While the Germans were having considerable success with their new machines and superior armament, the Allies were not bemoaning their fate and doing nothing. Although their task was unenviable, they faced it with determination. What Oswald Boelcke and Max Immelmann were doing for the German fighting spirit, a mild-mannered gentleman named George Lanoe Hawker was providing for the British. Hawker has not been widely known, but whenever World War I airmen foregather in reunion, the name of Major George Lanoe Hawker, V.C., D.S.O. is certain to crop up. While he was Britain's first ace, his official record is something of a mystery, since—as explained before—the British did not keep any reliable accounts of "enemy aircraft destroyed" until late in 1915. However, several unofficial records credit him with more than thirty kills, all accounted for between October 1914 and November 1916. His influence on combat flying in the R.F.C. cannot be overemphasized.

George L. Hawker was of medium build and height, clear of eye, and had a shy smile that shielded an iron will and the heart of a lion. On the ground he displayed a lovable nature and few could resist his friendship. He was born in December 1890, educated at the Royal Naval College, Dartmouth, and later at the Royal Military Academy. He secured a commission in the Royal Engineers and was one of the small group of officers selected for training as pilots in the new Royal Flying Corps. He was an adept pupil and on March 4, 1913, was awarded Aero Certificate No. 435, making his final test flight on a Deperdussin monoplane.

On the declaration of war, he flew an R.E.5 of No. 6 Squadron across the Channel and was witness to the fall of Antwerp in October.

Once firmly planted on Belgian soil, the Germans lost no time in setting up Zeppelin hangars to bring their raiders within shorter range of England. These bases naturally became a sharp thorn in the side of the Allied command and an immediate decision to bomb them out was first attempted on April 18, 1915. On that day Hawker climbed into a B.E.2c and took off for the Zeppelin hangar at Gontrode. Arriving over his target, he was welcomed by a veritable curtain of fire from ground machine guns. He also noticed a kite balloon up for the express purpose of signalling the approach of enemy aircraft. Ignoring the ground fire, Hawker went in for his attack. All he had were three French melinite bombs, the power of his wrists for eventual delivery, and in his lap a haversack of hand grenades.

His first two bombs missed by an Irish mile, so he flew lower and distributed most of his hand grenades. Again he missed, and a sudden pounding aft made him zoom for altitude, at which point he discovered that the balloon observer had a Parabellum gun and was blazing away over the edge of his wicker basket.

Hawker decided on new strategy and went at the balloon from a blind side and put it out of action with two hand grenades. The damage caused the gasbag to deflate slowly, and as it gradually dropped earthward he used it as a shield, spiralling down with it until he was a few feet above the main hangar. His last melinite bomb was hurled over the side, falling straight and true, and one brand-new Zeppelin shed went up in a gout of flame.

When he returned to his field at Abeele after being away for more than three hours, Hawker counted no less than thirty-eight bullet holes in the old B.E. For this one-man raid he was awarded the D.S.O., and, shortly after, Gontrode was abandoned as a Zeppelin base and was turned into a Gotha bomber field.

In June of 1915 Hawker flew a Bristol Scout, on the fuselage of which he lashed a Lee-Enfield rifle and went Hun hunting. The arrangement failed to come up to his expectations, so he rigged on a crude top-wing bracket that carried a Lewis gun firing over the tips of the propeller.

Apparently there were few enemy aircraft in his area, so Hawker established an intelligence warning system of his own by posting a number of mechanics up at the front line who were to telephone him whenever a German machine moved into Allied territory. He also used a number of clumsy B.E.2c's as decoys, and if an L.V.G. or an Aviatik pounded on these unarmed biplanes Hawker would sweep out of the skies with his Bristol Scout and soon had the Abeele front littered with skeletons of German aircraft. He became the idol of the admiring infantrymen.

Along with all this, Hawker still had to accept his share of daily bombing and reconnaissance patrols, and during one of these he almost came to an early finish. On April 22, 1915, when the Germans launched their first poison-gas attack, Hawker and several other fliers were sent out to investigate a rumour that the enemy had withdrawn to a reserve line beyond Ypres. The rumour was confirmed and every available aircraft was sent over to bomb this new position. While flying low, Hawker ran through a tornado of rifle and machine-gun fire; one bullet penetrated his foot and others wiped off his instrument panel. The wound turned out to be superficial, however, and he was back in action within a short time.

Early in the morning of July 25 one of his observers reported that an Aviatik was prowling over the British lines, and Hawker took off. His intial attack with the Bristol Scout was so fierce that the German stuck his nose down and did not remember to pull it up again until he had ignominiously crashed inside the German lines.

Returning to the air later that same afternoon, Hawker found another Aviatik photographing the area around Houthulst Fôret. One short burst from the high-rigged gun sent the photography ship crashing within the British lines. On his return to his own area, Hawker encountered another enemy aircraft, this time a Rumpler. The observer sprayed Hawker with his Parabellum until the Bristol dived below the two-seater to come up under the blind spot. Thirty rounds from the Lewis gun sent the Rumpler down in flames.

George L. Hawker received the Victoria Cross for that day's work and the citation mentioned: "The personal bravery shown by this officer was of the very highest order, as the enemy's aircraft were all armed with machine guns, and each carried a passenger as well as a pilot."

Whether we consider that particular day worthy of such high honour or not, we must remember that this was 1915 and values were entirely different than they were in following war years. At any rate, the R.F.C. officials recognized in Hawker the born fighter pilot, and he was promoted to a squadron commander (major) and sent back to England to assume command of No. 24 Squadron which was being equipped with the new de Havilland 2—a single-seater pusher fighter which had been expressly designed to combat the Fokker monoplanes and their fixed guns.

Hawker put No. 24 through five months of intense training, building up confidence, formation flying, and keen gunnery. When the group went out to France in February 1916 it immediately ran up a most impressive record. Although the D.H.2 did not have a fixed gun firing through the propeller, this "mark-time" arrangement of a Lewis gun nosing out of the streamlined pusher nacelle was in many respects more convenient for the pilot to handle. At any rate, this little single-seater did more than its share eventually to erase the first Fokker scourge.

It has been shown that there was not too much air fighting throughout 1915, but there was plenty of war flying. The men who in 1916-17 were to become national heroes and multi-decorated aces were all testing their fledgling wings over the latter months of 1915. There were not enough "fighter" aircraft to produce the deadly dog-fights, and the training schools were not producing pilots fast enough to justify the organization of specialized-duty squadrons. Indeed, most air services were short of trained gunners and observers—rather than pilots—and toward the close of 1915 the appeal went out for volunteers from the ground services.

Hundreds responded willingly in spite of the general belief that the Flying Corps was a suicide club. The stalemate along the Western Front during the winter of 1914-15 discouraged many who had imagined war as portrayed on the canvases of the old masters or in the celebrated accounts of the poets and writers. There were no gleaming rows of Lancers, no sabre charges of Hussars and Dragoons, no epic stands of the Thin Red Line, no stirrup charges staged by the Scots Greys and the Black Watch. The Great War had provided none of these glorious military tableaux. It was drab khaki, mud, blood, and apparently there was no end to the carnage. Only the bright-blue sky seemed worth fighting for.

Because of these disappointments and grim realities, many fine young soldiers were lost to the famed European cavalry regiments. After the first few weeks cavalry had no place in the war and mounted regiments that had been "the pride of the service and the right of the line" were ignominiously discarded and sent to the rear; many of them further dishonoured by being dismounted and given rear-area menial tasks to perform. When the flying services appealed for volunteers practically every cavalryman took one step forward. This was particularly true in the French and German services, where regimental traditions still cast a very beguiling spell.

There was the Marquis Alexandre de Turenne, once a

sub-lieutenant in the 2nd French dragoons who transferred to the Air Service in July 1915, subsequently becoming one of France's greatest to survive the war. Charles Nungesser (sometimes spelled Nungessor), third-ranking French ace, came out of a famed French cavalry regiment and gained fame as a balloon-buster. Albert Heurteaux, a former sub-lieutenant of Hussars, was wounded twelve times, downed twenty-one enemy planes, and became the leader of the famed "Storks" before he was twenty-one.

And there were other nationals who played a great part in this first war in the air. The leading ace of the Belgian Air Service, Major Willy Coppens, transferred from the 2nd Regiment of the Belgian Grenadiers to the Motorcycle Machine Gun Corps. But even that form of excitement did not suffice, and in January of 1915 Coppens applied for training in the Flying Corps. This boy fought more than fifty combats before he scored a victory, but he ended the war with thirty-six enemy aircraft to his credit, twenty-six of them being fiercely guarded observation balloons.

When Italy decided to join the Allies in May 1915, Major Francesco Baracca transferred out of the Italian cavalry and scored thirty-four victories for the Italian Air Service, meeting a gallant end in June of 1918. Lieutenant Silvio Scaroni saw little glory in hauling artillery pieces and ammunition up and down the Alps, so he transferred to the Air Service and scored twenty-six kills over the Austrians. The Italian air effort in World War I is seldom mentioned by historians, but no less than forty-one Italian airmen racked up at least five victories over their enemies. The same records also disclose that there were eight Belgian aces, three who fought for Russia, five Austrian aces, and one Rumanian.

The year 1915, which produced Roland Garros's deflector propeller, Fokker's interrupter-gun gear, the first of the Nieuport scouts, and two men who were to become the spiritual heroes of the British and German air services, also gave the war its most controversial and France her greatest aerial figure. A great hero, and yet the war's most pathetic person.

Georges Guynemer was the son of a prosperous French legal expert. All his life he had been sickly, sensitive to any reproaches, and most ill-equipped for the hardships of a war. As a baby he almost died of infantile enteritis. His childhood was spent in the hands of nurses, doctors, and anxious women relatives. He was curly-haired, pretty, and very frail, and so dainty in fact he was often mistaken for a girl. By the time he was ten he had rid himself of the curls, but he was much thin-

98

ner and paler than his schoolmates. He won all the first prizes in Latin and mathematics and picked up honourable mentions by the dozen. But in spite of his frailties and scholarliness young Georges always wanted to play at soldiers. He had little strength, but much agility, cleverness, a quick eye, caution, and a talent for strategy. When his father inquired of his sickly son what profession he wished to follow, young Guynemer proudly said he wished to be an aviator. His father argued that that was not a career, only a sport and that one travelled in the air as a motorist rode on the highways. But Georges persisted in his desire and asked his father's permission to become an aviator. His father thought he had not even seen an aeroplane, but in that he was mistaken, as Georges had gone up in one at Corbeaulieu.

And so at the outbreak of the war Guynemer, hardly nineteen years of age, induced his father to sign a permission for his enlistment, but the recruiting officer turned him down saying that he could not carry an infantryman's knapsack, and his former enteritis forbade him from becoming a cavalryman.

Guynemer stewed and fretted over the following weeks and then suddenly remembered his aeroplane flight. He hurried down to Pau, sifted past several sentries, and rushed up to the startled commandant, Captain Bernard-Thierry, who was in command of the aviation camp.

"Captain, you must help me . . . employ me . . . employ me at anything, no matter what. Let me clean those aeroplanes over there."

Captain Bernard-Thierry was taken aback but reflected gravely, for he could not rebuff such a supplicant.

"Maybe I can take you as a student *mécanicien*."

And so by November 14 Guynemer began his military career as a student mechanician at Pau, but the future knight of the air was the humblest of grooms. He slept on the floor, was assigned the dirtiest work about the camp, cleaned cylinders, and carried cans of *essence*. During his few hours of leisure he took two school aeroplanes apart and put them together again. He haunted the repair shops and watched experts make wings, fit ailerons, and adjust landing gears; but to the crude, hard-boiled mechanics he associated with, he was still "a little girl dressed in a private's uniform."

At the same time the "little girl" approach won him his way into the affection of several pilots, regardless of their rank. "Couldn't you help me get a pilot's diploma?" he would inquire of them day after day. All this, combined with the influence of his father, eventually moved him into a class of "learners" who were promoted from mechanicians to student pilots. This blissful reward came on January 26, 1915.

His first mount was a Blériot "roller," an underpowered monoplane that simply fluttered up and down the field, giving the students some feel of the engine and the controls under taxiing conditions. From the "roller" he went to a 25-h.p. Blériot, which could fly to about 100-150 feet. His first true solo flight took place on March 10, and by June 8 Corporal Georges Guynemer had passed out on Blériot Gnomes, Morane Parasols, and a dual-control school Nieuport. He was then sent to Morane-Saulnier No. 3 Squadron, which was to become the famed "Cigognes" or Storks Escadrille.

No. 3 Squadron was commanded by Captain Brocard, under whom the Storks were destined to become illustrious. Vedrines already belonged, and another cavalryman, Deullin, joined with Guynemer; and later on Heurteaux, Dorme, Auger, Raymond, and many others who blazed the glory of France across the war skies.

Guynemer began his front-line flying from a field at Vauciennes near Villers-Cotterêts in the Valois country, a region of beautiful forests, châteaux, fertile meadows, ponds, and fields. His artistic nature was entranced with the lovely surroundings and he wrote to his parents, "One would think oneself in the Midi, except that the inhabitants have seen the beast at close range and know how to appreciate us. . . . I have had a machine-gun support mounted on my machine and now I am ready for the hunt." Since his own home was nearby, he often flew over and gave the villagers a terrifying series of stunts but soon desisted when he learned his mother had fainted when she saw her frail son do a loop over the family château.

On delving into the history of Guynemer one finds the legends still continue, since his biographers were most careless of their facts and aeronautical details. Most of them were so occupied with presenting the effeminate side of his nature, they lost track of the equipment he was flying. One can never determine whether Georges was handling a two-seater Morane-Saulnier, or a single-seater Nieuport, for in order to provide conversation the accounts have an observer on board either type of plane. In his fights, too, Guynemer runs out of belts when flying an aircraft fitted with a Lewis gun. In others he actually changes belts, something of a trick when it is realized that the guns of those days were supplied by one single 500-round canvas belt. Of course, he may have worn another around his neck like a Hawaiian lei.

Some historians insist that Guynemer ran up an excessive

amount of crashes in his early days, but his logbook makes mention of only one when he wiped off an undercarriage hitting a ditch.

His closest friends recall the unending hours he spent sitting in his cockpit working the various switches and levers. He would make take-offs and landings until he had everyone on the field frantic with the unending engine roar and undercarriage thump. He kept minute details of the plane's reactions to various arrangements of the controls. His rapidity of conception and decision was astounding, and he seemed to become an integral part of the machine the minute he tightened his safety belt. Every sound, every twang of wire, every hiss of the slip stream over the taut linen brought him reliable information. So natural a pilot was he that several of his instructors were convinced he had taken flight training before entering the service. Others said he wore himself out trying to become a centaur of the air.

The aircraft of M-S.3 were, of course, two-seaters, and Corporal Guynemer usually carried an observer, and most of the time this team flew in search of enemy guns that were pounding the French forward area. By mid-July of 1915 the first Nieuport scouts equipped with a forward-firing machine gun (one firing over the tips of the propeller) were being delivered to the Storks. Guynemer was one of the first assigned to one of these gadflys and again he spent hours of dry-run time sitting in the cockpit, working out problems, possible stoppages, and making himself expertly familiar with the new mechanisms.

On July 19 Guynemer registered his first kill, but not with the Nieuport. He was flying with an observer named Guerder, and they were looking for a German marauder which had been reported over Courcres. The visitor cleared off, but then Guynemer encountered a two-seater Aviatik. It must be presumed that the Morane-Saulnier had been equipped with one of the experimental British interrupter gears, for his report states that he shot down the enemy plane after firing one complete belt. Before going down in flames the Aviatik crew fought bravely with a rifle and the M-S. did not get off scot-free, as Guynemer had to make a forced landing at Carrière l'Evêque. Observer Guerder had been grazed across the head and hand by a rifle bullet. Getting down amid following German shellfire, Guynemer ploughed into a haystack and broke off his propeller. Both Guynemer and Guerder were awarded France's *Médaille Militaire*.

Guynemer became a national hero overnight, but it was nearly six months before he scored his second victory. He had also to conserve his strength, and his C.O. granted him leave whenever it was possible. There was plenty of two-seater work to be carried out, and from all accounts he flew as an observer on many occasions. Some of his missions were hardly routine, for they were concerned with flying intelligence agents across the line, landing them in isolated areas, and going back and picking them up later on. He carried out two of these double-trip duties for which he was promoted to a sergeant.

While carrying a Captain Siméon with him above Chaulnes on November 6, he waged an epic combat with a German L.V.G. Moving in to get behind and below to give his observer a good shot, Guynemer became enraged when his observer's gun jammed and while trying to advise his companion how to clear the stoppage, Georges suddenly found that his wing had interlocked with that of the German. He stared around in amazement and saw the Jerry gunner aiming point-blank at him with a Parabellum. However, he ducked that storm with only one bullet clipping his leather helmet. Needless to state, both pilots veered off home and tried to forget the harrowing encounter.

On December 8 Guynemer was aboard a Nieuport single-seater and cut off another L.V.G. at Beauvraignes. Moving in to within 60 yards, he poured thirty-seven rounds into it and set it on fire. A few days later Sergeant Guynemer attacked a two-seater Fokker and broke it up in mid-air. A single-seater Fokker with a fixed gun next dived on him, and they staged a battle at the height of 30 feet, to the delight of the men in the trenches. Guynemer roared at this adversary and they almost crashed head on, but the French lad zoomed in time, and the Fokker pilot evidently decided he'd had his luck for that day and flew off home. Guynemer's Nieuport was riddled with bullets.

When Georges Guynemer came of age, December 24, 1915, he was awarded the Cross of the Legion of Honour and was credited with four air victories. He went home for the holidays and that ended his record for that year. He fought for almost two more years before he went to his legendary end.

This is the history of that year of trial and error. War in the air was taking on a new format. Machines were being designed for specific purposes. Engines were being produced to provide greater power, and young pilots were having to think in new terms of airmanship. The next year would see the fuller development of aircraft, weapons, and tactics. Strangely enough, the French seemed to lag in aircraft development, as will be noted in the following list of their newest types, as compared with the military planes being designed and produced by their British allies.

FRENCH WARPLANES OF 1915

Make	Engine	Speed m.p.h.	Purpose
Bréguet 5	Le Rhone 110 h.p.	75	Bomber
Caudron G.2b	Mono-Gnome 160 h.p.	85	Reconnaissance
Caudron G.3	Anzani 100 h.p.	90	Bomber
Farman	Le Rhone 60 h.p.	70	Reconnaissance
Morane 27 C.1	Le Rhone 110 h.p.	98	Fighter
Morane 29 C.1	Mono-Gnome 160 h.p.	102	Fighter
Morane Bullet	Le Rhone 110 h.p.	100	Fighter
Morane-Saulnier	Le Rhone 110 h.p.	90	Bomber
Nieuport 12	Mono-Gnome 80 h.p.	90	Fighter
Nieuport 13	Le Rhone 110 h.p.	105	Fighter

4

THE YEAR OF INDECISION—
1916

☐ Whatever superiority the Fokker fixed-gun fighter had given the German Air Service in the latter half of 1915, the French and British were able to maintain a brave show with the help of extemporaneous devices and pusher-type aircraft. Although the Fokker Eindekker was clearly a superior mount, it was woefully exploited. Its surprise factor was completely sacrificed as was the same feature in the introduction of poison gas, the flame thrower, and the armoured tank.

Had the Germans first organised a complete squadron or group of these early Fokkers and trained a special corps of destroyer pilots to introduce the weapon, the effect might have been devastating. As it was, Fokker's synchronised gun was to a great extent wasted. The Allies knew about it within days after Oswald Boelcke first flew the machine. Most certainly no German airman had employed the front-firing gun as efficiently as had Roland Garros, who destroyed five enemy planes in seventeen days. It took Immelmann nearly six months to score seven times and the great Boelcke downed only five in the same length of time.

Actually, few German airmen liked the Fokker E.1 in spite of its superior armament. Most of them preferred the new Halberstadt or the Albatros D.1. When Boelcke temporarily turned his attention to the Halberstadt, the day of the Fokker monoplane was over.

The early part of 1916 saw a race for aircraft production as well as the first probing efforts toward fighter-squadron development. Throughout 1915 British factories had produced

2,656 war planes of which 2,003 were two-seaters, 391 single-seaters, and 262 were seaplanes or flying boats. In addition 1,721 aero engines had been delivered in France, and 371 were held in reserve as spares. These figures may seem trivial in the light of modern production, but they do indicate that workers on the home front were appreciative of the part the fighting plane was playing and the workers were soon to give the R.F.C. and the R.N.A.S. a tremendous numerical superiority, of which the British fliers were to make spectacular use.

We are also reminded that General Hugh "Boom" Trenchard had taken over the command of the Royal Flying Corps and his stern hand was soon noted in the manner in which the corps was to be used. On January 14, 1916, he issued the following order:

Until the Royal Flying Corps is in possession of a machine as good, or better than, the German Fokker, it seems that a change in policy and tactics has become necessary. In order to ensure that reconnaissance and photography patrols are allowed a fair chance of success, all fighter aircraft will raid prominent enemy aerodromes and attack any hostile machine that offers combat.

Regardless of the tactics and strategy previously used, there was no question but that the British were expected to take the initiative. As a result, throughout the war, Allied aircraft had to intrude on enemy territory, whereas the Germans had adopted the economic policy of fighting only over their own areas. British two-seater squadrons were gamely attacking with the F.E.2b and the Vickers Gunbus, which provided cockpit arrangements in which the gunner fought from a forward position. How well they fought makes glorious history.

To get the full value of the available fire power, infantry machine gunners were being enticed from the trenches by the offer of flight pay (six shillings a day). History records that these youngsters, with absolutely no previous in-air training, still wearing their infantry uniforms and in many cases Highland kilts, did more than their share to stop the Fokker menace.

The 1916 period of Boelcke's career gives a sharp review of these volunteer gunners. All told, the Dessau expert scored forty official victories between July 6, 1915, and October 26, 1916; thirty-one of which were French or British two-seaters. Only four were Sopwith two-seaters. Most of his proficiency was displayed against old Farmans, Voisins, B.E.'s, and

R.E.8's. This is no reflection on Boelcke's courage or methods, but it does show how the fixed gun prevailed against slower and poorly armed machines.

Boelcke started the year well by destroying four British machines in January; in turn, a B.E., an R.E.5, a Morane Parasol, and a Vickers Gunbus. It should be explained that the latter was a pusher like the F.E. but powered with a rotary engine instead of the in-line Beardmore. The Gunbus in this case gave Boelcke an unforgettable scare. He had never encountered one before and probably had expected to make short work of it. However, the British plane flipped around so fast and the gunner was so skilled and alert that Boelcke had to wing over and study this new situation. Going back, he tried to outmanoeuvre the Vickers but found the pusher a veritable gadfly. For twenty-five minutes they jousted, and the British gunner was giving Oswald a bad time. Gradually both ships lost much height until they were practically down over Boelcke's Douai aerodrome. At this point the British pilot became alarmed and made a foolish dodge. Boelcke took advantage of it. A short burst killed the pilot, and the Gunbus piled up on the edge of the Douai field.

Boelcke was very shaken by this particular experience but fortunately he had an official appointment with the Kaiser, who had decided to reward him with the order *Pour le mérite*. The emotion of the award and the dinner with his Emperor erased the scare he had had and perhaps helped him to forget the experience.

The month of March did not bring further reward, but Boelcke was transferred from Douai and sent down to the French front to take part in a proposed aerial offensive over Verdun. Germany was determined to take the old fortress, first for the moral effect and second, to clear the path to Paris. No sacrifice was to be too great, and the cream of the crop, land and air, was moved into the area. Every airman was expected to take part in an over-all programme of aerial reconnaissance and rear-area bombings. Air fighting, as such, was to be ignored.

Young Boelcke made it clear from the beginning that he had no use for such a theory. On March 13 he spotted a creaky old Voisin squadron returning from a raid over German territory. Since he was alone, he moved cautiously until he spotted a laggard. One of the Voisins seemed to be experiencing engine trouble, and when most factors were in his favour Boelcke moved in like a shrike. The Voisin struggled up in agony, fell off as it stalled, and started down in a spin. But he had seen such trickery before, so he followed the big biplane down. Both machines slithered through a thin layer of cloud, and as Boelcke dove into the clear he found the Voisin floundering in a wide circuit with the French gunner clambering along the lower wing to provide weight leverage, thus hoping to right the plane. Boelcke was so close he could see the French boy's face, his fear-stricken eyes flashing like brilliants in a chalk skull.

A touch of humanity softened Boelcke until several Archie bursts snapped him back to reality and he sensed it would be folly to act humane when he himself might be shot down in hostile territory.

He realized his first burst had damaged the cable controls of the bomber and that the gunner had tried to provide temporary equilibrium in order to get down—and perhaps save two lives. It was a gallant gesture and deserved its reward.

Boelcke never fired another burst. While he probably was considering the quality of mercy, Fate solved his dilemma. The left wing of the Voisin dropped toward earth, and the plane rolled like a great bird in a torment of agony. There was a swift flash-scene of a helpless man being hurled from his frail security and tumbled into the dreadful nothingness of the sky.

With an ache in his heart Boelcke turned back for his own lines.

In successive days this German flyer shot down three more Farmans and now had thirteen planes to his credit. He became the idol of his Fatherland and only Max Immelmann came anywhere near him in the victory lists. It should be pointed out that Immelmann was a more spectacular showman and possessed that personal magnetism which attracts the interest of the masses. He won more headlines and columns of news, but Boelcke was entertained more often by the German nobility.

Max Immelmann, who was Germany's Bad Boy of the war skies, did not live long to enjoy his fame. After getting off to a sensational start late in 1915, proving that the fixed-gun fighter was a more efficient weapon than the anti-aircraft gun, he was slow in adding to his score following the Christmas holidays. At the same time, determined to keep his monoplane in favour with the scoring aces, Anthony Fokker made sure that Immelmann was personally provided with the absolute latest model. He was given the first Fokker equipped with two fixed machine guns and later a model, sometimes listed as the Eindekker 4, that actually carried three. There were many undercover complaints about these multi-gun models, many of them valid, but a great deal of this propaganda was being distributed by envious German aircraft manufacturers. They argued that the Oberursel rotary engine was not a suitable power plant for a war plane, pointing out that it was not too sturdy and completely broke up whenever rocker arms were damaged in action, a feature typical of all rotary engines. They also made a point of criticizing Fokker's gun gear (with some justification), saying that it was far from perfect and that many propellers were being pierced by bullets when the aeroplane carried but one gun, so what might happen if these scouts carried two or three?

Imbued with the spirit of the times, Immelmann was brash enough to ignore all these warnings and criticisms. As a result he enjoyed further success, and as the hectic weeks went on both he and Bolecke were frequently wined and dined. Several German historians have pointed out that these gay times were too frequent and much overdone. Immelmann revelled in the homage, however, and when Fokker suggested that perhaps *three* fixed guns might speed up his score, he jumped at the idea. On April 16 he took the new E.4 into the air and pressed the trigger, but unfortunately the synchronization gear was not selective enough to control three weapons, and Immelmann's prop dissolved into a pattern of splinters. The engine ran wild and almost ripped itself out of the bearers.

After that the Eagle of Lille, as he was being headlined, had to be contented with a two-gun mount, but even with this precaution he was ill-destined, for again on May 31 he "shot himself down" while attacking a British bombing formation. This time the gun ran amok, blasting the propeller to kindling, and a large chunk flew back and tore a gash in his leather flying helmet.

The month of June was very rainy and during this time the Germans captured Fort Vaux on the French front. Their High Command also decided to employ these new single-seater fighters in what was to become the first fighter command. It is understood that Boelcke had a great deal to do with this decision, for about this time he was away from his field making a tour of German aerodromes over the whole war front.

Immelmann, of course, was selected to lead one of these new fighter sections when the plan was ironed out, but on the morning of June 18 he took off with Sergeant Prehn, and two brothers named Heinemann. Once more we come up against the typical ace mystery that marked the end of so many World War I heroes. The generally accepted version is that this foursome ran into two F.E.2b's of No. 25 Squadron,

R.F.C. The first, manned by Lieutenants Robinson and Savage, went down before the concentrated fire of all four German machines. But the second F.E., piloted by Lieutenant G. R. McCubbin, put up a stiff battle. McCubbin's gunner, Corporal J. H. Waller, who was just out of the trenches, had little respect for these four Fokkers, and his first burst killed Immelmann immediately and the Fokker went down like a dart and then broke in two in mid-air. All these facts, the time bracket and details, have been confirmed by the R.F.C. and the anti-aircraft gunners in the area. The Germans, however, immediately put out a different version; one based on the possibility that again Immelmann had shot himself down and so damaged his machine that it was uncontrollable.

Some years later—in the 1930s—Rudolph Heinemann, writing in the *Berliner Nachtausgabe*, provided the following version:

"According to our instructions I flew close to Immelmann. On the further side of him I could see the machine of my brother, who waved at me. I knew he was feeling as happy as I was at that moment—and unbridled joy had taken possession of us.

"We approach (the oncoming English squadron) and the fight began. I wondered why the Archies of both sides continued to shoot when we were all mixed up with the Englishmen. Then suddenly—what has happened to Immelmann? His tail keeps going up and down and he has not fired more than a couple of bursts. But the pitching of his machine becomes more violent and pronounced. Damn it all, this seems to be bad business! But I must look after myself and pay some attention to my opponent. When I look around again—Immelmann has vanished!

"Later, they found two shattered parts of a machine. One was half a fuselage with the engine, the wings, and the dead pilot. The rest was several hundred metres away. So the machine had broken up in mid-air, and only a direct hit from an anti-aircraft gun could have split it in that way. Immelmann had been shot down! So, at least, we were told when we landed and a report to that effect was sent to our Army Corps and to G.H.Q. The German nation and the world read it in the official communiqué.

"But my last observations allowed me no rest. I went off in a car to the scene of his crash and made a thorough examination of the remains of the machine. There the closing stages of the tragedy rose up before my eyes and I visualized them as follows:

"Once again Immelmann had shot his own propeller to

pieces; once again the engine broke away from its support and hung on the upper tubes. This time Immelmann was as swift as lightning in cutting off the ignition, but the forward lurch of the engine caused the machine to dip into a nose dive. Immelmann instinctively applied the elevator, but when the machine was pulled up the engine slid back and aggravated the upward movement. The pilot checked this by putting his stick down again; once more the tail went up, and—more quickly than I can express it in words—the fuselage rocked up and down with ever-increasing force, like the writhing of a fish in its death agonies. After a while the fragile construction of the machine proved unequal to the strain, and one of the four steel tubes cracked. Then the fuselage began to slew around as if it had a propeller fixed behind it. Another tube cracked and after a few more blows of the tail both tubes were completely fractured. Then the end was not long in coming. The remaining supports were unable to check the turning movement and the air pressure on the rudder twisted the rear half of the fuselage until it tore right away.

"All this happened in a few seconds, while the machine was at a great height; then the two parts of the fuselage fell separately.

"My investigation of the debris showed that this was the only way in which the calamity could have occurred. The report which I sent in to the chief of my section was forwarded by him to his superior. To this latter I had to prove my theory at the scene of the tragedy. I showed him that one propeller blade was practically sawn asunder by the shots, that there were the halves of bullet holes along the line of breakage, and that the length of the blade's stump reached exactly to the machine guns' lines of fire. Moreover, the steel tubes of the fuselage were flattened at the point of breakage, thus showing clearly that they had been sundered by pressure exerted in two directions. The breakage would have been quite different had it been caused by a direct hit from an anti-aircraft gun. There was likewise evidence that the tail had been twisted off.

" 'You are quite right,' said my co-investigator thoughtfully, 'but we will let the world continue in the belief that has now become current.' "

This anti-aircraft-gun version may have been current in Germany, but Great Britain chose to believe that Corporal Waller had shot down Oberleutnant Max Immelmann, the Eagle of Lille, ending his career after he had been credited with thirteen victories.

In a letter home a few days later Oswald Boelcke explained Immelmann's death this way: "Immelmann lost his life by a silly chance. All that has been written in the newspapers about a fight in the air, etc., is rot. A bit of his propeller flew off; the jarring tore the bracing wires connecting up with the fuselage and then broke away."

By the beginning of September Boelcke was burdened with a Staffel of his own, the basic organization that was to hatch the famed Jagdstaffel 2. With the honour came the administrative strain, reams of paperwork, responsibility for advanced flight training and a continual round of dinners and formal ceremonies. Whenever possible he went home and enjoyed the quiet sense of security with his father. They had much in common and took long walks together, and Oswald would attempt to explain the role of military aviation.

Herr Boelcke understood none of this and pointed out that Wilhelm was not taking this war so seriously. He was serving on the desultory Russian front and had suggested over and over that Oswald get himself a sinecure on some inactive sector. Wilhelm felt that his much-decorated brother was a fool to still risk his life on the Western Front when he already had all the honours a German military man could gather.

Oswald was disgusted with Wilhelm's attitude and quickly changed the subject. Papa Boelcke always went back to his chief hope: that soon the war would be over and that Oswald would come home and become a teacher. In his heart the old man knew this boy had been a fine pupil and with this war as a background he would have great success in the academies.

But Germany's premier airman generally shook his head slowly. Like so many others, he knew civilian life would never match up to this and he made pathetic little jokes about the possibility of becoming a schoolteacher.

These at-home confidences generally ended with their mutual agreement that Fate would take its course, a precept with which Oswald had no complaint.

After his routine inspection of the complete German Air Service, Boelcke returned to Douai to learn that his war birds were no longer having things all their own way. The British were putting up a gallant stand with their two-seater pushers, and the D.H.2, the single-seater variant of the Fee, was giving the Fokker fighters a new lesson in air combat. In truth, the R.F.C. was outflying the Boelcke fixed-gun machines. It was a new interpretation of what you can't see, you can't hit.

At the same time Boelcke realized that the Aviation Staff was handling their two-seaters with little understanding of their full capabilities. They had been practically useless during the siege of Verdun, a long-drawn-out struggle that threatened to endure for months. Their observation planes had been sent into the air with little or no air protection. There was no real cockpit co-operation between the pilots and gunners, and as a fighting element they were not worth the fuel they were consuming.

However, since Boelcke was temperamentally a fighter pilot, he could not devise or suggest any acceptable two-seater strategy. The fixed gun had created a mental block so far as two-seater fighting was concerned.

The loss of Immelmann was a psychological blow, not only to the German public, but to Boelcke in particular. In spite of their newspaper rivalry they had enjoyed a warm personal friendship. Regardless of the official German explanation of Immelmann's death, Boelcke now realized that war in the air was no longer a one-sided sport. It was becoming a very deadly gamble in which many factors played vital roles.

This new concern needled Boelcke into making childish denunciations and braggart threats against the hated English, and the German High Command took advantage of his tirades and offhandedly encouraged him to devise new tactics and assume a more disciplined leadership to employ against the British. His new fighting manoeuvres were very productive and in a short time the Boelcke Staffel became the outstanding squadron for initiative, dash, and boastful confidence. All this was grist to the German press, and Boelcke as the focal figure found himself in an unenviable position. Unless he shot a Britisher down every day he was looked upon as something of a slacker.

To his credit it must be said that he put up a great effort. During the month of September, while showing his fledglings how it should be done, Boelcke destroyed eleven British machines. His bag included three D.H.2's, two Vickers Gunbus two-seaters, and two Sopwith one and one-half Strutters.

Between patrols or during bad weather he made hurried visits to Berlin to push his fighter-squadron ideas and theories, hoping to inject some up-to-date viewpoint into the minds of the General Staff, which still thought in terms of kite balloons and long-range artillery with which to fight this stalemated war.

While on one of these visits he became acquainted with a little-known pilot named Baron Manfred von Richthofen. Boelcke had been holding consultations at Koven when he heard of a headstrong young Prussian who, although a member of an Albatros two-seater Staffel, wished to become a single-seater fighter. Boelcke needed all these ambitious men he could lay his hands on, for the British unquestionably held the intiative now. In fact, they had become an absolute menace since the Battle of the Somme.

Boelcke must have drawn a very attractive picture of the action and glory his Staffel was enjoying in front of Douai, for Manfred von Richthofen was more than interested. After all, to fly behind the great Boelcke, wearer of the *Pour le mérit!* Would he be interested in flying a single-seater? He'd be greatly honoured.

Three days later von Richthofen was heading for Jagdstaffel 2. He was in Boelcke's formation when the master scored his next three victories. On September 17 under the guidance of Boelcke, this young Prussian from Schweidnitz scored his first kill. He was to claim seventy-nine more before the inexorable fate of war overtook him.

Boelcke's visits to Berlin resulted in another great service improvement. He insisted that his fighters be equipped with the new Albatros D.1, a tough, sleek-bodied biplane that carried two fixed guns. He had had enough of Tony Fokker's frail monoplane with its sportsplane structure and untrustworthy guy wires.

Flying this snarling two-clawed vulture, Boelcke set out to stem the new British air offensive. Beginning on September 17 Jagdstaffel 2 was flown as a flying circus, meaning that every available pilot and plane went into the air in one tight formation sweep with Boelcke leading. Anything intercepted by this armada was doomed, and as the days slipped by Boelcke brought his score up to forty. What the rest of the German Air Force was doing was something else, but Boelcke was surely holding his sector of the line above the Somme.

He always led the first morning patrol when the upcoming sun was in their favour, and as long as they maintained a tight formation they enjoyed perfect protection and security. Any Allied plane trapped in their three-dimensional charge was downed by someone. The new youngster, Manfred von Richthofen, was credited with fifteen victories during the last four months of 1916.

Boelcke no longer cared about his own fortunes or his score. The schoolmaster destiny had caught up with him. He spent every waking hour drilling his newcomers, lecturing his flight leaders, devising new fighting tactics for the men who were flocking to his banner. He wrote out his views, attached tactical drawings, and toured the whole area giving talks and spreading his experience. He set up skeletal formations that

114

were to become other Jagdstaffels and to make sure his pupils recognized him in the air he had his plane painted all black; a feature his understudy, Baron von Richthofen, was to adopt and take credit for.

Another up-and-coming youngster was Erwin Bohme, who was doing particularly well. As a matter of fact, Boelcke considered Bohme a superior pilot to von Richthofen, and had not tragic events cropped up to break Bohme's spirit, Boelcke's opinion might have been well justified. At any rate Bohme showed rare maturity for a beginner.

On October 28 Boelcke led a six-ship element on a formation drill. Von Richthofen and Erwin Bohme flew close behind on his right and left. They were there to observe the master's technique. Near Poziéres, inside the German lines, two D.H.2's of No. 24 (Hawker's) Squadron, flown by Lieutenants A. G. Knight and A. E. McKay, were out on an offensive patrol.

The Staffel leader raised his hand, folded his fingers down, and signalled the attack. Moving in from behind, he led his formation up and under the blind spots of the D.H.2's. In trying to maintain his protective position, Bohme somehow slithered into Boelcke's Albatros. To the pilots in the rear it seemed that the two planes hardly touched, but the machine in which Boelcke had so much confidence was stricken immediately; Bohme's upper wing tip had sliced through the two interplane struts, collapsing the wing of the famous black plane. As the wing folded back slowly, the leader's Albatros turned with the drag of the broken airfoil. The stick went dead in Boelcke's hand, and there was very little height in which to attempt a recovery. The ponderous 160-h.p. Mercedes took the crippled Albatros to its doom, ploughing into the blood-drenched territory of the Somme that had seen so many of Boelcke's victories.

They say they had a hard time with Erwin Bohme. He was heartbroken and when he landed begged for a minute alone with a service Luger. Wiser heads talked him out of suicide, and eventually he went on to command the Boelcke Jagdstaffel. His fate, too, was explicit, for in December of 1917 Erwin Bohme was killed—the day before he was to be decorated with the *Pour le mérit*.

Oswald Boelcke was buried from the cathedral in Cambrai with the staff of Germany's Imperial Forces and the ruling princes of the Empire in attendance. Among the floral offerings was one that might have meant much to Boelcke could he have known. It bore a card which read:

To a much admired and honourable enemy.
FROM: *British officers who are prisoners of*
war at Osnabruck.

The year 1916 saw the zenith heights and doleful lows of several star performers. Less than a month after the death of Oswald Boelcke, his leading pupil, Manfred von Richthofen, evened the score by downing Major George L. Hawker, Britain's V.C. airman, who was playing much the same role as had Boelcke.

By the middle of 1916 Hawker's No. 24 Squadron, which was equipped with D.H.2 pusher-fighters, was perhaps the best known on the Allied side of the line. Under his able leadership the twenty-fourth went from victory to victory and was noted as a "killer squadron." In June it was responsible for the destruction of seventeen enemy aircraft, indicating that the D.H.2 was as deadly a fighter as the Fokker monoplane. In July twenty-three more Germans went down before their guns and fifteen more in August; fifteen were also destroyed in September and ten more the following month.

But on November 23 Hawker met his end when he engaged in a duel with Manfred von Richthofen between Bapaume and Albert. This was one of the famous air battles of World War I, and in his official combat report von Richthofen told the story as follows:

"My eleventh Britisher was Major Hawker, twenty-six years old and commander of an English squadron. According to prisoners' accounts, he was the English Boelcke.

"He gave me the hardest fight I have experienced so far, until I finally succeeded in getting him down. . . ."

What von Richtofen failed to add was that this duel was fought for more than thirty-five minutes. He was flying a new two-gun Albatros, while Hawker had but one Lewis gun. Actually von Richthofen fired nearly 900 rounds of ammunition before one lone bullet creased Hawker's skull, knocking him unconscious. Unable to help himself, he went down and fell inside the German lines. It was one of those thousand-to-one shots that finished the great Hawker and brought an end to a brilliant air record.

A man named Hermann Goering became a pilot in the Imperial German Air Service during the spring of 1916. Later he was one of the most controversial figures in modern German history and today's readers remember him as the fat, boastful head of the German *Luftwaffe* of World War II, who, when eventually brought to trial, evaded the bitter consequences by taking his own life.

The full career of this man will perhaps explain something of his deplorable political history. A typical Prussian of the old school, he was born in 1893 at Rosenheim, Bavaria, the most unwarlike of the German states. His father saw service as an officer in the 1866 conflict against Austria and in the Franco-Prussian war of 1870-71, later becoming the first governor of German South-west Africa.

Young Hermann was not originally selected for a military career, but he was so reckless and high-spirited that the Goering family decided a few years of military life and discipline would do some good. In 1912 he came out of a German cadet school with the rank of Leutnant (second lieutenant) and was posted to the 112th Infantry Regiment. During the autumn manoeuvres he had the audacity to insult his commanding officer, who had questioned the wisdom of Goering's tactics during an exercise. Had it not been for his father's influence, Hermann's career might have ended then and there.

About this time he met Bruno Loerzer, who later on was one of Germany's premier air fighters. They became firm friends; their association surviving the post-war upheaval in Germany, where Loerzer played a part in Goering's subsequent rise to fame.

World War I gave Goering a chance to capitalize on his recklessness. When he was sent to the Alsace front he formed a cyclist corps from his own platoon and proceeded to harass the Allied outposts. On one occasion he set out to reconnoitre an enemy force with strict orders to avoid actual contact. This, Goering intentionally disobeyed and with seven men rode into a village containing nearly a hundred French troops. But for the fact that an over-anxious soldier opened fire from a hayloft before Hermann had placed the rest of his men into position, they might have captured the complete French force. Goering was awarded the Iron Cross Second Class for this daring foray—and in turn severely censured for his disobedience.

While in the hospital early in 1915 with an attack of rheumatism, Goering was visited by Bruno Loerzer, who sold him completely on the glories of the Air Service. When Hermann returned to his regiment he applied for a transfer, but his commanding officer would not countenance such disrespect for the infantry service, so Goering took matters in his own hands and when Loerzer next visited him, by a strange coincidence with a two-seated Albatros, Goering packed his bags, tossed them into the aircraft, and took off with his pal.

To the amazement of everyone, this heavy-handed stratagem worked! Goering became Loerzer's observer, and within two months this flamboyant duo was cited for the Iron Cross First Class. In February 1916 five French Farmans raided the German Crown Prince's headquarters at Stenay, and Loerzer and Goering "just happened" to be passing while the Farmans were unloading their eggs. The old Albatros dived through the formation, Goering firing in all directions with such effect that the raiders turned for home quicker than they had planned. One unfortunate who lagged behind was shot down by Hermann's exhibition of salvo fire.

A short time later they were attacked by a Nieuport, but Goering drove the Frenchman off, blazing away with a pistol when his Parabellum jammed.

In the spring of 1916 the Imperial Air Service was in dire need of pilots, and Goering was one of thirty hurriedly trained at a school outside Courtrai, where he again ran into trouble. While flying with Loerzer he had naturally picked up considerable basic knowledge of flying; so after less than two weeks of formal training he decided he was ready for the front. His instructors thought otherwise, but Goering closed the matter by appropriating a brand-new Rumpler, a type that had not as yet been selected for active service, and headed for the front line.

Headquarters, which had spent months trying to tame Hermann Goering, decided that the best way to eliminate this problem was to let him kill himself. When he turned up at a flying section in the Verdun area, they allowed him to stay there—hoping for the best. Instead, Goering did more things with the Rumpler than anyone believed possible, so he was allowed to rejoin his pal Loerzer, who by now was flying Fokkers in Staffel 5. Before the year was ended Goering had accounted for three French machines—and had saved Loerzer's life!

One crisp day in December 1916 Staffel 5 took on a flight of Nieuports, and Loerzer was forced out of the action with a gun stoppage. Two Nieuports spotted his difficulty and went down after him. First they shot one pair of elevator cables through, and Loerzer was really in trouble. Goering, who was having a glorious time, suddenly noticed his pal in difficulty. He went to his aid immediately, shooting one Nieuport into a tumbling bundle of wreckage while the other sought salvation in a speedy dive.

Staffel 5 carried out few patrols over the rest of the month owing to the continual bad weather; but when Bloody April opened in 1917 both Goering and Loerzer performed valiantly.

The year 1916 saw many interesting improvements in German aircraft. The early success of the Fokker E.1 was not long-lived, for it was discovered that the guy-wire-stressed monoplane wing was not suitable for wartime conditions, and the Halberstadt and the new Albatros D.1. took over. By the end of the year Germany had thirty-three squadrons of Albatros or Halberstadt scouts fully equipped and in action. At the time, the strength of a German squadron was fourteen planes.

The D.1. scout was a beautiful machine; its sharklike fuselage was in marked contrast to contemporary designs. It also set the pace in aircraft armament, and after the advent of the Albatros twin synchronized guns were standardized in both German and Allied types. An Albatros D.2, which was a slightly improved version of the D.1, was also produced in 1916. The designers revised the centre-section struts to allow better vision, and it also had ailerons on both upper and lower wings.

In 1916 the Germans used the Aviatik C.2 for short-range bombing attacks and later for artillery observation work. It was not as sleek a craft as the Albatros C.3, but it apparently was a good fighter. Twice in his flying career Georges Guynemer was downed by the gunners on Aviatik C.2's. Another French ace, René Dorme, rose to fame when he attacked and dispersed a formation of six Avaitiks that were bombing Paris. Later he created a sensation when he rammed an Aviatik with the undercarriage of his Nieuport scout, ripping its top wing away; at the same time he managed to flutter back to his own field and make a respectable landing.

Soon after Immelmann's death, Tony Fokker designed a new biplane fighter. It had some interesting features, and in July 1916 the German government ordered twenty-five of these new D.1. scouts, but they were never very popular with active-service men. Fokker next tried a D.2. model with the Oberursel rotary engine. However, the Albatros D.1 so outperformed it, there was little demand for full production. Fokker's problem in competing with the Albatros machines seemed to be based on the fact he couldn't get enough Mercedes engines for any continuous production of an in-line engine aircraft.

His D.4 model powered with the 160-h.p. water-cooled Mercedes had a far better performance than the Halberstadt Scout, although it looked somewhat similar in design. It was obvious that Fokker was in something of an eclipse, and he was not completely in the aviation picture again until August 1917 when he produced the D.R.1 triplane—an out-and-out copy of the British Sopwith triplane. But copy or not, the Fokker Tripe turned out to be an amazing dogfighter and made aces of many fair-to-middling performers.

The famed Halberstadt D.2. scout was one of the finest fighters on the front. Oswald Boelcke was the first to appreciate its design and sharp manoeuvrability, but he seemed to be the only German airman of any prominence who enjoyed flying it. For this reason, the Halberstadt was never a favourite, and after Boelcke's death it was withdrawn from the Western Front early in 1917.

The following is a complete list of military aircraft developed and produced for the German Air Service in 1916:

GERMAN WARPLANES OF 1916

Make	Engine	Speed m.p.h.	Purpose
Albatros D.1	Mercedes 160 h.p.	115	Scout
Albatros D.2	Benz 160 h.p.	110	Scout
Albatros C.3	Mercedes 160 h.p.	95	Bomber
Aviatik P	Mercedes 170 h.p.	82	Bomber
Aviatik	Mercedes 160 h.p.	90	Reconnaissance
A.G.O. C.2	Mercedes 160 h.p.	90	Bomber
D.W.F. B.2	Mercedes 160 h.p.	95	Reconnaissance
Fokker D.1	Mercedes 170 h.p.	110	Scout
Fokker D.2	Oberursel 100 h.p.	112	Scout
Fokker D.3	Oberursel 110 h.p.	110	Scout
Gotha G.1	Twin-Benz 160 h.p.	60	Bomber
Gotha G.1A	Twin-Mercedes 160 h.p.	65	Bomber
Halberstadt	Opel-Argus 160 h.p.	115	Scout
L.V.G. C.3	Mercedes 170 h.p.	90	Reconnaissance-bomber
Roland D.1	Benz 160 h.p.	100	Scout
Roland D.2	Mercedes 170 h.p.	105	Scout

On the British side of the line General Trenchard was taking measures which would cope with the Boelcke Circus threat, although at the time he could have had no idea what was in the German leader's mind. On January 14 he issued another order to the effect that:

"Henceforth, all machines must fly in formations of not less than four units."

Shortly afterwards this policy was amplified so that entire squadrons took part in bombing and fighting attacks, a marked improvement that soon achieved striking results. Indeed, there are some who declared that the much-praised German *Jagdgeschwader* was created from this R.F.C. idea. The new system also proved effective in discouraging attacks by hostile aircraft, and for a change the R.F.C. now could show a victory report figured on the right side of the ledger. In fact, between January 10 and April 30 forty-two enemy aircraft were brought down as against a loss of thirty-two British machines.

Another order was issued in March decreeing that squadron strength should be increased from twelve machines to eighteen, and by the end of June no less than twenty-seven such complete squadrons were in action in the British cause. The equipment was made up mainly of F.E.2b fighters, Sopwith one and one-half Strutters, and D.H.2's, with the pusher types bearing the brunt of the fighting.

During the first six weeks of 1916 very little was actually accomplished by the British in the way of air fighting and bombing. Much of this period was spent in experimenting with wireless and other systems of artillery co-operation. Later on, this air-artillery alliance reached a high stage of efficiency and proved most valuable during the grim Somme battles.

On January 5 a formation of fifteen B.E.2c's made a raid on Douai airfield and only one machine was lost. However, the Fokker scourge became serious during these operations and it was decided to try night raiding. Thus, on the clear moonlight evening of February 19 two B.E.2c's from No. 4 Squadron attacked a German field outside Cambrai with considerable success and encountered no opposition. It was the first night raid by the R.F.C. of that war. One of the pilots, a Captain J. E. Tennant, flew so low over his target that splinters from his own 20-pound Hales bombs penetrated his machine in several places. The success of this initial attack proved the practicability of night operations, and many squadrons were ordered to gain night-flying experience with a view to carrying out mass nocturnal raids on the enemy back areas.

Very few air-fighting records are available up to August 1916, and other than Hawker, Cruickshank, and one or two others, few British pilots won any outstanding distinction as air fighters. It should be pointed out that most air fighting was carried out by the two-seated pushers, and the gunners or observers were doing all the killing, but since most of them were N.C.O. airmen they were seldom, if ever, credited with their individual scores. Those who were particularly successful were, of course, rewarded with promotion and decorations, but in all cases their citations produced only the routine "devotion to duty and heroism in the field" announcements. Nothing about the number of enemy planes they had destroyed.

Because of this, the French and German airmen held the spotlight during the first two years· of the war; a point that probably attracted so many Americans to the French colours in the early months of the conflict.

Toward the end of March the first Nieuport Scouts were delivered to Nos. 1 and 11 squadrons, and a great deal was expected of them. However, at first the Nieuport proved something of a disappointment, since it was lacking in speed and in the hands of ham-fisted pilots was somewhat fragile during violent acrobatics. It had a good rate of climb, but never could catch the Albatros or Halberstadt, and by the same token never could run away from them.

While the Nieuport was being improved, the doughty D.H.2. had to bear the brunt of the single-seated fighter work, and we know how well they carried out this duty by a previous reference to the work of Hawker's No. 24 Squadron. In fairness to everyone concerned it must be admitted that the bulk of the offensive air-war was being contested by the pilots and gunners of the Fee (F.E.2b) squadrons; No. 25 in particular running up a splendid record.

On the afternoon of June 25 a young curly-haired second lieutenant, Albert Ball, broke out of obscurity and won the Military Cross. One of the most fabulous characters in British air history, this young man had transferred out of the Sherwood Foresters, a noted Nottingham infantry regiment, after buying pilot training out of his own pocket. In order to do this he had to rise at 3.30 every morning, motorcycle 60 miles to Hendron, take a one-hour training flight, and hurry back to be on parade at 7 a.m.

Ball was first sent out to No. 13 Squadron, which was flying ancient B.E.2c's, and his chief job was to take intelligence agents over the line and retrieve them a few days later. His passenger on one occasion refused to disembark when Ball had deposited him on the selected field, so the youngster (he was not yet nineteen) gave him a lecture on patriotism and then unceremoniously booted him out of the cockpit.

But such trivial events were too tame for Master Ball, so when his duties with No. 13 were done for the day he usually walked across the field and volunteered to do patrols with No. 11, which by then was flying the Nieuport of ill repute. No. 11 had been slated to get a series of kite balloons that were annoying their front, and only Ball was successful. He had taken up a lapful of highly sensitive phosphorus bombs, and by dropping three where they would do the most good, he scored one for No. 11. A few days later he "borrowed" another Nieuport and went hunting. A Roland two-seater fell across the Mercatel-Arras road and blocked traffic for some time.

Within a few weeks his name became a household word throughout the British Empire.

About the same time, on July 10, a British sergeant named James B. McCudden made his first flight as a war pilot from a field outside Clairmarais, which sheltered No. 20 Squadron. They were flying Fee pushers and were to become a squadron to be reckoned with, being credited with destroying more than 600 enemy planes during the war.

McCudden had been on flying status since the outbreak of hostilities, acting as a gunner-observer on anything that could get off the ground. During the spring of 1915 he was sent back to England for pilot training and for a short time was kept there as an instructor. Now he was an N.C.O. pilot with a glorious career ahead of him.

On August 3 he was transferred to No. 29 Squadron, flying D.H.2's out of Abeele and, as did von Richthofen, who was hunting over the same area, began to run up his amazing score early in September. On the morning of the sixth he was up alone at 14,000 feet between Armentières and Ypres when he spotted a German two-seater approaching. He gave chase and the intruder turned east, nose down. He flew to within 400 yards, but could get no closer, so he fired a full drum of Lewis ammunition. The enemy gunner did not put up a fight of any sort. Then McCudden rammed on another drum and continued firing until the enemy plane went down steeply through a cloud bank at 4,000 feet. That was the last he saw of him, so he flew back to his field and made a routine report but did not claim a victory.

Three days later an anti-aircraft crew in that area and a British agent in the enemy lines reported that a white two-seater had been brought down on the Menin road near Gheluvelt. The time and location coincided with McCudden's report, so he was credited with his first Hun.

This was a typical flight for young McCudden. He did his routine patrols each day and then would go off alone, climbing as high as his mount would take him, where he would sit and wait for the unwary.

The writer knew Jimmy McCudden in 1917 and remembers well his references to those early days.

"The astounding thing to me," he once told me, "was the number of rounds we would fire and still have nothing happen. Once six of us got in a fight and we battled away from 10,000 feet to 800 feet. We fired every round we had, but no one seemed to bring back a bullet hole. We all must have been awful duds as marksmen.

"Then again, I can't imagine what the Germans were doing during those days in 1916. Oh yes, Boelcke, Immelmann, and Leffers were apparently doing very well, but I can remember flight after flight of old B.E.'s flipping about all over Germany taking pictures, spotting for the guns, or just doing routine observation shows, and no one bothered them. We never had any such targets on our side of the line."

McCudden had a harrowing accident that autumn. He was flying alone making for his height, and he felt "particularly blood-thirsty," as he wrote in his enchanting autobiography, *Flying Fury*.

"I decided to do a loop, for no particular reason. I nosed down to get some speed, and then just as I was coming up I foolishly decided to snap back into straight flight. The change of pressure lifted all four drums of ammunition out of the boxes at the sides of my cockpit and they all went past my head, past the engine and—through the propeller. Three of the four blades were smashed too, and one cut through the right-hand lower tail boom. I tried to switch off quickly, but the remaining prop blade did surprising things to the engine and practically lifted it out of the 'spider' that carried it.

"I don't remember much of what I did after that—except pray. As far as I could make out only a diagonal cable was holding my tail on. I just hoped the controls were in order and gingerly turned her around and looked for a landing space. I kept her at about 65 m.p.h. and somehow she held together. It was my nightmare for weeks to come."

Of all the ranking aces, Jimmy McCudden was one of the few who told his story honestly, admitting his faults, weaknesses, and mistakes.

When the Germans began to get their new Albatros machines and work out the Boelcke Circus formations, matters became somewhat critical for the British fighters. Their planes did not have the altitude at which the Germans worked and most of them had to be content with a single gun, whereas the Albatros was now hunting with two.

Lieutenant William Avery Bishop, a Canadian, was serving as an observer with a British B.E. squadron in May of 1916. He had transferred, as did so many others, from a Canadian cavalry regiment "to get out of the mud" and had to undergo a short period of front-line experience as a P.B.O. (Poor Bloody Observer). One day on a return from an artillery shoot his pilot overshot what stretch of turf was available and wrapped up the hulk, and Bishop suffered a badly damaged knee. During his four months of back-seat flying he had never seen an enemy plane and had never fired his machine gun. All he had done was spot for the artillery.

After a period of convalescence in England, Billy Bishop was permitted to take flight training and for a time was kept in England doing night patrols against the Zeppelin menace; but again very little happened and he began to wonder about the headlined glory and romance of the flying services.

It was not until March 7, 1917, that Bishop was allowed to "get at" the enemy, but when he did he certainly made history.

In August of this memorable year, 1916, a one-eyed man with a consuming hatred of the Hun entered a flying school in England where Sergeant McCudden was instructing. The pupil was one of the prize duds of the era. However, Edward Mannock had more than the necessary dexterity to become a great pilot.

He was born in a military barracks, the son of a Scots Greys cavalryman, but his father was a complete wastrel and when Edward was only twelve years old deserted the family. After weeks of bitterness, months of destitution, and years of dreary toil, young Mannock signed on as an apprentice lineman with a British telephone company. He worked hard, studied in his spare time, and became an expert in the communications field.

At the outbreak of the war he was in Constantinople, installing a telephone system, and when Turkey joined the Central Powers, he and the other Britishers in his group were of course interned. As the months wore on the Turks discovered that Mannock had but one good eye and in April 1915 his captors, feeling that an "old crock," as they termed him, could not give them any trouble, repatriated him in an exchange of prisoners. Little did they realize that they were releasing a dedicated man who was to become one of the greatest of all air fighters. A "crock" who was to destroy the equivalent of several enemy squadrons.

On his arrival back in England, Mannock joined a Royal Army Medical Corps regiment. His new comrades nicknamed him "Jerry"—probably because he was continually expressing his bitterness toward the Germans. Later he was induced to

125

transfer to the Royal Engineers, where he spent a few months learning the job of sapper (one who digs tunnels) and with his combined telephone experience became a valuable engineer. His superiors hoped to keep him, but Mannock had been reading of the deeds of Major George Hawker, so he applied for a transfer to the Royal Flying Corps. In order to slip past the eye examination, he did a tricky double shuffle. When asked to read the card, one eye at a time, he raised his right hand and covered his blind eye—and read clearly. Then changing hands, he simply covered the same eye, completely fooling the examiner. However, he did not reach a flying school until August 1916.

As stated before, he was an inept pupil but fortunately was turned over to an instructor who understood Mannock better than Mannock knew himself. This was the famed Jimmy McCudden, also the son of a time-serving British soldier. For years both of these air heroes deeply resented the appellation "Irishman" as it was applied to them. Both had been born of British fathers on British soil. McCudden's mother was said to be French. Mannock's was a Liverpool girl his father met while stationed in Ireland. Neither young man had ever seen Ireland and both were the complete antithesis of the belligerent "Fighting Irishman."

When American fliers who became associated with Mannock a few years later attempted to call him "Mickey," he would not permit such familiarity. However, in his letters to his closest friends, Mr. and Mrs. A. E. Eyles of Wellingborough, Northamptonshire, he sometimes signed himself "Paddy," "Ed," or "Pat." Among his associates in the Royal Flying Corps he allowed only a select few to address him as "Mickey."

Mannock was apparently good in the air, but his landings were horrors. He was not a "stunt" pilot—but few great airfighters were. Von Richthofen once admitted that he had never looped in his life. Ball and Bishop were far from being star turns with the joy stick, but—one and all—they were great marksmen.

It must be remembered, too, that Mannock was much older than his flying-school comrades, being thirty-four at the time and considered very serious-minded. Later he explained that he was working on a self-imposed drill in which he aimed to perform every manoeuvre perfectly. To his flight mates he seemed a mixed bag of schoolboy impetuosity and veteran conservativeness. It must be admitted that his logbook presents more than his share of buckled undercarriages.

He finally got to France as a fighter pilot with No. 40

Squadron on March 31, 1917—about the same time that Bishop was joining No. 60 Squadron. Both were flying Nieuport Scouts.

The titanic struggle which opened on July 1, 1916, and was to go down in history as the First Battle of the Somme, found the Royal Flying Corps with a complete ascendancy in the air, and it was not until the closing stages of the battle five months later that the German Air Service could claim any real measure of success.

During the preparations for the battle the R.F.C. had undergone a period of considerable activity, for in addition to their everyday work, numerous pilots and observers had put in many hours training in a new duty known as infantry contact-patrol work. In this, the object was for the aircraft to keep in close contact with the advancing troops and to report on their progress, or to take note of and action against any obstacles such as machine-gun nests, concealed batteries, large enemy concentrations, etc., that might hinder the advance.

Many thrilling adventures befell the lot of the contact patrols, and innumerable lives were saved by their daring and initiative. On the other hand many good men lost theirs—victims of their own daring and the terrible ground fire they faced.

The value of this contact work was proved on the first day of the offensive when Captain J. R. P. Whittaker and Second Lieutenant T. E. C. Scaife, spotting a German light field battery busily enfilading the advancing British infantrymen from the cover of a small wood, attacked the gun crews at once with machine-gun fire. Flying only a few feet above the tree tops, the two men poured a hail of lead into the panic-stricken gunners, and within a few moments the guns had been abandoned and left to their fate in the hands of the advancing troops.

Another example of the valuable aid afforded by these machines was given by Captain A. M. Miller and Second Lieutenant C. W. Short. They were searching for their own infantry when they spotted a large enemy concentration. Closer investigation disclosed that a dangerous ambush was being set up in a wheatfield. After treating the ambushers to a few well-placed bursts from his Lewis, the observer signalled his pilot to fly over to a nearby British battery. There he dropped a marked map showing the position of the German ambush and some camouflaged machine-gun nests. The few Germans who escaped the torrent of high explosive were quickly rounded up by—of all things—a squadron of cavalry which had charged into the scene.

It was this same Captain Miller who dropped a note over the German lines after Immelmann had been killed, which act of chivalry stood him in good stead when sometime later he was forced to land in enemy territory. The Germans treated him with especial courtesy.

The British bombers were also in the thick of things and their persistent attacks on enemy railway centres and other lines of communication helped retard the arrival of reserve troops and munitions during the initial assault. The St. Sauver station at Lille was bombed by six Martinsyde Elephants from No. 27 Squadron. After dropping their load of 112-pounders dead on the target, the Elephants were attacked by a large Fokker formation, but the sudden appearance of five Fees saved the day, and two Fokkers were shot down.

Another bomber pilot, Second Lieutenant A. L. Gordon-Kidd, set fire to a train loaded with small-arms ammunition and on the same day Second Lieutenant L. A. Wingfield scored a direct hit with a 112-pounder on a train at the Saint-Quentin station, a hit that was to prove the biggest one-man "bang" of the war. The blazing train had been made up of sixty cars, each loaded to the brim with heavy shells. When the whole lot went up the explosion almost wiped out a regiment of troops which had lined up in the station waiting to entrain. Reports on this raid stated that 180 men had been killed or wounded, and their equipment was so badly damaged that even those who were unscathed had to be withrawn from the war area until they could be completely re-equipped. Wingfield was shot down with a single bullet in his engine and taken prisoner, but later escaped. Unfortunately the success of this operation was confined to his individual strike, for the carefully planned follow-up raid was a failure and of the seven machines that followed Wingfield, only three managed to limp home.

Between July 1 and November 17 no less than 298 raids were carried out and the 17,600 bombs dropped weighed some 292 tons. On July 2 six R.E.7's of No. 21 Squadron bombed Bapaume, each machine unloading one of the new 330-pound bombs. These missiles were remarkable inasmuch as the explosive charge accounted for only 70 pounds of the gross weight; the balance being made up of very heavy bands around the outer casing. The explosive effect of the bomb was extremely deadly, for the banded case disintegrated into countless fragments which travelled laterally at a velocity of

2,000 feet per second. The effect on massed troops or a loaded small-arms ammunition train can only be imagined.

During the Battle of the Somme, British scouts appear to have devoted most of their effort to contour-fighting, bomber escort, or general observation. Very little air fighting was recorded. One pilot of No. 32 Squadron, however, found enough opposition to keep him very busy. He was Major L. M. B. Rees, and while on an offensive patrol aboard a D.H.2 fighter in the region of Festubert he sighted what he took to be a squadron of British bombers returning from a raid behind the German lines. He obligingly flew up to escort them home. Within a few seconds he found out he had made a grievous error, for it was a German formation which only a minute before had shot down a British plane in flames; the pilot being one of Rees's own squadron mates, Second Lieutenant C. J. Simpson.

On Rees's appearance, an enemy machine left its formation to attack him, but a short burst from Rees's gun sent it spinning earthward. Three more two-seaters then took up the attack and Rees was hit in the left thigh, a wound which caused him to lose control for a short time. Seeing his predicament, two more enemy planes moved in to finish him off, but a rush of cold air revived him and he turned on his tormentors and drove them off. Encouraged by this success, he then attacked the whole formation, but because they were carrying bombs, they decided not to press the issue and returned to their field. At least this is the only logical explanation Rees could give for their strange action. For this, and an accumulation of other daring deeds during that period, he was awarded the Victoria Cross.

Carrying out the "Boom" Trenchard theory, the British next began a series of attacks on German aerodromes. During one raid Second Lieutenant A. S. C. MacLaren saw a two-seater about to take off. Diving down to within 100 feet, he planted a small bomb directly on the machine and blew it to smithereens. Turning back, he next machine-gunned a hangar and set fire to a Fokker sheltered there.

In the course of another raid a British plane was forced to land in German territory with a punctured fuel tank. On seeing it go down, Captain S. Grant-Dalton landed alongside it and while his observer, Second Lieutenant R. Paris, held off the enemy, he burned the stranded machine and squeezed the pilot in with Paris. Although they were twice attacked by Fokkers, they arrived back safely with their overloaded aircraft. Grant-Dalton was rewarded with the Distinguished Service Order and his observer with the Military Cross.

The Germans appeared to rally during the latter part of July and air fighting became very bitter again. It was British two-seater Fees and D.H.2's against Fokkers and Rolands, and from a study of the records the British pushers were getting the better of the deal.

A pilot in No. 60 Squadron, Lieutenant Claude E. Ridley, embarked on a spy-dropping expedition that was to involve him in a series of remarkable adventures. Shortly after crossing the enemy lines in the vicinity of Cambrai, he had to land due to engine failure. The agent he was carrying procured some civilian clothing and then left Ridley to his own resources. Unable to speak a word of French or German, Ridley wandered about the enemy back areas posing as a deaf-mute. On one occasion he saw a British B.E. brought down near Douai and watched its crew being hauled off to captivity. On another, he was riding a tramcar when the conductor began to eye him with suspicion. Fearing the game was up, he clouted the ticket taker and escaped to hide in a field of standing corn. During the course of his wanderings he had picked up much valuable information and was determined to make some attempt to reach his own lines. Joining forces with a Belgian spy, he eventually reached the Dutch frontier and shortly before dawn of October 8 he and his companion placed a small wooden ladder against the electric wire and so crossed the border. For his daring and the information he had gathered during his "tour" in occupied territory he was awarded the D.S.O.

During this period No. 60 Squadron recorded a victory that was unique, to say the least. Albert Ball, who had contrived to transfer to this famous Nieuport squadron, had gone out with Lieutenant A. M. Walters with orders to destroy a certain observation balloon. Walters was carrying eight Prieur rockets mounted in tubular casings lashed to his interplane struts. Ball was to cover him during the attack, but the mission had to be called off when it was found that the offending gasbag had been drawn down into its ground bed. So Ball went off on his own, and Walters, wishing to get in logbook time, decided to cruise about and enjoy the scenery. Thus absorbed, he blundered into a lumbering L.V.G. two-seater and attacked it with his Lewis gun, but that temperamental weapon jammed up, so he flew up to within 20 yards of the enemy observation plane and released his rockets. By some amazing chance he scored a direct hit and the L.V.G. fell in flames. As a rule, these early missiles went skating all over the sky like tracer bullets, but on this occasion Walters was lucky.

And rocket-fighting was considered new in the latter part of World War II!

A representative group of air actions staged by the Royal Flying Corps has been offered; the following is a full list of the various types of machines produced by British manufacturers during 1916:

BRITISH WARPLANES OF 1916

Make	Engine	Speed m.p.h.	Purpose
Armstrong-Whitworth F.K.3	R.A.F. 90 h.p.	81	Trainer
Armstrong-Whitworth F.K.8	Beardmore 160 h.p.	88	Reconnaissance
Avro 504L	Clerget 130 h.p.	90	Trainer
Avro Pike	Sunbeam (2) 160 h.p.	85	Bomber
B.E.12	R.A.F. 150 h.p.	97	Fighter
Beatty	Beatty 60 h.p.	65	Trainer
Blackburn G.P.	Rolls (2) 250 h.p.	97	Bomber
Bristol Monoplane	Le Rhone 110 h.p.	122	Fighter
D.H.4	B.H.P. 240 h.p.	120	Bomber
D.H.5	Le Rhone 110 h.p.	102	Fighter
Fairey F.2	Rolls (2) 190 h.p.	95	Bomber
Fairey F.16	Rolls 250 h.p.	90	Bomber
Fairey F.17	Rolls 275 h.p.	94	Bomber
Fairey F.22	Sunbeam 250 h.p.	92	Bomber
Fairey F.129	Clerget 110 h.p.	97	Bomber
Grahame-White 20	Le Rhone 80 h.p.	70	Trainer
Handley-Page 0/400	Rolls (2) 275 h.p.	102	Bomber
Martinsyde Elephant	Beardmore 120 h.p.	95	Scout-bomber
Morane Destroyer	Le Rhone 110 h.p.	102	Fighter
Nieuport	Le Rhone 110 h.p.	107	Fighter
R.E.8	R.A.F. 150 h.p.	104	Reconnaissance
Sage 2	Gnome 100 h.p.	100	Fighter
Sage 3	Rolls 75 h.p.	72	Trainer
Short N.2B	Sunbeam 275 h.p.	91	Coast Patrol
Short-1916	Sunbeam 320 h.p.	83	Torpedo-bomber
Short Bomber	Rolls 250 h.p.	78	Bomber
Sopwith Pup	Le Rhone 80 h.p.	107	Fighter
Sopwith Triplane	Clerget 110 h.p.	109	Fighter
Supermarine P.P.	Gnome 100 h.p.	90	Sea Scout
Vickers F.B.12c	Le Rhone 80 h.p.	130	Fighter
Vickers F.B.19	Le Rhone 110 h.p.	109	Fighter
White R.R.	Sunbeam 225 h.p.	81	Bomber

At 6 a.m. on the morning of May 14, 1916, seven Nieuport *chasse* planes stood on the turf of a gloomy field near Luxeuil-les-Baines, high in the folds of the Vosges mountains. These insect-like machines were powered with 80-h.p. Le Rhone engines and were armed with a Lewis gun mounted high on the top plane. There are a few on view today as museum pieces, but in that summer of 1916 the 13-metre Nieuport was considered a full-taloned war bird.

The pilots were aglow with restrained excitement as they preened over their new planes like kids with birthday bicycles. All seven of them were Americans, that breed of men who up to now had taken little active part in this Great World War. One or two wore the horizon blue of the French *poilu*, for they had volunteered early in 1914 and had seen bloody action with the French Foreign Legion. One or two had had better luck, or had been better advised, and had served with French Voisin bomber squadrons. But this was the first time an American unit was to wing together in combat against the Germans.

One man in particular nurtured a keen personal interest in these preparations, darting up and down probing and questioning. He was comparatively short with massive shoulders, blond hair, and a round kindly face garnished with a spread of oversize moustaches. This was Norman Prince—Sergeant Norman Prince, for the French were frugal with their commissions and the accompanying scale of pay. The scion of an honourable New England family, he had spent many summers in and around Pau in the Pyrénées and had many close friends in France and spoke French fluently. When war broke out it was natural that his sentiments were for France and he was amazed when a hundred million other Americans did not feel the same.

To be sure, a few other Yanks had made a gesture of repaying their ancient debt to France by joining the Foreign Legion or the volunteer ambulance service, which later became the American Field Service. But Prince wanted to be a flying man. He knew all about the French *poilu* with his lowly pay and heavy pack, so in November 1914 he returned home and enrolled in the Burgess Flying School at Marblehead, Massachusetts, where he learned to fly hydroplanes (seaplanes). At this flying school he met an older man, Frazier Curtis, who also believed in the Allied cause, and between flights Prince confided to him his dream of organizing a squadron of volunteer American airmen to fight for France.

Curtis was in favour of the idea, but since he did not speak French he decided to stick with his mother tongue and offered

132

his services to the British Royal Naval Air Service. In England he found that the enlistment papers carried an ominous phrase about "swearing allegiance to the Crown for the duration" and, fearing he would be forfeiting his American citizenship, withdrew his application.

By March 4, 1915, Prince had signed his enlistment papers with the French Army and because of his Marblehead flying-school training was sent to the Pau Aviation School, but in the meantime he had been needling every American he met in Paris to join him. Two who did were Southern coloured boys —Bob Scanlon, who was shining shoes in the corridor of the American Express Company, and Eugene Bullard. Scanlon had been stranded by a touring troupe of boxers headed by the famous Jack Johnson.

Bullard gained his pilot wings, a commission, and several decorations, but apparently lost interest in the cause, was demoted, and wound up in the trenches with the French infantry. Scanlon is said to have become a gunner on a Voisin bomber flown by Norman Prince and some reports have it that Bob was the first man to fire a 37-mm. air cannon from the creaky nacelle of a Voisin, but this has never been fully substantiated.

Prince's greatest obstacle in forming his unit was America's neutrality. The French were reluctant to waste time and money training men who might later be withdrawn by their government. The Germans were raising serious objections both in Berlin and Washington. At the same time a few Fifth Columnists of the day were circulating reports that most of these American volunteers were nothing more than German spies masquerading as sympathetic neutrals.

But in spite of these distractions Prince became a very apt pupil and was soon brevetted as a pilot to No. 108 VB. Squadron, flying day or night patrols where he turned in more than his share of combat time. For eight months he dared the Grim Reaper, taking on any assignment from long-distance raids to trench strafing. One of his gunners was killed and another badly wounded, but he seemed to lead a charmed life and was eventually raised to the grade of sergeant and sent to No. 113 VB. Squadron, which carried out missions requiring experienced air crews.

Meanwhile Frazier Curtis was in Paris winning the support of an American physician there, Dr. Edmund Gros, who devoted much of his time, office space, and advice in forming the proposed Escadrille Américaine. By July 1915 General Hirschauer of the French Air Service gave his approval for grouping all American flyers in the French service into one organization. However, movement in any military service being what it is, the Escadrille Américaine did not actually get together until April 20, 1916. By that time Prince had collected Bill Thaw, Victor Chapman, Kiffin Rockwell, James R. McConnell, Eliot Cowdin and Bert Hall. Bert had already seen some flying service as an international barnstormer and had acquired a doubtful reputation as a soldier of fortune with a few days' service with the Turks against the Bulgarians. Bill Thaw had fought with the French infantry. Victor Chapman had been a machine gunner with the Foreign Legion. Claiming he had shed blood in the Mexican War, Kiffin Rockwell had no trouble making corporal in the French infantry and fought well until he heard of Norman Prince's plan and transferred to the flying service. McConnell had enlisted in the Foreign Legion but was allowed to join the aviation service without previous action in the trenches.

This was the group Prince had assembled that morning of May 1916. Two French officers, Captain Thenault and Lieutenant de Laage de Meux, were assigned to them for combat leadership and the necessary liaison work.

Practically rookies at single-seater fighting, they were more than willing that Thenault should be their guide for a time and after a final lecture stressing the importance of a tight formation, obeying orders, and being satisfied to inspect the front line, the American formation took off. It was to be just a familiarity patrol.

They went aloft, taking in the beauties and wonders of the Vosages until they flew through a cloud layer at 6,000 feet. To the south the Alps poked their peaks up through the vapour with the appearance of alabaster icebergs. The course took them over Belfort and the trenches bordering the Hartmannsweilerkopf, which was undergoing a furious bombardment. Beyond in the misty distance flowed the Rhine as appealing as any gay tourist-folder pictorial.

But this was war and the first snarling attack of German Archie coughed its blotches of black smoke-puffs all around the tightly-knit patrol. Thaw, Prince, and Bert Hall had experienced this before, but the others looked on the venom with awe and huddled deeper in their cockpits.

For nearly an hour Captain Thenault toured up and down just inside the German lines, where they were constantly plastered by the anti-aircraft hate. It was part of the familiarity process, and the leader made the most of it. The solid cloud layer finally broke up into small detached designs of fleecy white.

Thaw, who was wondering about a jagged tear out near his

wing tip—an everyday souvenir from Archie—suddenly noticed that Thenault's wing tips were flipping an "alert" signal. The captain's top gun flicked a series of indicating flame fingers, warning them of enemy planes. Most of the Americans were as blind as bats, as are most newcomers during the first harrowing days of air warfare.

Finally both Prince and Thaw spotted three all-white Aviatiks cruising 3,000 feet below. Thenault signalled again, and the patrol dived to intercept the slow-flying two-seaters, but the Jerries spotted them and turned away, heading back for their own safer areas. Thenault decided to follow them, and one or two over-anxious Americans were soon firing wildly from a ridiculous distance.

The perfect formation was broken by now, and two or three Nieuports wisely turned back for the French lines. Thenault signalled to the others and tried to reform, but Prince and Rockwell either didn't notice or were determined to chalk up a "kill" for the new American unit. The enemy anti-aircraft plastered them, and the Aviatik gunners punctured their taut fabric with burst after burst.

Prince fired a short spurt, but his gun jammed. He tried every immediate action he knew but could not clear the feed. He then attempted to stand up and remove the offending drum, but he lost the joy stick and his plane went fluttering off completely out of control. It took him 1,500 feet to level off again and take stock of the situation.

Rockwell was nowhere to be seen, and the three Aviatiks had disappeared in the north-eastern mists. Both Prince and Rockwell eventually returned to their field, ruefully displaying tattered Nieuports for their indiscretions. Captain Thenault was relieved that his flight had returned safely but bawled them out for breaking formation and disobeying orders.

Thus the first patrol of the Escadrille Américaine was something of a fiasco, but Thenault was more than satisfied that these volunteers had demonstrated a true aggressive spirit; of course he had no idea what national heroes most of them were to become.

After the first patrol Prince tried hard to score the escadrille's first victory, and from his enthusiasm it will be noted how the "ace" fever had spread in the French and American services. Downing enemy planes was their prime effort. Throughout 1916 and 1917 whenever the French wanted vital photographic or observation reports they usually called on the British to provide them. Routine formation patrols by flights and tight schedules of all-inclusive operations were totally foreign to them.

Prince went out on every patrol and on a dozen others he contrived for himself, striving hard to shoot down a black-crossed aircraft, but the gods jested grimly with him. Either his gun or his engine tricked him at the opportune moment. He seemed to be completely jinxed, and so it was Kiffin Rockwell who scored the first American victory on May 18. While doing a voluntary lone eagle patrol over Thann, he caught up with a German observation plane and crashed it with only four bullets. Not until August 23, 1916, did the Fates relent and put Norman Prince's name on the victory list, when the New England youth hung up one that astounded the whole front.

He was cruising over the German lines at 10,000 feet, twisting and turning through the Archie barrage, when he suddenly spotted a lone enemy ship 5,000 feet below but deeper inside the German lines. He watched it carefully for some minutes and determined it was not out as a decoy and then tested his gun to make certain it was operating properly. He went down in a sharp dive and noted it was a two-seater Aviatik. His first burst stitched a leaden seam all along the fuselage from the tail to the centre section. The observer, evidently busy over a floor camera, bobbed up just in time to stop a chestful of bullets. Prince continued on and came up under the tail blind spot and pumped another long burst into the underside. The observer never appeared again to fire a shot.

Prince then zoomed from below and sat about 50 feet behind the Aviatik's tail assembly. With the rear gun out of action, the two-seater was at his mercy. He fired another burst and then saw the pilot turn around with a look of abject terror. The German started to dive sharply and then for some reason pulled up level and raised both hands in a token of surrender.

Prince reported later that his first impulse was to give no quarter and shoot down the German in cold blood, but since he was far over the German lines he might have a difficult time getting a confirmation of his victory. If he brought his victim home there could be no question. So he nodded and pointed in the direction of the French lines and the German pilot nodded back, probably figuring that imprisonment was preferable to death in a flaming cockpit.

Firing a warning burst every time the German showed any sign of making a sudden dash for it, Prince herded the Aviatik back across the lines and made it descend in an open meadow behind Verdun. The pilot was unscathed, but the observer was dead,

It was the first enemy aircraft to be brought down by an American inside Allied lines and at last Prince was content. He was on the honour roll, and the French soon promoted him from sergeant to adjutant, the last rank before being granted a French commission.

The escadrille was next moved to Bar-le-Duc, where Raoul Lufbery joined them. Shortly after, Clyde Balsley from the Foreign Legion, Chouteau Johnson, who had been flying with an outfit called the Paris Air Guard, Dudley Hill, Larry Rumsey, Didier Masson, and Paul Pavelka were accepted, and soon the small force of American volunteers was making a name for itself. So much so in fact that once more the neutrality point was raised and they had to fight under another name, eventually becoming known as the Lafayette Escadrille.

Late in August they were shunted back to Luxeuil, where they were furnished with the 15-metre, a more advanced Nieuport equipped with a fixed gun firing through the propeller as well as a top-wing Lewis gun. Kiffin Rockwell and Raoul Lufbery were the first to be entrusted with these new aircraft. On September 23 these two went on a two-ship foray and became separated during a terrific combat with Boelcke's squadron. Rockwell was shot down and killed, and the escadrille tasted the first bitter dregs of defeat. Kiffin was their first casualty and his going left them grief-stricken.

Prince was especially upset, for he and Rockwell had worked as brothers on many squadron projects, and to gain some personal revenge Norman formed a partnership with Lufbery and together these two began a new epoch of Yankee aerial offence. During this programme of vengeance Lufbery nailed four in a row, but Prince was not so lucky.

However, on October 10 Prince bagged his second victory against tremendous odds in a melee that almost ended in disaster. Raoul was circling low over Habsheim aerodrome, taunting the German airmen to come up and fight while Prince sat above waiting for the birds that were flushed out. The scheme worked well for a few minutes, but unfortunately another flock of Fokkers took off from a neighbouring field at Colmar. Before Lufbery and Prince knew what they had started they were trapped between two layers of annoyed wasps.

They fought for their lives and, with their speedy new ships, hoped to outdistance the Fokkers, but the odds were terrific. Flying side by side, completely hemmed in, they swooped, zoomed, twisted, and darted like streaks of light. Whenever they could trigger off a burst, they spattered the enemy and slowly battered their way to an area near Mulhouse. By then only two Fokkers stood between them and safety. One was flown by a master pilot whose Spandau slugs were gradually shooting Prince's plane to kindling. The other was fastened to Lufbery's tail like a leech. Prince turned suddenly and pooped off a burst which eliminated Lufbery's annoyer. Thus relieved of his problem, Lufbery twisted in the opposite direction and drove off the remaining Fokker that was clawing at Prince's tail.

Lufbery was forced to land just inside the French lines; three bullets had smashed up his Le Rhone engine, two had passed through his flying suit, one boot was cut wide open from the instep to his knee, and one of his elevators just wasn't there.

Prince managed to get back to Luxeuil with a Nieuport that wasn't supposed to fly. An explosive bullet had broken the main spar of his lower wing and another had shattered one of his centre-section struts, several flying wires were cut through, and what was left had to be junked. Nevertheless, Norman Prince was very happy; he felt he had avenged Kiffin Rockwell's death.

In October a group of British bombers of all types was brought to Luxeuil to carry out one of the most destructive blows of the war, and the Lafayette Escadrille was selected to give cover support to their English comrades. A few French Farmans and Bréguets were also included in this raid which resulted in the complete destruction of the Mauser ammunition factory at Oberndorf.

One flight of escort planes, including Lieutenant de Laage de Meux, Masson, Lufbery, and Prince, went with the bombers as far as their fuel would allow, saw them across the Rhine, and then flew back to quickly refuel. When the harassed bombers returned, the escadrille Nieuports were on hand to see them safely home. Lufbery got into a tangle with three Fokker fighters and brought one of them down, racking up his fifth victim and becoming an ace. Prince came in contact with a group of seven, but he was well above them and despite the odds, recklessly swooped down. His first burst paid off. Then with both guns roaring he plunged into the middle of the enemy formation; his bullets drilled the cockpit of the enemy leader, and the front Fokker turned two complete wing-over flips and fluttered to earth in erratic circles. Halfway down a wing ripped away, completing the job.

Although facing a torrent of enemy fire, Prince nevertheless stayed with the attack. He swooped in and out, triggering devastating bursts at the Fokkers from every angle, and in a few minutes had broken up the formation and driven the planes deep into their own lines. The daylight was beginning to fade by now, but Prince and Lufbery stayed aloft as long as there was a straggling bomber to be brought to safety. Then Lufbery took refuge in a small emergency field at Corcieux, making a safe landing. Minutes later Prince spiralled down and levelled off beyond a stand of trees bordering the turfed area. In the half-light he failed to see a high-tension line that swung just over the treetops. The wheels of the Nieuport struck the cable and the plane stumbled forward and rolled over twice. Lufbery stood transfixed as he watched Prince thrown clear when the safety belt broke. Norman had both legs broken and suffered internal injuries, but regardless of his injuries when he saw another Nieuport circling to come in he screamed at the mechanics to set out flares to mark the area.

Raoul Lufbery climbed into the ambulance that carried his pal to the hospital and on the way he refought their glorious battle, trying to keep up Norman's spirits. For a few hours it seemed as though Prince would recover, but the next day a blood clot formed on his brain. The French commander of aviation at Luxeuil hurried to the hospital and, standing at his bedside, he commissioned Prince a second lieutenant and decorated him with the Legion of Honour. These were the last words Norman Prince heard. He died on October 15, 1916, leaving a fabulous organisation that became the nucleus of the United States Aviation Service, which performed so gallantly in the months that followed.

Because of the atrocious weather along the southern end of the battle line, 1916 opened up quietly for most French airmen. As we know, Germany was massing her ground forces for the attack on Verdun.

Of five enemy aircraft downed during January, three had fallen before the guns of bomber observers and two had been shot down by Lieutenant Jean Navarre, another legendary flier whose end is not actually known. When he died he was credited with twelve victories and had held the imagination of the French people for weeks. He was one of the first to fly the Nieuport Scout, and how well this machine performed can be gathered from its enemy bag over the following months. In May forty-one Germans were shot down by the wing-gun Nieuport; in June, eighteen; July, forty-nine; August, sixtynine; September, eighty-seven; October, forty-one; November, thirty-nine; and December, fifty-six.

Georges Guynemer was scoring wildly during these

months, but on March 12 with eight victories to his credit he was wounded and almost became a prisoner of war. He had been given a new 120-h.p. Nieuport, and on encountering two German aircraft had attacked from behind; but the new mount's speed almost betrayed him, for he was up to and zooming over the two-seater before he had time to draw a bead on his target. He thus put himself in a perfect-shot position for the enemy gunner who plastered him and riddled the engine's accessory grouping and sent two bullets through his left arm. Guynemer was lucky to get into his own lines, and it was only by the daring of the French ground troops who swarmed out of their trenches that eventually he was carried to safety.

While the French ace was in the hospital for a couple of weeks, Jean Navarre took the lead. There were other fliers, too, who were commanding attention. Men like Nungesser, Jesser, Rochefort, and Chaput were entering the lists of the knights of the blue. In all probability the month of April 1916 might be accepted as the real beginning of "ace" warfare.

The handsome Navarre was now the uncontested aerial champion of France and on May 18 downed a Fokker, his tenth victory, and on the next day caught an L.V.G. over Chattancourt, sending it crashing in flames.

And now legend befuddles history once more. On June 16 Navarre was shot down and badly wounded. According to one version Navarre escaped from his hospital bed, made his way back to his field, stole a plane, and was never seen again. Another rumour is that while he was in the hospital his mind became deranged and when he was discharged from the hospital he borrowed an automobile and in a disturbed state of mind charged into a crowd of civilians. Some people think that Jean Navarre still languishes in a French asylum, but the romanticists believe he met an end more befitting a brave hero and was lost without a trace somewhere over Germany.

At times the "ace" race went to ridiculous extremes in the French service. While Guynemer, Nungesser, Jesser, and Chaput were engaged in their fantastic rivalry, Sergeant de Terline died while scoring his second victory. On July 27, accompanied by two companions, de Terline attacked an Albatros two-seater. Both of de Terline's fellow flyers were sent down out of control, and in a blind fury the sergeant pilot rammed the two-seater, and he and the two Germans, Leutnant Freytag and Korporal Finke, were killed instantly. In the French report of this action it was stated that de Terline had once remarked that if his gun jammed he would ram the enemy plane. This might appear as a senseless form of suicide, but the French thought otherwise and awarded Sergeant de Terline a posthumous *Médaille Militaire*.

This single-seater fighter savagery continued all that summer, and by September Escadrille No. 3 (the Storks), commanded by Captain Armand Brocard with Guynemer, Heurteaux, Dorme, Deullin, and Sauvage on its roster, spurred all French scout pilots to fantastic achievements. Between March 12 and August 18 the Storks engaged in 338 combats, destroyed thirty-eight aircraft, burned three observation balloons and had sent an additional thirty-six enemy aircraft down out of control.

Georges Guynemer scored his fifteenth, sixteenth, seventeenth, and eighteenth victories during September, but the wild-flying Nungesser of No. 65 Escadrille was in hot pursuit with seventeen. Nungesser was an exhibitionist and always flew in a gaudy uniform with all his military decorations—not just the ribbons! I met him in 1917 at Izelle-Hammeau when he was wearing his *Croix de guerre* with a ribbon at least 20 inches long to carry all the additional "palms" that had been added to his decoration. He always wore every one of them, and, running his thumbnail along all this gaudy metal, would cry: "Me, Nungesser! Legion of Honour, *Médaille Militaire, Croix de guerre avec cinquante palms!*"

On September 26 Nungesser shot down a balloon near Le Transloy and then bagged a Fokker on the way home. Going aloft again in the evening, he attacked two L.V.G. bombers, sent one down in flames, and then had to make a forced landing on top of the French front-line trenches when the other L.V.G. put a burst through his fuel tank and shot the drum off his machine gun.

Toward the middle of October the new German Albatros and Halberstadt began to appear in increasing numbers, and, in spite of their forty-one victories that month, the French *chasse* pilots were having a very rough time. More than sixty of their machines were listed under the ominous heading of "missing" durig the same period.

In an effort to provide two-seater opposition for the new German fighters, the designers at the Spad plant brought out one of the flying freaks of the war. They were striving for a *biplane* machine that provided a front gunner without using the pusher-mounted engine. The gunner and his front nacelle were separated from the pilot by the propeller itself!

This may be difficult to visualize, but the front cockpit was supported out in front of the propeller on two tubular mem-

141

bers bolted to the landing gear. Two steel cables, fastened to brackets on the top wing, kept it from falling forward. How the propeller found any air to "bite" on is a mystery.

The machine was fairly successful in its early trials, but when one was shipped to the front for a demonstration the guy wires broke and the nose cockpit fell forward, tossing out the unfortunate gunner; the whole structure hung below like a ditch digger, killing all forward speed, and the plane stalled and spun in. This aircraft had to be seen to be believed.

Late in October the Spad company (Société Pour Aviation et ses Dérivés) produced a scout that was as good as the two-seater had been bad. Powered with a 150-h.p. Hispano-Suiza engine, it was something of an answer to a fighter pilot's prayer. It was tough, fast, and had a Constantinesco gun gear with its fixed Vickers gun. More important, it photographed well and one look at it made most airmen of the time drool. Some years later its general bulldog appearance made it the dreamboat of the American services.

In all honesty, however, compared to the British S.E. 5 and the Sopwith Camel, the Spad—just photographed better.

Georges Guynemer received the first single-seater Spad to leave the factory and his success was phenomenal, for between November 9 and 27 he destroyed 2 L.V.G.'s, 2 Albatros Scouts, 2 Albatros two-seaters, and 1 Fokker. Group 13, which included the Storks and Escadrilles 68, 83, and 103, was at once assigned the first full delivery of these snub-nosed fighters, and it was the Spad which won the Storks their second escadrille citation. This was announced on December 5 and stated that the organization, now Spad 3, had destroyed another thirty-six enemy aircraft between August 19 and November 29.

At the end of 1916 Guynemer led all the "aces" with a score of twenty-five. Nungesser was a close second with twenty-one, while Dorme with fifteen, Heurteaux with fifteen, Lenoir with eleven, and Tarazcon with nine were also in the running. Tarazcon's career is notable in that he had lost a leg in a crash before the war and now flew with a specially rigged rudder bar. On the occasion of his fifth victory on September 17 he swooped low to look at the crashed L.V.G. and a shell passed through his cokpit smashing his wooden leg. Undaunted, he flew over the nearest enemy aerodrome, dropped the broken limb and with it a note reading, "Now pull the other one!"

Having proved that they could hold their own against the new Albatros and inspired by the news that the new year would bring them fighting Spads in unlimited numbers, the scout pilots of France were in high spirits and had little fear of the future. Unfortunately, the Falcons of France and the War Birds of Britain were in for a rude awakening. Bloody April was only just around the corner.

Although the single-seaters were being headlined all over France, the bombers still ranked first in the opinion of the headquarters staff, and while the bombardment work was not carried out with the same marked detail and formation as was that of the British, the French airmen managed to do everything with Gallic verve and it was more newsworthy.

On January 10, 1916, three Voisins made an attack on the German balloon line along the edge of Houthulst Fôret. Just as they started to deliver their bombs, three Fokkers came down out of the sun, and one raider was shot down. A second Voisin, with Corporal Padieu as pilot and Sergeant Fulber as gunner, immediately attacked the victorious Fokker and sent it down to join its victim. Ignoring the other Fokkers, the Frenchmen carried on with their mission, destroyed a balloon, bombed the winch crew, and then were attacked by three more Fokkers and two L.V.G.'s, but in the running fight they drove three of the enemy to cover and were able to land unscathed.

On the first day of February a French bombing squadron stationed on the Bulgarian front decided to raid a Bulgar military camp at Petrich. They went in their old Farmans, carrying anything that would explode or burn. In less than half an hour the camp was a shambles after more than 200 bombs and grenades had been dropped. Very few raids of the aerial dreadnoughts in 1918 could rival such wholesale destruction in the course of a single action. No less than 476 soldiers were killed outright and fifty-eight were seriously wounded.

Along the Western Front the German High Command had staged a series of feint attacks; and bombers, scouts, observation ships, and in fact anything that would fly, was put up to trace the real German objective. This turned out to be wholesale murder, for not one plane got through, and the German Air Force had a picnic. Every French machine was either turned back or shot down. By February 21 there was no doubt where the push was to take place, and a nine-hour barrage heralded the opening of the Verdun offensive. At the beginning of this battle French bombers fought their way over the German lines and made the war a misery for the enemy artillery, rest camps, and machine-gun nests. In turn the French infantry were strafed by the German airmen and the

French air offensive had to be called off. The Germans took every advantage of this and swarmed all over the Verdun back areas.

This state of affairs went on until mid-June, when the French, disgusted with being always on the defensive, ignored the protests of their infantry and took up the offensive again. One pilot actually flew to Berlin.

The hero of this long flight was Lieutenant Pierre Marechal, who took off from a field outside Nancy at 9.20 p.m., June 20, in a specially-built Nieuport that carried oversized fuel tanks calculated to give it a flight range of fourteen hours. Marechal reached Berlin, a distance of about 450 miles, and showered the German capital with propaganda leaflets that read:

We might have bombed the open town of Berlin and killed innocent children, but have contented ourselves by throwing this proclamation.

But unfortunately Marechal was forced down in Austria with engine trouble, where he was taken prisoner. The Austrian officials were sceptical of his story, but eventually the truth came out. He wrote from his prison camp that sparkplug trouble had been his undoing and that he had landed, changed two plugs, and started the engine again, but two more needed replacement and he was captured while attempting to clean them. All in all Marechal had covered 816 miles in his long night flight, a remarkable effort of piloting and navigation in those days.

A few days after this episode Adjutants Barou and Emmaneulli made a 230-mile flight across the Vosges, dropped 350 pounds of bombs on a German powder factory at Rottweil, and set two magazines on fire. Later they made still another raid on this plant and destroyed a complete powder train.

On the night of June 21-22 French bombers dropped fourteen tons of explosives on German military establishments.

As the autumn months drew on, long-distance night raids became commonplace with the French. On September 24 Captain René de Beauchamp and Lieutenant Daucord made a 500-mile flight to Essen and did considerable damage to the munitions plants in that vicinity. On October 10 Adjutants Barou and Chazard bombed the famous Bosch magneto factory at Stuttgart and set fire to storage sheds. Sub-lieutenant Loste and Sergeant Vitalis inscribed their names on the "ace" list from the gun pit of an old Farman bomber. Both men scored their five victories from the orange-box cockpits of these old machines and were to register several more before their fate caught up with them.

On November 17 a Morane from M-S. 23 with the above-named Captain de Beauchamp at the controls bombed the railroad station at Munich, destroying the engine turntable and several sheds. In order to escape enemy planes awaiting his return, he flew across the Alps and landed in Italy after a flight of 438 miles. Returning to action on December 16, he was killed two days later when six Albatros scouts shot down his Morane in flames.

The bombers' year closed with the promise of new and more efficient aircraft, and pilots who had seen the new Bré-guets, Caudrons, and giant Letords were most enthusiastic, and their hopes for the future soared high.

Here is the complete list of aircraft provided by French manufacturers during the year 1916:

FRENCH WARPLANES OF 1916

Make	Engine	Speed m.p.h.	Purpose
Astra D	Renault 160 h.p.	95	Reconnaissance
Caudron G.4	Le Rhone (2) 110 h.p.	95	Reconnaissance
Deperdussin	Mono-Gnome 160 h.p.	105	Bomber
Dorand A.H.	Renault 160 h.p.	98	Fighter
Farman N	Renault 160 h.p.	105	Reconnaissance
Letord	Hisso (2) 150 h.p.	85	Reconnaissance
		78	
Letord	Salmson (2) 90 h.p.		Bomber
Morane T	Le Rhone (2) 110 h.p.	85	Bomber
Morane S	Renault (2) 250 h.p.	96	Bomber
Morane C	Mono-Gnome 160 h.p.	110	Bomber
		108	Fighter
Nieuport 15	Le Rhone 110 h.p.	95	Fighter
Nieuport Triplane	Mono-Gnome 160 h.p.		Reconnaissance
		90	
Spad T.P.	Hisso 150 h.p.	110	Fighter
Spad S.5	Hisso 150 h.p.		Fighter
Voisin	Renault 160 h.p.		Reconnaissance
		98	

5

THE YEAR OF
THE SKY GODS—

1917

☐ The air war, 1914-18, was a fighter pilot's war. Practically all action that resulted in any vital objective was dominated by the men of the fighter squadrons. What bombing was completed, came as the result of the failure of fighter defence. What artillery co-operation and ground co-operation was accomplished, was that carried out by airmen who had evaded the enemy fighters. Anti-aircraft guns played a lesser role than adverse winds or engine malfunctions.

The fighter pilots' big year was 1917; almost all the greats ran up their scores over this bloody twelvemonth. A glance through the history of this eventful year will bring to light such names as von Richthofen, Guynemer, McCudden, Bishop, Lufbery, Voss, Gontermann, Wolff, Ball, Baracca, Dorme, Mueller, and many others.

New machines, new tactics, and a new brood of inspired fledglings were making their way to the various fronts; skilled and warwise volunteers were coming from the infantry regiments to put new spirit and blood into the fighting squadrons. In the case of Great Britain keen youngsters were volunteering from all over the empire, and the selection boards had a wealth of adventuresome material to screen and filter through to the various types of aircraft. Even America was contributing to the cause by allowing hundreds of young college men to cross into Canada, where they could be given Royal Flying Corps training. Britain's stand during the latter part of 1916 had been a great stimulus to R.F.C. recruiting.

Those early days of 1917 witnessed the ground forces making great tactical strides. The British Army was about to follow up their success along the Somme by striking new blows along the Ancre, around Arras, and up the bloody slopes of Vimy Ridge. At the same time it was hoped the French would make a simultaneous assault in the Aisne area.

In order that the Royal Flying Corps should have the advantage of springing an aerial surprise all the new 1917 models—including the Bristol Fighter, D.H.4, S.E.5, and the much improved Spads and Nieuports—were withheld from the front-line squadrons until the end of April. We have commented on the value of striking with large numbers of any new weapon in order to make the most of the surprise element, but in this case holding back so much new equipment turned out to be a grave error.

The plans for the British-French offensive were suddenly disrupted when the Germans carefully withdrew to the new Hindenburg line. This should not have been such a surprise, for the Allies knew of this line of fortifications as early as November of 1916, but they had assumed it was nothing more than a reserve position, instead of the enemy's future first line of defence, which turned out to be one of the really impregnable systems of the whole war.

The combined mistakes of withholding the latest aircraft and misinterpreting the German intent regarding the Hindenburg line contributed largely to the British air losses during "Bloody April" of that year. Only the determination of the R.F.C. pilots and observers prevented wholesale slaughter, and the flower of the empire's youth flew endless hours in outgunned and outpaced machines. So serious was this situation that there was one report going the propaganda rounds that the life of a British flying man during "Bloody April" was roughly three minutes.

Like all such *canards*, this is disproved by the available records. Over this anxious period 315 pilots and observers were lost in a total of 29,500 flying hours; thus the actual number of hours flown per man killed or captured was approximately ninety-three.

During these months in 1917 Germany reached the height of her aerial supremacy, and at no other period throughout the whole war was the Imperial Air Force so strong in morale, so well organized, and so completely equipped. Their Albatros and Halberstadt scouts were almost invincible. January and February were months of cold dark mists and heavy rain fell almost continually, so few flying hours were racked up; the Germans claiming only nineteen victories in January. February was marked by zero weather day after day, but the German pilots knocked down 33 more Allied planes.

At this lowest ebb in the fortunes of the Royal Flying Corps a number of front-line infantrymen who had been clamouring for a transfer to the flying services were hurriedly brought back from the trenches to fight as machine-gunners aboard the two-seaters. I was a member of this emergency force and one of the few of my particular group to live out the war.

I was advised of my good fortune early one Saturday morning shortly after the winter closed the bloody campaign along the Somme. I had applied for this transfer more than six months before, but at the time had no idea what I had volunteered for. I simply wanted to get out of the mud and discomfort of the front line. No one could tell me that Bloody April was just around the corner.

Packing up my infantry gear, I left my machine-gun team in a support trench behind Arras and hopped any available transport until I found No. 22 Squadron located at a village called Chipilly just behind Péronne. I arrived there shortly before noon and just in time to see a stunting Nieuport of No. 24 Squadron, which shared the same field, pull its wings off and corkscrew into the ground less than 20 yards from where I stood. Totally ignorant of the danger, I ran up to the wreckage and tried to pull out the unfortunate pilot, not realizing that his burning fuselage carried a large aluminium box of .303 ammunition. I was roughly hauled away by wiser and more experienced men, who demanded to know what the hell I was doing on an R.F.C. field wearing some nondescript infantry uniform. I explained that I had been sent there as an aerial gunner.

A flight sergeant spotted the cross-rifles insignia (sniper) and machine-gun badge on my sleeve and accepted my explanation. "Cool So you're to be a gunner, eh? Well, you'll see plenty of crashes without going looking for them," he bellowed. "Get over to the orderly room and report in—and listen, son, don't ever go poking around crashes like that again. You'll lose all your enthusiasm in no time!"

Frankly, I expected to be sent to England for some in-air training. After all, I had never seen an aeroplane at close range; but within an hour I had been booked in, given a complete flying outfit, and taken up to fire a few bursts at a white canvas target spread out on the ground. I never did get my lunch that day, for immediately after my target shoot I was assigned to go on patrol and before we returned to Chipilly I had destroyed my first enemy plane from the front cockpit of an F.E.2b pusher-fighter.

I was told I had to put in fifty hours over the line as an aerial gunner, after which I would be sent back to Britain for pilot training and a commission. Instead, I flew practically every day, weather permitting, until January 18, 1918, putting in more than 1,300 hours of active-service flying over the line. It turned out that the "fifty hours over the line" qualification was intended for commissioned officer observers—not N.C.O gunners. Over those harrowing months I flew with any pilot available. I fought with one Lewis gun, whereas officer observers had two. Although only a corporal gunner, I acted as flight commander for weeks and weeks, since I was the only airman in my flight who had lived long enough to know our sector with any degree of familiarity. I became a skilled observer and could be trusted with aerial cameras, long-distance navigation, leading bombing and gun-strafing raids on enemy trenches, and in addition was generally selected to take new and very scared young pilots over the line to show them where the war was—and how to get home again.

Whatever enemy aircraft I downed were credited to the squadron records—not to me. Any shot down by our fixed-gun pilots were duly credited to them and they were decorated accordingly. You will find no N.C.O. pilots or gunners in the official British records of their aces. Whenever we were awarded military honours it was usually for devotion to duty, gallantry in action, or integrity of spirit—never for any success we might have had as air fighters. When I left No. 22 Squadron early in 1918 to receive training as a Camel pilot, our recording officer confided that the squadron records credited me with destroying sixteen enemy planes and six kite balloons; but you will not find my name on any official "ace" list.

But I was not alone. Through 1917 dozens of infantry machine gunners of all ranks gladly made the transfer to the Royal Flying Corps. They were rewarded with Distinguished Conduct Medals and Military Medals for their gallantry but were never credited with destroying enemy aircraft. They fought and died as nobly as any pilot, but they had been assigned the wrong seat in the aircraft. They were known from one end of the front to the other as only P.B.O.s—Poor Bloody Observers.

Early in March the majority of the German fighting squadrons had been re-equipped with the new Albatros D.3, and those pilots who had performed so well in 1916 with the D.1 outdid themselves when the weather improved. For the first time the massed circus formations took the offensive inside their own lines, and the skies were black with Maltese-crossed fighters. As usual, the British had to bear the brunt of this because they insisted on carrying out scheduled patrols well within the enemy's territory, and their battle-scarred pushers that had once whipped the Fokker menace were shot to pieces. In the last three weeks of March not less than 171 British planes were destroyed.

A new figure stepped into the German picture of victory. This was Werner Voss, then known as the Hussar of Krefeld, who had gained twelve victories during this agonising period, running his score up to twenty-two. This lad won the admiration of the British and when he died in a grim one-sided battle later that year, there was sincere regret through all squadrons of the R.F.C. For one thing, Voss was one of the few Germans who risked fighting over the Allied side of the line. Next, he was unafraid to have his plane marked distinctively with a bold red-and-white chequerboard design, and for weeks was known only as The Chequerboard Ace.

Voss's family was Jewish, his father being a dyer in the town of Krefeld, and Werner's prewar military background was confined to service in a militia Hussar regiment. Throughout the early months of 1917 Voss often threatened Manfred von Richthofen's lead in the ace sweepstakes, but whenever he caught up with the Red Baron he was quietly withdrawn from the front or sent off to some unimportant Russian area where there were few enemy planes to destroy. In that way the dignity of the German nobility was maintained and von Richthofen always kept his lead.

On March 9, 1917, von Richthofen had a very narrow escape. In his personal report he is careless about details, but one gathers that he had come upon a flight of British pushers (he does not say whether they were single- or two-seaters), and, noting one machine leave the formation, von Richthofen left his. Whenever he did this the Red Baron seemed to get into trouble. He manoeuvred carefully to bring the Britisher in his sights and saw that his enemy was firing a series of mixed ammunition, including tracer. He says he ignored the gunfire and prepared carefully for the kill. Instead, his Albatros was suddenly hammered with a direct burst, and, while not hit himself, he smelled petrol and knew it was time to play it safe. The unknown Britisher followed him down from 9,000 feet, with von Richthofen trailing a stream of petrol vapour. The chase took them well inside the German lines, and eventually the British pilot decided he had more than played his part, and returned to his formation. Richthofen made a safe landing and discovered that besides the damage to his fuel tank he had taken many bullets in his engine and fuselage. This did not make much of an impression on him, however, for he was in the air again later that day and shot down another R.F.C. single-seater pusher D.H.2.

Other German aces who scored heavily during this period were Schaeffer, Wolff, Bernert, and Allmenroeder. When Bloody April was over von Richthofen had fifty-two victories; Wolff twenty-seven; Bernett twenty-six; Voss twenty-five; and Schaeffer twenty-five. It is worth noting that all these pilots were members of Richthofen's Staffel 11, and much publicity was given to their accomplishments. Another interesting feature of these stars is that practically all of them had once served in the German ranks.

But it was not all beer and skittles, for Staffel 11 suffered several grievous losses. Leutnant Hartmut Baldarmus, who was credited with eighteen victories, was shot down on April 21. Adolph Schultz, with six confirmations, was killed the same day. One of Germany's leading aces, Karl Schaeffer, went to the aid of Lothar von Richthofen, brother of the Red Baron, and had his tail practically shot away by a British gunner aboard an old B.E.2c. Schaeffer crashed in no man's land but luckily escaped serious injury and had to hole up in a shell crater most of the night. German infantrymen rescued him eventually, and he returned to his squadron at 3 a.m.—just in time to join in a last toast to his gallant end.

Loaded with laurels and agleam with military decorations, Manfred von Richthofen was given a well-deserved rest at the end of Bloody April. He had no sooner arrived in Berlin than bad news began to seep back from the front. The British had finally decided to unleash their Bristol Fighters, S.E.5's, and the deadly Sopwith Camel. During the month of May these newcomers batted down 255 German fighters, while the French with their souped-up Spads and Nieuports bagged ninety-five more. Against this, the German Air Force could claim but 136 victories.

There was one doleful note, however, for the British lost Captain Albert Ball and another mystery finish was recorded that ignited heated arguments for a long while.

When he had nearly forty victories to his credit Ball had been sent home for a rest in October of 1916. He had fought against the decision, but the British officials were adamant. They decided to send him on a lecture tour through the flying schools, but Ball had nothing to talk about. He had no rules, laws, or secrets of success. He was just a headstrong schoolboy who did what he considered he was being paid for. They tried to make an instructor of him, but young Albert had no patience with quirks and beginners. They wrote out a gunnery lecture for him to recite, but none of it made any sense to him.

He haunted the British aircraft plants and while a guest at the Austin factory outlined his idea of what a modern fighter should be. Blinded by the young man's career and decorations, the company designers made a mockup of his crude drawings and in time turned out a prototype that was a Spad-like item, which was powered with a Hisso engine and had a corpulent fuselage. It was never taken seriously, but its production gave Albert Ball a few more weeks of life.

Late in February of 1917 he managed to get back to the front, where he arrived carrying two rabbits in a box and a squeaky violin. This time he was gazetted to No. 56 Squadron, one of the most famous fighter groups in World War I. Captain Billy Bishop, who had taken Ball's previous position with No. 60 Squadron, was enjoying a wild victory spree. No. 56 included such famous names as Captain Jimmy McCudden, Lieutenant Rhys-Davids, Captain Meintjes, Major Bloomfield, Lieutenant Barlow, Lieutenant Maxwell, and the gay-hearted Lieutenant Knaggs. Ball immediately expressed his low opinion of the S.E.5, so for a time he was given a new Nieuport and allowed to continue his lone-wolf hunting.

His career began all over again and his wild patrols were the talk of the whole front. Eventually he learned to accept the S.E.5 and agreed it was much stronger in every respect than the Nieuport. His conversion was complete when he had the red nose-spinner from his Nieuport moved over to an S.E.5. Ball and Billy Bishop were the only two British pilots allowed to give their mounts a distinctive marking. Bishop, who had inherited Ball's mechanic at No. 60 Squadron, a Corporal Bourne, was presented with a blue nose-spinner the day he was awarded his Distinguished Service Order.

Ball came to the end of his flying career on the evening of May 7. You can get one version of his death any day of the week in any British town. You can get several others in the Tempelhof Hotel in Berlin, where ghosts of a hundred German aces prowl nightly.

After many years of research, questioning, and authentic documents, the writer offers this as what probably happened.

Officials of the British 9th Wing ordered a formation of six Spads, six Camels, and six S.E.5's to be concentrated in the Douai-Cambrai area throughout the day, presumably looking for the von Richthofen mob. At 5:30 p.m. a squadron of three S.E.5 flights led by Captains Ball, Crowe, and Meintjes rendezvoused as arranged. They were stacked up in three tiers and crossed over the line through heavy clouds and rain. Over Burlon Wood just west of Cambrai they ran into worse clouds and were badly dispersed. However, Meintjes's flight piled into a German Albatros and shot it down.

Next, the whole formation, Spads, Camels and S.E.5's, roared out of the clouds and came upon a Circus of red Albatroses. Everyone went into action. There was no system or order once the first bursts were fired. There never is.

Meintjes had to spin out when two Germans got on his tail. His flight man, Cecil Lewis, who later became a noted author, got into the same trouble, and Ball and Knaggs had to go to their rescue. Meintjes returned to the fray, shot down a red fighter, and watched it fall east of Gouy-sous-Bellone. Hoidge, another S.E.5 pilot, knocked down an Albatros smack into the streets of Cambrai.

After being scattered by the action, the British fighters finally re-formed over Arras. More intensive fighting took place every few minutes until one by one the S.E.5's broke off, either with engine trouble or the lack of ammunition. Ball, Crowe, Lewis, Hoidge, and Knaggs, who had started out together, were widely dispersed. Crowe saw Ball fire two red lights indicating he had spotted more enemy aircraft. Crowe searched but couldn't see anything to shoot at, so he followed Ball, who was heading for Lens. Suddenly Ball went into a dive, and Crowe saw him shooting at an Albatros single-seater below. Crowe joined this fight until Ball took over and followed the German eastward into a heavy cloud. That was the last Crowe saw of the young British ace.

The truth is that Ball went on to finish off his forty-third victim and then, since he was out of ammunition—he had been in the air for more than two hours—he dropped through the clouds and came out just east of the village of Annoeullin. He recognized the hamlet immediately, and, following an old formula, decided to check on the time. He wore a wrist watch and his aircraft had a small clock set into the instrument panel, but Albert Ball, the Sunday-school boy, would rather put his faith in a church clock. Whenever he was in that area or on his way home, he always sped past the Annoeullin church and checked with the time-crusted hands of its tower clock.

The villagers knew this and always waved to the British plane with the red nose. The occupying Germans learned eventually of this friendly habit and early in May they set up a machine gun in the church tower—and waited.

On this particular evening Albert Ball flashed past to glance at the church clock. A few seconds later he crashed in the village of Annoeullin. A spray of bullets from that sanctuary had accomplished what the whole German Air Force had failed to do throughout Bloody April.

Three weeks later the German newspapers were celebrating the death of Captain Albert Ball, saying he had been shot down and killed by Lothar von Richthofen, brother of the famed Red Knight.

But the villagers of Annoeullin knew better. They signed a full statement later, explaining how Ball had died. And the British knew better, since Lothar von Richthofen had stated in his "combat report" that he had been victorious over Captain Ball and had shot down his *Sopwith triplane* near Annoeullin. (There is some question whether the Sopwith triplane had as yet been sent to the front.) Lothar von Richthofen somehow had the motor number of Ball's S.E.5, but he could not give the aircraft number. When he was charged later with the mistake of calling Ball's S.E.5 a triplane, he blandly stated that in the heat of action he *often* mistook biplanes for triplanes!

Lothar von Richthofen's movements on this particular day are most bewildering. One set of German reports state that on May 7 he was on leave in Berlin. Another report has it that he was in the air on that date with Karl Allmenroeder, and after downing an old R.E.8 was attacked by an S.E.5 and shot down. Thus, he could have been in the hospital when Albert Ball was trapped by that gun in a church tower.

As was to be expected, the German propaganda machine found it convenient to award this kill to one of the von Richthofens. Details mattered not at all. Facts could be woven and twisted into any pattern. All that was required was a glory-story to bolster the morale of the German Air Force.

The Germans have never denied the fact that Ball's identification tag was on view in a German hospital. There it was shown to dozens of wounded British airmen with the contrary boast which, in effect, went thus: "Well, there's the end of your great Captain Ball. He was shot down the other night by a lowly infantryman who was hiding in a church tower. He knew the Britisher usually passed that way . . . and . . . Well . . . here's the evidence."

On June 3, 1917, less than a month after Ball's death, a grateful British government awarded him the Victoria Cross

155

posthumously, it being the tenth V.C. awarded to British airmen after nearly three years of fighting.

Nineteen-seventeen was most profitable for Baron von Richthofen. Over those twelve months he was credited with destroying forty-seven British planes and became Germany's ace of aces.

What kind of man was this air warrior? Why has his record of eighty victories been questioned by many airmen who fought on the same front? This is an interesting point because, of all the leading aces, no other has had his claims questioned. No war ace has been more publicized. None has proven such an enigma. None has provided more bitter inter-service arguments.

Among British airmen of World War I there are two definite schools of thought concerning the Red Knight. One side stoutly defends him as the *beau idéal* of the wartime airman. He was a gentleman in the air and on the ground. He was a distinguished leader and a gallant foeman.

The other side will tell you that the Baron was a confirmed liar, a braggart, a military martinet, and a most cautious fighter who hugged the security of his Circus formation, that most of the victories he claimed were won by unimportant members of his Staffel, but were credited to their leader.

I have talked to World War I pilots in Germany and in private conversation noticed the same difference of opinion. These men either worshipped the name of von Richthofen or they displayed contempt for his record or the honour in which he is still held by the German public. A few admitted that he was a "manufactured" hero who was built up to strengthen the flagging spirits of the German Flying Service during their black days following Bloody April. Whether either view was expressed for my reportorial benefit, is, of course, a matter of conjecture.

To compare von Richthofen with Britain's Edward Mannock will give perhaps an inkling of the difference in two national mentalities. Both were killed in 1918 within a few weeks of each other, but Mannock was more than five years older than the German Baron. Von Richthofen like Boelcke, realized fully the importance of applying definite tactics to formation flying. Right from the start he had been trained in these tactics under the guidance of Boelcke, but he was definitely a defensive fighter and a study of his claimed eighty victories shows that fifty of his victims were ancient two-seaters carrying out detailed reconnaissance jobs well within the German lines. They were much slower than his scarlet Albatros and they were usually working alone, whereas the Red Knight was supported *always* by a strong formation. Of the remainder of his kills, practically all were inferior in performance and again caught well inside the German lines. Very few S.E.5's, Sopwith triplanes, and Camels fell before his guns.

It was his practice to attack isolated two-seaters whose pilots were too venturesome, and he once wrote: "It is better for one's customers to come to one's shop than to have to look for them." Aggressive though he was, von Richthofen made more than one exaggerated claim and never, if he could avoid it, gave credit to a comrade for a victory. He was notably jealous of his own brother Lothar and disgustingly arrogant before young pilots of his Staffel.

One day while instructing a number of newcomers on the Douai airfield, a flight of S.E.5's appeared overhead. Beckoning to a newcomer, he pointed to the R.F.C. machines and snarled: "You see those Britishers up there? Go and kill them, or be killed!" A few minutes later the young pilot had obeyed the second part of the order.

Mannock presents a startling contrast. When he joined No. 40 Squadron in April 1917 he showed nothing that presaged his amazing career. He was a poor marksman, and only by continual practice was able to keep his place in formation. But with perseverance he gradually acquired a reputation. Once he was in command of a flight, he was a stickler for tight formation flying and refused to allow his men to leave the element except for engine trouble. He was never afraid to admit he *was* afraid and, like so many others, had a grim dread of fire in the air—but wished such an end on every German he encountered.

As his flying experience developed his idea of attacking in formation proved more and more successful, and for weeks he was downing an average of one enemy plane a day. His feelings for the enemy tended toward undisguised hatred of everything German and of what Germany represented. Toward the end of his career Mannock thought of nothing but killing Germans, whom he regarded as degenerate vermin. He had little use for so-called chivalry and was frankly delighted when the news of Richthofen's death reached his squadron. He refused to drink a toast to the dead Baron. Instead, according to those men who served with him, Mannock growled: "I hope he roasted all the way down!" and sat down to his meal.

Mannock was no Knight of the Air and he openly insulted contemporary journalists who tried to present him in such a light. Subsequent magazine writers of the sentimental, mawkish school often tried to renew this unrealistic theme, but those who were there know that little mercy was ever shown in combat. These men fought to kill and neither expected nor received quarter. Both sides, at one time or another, fired on balloon observers after they had jumped from burning kites with their parachutes.

But in his association with his comrades Mannock was the complete opposite to von Richthofen. He would never make a claim for a personal victory if it could be given to someone else and his logbook, showing he had shot down seventy-two German aircraft, was most conservative. His solicitude in teaching and encouraging young pilots was most admirable, and it was while initiating one of them in the tricks of air fighting that he received his own death wound. He did not fear dying, and a few days before his end had said to a friend, "Old lad, if I am killed, I shall be in good company."

For some strange reason American authors have always been starry-eyed about Baron von Richthofen and for years newer and more elaborated versions of his Western Front career have appeared in U.S. publications. He has enjoyed greater adulation in American print than either Captain Eddie Rickenbacker or Lieutenant Frank Luke, and as for the British or French heroes, few, if any, have been exploited in any such manner. Shortly after World War I a book written by Billy Bishop received only mild acclaim. Books depicting the lives of Guynemer, Mannock, Ball, McCudden, or Boelcke have never been published in the United States. In 1956 I wrote a motion-picture scenario on the career of Major Bishop for a Hollywood syndicate, but they could not raise the modest amount of money needed to finance its production, because it was believed that "no one had any idea who Major Billy Bishop was."

A very detailed report on Baron von Richthofen's flying life is to be found in Floyd Gibbons's book titled *Red Knight of Germany*. In these pages Mr. Gibbons went to great effort to present in detail each battle and victory claimed by the German ace. It should be added here that twenty-one of these victories have never been substantiated in the German Aviation archives in Berlin. In many instances his "victims" were shot down inside German territory, where engine and plane numbers could be determined. In many cases he talked to the surviving pilot or crew member, but not all of Richthofen's battles ended so conclusively.

Let us consider victory No. 42, scored on April 13, 1917. In his report von Richthofen stated that this fight took place at 12.45 p.m. between Monchy and Feuchy. The plane, a

Vickers two-seater, was downed behind the enemy (inside the British) lines. The Baron added the following: "Together with Lieutenant Simon, I attacked a Vickers two-seater coming back from German territory. After a rather long fight, during which I so manoeuvred that my adversary could not fire a single shot at me, the enemy plane plunged to the ground between Monchy and Feuchy."

In this report we have at least one example of a Richthofen victory that was no victory at all.

I was the gunner aboard that two-seater. It was an F.E.2b, not a Vickers, but as mentioned before the Germans often made this mistake since both planes were almost identical. We were not shot down by Baron von Richthofen. We did not "plunge" to the ground. In my wartime notebook, beside me now as I write are our corresponding details.

```
      11:30 ............... A-7244
      4/13/17 ............. Captain Bush
      Clouds at 4,000.
      6 E.A. .............. 12.30 over Lille.
      10 E.A. ............. 12.50 over Roulers.
      Engaged ............. 12.55
  Shooting at us ............. 4 E.A. over Roulers
  Shot down near Monchy .... A red plane
```

The interpretation of these notes indicates that we took off at 11.30 a.m. in a Fee No. A-7244. My pilot was a Captain Buss. The terms "6 E.A." and "10 E.A." refer to enemy aircraft. They were the simple details written in the air from which I later wrote my routine account of this particular mission.

Our six-plane flight was led by Captain Carleton Clement of Vancouver, B.C. We were slated to carry out a photography patrol in co-operation with a number of R.E.8's which we had picked up over Arras. The clouds were no help for good reconnaissance work, and evidently I was watching for enemy planes, for later I wrote: *"There are the camera planes—over Arras. I see several E.A. coming up from behind Douai. Better keep our eyes open."*

While the phrase "Richthofen's Flying Circus" is widely understood today, we had not heard of it, nor did we know of von Richthofen. How could we? The Red Knight was just another successful fighter pilot and had not as yet won continental renown. Later, however, I learned that his Staffel was operating from the village of Marcke, a few miles north of Courtrai.

159

There is always something hackle-raising about a photography patrol. You seem to be continually held up by some situation that is never quite clear or justified. But there we were over the German lines with half a dozen Fees and three slogging old camera craft bunched below us. The Boche planes were moving parallel and watching us like vultures. I was fairly experienced by then and I sensed they were climbing for height, but since we had nine two-seater aircraft with alert gunners we stood a reasonable chance of holding them off.

When at last the camera planes signalled that they had their pictures we turned back towards Arras and escorted them up to our line. A few Jerry anti-aircraft guns belched at us, but we ignored them and prepared to devote the rest of our time to offensive operations.

Suddenly out of nowhere came a cavalcade of Albatros D.3's that did not fire a slug until their props were almost chewing up our rudders. I was soon up on my feet, firing frantic bursts over our top plane. To do this we had to stand with our feet on the upper edges of the plywood nacelle and hang onto the gas-pipe gun mounting.

A green-and-white Albatros went down with blue smoke trailing after and disappeared. I have no idea who got him. I know I didn't. They came back and charged again, and I became fascinated by their blue noses, red wheels, green prop bosses and yellow-striped wings. I had never seen such aerial gaiety. Two came at us from a stiff angle that left me blocked off by my own wing tip. I tried shooting through the struts and risked clipping our flying wires until Captain Bush screamed at me to stop.

Another Jerry went down in flames, throwing away his tail on the way through the battle debris. Bush was flinging our Fee all over the sky, and dust, splinters, and loose items were swirling around my feet and legs as I darted from one gun to the other. When it all settled down I discovered to my dismay that we were all alone. Neither of us had any idea where the other Fees had gone, but I presumed they had hurried back to our side of the line to re-form.

Instead of taking the same precautions, my pilot, a very aristocratic Britisher who had already been decorated for his work in the trenches, immediately started off on an offensive patrol on his own. I was an unwilling participant and I tried to warn him.

"You're heading for Roulers, you know."

He nodded—and smiled.

"Those aircraft over there are 'theirs' not 'ours.' " I pointed out the ten E.A.

He smiled again and turned even deeper into enemy territory.

Since I was the observer and to a great extent responsible for this pilot, who was somewhat a newcomer, I asked what was his idea. He explained that he was going round the back of them. When I asked him why he said, "They'd never expect anything like that, would they?"

I again reminded him that we were well inside the German lines as it was, but that point didn't seem to interest him, so I gave up and hoped for the best.

Of course we were warmly welcomed. Four Albatroses took us on, and I had a very exciting time keeping us in the air. Some of this seemed to warn Captain Bush and he finally nosed down and tried to head for our line.

At that point a Jerry scored. From somewhere below came a terrific burst that slammed metal through everything we had. The Fee dipped and jerked. Bush sat a second or so in deep concentration and then reached over and snapped off the ignition switch. I looked back to see if the prop had stopped, but there was no prop! Between snap bursts at the Albatroses I looked again and discovered it had broken away, taking a portion of the engine crankcase with it, and lay entangled with the lower tail booms and their cross-bracing wires. I wondered what had caused that but was soon roused out of that reverie by the four Albatros pilots, who could probably sniff victory.

I took a quick glance down at the area below and then yelled at Bush: "Head *that* way—and dive like hell!"

We dove.

All the way down I noticed that I was now fighting but two German planes, a bright-red one and a green-tailed devil. They both sprayed us with everything they had, and Bush sat in the shelter of our disabled engine—actually laughing at me as I popped up and down from the front gun to the one used to fire over the top wing. Von Richthofen stated that I had not been able to fire a single shot at him, but I remember my cockpit floor being littered with empty gun drums and the canvas bag that caught the spent cartridge cases was bulging.

It must be remembered too that we were not running away from two Albatros scouts. We were going down with a disabled engine which had been struck by a large chunk of *anti-aircraft* shell casing. This had clipped a connecting rod which had whirled long enough to shear off the rear section of the

161

engine—and the propeller had fallen down on the tail booms. No aircraft had shot us down, but I learned later that I had torched one of the four Albatros scouts, a matter von Richthofen failed to mention in his report.

We held them off long enough to glide into our own lines, and we did land near Monchy, where we both sat wondering just what had happened to the engine. We had little or no thought for the Albatros pilots who had followed us down, and it wasn't until a couple of British tommies sauntered through a hedge that we were congratulated for escaping an everyday routine demise.

A Cockney corporal said, "Coo, you ain't 'arf lucky. Know who it was you was fightin'?"

"Oh, a couple of giddy Albatros blokes," Captain Bush grinned.

"Albatros blokes! Look 'ere, mate, that was the Bloody Baron. Didn't you see 'is red plane?"

"Oh, stow it!" smirked Captain Bush.

The Cockney persisted. "I know it was. We've seen 'im dozens of times."

"Who?" I broke in on the chitchat.

"The Bloody Baron!" he growled. "Don't you know who 'e is? Gawd! I thought all you Flying Corpse chaps knew 'im. Mark my word, mate, you ain't 'arf lucky!"

"So now it's a Bloody Baron," Bush muttered. "Leave it to the gravel-crushers. They'll find someone to idolize. Tomorrow it will be a Mad Major and the next day a Red Devil of some kind. I know them."

And that is how I became acquainted with the Red Knight of Germany and a small portion of his Flying Circus. I was to go on flying for many more months and meet these gaudy gulls almost daily throughout, but this incident is offered to show how easy it was for Baron von Richthofen to become confused about his "victories."

No one will deny that Baron von Richthofen was a fine pilot, a good leader, and an outstanding figure during this period. He was more than fortunate in some respects. He came to the Western Front in time to assume Boelcke's role. He had a fine family background that always impressed the German public, and when he wasn't commanding his Staffel 11, his brother Lothar was given the post, the heads of several more deserving members being passed over just to keep the von Richthofen name in the war news. Manfred played his part exceedingly well. Whether he was the greatest war pilot is another matter.

Let us remember that on the three occasions when he left

the security of his formation, he was shot down—twice by lowly two-seater gunners, and finally by a none-too-experienced Sopwith Camel pilot.

Through the heat and battle of 1917 roared one German fighter who never had to fake any reports, nor was he included among the Prussian elite when it came to publicity. Bruno Loerzer was totally unknown on the Allied side of the line and on his own he was simply an ex-farmer turned airman who, because he had felt that perhaps the Aviation Service might add some prestige to his colourless life, had joined early in 1913 as an engineer officer. His being selected for pilot training had been something of a comedy of errors. He had made his first flight on a dare, and later when volunteers were sought for aviation training Loerzer had put his name down, thinking he was volunteering for a card tournament to be held at a nearby officers' mess.

We met Loerzer in a previous chapter when he induced Hermann Goering to switch from the cyclist corps to flying. By 1917 Bruno had performed no particular acts of valour; he had but three planes to his credit. He had been shot down by a French two-seater and nearly killed. Again, flying as an observer with the forty-six-year-old Jacob Wolff, he suffered another frightening defeat at the hands of a couple of old Caudrons. Following that, he settled down to business and after two months on the Lorraine front as a two-seater pilot leader was told to form a Staffel of his own.

He began this task in January of 1917, and the first man he selected to follow him was Hermann Goering. His brother Fritz, then known as the Flying Pastor, was second, and Walter Blume, another veteran, was third. It was finally built up to strength with Albatros fighters and known as Jagdstaffel 26. They fought so well under Loerzer's leadership on the Arras front that von Richthofen urged Bruno to adopt some special squadron marking. It was the thing to do. Be identified as a unit upon which all other German flyers could depend.

Loerzer put the question to his pilots, and Walter Blume, a chess player, reminded him that he had trained his men to fight with their heads and fly always one thought ahead of their opponents. It was something like chess, so why not have a chessboard for an insignia?

It satisfied everyone. It had a certain dignity and could be recognized at a good distance. No one would mistake the Chess Players, so on the sleek sides of their Albatroses they painted the sharp black and white squares of a chessboard.

Loerzer further capitalized on the idea, devising moves

based on chess strategy. His pilots were taught to be far-sighted, daring, quick to move forward at the right time, and retreat when victory had been attained. Above all, he stressed that victories alone were no evidence of success but must stand in the right proportion to losses.

The area around Arras provided a hundred combat situations. For instance, a British D.H.2 patrol was flying above a cloud layer, unaware of the Chessboards or their new programme of tactics. They were watching the upper sky and were completely off guard when Loerzer's Staffel 26 zoomed up through a rift in the layer to riddle the de Havillands from below. The leader went down with a shattered propeller; another curled out of the formation with his engine smoking badly, and three others dived for the security of the cloud below to get away from this weird unorthodox attack.

From that day on, a signal went out along the British lines: "Watch out for those Huns flying chessboard-design Albatroses!"

Loerzer downed his fourth aeroplane in that skirmish and added four more to his score in the next two weeks. In quick time he received the Iron Cross and the new Order of the House of Hohenzollern and by midsummer had twelve enemy planes to his credit.

Bitter air fighting took place at this time. The armies on the ground were locked in deadly combat. They were struggling for Passchendaele, and the Third Battle of Ypres was to open on July 31. The air offensive was released on the eleventh, and although the major portion of the sky combat took place within the German lines, the British lost but 217 aircraft while downing nearly five hundred black-crossed planes.

An item of interest occurred in July when German scout pilots were equipped with parachutes for the first time. These were known as the Heinecke type and were packed in a bag fastened to the pilot's shoulders. A release cord ran from the parachute and was attached to a snaffle inside the cockpit. All the pilot had to do was to breathe a prayer—and jump. It was several months later before the Italian Paulus seat-pack parachute came into general use. The French and British airmen had no parachute of any kind throughout the whole war. Several ideas had been proposed, but while most of them would open under these emergency conditions, all were too bulky for aircraft use and none was adopted.

The Chessboards flew all through this bitter period and before the year was out Loerzer had brought down twenty planes. Early in 1918, after being awarded the *Pour le mérite*, he was given command of a fourteen-squadron Jagdgeschwader—a flying circus. Promoted to Oberleutnant, he fought out the war with his Jagdgeschwader 3 and was finally credited with forty-five victories. His organization was the last to disintegrate with the final thrust in September of 1918. When it was all over Loerzer and his top lieutenant, Hermann Goering, were left alone to ponder on their doubtful future.

The German Air Service took on a new lease of life in August, claiming three hundred victories, most of which went to the credit of the Flying Circuses. Oberleutnant Edward Dostler, in command of Staffel 6 and with twenty-six kills, was actually struck down while flying low through an artillery barrage. A shell, no one knows from which side, struck his aeroplane and it disintegrated in mid-air. Walter Hohndrof, who had scored twelve victories, was shot down on the twelfth of September. Kurt Wolff, leader of Staffel 10 and just out of the hospital, was cut down in flames over Wervicq, and then came one of the severest blows of all.

On September 23, while flying his red-and-white chequered Fokker triplane, Werner Voss boldly crossed the line alone and piled into a large formation of S.E.5's led by Captain Jimmy McCudden of No. 56 Squadron. It was one of the most daring attacks ever staged by a German pilot. Utterly foolhardy. For more than twenty minutes the gay Hussar of Krefeld held the British S.E.5's even, but finally an equally bold and headstrong young nineteen-year-old, Albert Rhys-Davids, roared through the whole swirling formation and poured a long burst into the scarlet-and-white triplane. Werner Voss went down to his last landing with a squadron of British pilots actually regretting his end.

McCudden wrote in his book *Flying Fury*: "Werner Voss was the greatest pilot any of us had encountered. We all came out of the fray bearing scars of the battle. It was a shame to see such a brave man die."

In the summer of 1917 the Germans decided to follow the lead of the R.F.C. and take up ground strafing. Suitable equipment had been designed for the purpose and early in September there came an opportunity to try out this type.

On August 6 German ground forces had been forced to evacuate Péronne, and in order to stem the tide of the British advance, a squadron of Halberstadt L.C.2's were loaded up with contact bombs and the potato-masher-type hand grenades. With this high-explosive opposition, they streaked over the heads of the advancing tommies. Four times the squadron went back for more bombs and grenades and when they were through had made a shambles of an entire British division. During the attack these Halberstadts also knocked down two low-flying Camels.

October was a bad month for flying, and both sides made the most of the respite. Friend and foe had been scoring high, but, by the same token, they also suffered serious losses. On the last day of this month the Germans lost a gallant airman when Leutnant Heinrich Gontermann, who commanded Staffel 15, was killed. Gontermann had enjoyed considerable success on the French front, and some of his history makes interesting reading.

Heinrich was of peasant stock and joined the army when he was fifteen. He was a good soldier and advanced rapidly. When he applied for a transfer to the Air Service his request was immediately granted and by 1916 he was posted to Staffel 5. At flying school he proved to be very skilled, a daring stunt flyer, and an unusual marksman. On his first flight on the front he performed the unusual feat of destroying an Allied plane over Ypres. But then his luck petered out and nothing of interest is to be found in his logbook until March 5, 1917. From that point on Gontermann scored heavily. By October 12 he had accounted for forty Allied aircraft, including fifteen kite balloons. During Bloody April he downed an even dozen enemy aircraft and the following August he added thirteen more, most of them observation balloons.

When Oberleutnant Reinhold, commanding officer of Staffel 15, was killed by a French Spad pilot on April 13, Gontermann was given his command. He was an able leader but made very few friends and appears to have been overbearing and distrustful of any well-intended advice. On one occasion he attacked a French balloon, but the observer had a light Hotchkiss gun in the basket. A snap burst practically shot away one of Gontermann's guns, but he went back with what he had left, and the French observer died under a burning balloon.

Throughout the summer Gontermann scored time and time again with but a miserly expenditure of ammunition. Like the Canadian Billy Bishop, he seldom spent more than ten rounds on a target and on several occasions he downed his opponent with but six bullets.

While in Berlin on leave, "wetting" his new *Pour le mérite*, Gontermann, who had flown practically everything, applied for a Fokker triplane for his especial use. When one of these unusual Fokkers was delivered to his field he decided to make a couple of test flights to get the feel of the machine. By now the Fokker Tripe was earning a bad reputation. Voss had died in one. Wolff had gone down in flames, and von Richthofen had had a bad experience fooling around with a Fee gunner while flying a triplane.

It was on October 29 that Gontermann climbed into a cockpit for the last time. He took off, and the Fokker D.R.1 zoomed like a rocket. The pilot enjoyed this new sensation and began to put the machine through its paces. He was a skilled and daring stunt flyer, but the triplane was not equal to his bidding. There was an ominous crack like a pistol shot and the wing section collapsed and the plane went down completely out of control, hitting hard. Gontermann was still alive but died within the hour: a hero with forty victories and not yet twenty-one years of age.

Once their air offence of spring 1917 petered out, the German High Command decided to attack Britain direct. Their gasbag Zeppelins had been grim failures, so they resolved to make their new raids with an improved version of the old 1916 Gotha which was ready by March of 1917 and listed as the Gotha G.3. This long-range machine was powered with two 260-h.p. Mercedes engines, had a top speed of 80 m.p.h., a ceiling of 12,000 feet, and carried a crew of three and 900 pounds of bombs.

At one Gotha field the Germans had established an L.V.G. two-seater fighter squadron for defence of the bombers' hangars. Late one afternoon a lone L.V.G. two-seater spotted six French Bréguet bombers obviously heading for the Gotha base. The gallant German pilot went into action and shot down two Bréguets in as many minutes. The observer shot off the wings of a third and then forced a fourth to land inside the German lines. Had they been much publicised scout pilots, they undoubtedly would have been promoted and decorated; instead they received a brief mention in the orders of the day.

By the end of March the new Gothas were ready to sing *Gott Strafe England*, and the honour of making the first raid fell to Battle Squadron No. 3, commanded by Captain von Brandenburg. They went out from Ghent on May 25 with sixteen Gothas and made a successful attack on Folkestone. On June 5 another formation, eighteen strong, raided Sheerness. Another, flying out on June 13, met so little opposition they decided to go for metropolitan London. Cruising over the famed Liverpool Street Station, they dropped seventy-two bombs, killing and wounding nearly 600 people. They toured over the metropolis unmolested for more than an hour, then calmly re-formed and headed back for Ghent. Their unusual

167

success was toasted in champagne by their Air Commander von Hoeppner.

The raiders suffered their first loss on July 7. This time, a formation of twenty-six machines raided London, and on the return journey one Gotha was shot down in the North Sea and another was so badly damaged that it collapsed on landing and two members of the crew were killed.

These daylight raids continued on through August with varying success until the twenty-second, when the British finally took up this new challenge. Thirteen Gothas led by a Captain Kleine tried to raid London but ran into a series of misfortunes. Three were forced down by engine trouble, two were destroyed by anti-aircraft fire, and one by a Home-Defence aeroplane.

For a time the Germans decided to hold off these raids until better equipment could be designed, but on second thought came to the conclusion that any easing off would only give the British time to improve their defences. The German High Command then considered experimenting with night attacks, and Battle Squadrons Nos. 4, 5, and 6 were organised and assigned to night flying.

Their first assault was made by two planes early in September when Dover was raided. The following night ten Gothas went to Chatham, and in this raid two 112-pound bombs hit the Naval barracks and 130 men were killed and eighty-eight wounded. On September 4 ten Gothas of Squadron 5 attacked London, and nineteen people were killed.

At the same time the German bombers on the Western Front were not having such success. Every time they attempted to cross the British lines the R.F.C. moved in like a swarm of wasps. Although they took off nightly, they were all too often forced back without dropping their bombs. New machines were called for. A better weather prediction system was also necessary. Long-distance flights were too precarious with the equipment available.

Late in November the German bomber crews got their wish. A new machine, aptly named the Zeppelin Giant, was being testflown. This behemoth had four Mercedes engines, a wing span of 130 feet, and carried a crew of eight.

On the night of December 6 Captain Kleine was allowed to take the first model on a raid on England. He was given an escort of fifteen Gothas. Germany had high hopes for this expedition, but it turned out to be most disastrous.

London and Sheerness *were* bombed, but two Gothas were shot down by anti-aircraft fire, two were forced down in Belgium, one disappeared in the North Sea, and another crashed into a hangar while attempting to land with a part of its undercarriage shot away.

Another raid was carried out on December 18 with not much better result. The last attack of 1917 was attempted on the twenty-second, and this time two Giants and a Gotha reached the English coast, but owing to a high wind, their two-and-a-half tons of bombs had to be dropped into the sea. The engines of the Gotha failed and it had to be landed in an open field near Margate, but the crew set their plane afire before the British could interfere and save it.

The flying equipment produced and supplied to the German Air Force during 1917 is as follows:

GERMAN WARPLANES OF 1917

Make	Engine	Speed m.p.h.	Purpose
Albatros D.3	Mercedes 160 h.p.	120	Scout
Albatros D.5	Mercedes 200 h.p.	130	Scout
Albatros D.7	Benz 195 h.p.	132	Scout
Albatros C.5	Benz 225 h.p.	112	Reconnaissance
Fokker D.4	Oberursel 110 h.p.	120	Scout
Fokker D.5	Oberursel 110 h.p.	122	Scout
Fokker D.R.1	Oberursel 110 h.p.	121	Scout
Hannoveraner	Opel-Argus 180 h.p.	96	Ground-attack
Halberstadt	Mercedes 180 h.p.	97	Ground-attack
L.V.G. C.4	Benz 225 h.p.	95	Reconnaissance
L.V.G. C.5	Benz 225 h.p.	110	Bomber-fighter
Rumpler C.4	Maybach 260 h.p.	98	Reconnaissance
	or Mercedes 260 h.p.	?	Reconnaissance
Rumpler C.5	Mercedes 260 h.p.	101	Reconnaissance
Sablatnig D.R.1	Benz 230 h.p.	122	Seaplane Scout
Pfalz D.3	Mercedes 160 h.p.	103	Scout
Pfalz D.R.1	Oberursel 110 h.p.	103	Scout

For the British, 1917 opened with bitter cold weather, outdated machines, and an enemy offensive that demanded the utmost in courage and devotion to duty. An unusual example of this was provided by Sergeant Pilot Thomas Mottershead of No. 20 Squadron. He was the ninth Britisher and the only N.C.O. to win the Victoria Cross for the Royal Flying Corps.

On January 7 as a pilot in an F.E.2b with Lieutenant W. E. Gower as his observer, Sergeant Mottershead was flying a lone offensive patrol over the line when he was attacked by a flight of enemy fighters. Gower put up a splendid show, but they were outnumbered, and a German tracer apparently torched the fuel tank beneath the pilot's seat. Within a few seconds Mottershead was enveloped in flames, and although Gower gave up his gun for a Pyrene extinguisher, nothing he could do would control the blaze. However, Mottershead sat it out and put the machine into a partial sideslip which carried the flames out at an angle past the wings and into the lower tail boom. How he did this sitting in a flaming seat cannot be imagined. The machine should have broken up in mid-air, but it hung together long enough for Mottershead to make a landing in friendly territory. The Fee rumbled along some uneven ground and then collapsed. Gower was thrown clear, but the sergeant pilot was entangled in the wreckage and died a few minutes after being lifted out. A few days later he was awarded the Victoria Cross posthumously.

Throughout this month No. 8 Royal Naval Air Service Squadron and No. 24 Royal Flying Corps played havoc with the enemy service. Flight Lieutenant E. R. Grange of No. 8 shot down five machines in four days. He kept up this offensive spirit for a couple of weeks until a stray bullet clipped his shoulder and he had to go into the hospital.

Late in February Major E. Graves, commander of No. 60 Squadron, was shot down in flames by Baron von Richthofen. The Red Knight reported this as a B.E.2c, but Graves was flying a single-seater Nieuport. However, on the same day a very new and very determined Canadian joined the squadron as a pilot. He had had experience the year before as an observer, but this was the first time Lieutenant William Avery Bishop was to fly on the front alone.

By August 11—exactly six months after he had flown his first Nieuport patrol—Billy Bishop had downed forty-seven enemy aircraft. He had won every decoration the British and French governments could award and hadn't suffered a scratch. After a period of rest—enforced by the British government—Bishop went back to the front at the head of his own squadron. In twelve days he hung up twenty-five more victories, bringing his total to seventy-two. Again the British government stepped in; Bishop was ordered back to London and his great fighting career was over.

Billy Bishop perhaps best represents the British single-seater pilot type, for he was typical of the group that willingly selected the service after a period of ground duty. He was a small compact young man who moved like a lightweight boxer. He did not always conform and was of no particular value in orthodox formations. In fact, he was not a good pilot

170

in the true sense, but he had two qualifications that made him the most picturesque of the very colourful Canadians. He was probably the greatest marksman in the war and like Mannock, honestly believed in the cause for which he fought.

He was born at Owen Sound, Ontario, on February 8, 1894. His parents were English and typical of the immigrant types that had moved to Canada late in the nineteenth century. Billy was a very active youngster, and his parents decided that the discipline of the Royal Military College in Kingston would perhaps curb him somewhat. On his graduation he joined the Canadian militia and received a commission in one of their Saturday-afternoon cavalry regiments.

Like his opposite number, Manfred von Richtofen, Bishop became bored with the dull drudgery of the cavalry service in the war and eventually transferred to the R.F.C. He put in a few months as an observer until he was injured in an aircraft crash, after which he was returned to England for treatment and eventual pilot training.

Before he was sent out to the front Bishop had overheard a portion of a lecture delivered by General Hugh Trenchard, then Commander in Chief of the Royal Flying Corps. The general was denouncing the publicizing of single-seater fighter pilots and their continual effort to make the "ace" lists. He argued that "aces" were four-a-penny and were actually doing very little to win the war in the air. In this lecture Trenchard was the first to advocate the objectives of a strategic air force.

"These aerial duels are a waste of time and manpower," he expounded further. "It would be much simpler and more efficient to destroy the enemy's equipment long before it ever reaches a front-line hangar. One strategic bomber, a trained bomber crew, and the proper type of armament would do more good in a week than all our multi-decorated aces can accomplish in a year."

Of course General Trenchard was soon in hot water and later forced to resign his post. The opinion, however, had a great influence on Bishop, for he went out to France fully determined to "make a fool" of that General Trenchard. A few months later Bishop had the pleasure of again hearing Trenchard's voice—over the telephone—telling him he was most proud to announce that he (Billy) had been awarded the Victoria Cross.

Bishop's record was the result of a daring plan conceived during his freshman days as an observer where his colourless experiences only whetted his appetite for more exciting action. Once he became a fighter pilot, he was immediately recognized as a Hun-hater. He had nothing but contempt for his opponents in the air or on the ground. The only fear he ever disclosed was that his unreliable rotary engine would one day betray him or that his guns would fail during a critical point of an air battle.

In the case of his power plant he relied on Corporal Walt Bourne, a crafty little British mechanic who apparently knew more about the Le Rhone than the man who invented it. Bishop took care of the guns himself and personally tested every round of ammunition before it was inserted in the drum. He became a master at remedying stoppages in the air and spent endless hours in gunnery practice against all types of ground targets. Besides taking part in routine patrols, he put in as many as six or seven hours a day stalking the enemy as far back as the limited range of his Nieuport would permit.

At No. 60 Squadron Bishop bored everyone stiff with his persistent questions concerning the tactics and strategy used by Albert Ball, who had just been sent back to England for an enforced rest. He had studied the work of Hawker, McCudden, and several of the French flyers who were high on the ace list. But young Ball particularly intrigued him, for the Nottingham lad employed the same daredevil resoluteness that was to mark this Canadian ace. Strangely enough, when Ball was relieved, Bishop was sent to the same flight and Ball's mechanic was assigned to his machine.

There never was so relentless a fighting airman in any war. When Bishop had gained every decoration the empire could bestow, King George V and Winston Churchill, then Secretary of State for Air, ordered him back home, but only through subterfuge were they able to enforce the command. A few months later Bishop had inveigled his way back again, supposedly to command a new S.E.5 squadron with strict orders to stay behind the line and engage only in administrative work.

It was over those next twelve days when he was presumed to be leading indoctrination flights inside the Allied balloon line that he collected his final twenty-five kills. The day he was ordered home he shot down five enemy aircraft during one afternoon's foray.

On August 11, 1917, Bishop received a telephone call from General Trenchard at R.F.C. headquarters. Without a word to his superiors he left the squadron office and sought out Corporal Bourne, who was at supper in the N.C.O. mess. Captain Bishop moved in and sat beside his grubby mechanic, who, to say the least, was somewhat startled.

"Anything wrong, sir?" he inquired.

"Not particularly."

"I replaced that interrupter-gear piston, sir," the corporal explained.

"It's not that. I just wanted to tell you that *we've* won the Victoria Cross."

Bourne showed no change of expression. "Thank you, sir. That means, of course . . ."

"Nothing of the kind!" Bishop snorted. "They'll not send me back. I have only four more than Ball, and Jimmy McCudden over at No. 56 is going like a house on fire."

Bourne moaned, "We've lost practically every V.C. airman so far, sir. There was Rhodes-Moorhouse, Warneford, Hawker, Liddell, Ball, and Sergeant Mottershead. Leefe-Robinson is a prisoner of war. They won't risk you any longer."

"I'll have something to say about that," Bishop stormed.

Bourne was right. The orders were explicit and Bishop was ordered back, ostensibly to have the Victoria Cross pinned on by the King at Buckingham Palace.

Not only was his V.C. awarded, but for the first time in British military history one man received the empire's three greatest decorations at one ceremony. While a hundred other heroes looked on, His Majesty pinned the Victoria Cross, the Distinguished Service Order, and the Military Cross on the breast of Captain William Avery Bishop.

The King smiled and said, "You *have* been making a nuisance of yourself out there, haven't you, Captain?"

Before daybreak on the morning of June 2, 1917, a slight young man just twenty-three years of age crawled from his disordered bed and without bothering to discard his pyjamas pulled on a pair of knee-length flying boots, an old football jersey, and a short leather jacket. With a final glance about the cubicle he tiptoed out quietly.

The mess sergeant in the cookhouse glared. "You don't expect to find any Huns up there at this time of day, do you, sir? It's still dark."

Bishop just grinned and took a long swig of tea. There was a low whine and a scratching sound at the cookhouse door. Bishop back-heeled the door open and an ugly-looking mongrel bounded in and smothered him with slobbery affection.

"I don't understand that dog," the sergeant muttered. "The horrible cur has never taken to anyone. He just scrounges his meals here. If anyone but you tried to stroke him he'd probably take an arm off. What is it he likes about you?"

173

"We're kindred spirits. Come on, Nig, let's go and rouse Jerry out."

Bishop and the dog wandered over to the hangar where Bourne stood by the wing of a dew-streaked Nieuport scout. Nig sat on his haunches and watched the rest of the proceedings.

"How's everything, Corporal?"

"The machine's all right, sir. Your guns are serviced and loaded, but I don't like any of this, sir," he grumbled.

"Don't worry. Keep an eye on Nig. I'll be back in just over an hour and I shall want the bus for a gunnery test after breakfast."

"Good luck, sir," Bourne said and looked like a worried bloodhound.

"Switch off . . . petrol on . . . suck in," Bishop chanted tonelessly.

Gulping the heavy morning air, the Le Rhone lifted the silver Nieuport off the turf in a few screeching yards. It was still far from dawn, but once Bishop climbed to 3,000 feet he could see the silver tracery of the new day plating the horizon. Ahead and below belched the scarlet and gold eruptions of the front line, where the artillery shelled the back areas and added to the predawn hate designed to try men's souls and further the dread of the war-weary infantryman.

Once he was clear of the balloon lines and their treacherous steel cables, Bishop dropped back to hedge-hopping level and scoured the obscure countryside. His objective was a certain enemy aerodrome. By now he was in a bad mood because of Bourne's concern and would have relished taking it out on anything—enemy planes, columns of infantrymen, or convoys of transport. It was that sort of a day for Captain Bishop.

Now he was 15 miles inside the enemy lines and roaring along at 300 feet. If his engine gave any trouble his case would be hopeless. From this altitude, too, finding his way back by simple ground contact was all the more difficult.

Suddenly he came upon a field that had been alerted. At least seven single-seaters and one two-seater were out on the line, and the mechanics were standing around in small groups. As his opening attack, Bishop nosed down and raked the machines until he was down to 50 feet. He concentrated on the two-seater, for among his war hates was the two-place aircraft that had a rear gunner. He had a healthy respect for two-seaters and rear gunners.

The scene below took on a new pattern as the German mechanics scattered or sprawled grotesquely. Bishop swung over

174

to one side of the field to await new targets. Uninjured men were darting in all directions like startled rabbits, while from a sheltered corner of the field two fixed machine guns opened up and peppered his wings.

Then unexpectedly a single-seater began to taxi down the field and wheeled into a take-off. Bishop pounced on it like an enraged hawk. The Nieuport swooped in close just as the unfortunate Jerry had gained enough speed to get his tail off the ground. Bishop opened up with both guns. The Albatros fighter took just fifteen rounds, tilted up on a wing, and side-slipped toward the ground wrapped in garish flame.

Another single-seater was taking off by the time Bishop was zooming from his first kill. Again he moved in fast but had to fire from a greater range and as he closed in he saw the frenzied pilot turn and stare back into the flickering guns. The second Albatros got off the ground high enough to crash headlong into a small clump of trees.

Bishop circled the hangars again and this time discovered the Germans were getting their aircraft off in teams; two were roaring down the field wing tip to wing tip. As he raced to blast them down they changed course slightly, and he sensed his morning's fun was over. He climbed fast and set out his last attack. One of the Albatros biplanes turned away to the east and the other zoomed with savage intensity. Bishop moved in on his adversary from 1,000 feet. The climbing Albatros was gaining on him, so he made two complete circuits of the area and then pounced. His third victim took a short burst of ten rounds, threw a wing strut away, spiralled down stiff, and crashed dead in the centre of the field.

The fourth biplane now attacked, and Bishop saw that the Jerries were still taking off from the field below and he also realized that the responsible officials might have alerted other aerodromes to intercept him on the way back. He emptied a full drum at long range, saw no immediate result, and, concluding that discretion was the better part of valour, headed for home.

By now the strain was beginning to tell, and he admitted later that he was terrified; so much excitement on an empty stomach left him limp and he fought spasms of nausea as he swayed back and forth from one wisp of vapour cover to another. He said that the thrill of his victories had completely dissipated, being replaced by dread and dizziness that left him almost physically helpless. He hung on, however, and by the time he reached his own field the nausea began to wear off.

When he crawled out of his cockpit Corporal Bourne asked

him how many Huns he had downed and Bishop made the understatement of the times. "Only three. One got away."

It was for this solo feat that he was recommended for the Victoria Cross. After long weeks of careful investigation as to the authenticity of his report, the decoration was confirmed on August 11, 1917. Agents inside the German lines discovered that the two-seater had been seriously damaged, several of the single-seaters had been put out of action and the fourth Albatros pilot had been lightly wounded.

This amazing young Canadian lived through the war, married a well-known Canadian heiress, went into many business ventures, but had none of the satisfaction that was his during the war days. He tried writing, was given important posts in several Canadian industries, but Billy Bishop was a born fighter pilot. During World War II he rejoined the service and as a commanding figure headed Canada's drive for aviation recruits—a role that bitterly disappointed him, for he had hoped to return to Britain and head a squadron or group of his own. It was not to be. Again, a man named Winston Churchill headed him off and sent him back to Canada.

Bishop pleaded, "I want to do more, Mr. Prime Minister. So far I'm nothing but a figurehead in uniform and decorations. I want to take a more active part."

Churchill said: "So do I. I'm a trained soldier, too. I could still command a brigade or a division out there, but I rather think I would be wasted, don't you?"

Bishop had no argument for that.

"I seem to recall, Air Marshal," Churchill went on with a smile, "that we had a similar interview in the last war. My answer is still the same. Men such as you can't be wasted. You have a far more important job to do at home. I must remind you, sir, that while the war at present is being fought in Europe, the Allied training programme—our most important weapon—is being staged in Canada, not Great Britain. Do you think you are entitled to ignore that?"

Bishop bowed to this authority and the Allied Air Training Plan became one of the most successful inter-Allied efforts.

Air Marshal William Avery Bishop died on September 11, 1956, in Palm Beach, Florida. He was sixty-two years old.

Any record of air action in World War I would be incomplete without a comprehensive reference to Major James B. McCudden, who was to become one of the most skilled wartime airmen of any service. As previously explained, McCudden was born in a drab military barracks and became a bugle boy long before most boys have entered high school.

His education must have been very sketchy, but before his flying career was ended he wrote his life story, *Flying Fury*, in a more satisfactory manner than that of any other airman of those days, probably because it was written during the time of his conquests.

Before the beginning of the war McCudden transferred to the fledgling Royal Flying Corps as a mechanic and subsequently went overseas with No. 3 Squadron, arriving in France August 12, 1914. Here he served as a mechanic, lorry driver, gunner, and observer under fire, and within a few months was one of the most efficient men in any air force in any war. His knowledge of every branch of military aviation was profound, his skill uncanny, whether with a gun, an engine, or an intricate airframe. Besides all this, he displayed courage of the highest order, cultivated his diction, personal appearance, and adopted most gentlemanly manners.

He knew more about truing up an aeroplane than the average rigger, was master of every available aero engine, and so was as much at home in the hangar as he was in the cockpit. He studied every aeroplane with intense interest and whenever possible he would sit for long periods in or actually fly captured enemy machines until he knew every feature of their construction and fighting capability. As a result, he was able to give very comprehensive lectures to pupils, whether they were mechanics, observers, or pilots.

As a pilot he was as near perfect as it is possible to be. He flew practically every type of aircraft in the R.F.C. under all conditions and could have accepted any job at any rank in the Flying Corps with the certainty of success. But Fate was most unkind; McCudden made only one mistake in his whole wartime service, but it was his last.

He was also unique in that he served in France as a flying man in every year of the war—1914, 1915, 1916, 1917 and 1918. Few airmen can claim the same. He served in every possible capacity from bugle boy to major before he was twenty-one years old and had won practically every decoration his country could bestow. He was awarded the Victoria Cross in April 1918 with a record of fifty-four enemy planes shot down, twice felling four planes in one day. Besides having been a daring high-altitude prowler, he had led seventy-eight offensive patrols and had fought duels with practically every noted German champion.

McCudden and Boelcke had an interesting coincidence in their flying service. On October 23, 1916, Boelcke came upon and engaged a formation of Fees. He attacked one and as it went down the observer fell out and dropped behind the German lines, but the Fee with a dead pilot in it crashed inside the British lines. It was Boelcke's last victory; five days later he was killed.

In February of 1918 McCudden attacked a Hannoveraner at close range and saw the observer tumble from the shattered fuselage and fall over the British lines. The Hannoveraner with the German pilot in it crashed inside the German lines. It was McCudden's fifty-eighth and last victory.

McCudden's most memorable days were passed in No. 56 Squadron (S.E.5's). With its record of two hundred enemy planes shot down in five and a half months it easily beat the von Richthofen Circus report of two hundred Allied planes shot down in seven months.

Because of his splendid achievements and long list of decorations Jimmy McCudden was sent back to England to conduct a lecture tour in the flying schools. In July he was returned to France to take the flying command of No. 60 Squadron. He crossed the Channel safely and landed at a nearby field to have lunch with some old friends. When he took off again his new S.E.5 engine quit and he made the mistake of trying to turn back to the field, and in doing so, he stalled his plane and spun in. McCudden was killed; his remains still lie near where he fell.

The following is a complete list of British military aircraft designed and delivered to active-service squadrons during 1917.

BRITISH WARPLANES OF 1917

Make	Engine	Speed m.p.h.	Purpose
Austin "Ball" *	Hisso 200 h.p.	138	Scout
Avro 504K	Le Rhone 110 h.p.	82	Trainer
Blackburn N.1B	Hisso 200 h.p.	114	Sea Patrol
Beardmore W.B.1	Beardmore 230 h.p.	97	Bomber
Beardmore W.B.2	Hisso 200 h.p.	120	Reconnaissance
Bristol Scout	Le Rhone 110 h.p.	130	Scout
Bristol F.2A	Hisso 200 h.p.	112	Reconnaissance
Bristol F.2B	Sunbeam 200 h.p.	121	Fighter
Bristol F.2B	Rolls-Royce 200 h.p.	125	Fighter
D.H.6	R.A.F. 100 h.p.	66	Trainer
D.H.9	B.H.P. 240 h.p.	111	Bomber
D.H.10	Rolls-Royce (2) 250 h.p.	117	Night Bomber
Fairey 3A	Sunbeam 260 h.p.	103	General Purpose

Fairey 3B	Sunbeam 260 h.p.	96	General Purpose
Fairey F.127	Sunbeam 260 h.p.	109	General Purpose
Fairey F.128	Rolls-Royce 190 h.p.	103	General Purpose
F.E.2B	Beardmore 160 h.p.	81	Night Bomber
Grahame-White 21	Le Rhone 80 h.p.	78	Trainer
Grahame-White R.1	Le Rhone 80 h.p.	55	Trainer
Kennedy Giant	Salmson (4) 200 h.p.	?	Night Bomber
Martinsyde F.3	Rolls-Royce 275 h.p.	128	Scout
Sage 4.A	Hisso 150 h.p.	94	Ship Scout
Sage 4.B	Hisso 200 h.p.	95	Ship Scout
Sopwith Camel	Clerget 130 h.p.	119	Scout
Sopwith Camel	Bentley 150 h.p.	121	Scout
Sopwith Camel	Le Rhone 110 h.p.	110	Scout
Sopwith Camel	Mono-Gnome 150 h.p.	125	Scout
Sopwith Cuckoo	Sunbeam 200 h.p.	104	Torpedo Bomber
Short Skirl	Rolls-Royce 275 h.p.	99	Torpedo Bomber
Supermarine A.D.	Hisso 200 h.p.	112	Coast Patrol
S.E.5	Hisso 120 h.p.	120	Scout
S.E.5A	Wolseley 200 h.p.	132	Scout
Vickers F.3.11	Beardmore 230 h.p.	103	Scout
Westland N.17	Bentley R.1 150 h.p.	108	Sea Scout

* Only a test model was made. It never went into full production.

The great conflict had been raging for more than thirty months before America declared war on Germany in April 1917. Previous to that time, a small group of Americans had participated as volunteers with the French and British forces. So far as is known, no Americans volunteered to fight for Germany.

The United States Army did not fire a shot on any front until October 22, 1917, and its Air Service did not go into action until March of the following year. The U.S. Navy, of course, was able to offer its aid and strength in the battle against the German U-boats in the North Atlantic immediately after declaration of war.

A view of America's war effort from the battle zone makes it seem that the loudly proclaimed know-how, initiative, and the New World's ability to get things done was but a fantastic myth. This lag in actual participation was a grim disappointment to the civilian public and the serving soldiers who had borne the brunt of the war so long. They had entertained high hopes of the arrival of "great fleets of aircraft," "fresh divisions of spirited troops," and "convoys of new and much improved military equipment." For months American officialdom produced nothing but boastful headlines and too many unfulfilled promises. Because of the vast manpower pool, they were able to raise and provide many first-class divisions of ground troops, but in most cases these had to be armed with French artillery, tanks, machine guns, and British grenades, mortars, steel helmets, and other military equipment. This is no reflection on the superb fighting qualities of the personnel concerned. These are simply historic facts.

In the sphere of aviation America produced no first-line military aircraft. During the first twelve months as a partner of the Allies a very doubtful power plant known as the Liberty engine was designed and put into production. This theatrically publicized effort, consuming millions of dollars and a tremendous output of manpower hours, was a dreadful waste. Had half the same amount of money and time been allotted to further development or manufacture of tried-and-true Rolls-Royce, Sunbeam, B.H.P., or the new British A.B.C. radial engines, the war might have been concluded in the early spring of 1918. A full production of S.E.5's, Sopwith Snipes, Bristol Fighters, and the Handley-Page two-engined bomber might have destroyed the German Air Force by the close of 1917.

Instead American politicians and lobbyists insisted on the production of all-American equipment, from which the Thomas Morse Scout and the Loening fighter monoplane appear to have been the best of the lot, but neither went into production early enough to get to the front. The Standard Aircraft Company undertook the manufacture "and improvement" of the Handley-Page night bomber by rebuilding it to take U.S. Liberty engines. Needless to state, this was a hopeless project.

American aviation officials refused to accept the manufacturing licence to produce the Bristol Fighter—unquestionably the finest two-seater developed during the war—without incorporating "improvements" of their own conception. One such change was the substitution of a Liberty engine for the Rolls-Royce, which added so much weight and structural change that the new machine could not get off the ground. These two-seater Brisfits could have been turned out on American production lines like flivvers at the Ford factory and U.S. aviators might have been in action on the front with a first-class mount months before they were able to participate.

Instead of building the British Handley-Page or any one of several French multi-engined machines, America decided to concentrate on a home-developed specimen known as the Martin bomber, the prototype of which was bolted together and photographed just in time to make the 1919 edition of Jane's *All the World's Aircraft*. None got to the front.

Many fine prototype models were turned out by several U.S. manufacturers such as Loughead, Vought, Packard, and the Curtiss plants. The fighters resembled Spads or Camels, and the two-seaters had many of the features of the British D.H.4—with certain "improvements." However none of them ever reached the war production line.

In the meantime thousands of willing and able volunteers were applying for aviation training. Four important universities opened aviation schools. Smart uniforms were available and there were plenty of open spaces where flying could be taught to these eager fledglings—but there were no available planes except the by now obsolete Curtiss Jenny. As a result those who had restrained their enthusiasm saw the writing on the wall and quietly crossed the Canadian border to join the British. Hundreds of them were eagerly accepted, given a fast training course, and they served with distinction in British Empire squadrons.

Because of the aircraft production delay, America was unfortunately slow in getting an air service together. The candidates were ready and willing, but a lack of foresight in the early years of the war kept them grounded for months when they could have been of great value on the Western Front. As explained above, no American Air Service squadron got to the battle zone until March of 1918.

However, the Lafayette Escadrille was still playing a sterling role with the French. The squadron had seen many ups and downs, and when the United States joined the Allies there was little hope of extending the Escadrille. As a matter of fact plans were soon under way to "borrow" these skilled and experienced aviators to provide cadre groups around which to build U.S. service squadrons.

Shortly before the death of Norman Prince, which occurred after the bombing raid on the Mauser arms factory, the squadron received newer and somewhat improved Nieuports. Raoul Lufbery and Kiffin Rockwell were the first to have their guns sighted and engines tuned, and together they went off on a two-ship patrol. By now the Germans had concentrated several fighter squadrons opposite the Luxeuil area to counter the sorties made by the American volunteers.

As usual, these two soon became separated and Lufbery went headlong after a Hannoveraner which turned out to be a decoy. He no sooner opened fire on the two-seater than he was attacked from all sides by a flight of Fokkers. He managed to wriggle out of this trap with much difficulty and hurried back to a field just behind his own lines, and the first news he received there was that Rockwell had been shot down and killed.

Kiffin Rockwell had also found an enemy target and if he only could nail him he would move into the ace list. Holding a position above the Fokker, he attempted to get into an up-sun spot from where he started his dive, but before he pressed the trigger the enemy pilot spotted him and turned to exchange bursts. Rockwell held true to his course and did not fire until he had the enemy clean in the ring sight. Before he could open fire, however, the Fokker sprayed him and a series of slugs cut his main spar at the wing root. Still he continued on, daring the Fokker to stay on course, and when they were about 30 yards apart he pressed his trigger. The German avoided a collision by swerving sharply and Rockwell went on through in a fairly steep dive. As he pulled out to continue the attack his wings broke away, and the new Nieuport spun in, a short distance inside the French lines. When the wreckage was inspected it was discovered that besides the damage to his main spar, Rockwell had taken an explosive bullet in his chest.

During the middle of October 1916 the Lafayette Escadrille was moved from the comparative calm of the Vosges to take part in the Somme offensive, where they played an honourable and conspicuous part. During that campaign they destroyed a total of thirty-eight enemy aircraft.

James McConnell was killed in the air on March 19, 1917, leaving only Bill Thaw of the original group of seven. Prince, Rockwell, Chapman, and McConnell were killed in action. Cowdin had to leave because of ill health. Bert Hall was somewhere in the Balkans training Russian pilots, so some records state. But there were many enthusiastic volunteers to take the places of those who went west, and by the time America declared war on Germany more than three hundred names were inscribed on the French aviation lists. The example of the original seven had borne a crop of fine fruit.

McConnell, in particular, was a splendid example of the idealistic American volunteer. Never a great pilot, he continued his efforts, ignoring several dangerous or amusing escapades. In his first flight over the Vosges he became lost and floated about for two hours trying to find a familiar landmark. Eventually he had to descend and fortunately selected a farm in French territory, and was soon returned to his squadron mates.

In quick succession he cracked up his machine twice on landing and was painfully injured both times, and as a result did not rack up flight time or fighting experience so fast as the others, but he never lost heart. Two weeks after the escadrille was moved to the Somme area he was back in routine action. At the time the Allied forces were superior to the German Air Service and it was not difficult to run up a score.

One of the newer pilots to join the Americans was Edmond Genet, a New Yorker, said to be a descendant of Citizen Genet, who became a very sincere friend of Thomas Jefferson shortly after the Revolution. Genet and McConnell teamed up immediately, and on March 19 flew together over the battle area beyond Ham. Edwin Parsons accompanied them on this flight for a time but later went off stalking on his own.

Within an hour McConnell spotted three enemy planes behind Saint-Quentin and signalling to Genet, he started his attack. During the heat of this melee Genet was struck in the cheek and had several bullets seriously damage his machine; with that he sensed he was in too tough a league and headed for his field, but McConnell never returned. Later McConnell's Nieuport was reported down between Saint-Quentin and Chauny. Three days later advancing Allied troops came upon the wreckage and what was presumed to be McConnell's body. It had been stripped of all articles of clothing and identification and was unrecognizable even to his friends. He was buried, just as he had requested, near where he fell, in a small garden plot in a coffin made of old doors taken from a wrecked house.

McConnell had been proposed for the *Croix de guerre* on the day of his death and in his diary he had written on his twenty-ninth birthday: "This war will perhaps be my death, but in spite of all, I owe it a profound gratitude." He was the last American wearing a French uniform who was killed while fighting in the air before the United States declared war on Germany.

Genet was killed by German anti-aircraft batteries on April 16. He had been feeling ill for some time but insisted on accompanying Raoul Lufbery on a duty flight, although other pilots had offered to take his place. It was a cloudy day and the two Americans had to fly low to keep in touch with the ground and as they crossed the lines they encountered heavy enemy fire. Almost immediately Genet went into a sloppy half turn, and Raoul thought his partner was returning to their field, so he tried to follow him to make certain but lost him in a low cloud bank. A short time later a message was received stating that Genet had fallen inside the French lines with a large chunk of anti-aircraft shell in his body. He had made a valiant effort to return to his field but apparently lost consciousness in the air, and his Nieuport crashed in the middle of a road with the engine running at top speed. He was buried during a blinding snowstorm, but the instant his body had been laid to rest and Captain Thenault had said the "Amen," the sun pierced the clouds for an instant and illuminated the bier "like a benediction from heaven," as one of the pilots remarked.

When the United States entered the war many of the American volunteers were too busy to celebrate the great event but a number naturally hoped to transfer to their expeditionary force once one had reached the front. One small group still serving with the Foreign Legion wrote a letter to President Wilson offering their services, to which they received the following reply from H. T. Dean, Adjutant General:

The subject of utilization of the services of Americans serving abroad has received the careful consideration of the War Department in a number of instances and the conclusion has been reached that it is not deemed for the best interest of United States for the War Department to request the discharge of Americans serving in the Allied Armies, except in special cases where it is clearly advantageous to do so.

After weeks of disappointment several Americans took their leaves in Paris where they appealed to the U.S. officials there, but they had the usual struggle with red tape and only a special few were accepted eventually.

Meanwhile the Lafayette Escadrille was moved up and down the front wherever their services were needed. As were all French squadrons, it was limited to twelve to fifteen pilots and any other American volunteers were dispersed among other French pursuit, bombardment, or observation squadrons along the front. Actually, only thirty-eight American pilots and four French guidance officers were ever on the rolls of the Lafayette Escadrille, although many more who served with the French often claimed that honour.

Among American volunteers who served valiantly with

other French squadrons was Frederick Zinn, who, while flying with the F.24 observation squadron, won the *Croix de guerre* for his *sang-froid* and daring while carrying out a number of photographic patrols. He was promoted to the rank of sergeant in the summer of 1917 and added another citation to his record.

Herman Chatkoff of Brooklyn, who had gone abroad after a family quarrel, became stranded in Paris and washed automobiles in order to eat. When the war erupted in August he told French officials that he had served with distinction in the Salvation Army and so was accepted in the Foreign Legion. He fought long and well until he was struck down with an illness while in the trenches. After a long period in the hospital he volunteered to fly and wound up with the C.11 escadrille, where he won the *Croix de guerre* for his skill, daring, and devotion to duty.

On June 15 he flew over to visit the Lafayette Escadrille field and after lunching with several American pilots agreed to take up a young American war worker, Benjamin Woodworth, for a spin. The exhibition, which was remembered for a long while, ended in tragedy. He put on such a performance with the old Caudron that the Nieuport pilots could no longer look at the wild spectacle. He finally lost control low down and they crashed. Woodworth actually was cut in two at the waist and Chatkoff so badly injured that he spent the rest of the war in the hospital and came home with a seriously impaired mind.

In contrast to the treatment accorded Americans in the French infantry and other air squadrons, a great deal of pressure was put on the pilots of the Lafayette to have them serve with the U.S. forces. Most of them were ready and willing, but many of them felt that they owed a debt to France, which had spent an average of $10,000 each to train them, and they also had become attached to their French comrades. They were disappointed at the pace at which American forces were being enlisted and trained and sincerely felt they could render the best service to the Allied cause by remaining where they were until the U.S. Aviation Service was ready to take its place at the front.

But after months of reflection and some outside pressure the Lafayette Escadrille flyers decided in the autumn of 1917 to offer their services to their own colours, but as they had feared there was considerable delay in cutting red tape and it was not until February 18, 1918, that they were accepted by their own country, at which time they became known as the

One Hundred and Third Pursuit Squadron. Since there were no other American squadrons at the front ready for active service, the squadron remained where it was, attached to the French Groupe de Combat 15, and under the command of Bill Thaw.

All of these Lafayette Escadrille pilots received commissions in what was then the United States Air Service. Lufbery and Bill Thaw became majors, Robert Soubiran was made a captain, and William Dugan, a first lieutenant. By early summer of 1918 most of them were scattered through the American squadrons as commanding officers or flight leaders. Thaw later took command of the Third Pursuit Group and ended the war as a lieutenant colonel. Raoul Lufbery eventually was attached to the First Pursuit Group and after weary months of sitting in an office at Issoudun finally got back into action near Toul, where he was killed on his first actual combat as an American flying man. He had won the French Legion of Honour, the *Croix de guerre* with ten palms, and the British Military Medal, as well as several other Allied medals.

Robert Soubiran succeeded Thaw as the commanding officer of the One Hundred and Third Pursuit Squadron and eventually was promoted to major and, although seldom mentioned in World War I history, had won the Legion of Honour and the *Croix de guerre* with two palms. He was not a great fighter with a lengthy record of kills, but his leadership and administrative ability were recognized by the French.

The air-war took several new turns for France in 1917, with new machines and new tactics being used on the various fronts. With a complete switch, they produced a new concept in bombing after General Lyautey was appointed Minister of War. Lyautey immediately made plans for a great Air Service expansion in which he proposed to weld the army and navy sections into one unit. He created the General Directorate of Aeronautical Services on February 9 and placed General Guillemin at its head, but just what plans these two men had in mind will never be known as a political crisis erupted and their ideas were not put into action.

However, the French opened 1917 with a dashing plan of bombing operations with Escadrille VB.101 conducting an offensive that continued unabated for three weeks. Ten machines delivered 8,500 pounds of high explosive to important targets on the first day, and before the operation was over more than 53,000 pounds had been dropped with the loss of but two machines.

French night bombers unloaded 100,840 pounds of bombs

throughout January and February, making life very difficult for German munitions workers.

What seems to have deposed the Lyautey-Guillemin combine was the failure of French manufacturers to deliver the new aircraft that had been promised. The French Deputies accused the War Council of slackness, and there was a swift change of government. General Lyautey relinquished his command and was quickly superseded by Guillemin. The proposed union of the army and navy services went by the board, but by April 1 M. Vincent was put in charge of Military Aeronautics and the French Air Service was soon back in collective action.

French bombers were unperturbed by the political hagglings and continued to carry on their difficult but rewarding work. Farman 25 dropped 6,000 pounds of explosive on the last night of April, and VB.101 outdid itself by carrying out more than one hundred raids during the same month when they delivered 25 and a half tons of bombs on important objectives. Then Caudron 46 hit the German Third Aircraft Park at Soissons with a full ton of explosives, and on the same evening VB.101 and VB.102 staged a joint raid on the same park, setting a large experimental shed on fire. Four other squadrons dropped 8 tons of bombs on the munitions factories around Metz, and their return journey was a thriller, for they were intercepted by fifty enemy aircraft. However, the French maintained a tight formation and fought their way back with only two losses, while three German scouts fell before the bomber observers' guns.

The French Naval Air Service was back in the news again early in June. A fishing smack wirelessed that it had sighted a U-boat moving on the surface in the channel, and in answer five French torpedo planes took off from Le Havre and within forty minutes had sighted the commerce raider. As they pounced, the submarine made a crash dive, but the French airmen were determined to get a kill. They bombed the area for half an hour and finally were rewarded with several great air bubbles and a satisfactory patch of oil.

On June 3 French bombers surpassed all their previous records by dropping thirty-seven tons of explosives on enemy redoubts at distances up to 250 miles away. Again VB.101 took the lead with a delivery of 21,750 pounds and every day throughout this month showed similar operations; on the fifteenth some seventy-three tons rained down on German railway and munitions centres.

The French air effort continued in this manner and now the names of the bomber crews were as widely publicised as those of the ace pilots in the honours lists. In fact, in 1917 the bombers received more decorations than did the scouts, a statement that cannot be made by any other air service.

On July 7 Sergeant Pilot Gallons was cited for extreme gallantry shown on a solo raid against the Krupp munitions factory at Essen, when, during the course of this flight, he covered 440 miles in seven hours with a bullet-shattered elbow. Exactly one week later Sub-lieutenant Giallet of the Brest seaplane station was awarded the *Médaille Militaire* for destroying an enemy submarine. In the first few moments of this action Giallet was wounded in both legs by shrapnel splinters but stuck to his target until a well-directed bomb tore the stern off the U-boat and it sank with all hands.

Most of the old Voisins and Caudrons were withdrawn from service by August and replaced with the new Bréguets, Letords, Caudron R.4's and twin-engined Farmans. Several hundred British Sopwith one and one-half Strutters, turned out under licence, were being issued to artillery and reconnaissance squadrons, and, although outmoded on the British front, these old Sops performed well in many French squadrons and later were handed over to a few American squadrons and were in service up to the Armistice.

The new machines received their baptism of fire during the second week in August, and in the preliminary operation to the battle of Saint-Quentin forty French bombers stayed in action for thirty-six hours strafing strong points, machine-gun nests, concentration points, artillery positions, and all reserve lines. When they withdrew, all the infantry had to do was to walk across no-man's land and consolidate the wreckage that had once been a strong line of defence.

This great offensive bombing was maintained up until the last few days of the year; neither the enemy nor the adverse weather conditions could hamper their activities and by the end of 1917 the bombers had dropped a total of 108 tons of explosive during their daylight raids and 600 tons at night. As impressive as this may seem for those days, the French Air Force more than tripled this effort the next year.

While the German fighter squadrons were scoring heavily during the first four months of 1917, they apparently gave little attention to the French fighters, concentrating their chief forces on the British front. It was just as well, for unfortunately the new French fighters had turned out to be disappointing duds. Their engines failed above 8,000 feet; controls were too slack for the type of precision flying demanded, and

247 French scouts were lost—most of them with engine trouble over the enemy lines—in a period of ten weeks.

Other troubles harassed the scouts too. Their observation and reconnaissance mates were taking a beating, complaining that the much publicised fighters were never to be seen. The reason of course was that the "aces" were unable to get into the air or stay there long enough to be of any protective use.

Despite the inclement weather in the opening winter months of 1917 the top-ranking aces were still doing their share. Georges Guynemer, miraculously still alive, scored five times in three days. Heurteaux, Doumer, and Madon were clinging to their positions in the ace list. New names such as Delorme, Gastin, and Hauss were appearing regularly in the news columns, showing that the scouts were at least trying under unenviable conditions.

During February twenty-three Huns were shot down; only one by Guynemer, his thirty-first, but it was a memorable victory. Georges came upon a giant two-engined bomber, a type he had not seen before, one of the new German Gothas. He made a clean job of it and French designers soon gave it a close inspection. Guynemer was promoted to captain for this kill, and Russia awarded him the Cross of St. George.

There was another political upheaval in France and an Inter-Allied Aviation Service was formed to exchange ideas with the Allied air services. A new plane-testing system was evolved in which war-front airmen were brought back regularly to check out all new machines to make sure they fitted active-service requirements, and from this point on French scout squadrons were much better equipped.

Most of the bugs had been eliminated in the new Spad's engines by the beginning of May, and the French scouts were again successful, downing 108 enemy aircraft that month. At the same time British fighters had been given their new Camels, S.E.5's, and Bristol Fighters, and the Albatros and Fokker scouts were openly on the run.

But these periods of success were generally bitterly paid for and prominent names began to appear in the French casualty lists. Captain René Doumer, a highly skilled bomber of the early days, had transferred to the Storks and run up a very respectable record. He shot down an Albatros in flames on April 1 and then received a slight wound that hospitalised him for a short while. On May 23 he went off on a lone offensive patrol and was trapped by five enemy scouts. He put up a brilliant battle, but a single bullet pierced his heart and he fell in his own lines. A few hours later two Stork pilots evened the score by downing Oberleutnant Reinhold, commander of Staffel 15.

The next French ace to be brought down was Lieutenant Sauvage, followed a few days later by Marechal des Logis Hauss. Lieutenant de Laage de Meux, who had been second-in-command of the Lafayette Escadrille, also lost his life in May. Albert Heurteaux, another ace of the Storks, was shot down and badly wounded on May 3, and the best-loved of them all, René Dorme, fell to his death on May 25. Along with Lieutenant Deullin, Dorme had left the Fismes field and flown deep into enemy territory, where they were attacked by five Albatros D.3's. Deullin saw Dorme send one down in flames, but in the closing fight he disappeared completely and his end and final resting place is still a mystery.

Burning with a mad desire to avenge "Papa" Dorme, Guynemer took off late that same afternoon and literally ran wild; flying over Goyencourt, he first shot down an L.V.G. two-seater in flames. This plane had been used as a decoy and immediately three German scouts poured down on the French flyer, and within five minutes two of the three were twirling down minus their wings and the third was scurrying homeward. Returning to Fismes, Guynemer caught a Rumpler and a Fokker directly over the aerodrome and with the last thirty rounds left in his belts he shot down both of them. Two combats, five victories—in a two-hour patrol.

Nungesser ran up his score to twenty-nine by downing eight (confirmed) enemy aircraft in this same month. Pinsard racked up five, Madon four, Matton three, and a new name was soon to rise to the top of the "ace" list. This was René Fonck, who downed his first five planes in a comparatively short time. He eventually became France's ace of aces with seventy-five confirmed enemy aircraft.

Only sixty-five enemy planes were accounted for in June, and at the end of the month Guynemer went to Villacoublay, where a new idea was brewing. It was hoped that gunpower might be stepped up by fitting a 37-mm. light cannon to a new Spad 22. This plane was powered by an Hispano-Suiza engine incorporating a reduction gear box which allowed the gun to be placed behind the short hollow prop shaft. This would give a pilot an air cannon which would need no interrupter gear, or the one-pounder shell would travel through the centre of the propeller boss. On paper it seemed like the ideal solution to an old problem.

After a short factory drill in the use of the weapon Guynemer took his new *Vieux Charles* into the air over the front on July 16, where he met an Albatros D.3, and a direct hit over a range of more than 200 yards blew both the Albatros and its pilot to smithereens. However, the recoil from the unwieldy gun was a menace, and the fumes from the expelled cartridges almost asphyxiated Guynemer, so for a time the Spad-cannon idea was discarded. Later René Fonck developed the gun to some advantage and scored many victories with the unusual weapon.

At this point in our history Georges Guynemer was dying a slow death from tuberculosis. He must have known he had a very short active life left, for he suddenly went berserk, and by August 1 had fifty planes to his credit. During this period he had fainted twice in the air at high altitude, and how he got down no one ever knew. His end came—if such it was—on September 11, a month when France lost more than seventy scout pilots.

On that day while flying over Poelcapelle with Lieutenant Bozon-Verduraz and Captain Deullin, Guynemer attacked a Rumpler two-seater, evidently acting as a decoy, for a few seconds later his companions were pounced on by eight Fokker D.5's. By the time the two Frenchmen had fought their way clear, Guynemer had vanished. That is the story in its briefest form. The details are part of history and worth repeating.

Guynemer had experienced nothing but bad luck over the previous three or four days; the weather was uncertain and when he went into the sky some wayward bullet seemingly from nowhere would set up some minor but annoying damage and his flights ended with emergency landings anywhere but on his own field. His illness was beginning to tell on him, and he moved about with a sallow complexion and the tense expression of a very nervous man. He would start for church and as suddenly decide not to go. He would head for the hangars, borrow a companion's plane, and almost immediately it would develop some unbelievable malfunction. He would pace back and forth from his tent to the hangars hour after hour. His friends begged him to rest, and a physician had him fixed up in a private room in a nearby villa, but he stayed there only a few days. The delivery of a new plane was delayed thereby hoping to encourage him to take things easy, but instead Guynemer went into the hangars, stripped off his captain's jacket, and worked like a man possessed on any available repair job.

The weather on September 11 was still uncertain, a seaside fog had blanketed the area, and after a restless night Guynemer was determined to rush off for Buc aerodrome to find out why his new plane was not available, but a train for Paris would not leave until afternoon, which meant another delay.

Then there was a report that Majors du Peuty and Brocard of the office of the Minister of Aeronautics were coming down by an early train, and someone suggested that a talk with them might expedite matters with reference to any new equipment. Guynemer accepted that, but within half an hour the weather cleared and he hurried off to the sheds, where he discovered that *Vieux Charles*, his personal Spad, had been somewhat renovated. The motor had been tuned, the guns checked, and a water pump had been replaced. Commander Heurteaux, who was in the hospital with a war wound, had left Guynemer in charge, so it was just a matter of making a decision in his own favour.

Lieutenant Bozon-Verduraz was available and most willing to accompany Captain Guynemer. Deullin wanted a Boche. Only some clod thought to mention the almost immediate arrival of du Peuty and Brocard. "Won't you wait until they arrive, mon Capitaine?"

Guynemer's answer was a wave toward the sky, and everyone who sensed his nervousness decided to say no more. When he was in these moods no one knew how to approach him. The two Department of Aeronautics majors had been met and greeted at the station and they hoped to be at the field in time to intercept Guynemer. They were five minutes late. He had left at 8.35 a.m.

Guynemer led his two flying companions south-east, picking up the Langemarck road and the smear that was once a railroad between Ypres and Thorout. From there they went along the Saint-Julien-Poelcapelle road. There were no German patrols in the area, so they turned in deeper, until Guynemer's keen sight picked up a German two-seater, and moved into a position behind and below the German's tail plane. He had great respect for a coolheaded gunner, so he approached with zigzag movement. His first burst was badly off and the German went into a spin. Bozon-Verduraz, who was waiting below, also missed. During this second attack Bozon-Verduraz noticed a formation of German scouts and, as previously arranged, he moved below them to act as bait. This trick had been used time and time again. The last picture of this fight that Bozon-Verduraz carried away with him was that of Guynemer trying to find the proper instant to shoot. The German scouts above made a pass at Bozon-Verduraz and then broke up, sensing the decoy idea, and the Stork pilot swept back to rejoin Guynemer. He never saw him again.

The harassed lieutenant stayed aloft until he had very little fuel left in his tanks, but there was no trace of Guynemer. When he arrived back at their field his first words were an inquiry for his leader.

"Not back yet," someone muttered, and Bozon-Verduraz knew Guynemer had been taken from them.

The great legend began to unfold. Anxious men got on a telephone or checked through every channel to the balloon lines. Hour after hour passed. Small flights of searching aircraft went out and scoured the whole Peolcapelle area, but there was no evidence of a shattered machine anywhere.

Dinner that night was a melancholy affair. French, British, and Belgian comrades burst in from neighbouring fields demanding reassuring news. There was no news of any sort. No one dared take Guynemer's chair. Some talked of the possibility of Guynemer's being a prisoner of war; yet they all remembered that he had always snarled: "Those Boche! They will never get me alive!"

Ten long days passed, and officialdom had to admit that Georges Guynemer, the idol of the Storks, was missing after an engagement with an enemy biplane over Poelcapelle (Belgium). Nothing had been heard from the German side of the line, and neither of the von Richthofens had him on their lists. He had simply disappeared. Then came the day when the Germans dropped some notes on a British field explaining that certain "English" flyers had been shot down in certain areas on such and such dates; then, as an afterthought, they added a note concerning a Captain Guynemer, stating that he had been shot down at 8 a.m. on September 10. The hour and day were wrong. Guynemer was alive and enjoying breakfast in his own mess at that particular hour. Obviously the Germans had heard the French report on Guynemer's loss and had quickly inserted his name in a list of British prisoners. If they *had* made a mistake on the day, the time was wrong, as Guynemer did not leave the ground until 8.35 a.m.

Bozon-Verduraz went over every detail of that fatal flight. No one could believe that Guynemer was dead, that the lad with the piercing eyes could ever die. He was superhuman, a man whom death could not vanquish. One poetic writer in Paris offered an idyllic solution which to this day is told to French school children.

"Guynemer flew so high he could not come down again!"

By October 4 the British had taken Poelcapelle, but the Germans counter-attacked and regained it. The village was once more in British hands by the ninth and they searched for Guynemer's grave, but no trace of it was ever found. In fact the Germans acknowledged officially that both the body of

193

Guynemer and his aeroplane had disappeared completely. There were vague reports that he was brought down from a height of 21,000 feet over the village and fell near the Poelcapelle cemetery. Three German soldiers were said to have sworn that they found the machine with a wing shot off, and the pilot had been shot through the head and his shoulder and one leg had been broken in the crash. How would they know? The Germans later published a list of French machines that had fallen inside their lines, but the numbers of Guynemer's *Vieux Charles* was not among them.

We shall have to accept the probability that Guynemer crashed somewhere in the Poelcapelle district and that, almost immediately after, the heavy ground fire, preliminary to the British attack on the village, completely obliterated all traces of his end. There had been no military funeral, so Guynemer had accepted nothing from his enemies—not even a wooden cross.

Various versions of his end were bandied about, and for a time it was generally agreed—in Germany at any rate—that Guynemer had been shot down by a Captain Wisseman, a Rumpler two-seater pilot.

Curiously enough Fonck, who later headed the Storks, killed Wisseman four days after Guynemer's disappearance.

But one of the most fantastic legends was persistently told about the mysterious end of France's most popular ace. This atrocious fable was a basic plot of pulp air-story writers for years. It went something like this.

Guynemer was not killed in an air duel with a German; after all, no German could kill Guynemer. Instead, he died ignominiously of the dread disease that had racked his body for months, in the back room of some disreputable *estaminet;* although Georges seldom ventured inside any of these pothouses. This could not be the traditional end for such a hero; heroes died in glorious action in the Great Tradition, and so his friends secretly carried the body of their hero out of the *estaminet,* and a small group of French pilots propped him up in the seat of his machine—*Vieux Charles*—the safety-belt was tightened and the controls tied in neutral position. The engine was started, the chocks pulled from the wheels, and the throttle opened wide. Thus, the famous Spad fighter took off with the earthly remains of the Great Guynemer to fly deep into the enemy lines where, after the fuel had been consumed, it crashed—no one ever found out where.

The Great Tradition had been upheld.

No war can compete with World War I in the origination of improbable legends, and this one concerning the death of

Georges Guynemer is probably the most improbable—and fascinating.

The last few months of 1917 were filled with heavy rain and fog, and flying on the French front was curtailed. Many pilots were lost when erratic engines failed and they were forced to land in enemy areas, but despite these deterrents French fighter pilots continued to invade Germany and hammer away at their adversaries. At the close of the year the leading *chasse* pilots were Nungesser with a total of thirty-two victories; Fonck with nineteen; Pinsard, seventeen; Madon, seventeen; and Boyeau had eleven. Among the unfortunate aces who had gone to Valhalla during the closing months were Sanglier who had a score of fourteen; Mathieu de la Tour, nine; Auger, seven and Tochard, five.

Up to December 28, 1917, the French Air Service claimed 2,192 enemy planes destroyed or captured, 1,075 claimed but not confirmed, and seventy-six observation balloons totally destroyed. Of these totals the Storks had destroyed 221 planes and eighteen balloons against a casualty sheet of forty-four pilots killed or wounded. No over-all casualty list has ever been published for this year, but a fair estimate would be about 2,500 killed or wounded.

The French manufacturers produced the following types of machines during 1917.

FRENCH WARPLANES OF 1917

Make	Engine	Speed m.p.h.	Purpose
Bréguet 14B2	Renault 310 h.p.	112	Reconnaissance
Bréguet 16B2	Renault 310 h.p.	110	Reconnaissance
Caudron R.4	Renault (2) 140 h.p.	96	Bomber
Caudron G.4	Le Rhone (2) 110 h.p.	95	Bomber
Donnet F.B.	Hisso 200 h.p.	72	Sea Patrol
Dorand A.R.2A2	Renault 200 h.p.	108	Reconnaissance
Farman F.	Salmson 260 h.p.	110	Reconnaissance
Farman F.30B	Salmson 260 h.p.	105	Reconnaissance
Letord 3	Salmson (2) 175 h.p.	85	Bomber
Letord 5	Lorraine 240 h.p.	100	Reconnaissance
Salmson 4 A.B.2	Salmson 230 h.p.	108	Reconnaissance
Salmson 5 A.2	Salmson 230 h.p.	105	Reconnaissance
Spad S.7	Hisso 220 h.p.	115	Fighter
Spad 15	Hisso 150 h.p.	115	Fighter
Spad 17	Hisso 200 h.p.	122	Fighter
Spad 178 B	Hisso 200 h.p.	98	Reconnaissance

6

THE YEAR OF
TACTICAL AVIATION—

1918

☐ This year, which was to see the total defeat of the German Air Force but an inconclusive victory over the German people, opened gloomily for the Allied airmen. A fourth spring in a row came in with a period of setbacks and defeats while the widely publicized German *Kanones* added to their scores. As we have shown, 1917 provided the arena, the airmen, and the machines for high-altitude combat which wrote amazing records for the fighter squadrons on both sides of the lines. It was the fighter pilot's greatest year, for he had been encouraged to duel instead of to carry out the less romantic duties of tactical warfare. While flying at 14,000-18,000 feet engaged in this knightly combat, he had furnished little support to the infantryman below.

The bloody battle of Cambrai, fought through November and December, received little true air support from the Allied flying services. Bad weather and fog conspired to keep routine reconnaissance to a minimum, but in all honesty little effort was made to give the infantry the air cover it required. As a result, although Cambrai was rightfully a British victory, it might have played a more vital role in the eventual triumph. Germany's March push in the following spring might never have been attempted had the R.F.C. devoted more of its heroism to tactical support over Cambrai rather than to striving for the false rewards of high-altitude air combat.

On the other hand Ludendorff and Hindenburg could not have considered their March push had they not been able to move forty-two divisions from the shattered Russian front and bring in more than 6,000 guns, one-third of which had been captured from the Italians in the Piave fiasco. The French armies had not recovered from their disasters of 1917, and the British ground forces had been cruelly weakened by the costly offensives of the two previous summers. General Haig had been forced to reorganize what divisions he had left on a nine instead of a twelve-battalion basis. Besides all this, Clemenceau had discounted the arrival of the first American forces and had appealed to General Haig to take over another twenty-eight miles of French front.

Before the Battle of Cambrai had ended in the mud around Flesquiers, Ribécourt, and Gauzeaucourt it was evident the enemy was planning a last-ditch attack that would take him to the Channel ports, to Paris, and to a dictated peace. As a result the Allies were forced to switch suddenly to the defensive and adopt a new over-all elastic movement. They were at last to assume a programme of tactical air warfare.

General Trenchard, who was about to become Chief of Air Staff of the new Royal Air Force, had left a memo at R.F.C. headquarters in France that the air offensive must be continued at all costs, but added that their first duty was to watch for any hostile ground movement and to gather all information concerning such movements. To carry out this order the R.F.C. was expected to provide all forms of air support at any moment.

General Salmond, who succeeded Trenchard, held the same opinion and early in February took measures to strengthen all squadrons available to the British Fifth Army. He predicted that the Germans would attack between the Sensée River and Saint-Quentin—the Fifth Army's front—and he was correct. He also believed the Germans were holding a great portion of their air force in reserve, but unfortunately his views did not coincide with those of General Headquarters, where as late as March 8 it was denied that the big blow would fall on General Gough's Fifth Army.

Thus, practically to a squadron, the Royal Flying Corps was taken off its regular duty of fighting in the air and put on low-altitude tactical missions. The Camels carried four 20-pound Cooper bombs, S.E.5's became two-gun trench strafers, and Nieuports did what they could to provide cover at low altitude for the planes carrying out these unfamiliar ground-attack duties. The Bristol Fighters, which had been sweeping the skies at 15,000-17,000 feet, were now trench-strafing, bombing enemy pillboxes, shooting up Germany's new tanks, or photographing enemy movement in the back areas.

As a result, while the German infantryman complained loudly that the sky was full of British machines and where was the German Air Force, the rebuilt flying-circus formations were having a glorious time. Their newspapers were full of the exploits of the two von Richthofen boys, a little-publicized airman, Ernst Udet, Hermann Goering, Carl Bolle, Willy Reinhardt, Erich Lowenhardt, Kurt Wusthoff, and several others. American papers reprinted these deeds, and the impression in the United States was that British airmen were doing nothing, Haig had his back to the wall, and the Allies were simply marking time until Uncle Sam came to their rescue.

As the fateful March approached, the weather added to the Allied difficulties, for low reconnaissance flying was almost impossible. The German ground forces were moved into strategic positions with no trouble. Between March 17 and 20 low clouds and rain obscured the whole area. What few captives were taken in trench raids provided the information that the big push would start on the twentieth. Late that day the weather improved somewhat, and a small R.F.C. patrol went out and noted that the German front-line strength was being relieved—a sure sign of an attack. When it came some hours later bad weather set in again, so the information was apparently ignored, and the offensive burst as a complete surprise. Onrushing Germans suddenly appeared out of a bank of fog and mist and for a time nothing could stop them.

It is not necessary to relate full details of that March push here. What interests us at this point is that the R.F.C. had gathered 579 serviceable aircraft, of which 261 were single-seater fighters. Against these the German Air Force stacked 730, of which 326 were fighters. Thus from the start the enemy had a numerical superiority and were not hampered with detailed reconnaissance duties, trench strafing, or tactical bombing. They simply stayed inside their own lines and attacked any British plane that appeared in their area.

The German superiority in numbers was the result, first, of a new unity of command, second, of tremendous efforts in their aircraft factories, and third, of the introduction of seventeen new artillery-spotting flights, provided with equipment far superior to anything previously used in gunnery cooperation. Much of this had been planned because of the great fear that America would soon be producing an overwhelming quantity of first-line aircraft.

Before the offensive started, British air operations had been largely confined to reconnaissance and bombing. Army Corps squadrons had flown hundreds of hours engaging enemy batteries and photographing stretches of wire, strong points, supply dumps, and other features of military importance.

For the first time, British aircraft were employed in a full programme of tactical and strategic operations. They were not in the air to shoot down enemy planes; they attacked only enemy planes that were interfering with the bombers, reconnaissance, artillery, and trench-strafing squadrons. To engage the enemy's air force and destroy his aircraft was not an end in itself but only a means to an end. They had to be destroyed in order that the tactical squadrons could carry out their task of engaging the enemy ground forces. By March of 1918 both sides had recognized the importance of a completely integrated air service, but only the R.F.C. was successful in forming it.

While German aces were adding to their scores as fighting airmen, they provided no air support for their infantrymen, and the German Army was beaten back after its March offensive and eventually lost the war. Germany perhaps had the most aces and ran up the most impressive scores, but the British in particular fought this last year of the war with every club in the bag, as golfers say. When it was all over the new Royal Air Force (the integration of the R.F.C. and the R.N.A.S.) had perfected the co-operative system. They had developed skilled trench strafers, night bombing, tactical bombing, and a method of artillery cooperation that finally blasted the German Army back across the Rhine.

I am not alone in this opinion. General William (Billy) Mitchell, who was to command America's Air Service, had listened carefully to the theories of General Trenchard and absorbed "Boom's" belief in the importance of both a tactical and strategic command. He believed as did Trenchard that the "ace" system of "swatting planes one at a time" was wasteful and that the enemy air service could be eliminated more effectively by striking at his factories, his aircraft pools, and his front-area hangars, where one bomb would totally destroy aircraft by the dozens before they could be flown into action. Mitchell was to work furiously to develop an air service of two separate commands—tactical and strategic.

Throughout the opening months of 1918 Germany continued to monopolize the headlines of the world's press, but in April she was to mournfully "lead" her own publications with a loss that certainly should have been avoided.

It will be recalled that Baron Manfred von Richthofen had received a serious head wound in August 1917 which kept him out of action for some time. He was never quite the war-

200

rior he had been after that and by the close of the March push the Red Knight was a very tired man. Why he was allowed to continue to fight at the front has never been explained. After all, he had more than served his time, giving generously of himself to the German cause. He held such a commanding lead as a flying-circus fighter that the decision to keep him on active service was sheer stupidity. His eventual loss had a greater effect on the morale of his service than any addition to his lengthy score could have added to his stature as an air leader.

The end, which was inevitable, came on April 21, 1918. The story has been told many times by popular press writers who were never at the front or in any way connected with World War I, with much mawkish sentiment and in most cases little consideration for actual facts. Some say that the British had actually formed a special neck-or-nothing squadron of fighters who were put on the front with the sole responsibility of downing a certain red triplane. Von Richthofen was never that important to friend or foe. Most airmen who were in the vicinity at the time have dismissed the Baron's end with very few words of sentiment. More often—particularly in the case of the British—the news was learned with some satisfaction, and many R.F.C. squadrons put on a special "guest night" in celebration. They did, of course, observe strict military courtesy and buried Baron von Richthofen with full honours.

The Flying Uhlan's end is as legendary as that of Georges Guynemer or Albert Ball. No one knows exactly how he died. It is known that he was shot down and crashed in the village of Sailly-le-Sec in the Amiens area of the Somme. Who shot him down is anyone's guess.

The popular version is that von Richthofen had left his main formation to chase Lieutenant W. R. (Wop) May, a native of Edmonton, Canada—not an Australian as often reported—of No. 209 Squadron. Von Richthofen was in turn attacked by Captain Roy Brown, also a Canadian, who had no idea who this opponent might be. Brown was May's Flight Commander.

From this point on the history of von Richthofen's end is very confused. The standard version is that Brown, flying a Camel, fired a long burst at a red Fokker triplane which happened to be flown by Baron von Richthofen. Brown did not see the red triplane crash, but two members of his flight claimed that they did. On the basis of this it is generally accepted that Roy Brown killed Baron von Richthofen, and recently I have talked with men who served with Brown and had spent some time with him and who declare that Brown was reasonably positive he shot down von Richthofen.

However, in Australia they have another version of von Richthofen's end. There they stoutly declare that von Richthofen was shot down by two Australian machine gunners who were guarding an Aussie artillery battery. As a matter of fact both these men were awarded the Distinguished Conduct Medal for their success. In this variation of the story the Australians claim a red triplane was following a British Camel down. A second Camel was firing at the German triplane, but the enemy ship did not leave its line of flight until converging bursts of fire from two ground guns caught it as it swept toward the Australian artillery battery. Then it half stalled, wavered, and finally piled up in an open space in the French village.

When British investigators examined the wreckage and discovered who the pilot was, they traced the bullets that had killed him. There were several in the framework of the machine, but two that penetrated his right and left breast had killed him. These must have been fired from the ground to have entered and left von Richthofen's chest as they did. Brown had fired a long burst, but he had been above and behind the red triplane. Another version is that Brown pulled out of his dive to come up beside von Richthofen and had fired at him from a sharp angle.

However, if you delve deep enough into the many explanations of this rather routine combat you will come across conflicting claims as to the direction of the bullets that killed the Red Knight. One report has it that a burst had come up through the bottom of the fuselage and had struck the pilot in the head. For years the German press claimed that von Richthofen had had to land in British territory and that he was mowed down by some unknown machine gunner as he stepped out of the wreckage.

Captain Brown, who had previously won the R.N.A.S. Distinguished Service Cross, was not rewarded in any way, whether or not the R.A.F. believed he had downed von Richthofen. The day following this combat he suffered a physical breakdown and was placed in a hospital for a rest, where he remained for more than two months. For a time he served as an instructor at a British fighter school, but during a training formation flight he fainted in mid-air and crashed. When he was pulled out of the wreckage he was pronounced dead, but he actually had a serious skull fracture, and survived.

Following this, he was awarded a bar to his D.S.C., but it is

not clear if this was an award for his fight with von Richthofen.

Lieutenant May went on to collect thirteen victories and
was awarded the new R.A.F. Distinguished Flying Cross.

And so, nineteen months after it had begun, von Richthofen's flying career came to this abrupt end; he had won every
decoration his country could bestow, he had risen from a
Leutnant to the rank of Rittmeister—an elevated post expressly designed for the new German Air Force.

Von Richthofen's brother Lothar lived out the war, but, although more popular than the Baron and given every
opportunity to fill his shoes, never enjoyed the national adulation or homage that was showered on Manfred. He did, however, provide many conflicting features in his air-fighting
career.

When the war broke out Lothar enlisted in the 4th Regiment of Dragoons as an officer aspirant and was fighting the
French a few days after the first shots had been fired. Long
before Manfred had reached the front young Lothar had experienced considerable front-line action and was proud of the
fact that he had been one of a small party that had seen the
Eiffel Tower from the outskirts of Paris. When this initial
German drive was checked Lothar was sent to the Russian
front, where he developed a dislike of trench warfare. At this
point his history is obscure, but he seems to have made a
transfer to the German Air Service in May 1916 and by November had taken part in thirty-eight bombing raids, both as
an observer and a pilot.

In the meantime his brother Manfred had become something of a prominent figure as a German ace and it was natural that his younger brother should request a transfer to a
fighter Staffel. By December Lothar was getting in a few
practice solo flights on an Albatros single-seater. From this
point on there are puzzling contradictions in Lothar's flying
record. One report discloses that he had his first combat as a
fighter pilot on March 25, 1917, when he was in a formation
attacked by a flight of Nieuports belonging to No. 29 Squadron, R.F.C. He did not score but apparently handled himself
well in this melee. Just when he did make his first kill is something of a mystery, for in other words it is stated that he
downed an R.E.8 and a Fee on March 13 and these were
chalked up as his eighth and ninth victories!

This becomes more puzzling, since in a letter to his mother
dated March 25 Manfred stated that Lothar was doing very
well "but as yet had not scored his first victory." If, as one set

of records claim, Lothar had scored ten victories in nineteen days, surely the German archives would have some record of the combats—but they do not! By May 7 he was credited with his twenty-second victory, which, if true, made his score equal to that of Manfred—which is highly improbable. Let us return to May 7, when Lothar claimed he had shot down Captain Ball's "Sopwith triplane," whereas the British airman was flying an S.E.5 biplane. When we consider all these contradictions, the best we can say about Lothar von Richthofen is that his hostorians were very careless with their facts and figures.

When Manfred went on leave May 1, 1917, Lothar took over his brother's command, a post he held for just six days. On the evening of May 7, the same day on which Ball was lost, the younger von Richthofen went out with Karl Allmenroeder and they were attacked by a flight of Sopwith Camels. The rest of Staffel 11 came down to help out and in turn were intercepted by a flight of S.E.5's. Lothar was immediately in trouble when an S.E.5 got on his tail and spat a burst of bullets at him; his instrument panel was shot out, and a bullet pierced his right hip. Apparently he fainted, but his Albatros miraculously landed itself inside the German lines, where he was taken to the hospital.

As stated before, somewhere in that dogfight Albert Ball had played his usual savage role, but when he was found later in a crash that piled up in the village of Annoeullin, Lothar von Richthofen was asked to write out a report concerning the dogfight. On the strength of this, Ball was credited to him as his twenty-second victim.

Young von Richthofen did not get back to the front until September 25, when he picked up where he had left off and ran up a very respectable score. During March of 1918 he tangled with a Camel pilot and went back to the hospital for another four months. When he returned to the front in July the von Richthofen circus was in a pathetic state; their leader Baron von Richthofen had been downed behind the British lines and many of the old reliables were missing, including Weiss, Hans Wolff, Nautter, Reinhardt, Friedriche, and Kirchstein. The Allies were moving fast, and hardly a week passed but that the Circus had to move its hangars back to stay out of the front line.

But Lothar apparently put on a good show during his last few weeks on the front, scoring eight victories in seven days. By August he was fighting manfully to keep the Jagdstaffel intact, although he must have seen the writing on the wall. He scored his fortieth kill on August 12, shooting down two

Camels. The next day he received his third and last wound of the war. Again a British bullet tore through his right thigh, and he had great difficulty in landing. His Fokker was so badly shot about it collapsed the instant its wheels touched the ground. He was still in the hospital when the war ended.

This ill-fated young man is not too familiar to those interested in air-war history, being overshadowed by the fame of his brother and usually neglected by war historians, but he was as great an air fighter as Manfred and a more likeable person. He had a firm belief in good-luck talismans and carried his riding crop in his cockpit whenever he went on patrol. He was killed in a commercial crash—the first and only time he flew without his goodluck charm.

By 1922 Germany was trying to get back into the commercial aviation business and several small passenger-carrying airlines were established. Lothar was hired as a pilot for one of them and on July 4, 1922, was chartered to fly an American film actress and her manager from Hamburg to Berlin. The machine was a converted bomber, and when halfway to their destination the engine failed and the aircraft tangled with an electric cable. The two Americans were pulled out seriously injured, but Lothar had been killed.

We now encounter an entirely different type of German air hero. We met Ernst Udet in 1916, when, as a lance-corporal pilot with a two-seater squadron, he was having a dull time. Eventually he became a member of Baron von Richthofen's Flying Circus and as a result ended the war with sixty-two confirmed victories and the respect of most Allied flyers.

He was a happy-go-lucky character completely alien to most German Air Force types. During his service with von Richthofen's Jagdstaffel he provided a continual series of dramatic or amusing episodes that make his career more interesting than that of any other top-flight German airman. He was the youngest ace in the enemy service and although he became a runner-up to the great von Richthofen, he was still considered a playboy by his dour companions.

Like McCudden, Udet fought through every year of the war, but in contrast to the ill-fated Englishman, was more fortunate in having his service provide him with a parachute during the last phase of the war. Twice he was shot down and had to take to this new aerial life preserver and both times was saved from certain death.

Having upheld the honour of the German Air Service throughout the closing months of 1917 by scoring his twenty-first victory, Udet was awarded the *Pour le mérite*. He later joined the Red Knight's entourage and was placed in command of Staffel 11. Later Staffel 4 was put under his guidance, and whenever the Baron was away and his brother Lothar unavailable, Ernst Udet generally led the whole Circus.

This youngster was always in the thick of things, and although he was supposed to be the Staffel leader, he often did lone-wolf patrols and added to his score. He tackled anyone and usually came back with dozens of bullet holes in his plane. Once he tangled with a British two-seater and after a short burst noted that the observer had apparently folded up and disappeared under his gun mounting. This was an old trick of the Bristol Fighter crews and in this instance Udet was fooled by it. The next thing he knew the gunner had popped up again and poured most of a drum of ammunition into the Fokker triplane.

Udet saw he was in trouble and decided to take to his parachute. It was a shoulder-bag type, and when he went out the canopy somehow became entangled with his battered engine cowling. He hung there roped to a falling triplane, and it was not until he was down to about 400 feet from the ground that he was able to jerk the parachute clear and have it open to let him down safely.

Soon after the March push had been halted and the front stabilized, the German Air Service began to again feel the impact of the Allied fighter force. On the first day of May 1918 a total of 240 German planes were destroyed. By July there was such a shortage of fighter pilots that bomber pilots were being given quick single-seater courses and turned over to combat Staffels. Nevertheless, during all this travail Udet carried on and bravely added to his score day after day.

Early in July of 1918 Udet encountered his first American opponent. The flyers of the 27th Squadron of the First Pursuit Group were out on patrol duty in the Château-Thierry area, the formation consisting of nine Nieuports led by Lieutenant Fred Norton. In the outer corner spot was Lieutenant W. B. Wanamaker of Akron, Ohio. They were flitting about at 16,000 feet and had patrolled back and forth over their assigned area several times when they suddenly encountered a German Staffel of eleven Fokkers. They had no choice but to fight and fight they did.

From his "coffin corner" position Wanamaker saw a Fokker swoop down on Lieutenant Grant and he went to the rescue, lining up his sights on the German who was hounding Grant. At the same instant a burst of fire stitched his Nieuport fuselage from rudder to crash pad. A bright-red D.7

biplane with black crosses was dead on his tail. He went into a tight spin and the German plane followed him down. As he tried to straighten out the German let him have it from two guns, and the Nieuport instrument panel was perforated with a dozen slugs.

Wanamaker tried another tail spin until he was only 3,000 feet from the ground, but his adversary triggered off another burst which put his fuel system out of commission. By now the American realized he was in serious trouble and decided to get down as fast as possible and try to destroy his plane before it fell into the hands of the enemy. Unfortunately, he must have fainted in the air and piled up. When he regained consciousness he found himself in the middle of a circle of enemy soldiers, not one of which had made any attempt to get him clear of the wreckage. Finally a German pilot stepped through the gathering and ordered some soldiers to help the unfortunate airman. When Wanamaker asked for a cigarette, the pilot, who said his name was Udet, gave him one and tucked the rest of the package into Wanamaker's pocket.

When he discovered Udet understood English Wanamaker mooned about his poor show, although he had a broken spine, leg, ankle, and severe cuts.

"Don't feel too badly. I already had thirty-eight to my credit. You are the thirty-ninth," he was told by Udet.

However, it was some time before Udet realized he was talking to an American. When that point was established he tore off the rudder fabric from Wanamaker's Nieuport and had the American autograph it before he was carried off to a nearby hospital. One wonders what Udet thought when he realized the Allies had at last been bolstered by the Americans.

Ernst Udet was one of the few pilots who deliberately rammed an adversary in mid-air and lived to tell it. On August 8, when he was flying with several companions at 2,500 feet, a British Camel roared in with both guns chattering to attack the lot from a tight angle. Udet banked, pulled a sharp turn, and came out on the Camel's tail. The Briton dived and Udet followed as he had with Wanamaker. At 1,000 feet the Camel suddenly zoomed and cranked into an Immelmann turn. Thus both planes were hurtling straight at each other. Udet stuck to his course, expecting the Englishman to give way, but the Camel pilot came on, refusing to give up the shelter of his Bentley engine.

Udet had no choice. He decided to see what would happen. The Fokker and Camel crashed. The Camel's wings folded back under the impact of the Fokker's undercarriage. When both pilots were able to take inventory the Camel was in a giddy spin and the Fokker appeared to have thrown away a great deal of her wing surface. It could have been a fatal double crash, but instead the Britisher somehow unwound the spin and pancaked the mess safely and was listed as Udet's forty-seventh victim. Forgetting he had a parachute, Udet stayed with his hulk and made a safe landing.

"Those crazy English," he is said to have grumbled, "you can't figure what they are going to do. He was supposed to give way and let me shoot him down!"

Udet flailed away throughout that bitter summer and soon scored his fiftieth victory and received a telegram of congratulation from the Kaiser and with it the award of the Cross of Hohenzollern. Twelve more planes were to go down before his accurate gunnery, his last falling as part of a "double" on September 3, 1918.

During the last five weeks of the war he was sent from the Argonne to the red-hot British front, and there the competition was so keen he did not score again. He flew high and often, but the new British Snipes backing up the Camels and S.E.5's were too much—even for Udet. He was the ranking German living ace, a fighter who had fought on every front and had dared every type of Allied machine. There wasn't a more glamorous figure in the German Air Service than Oberleutnant Ernst Udet.

The parachute device which had twice proved a guardian angel for Udet betrayed two of Germany's outstanding aces during 1918.

Willy Reinhardt, who took command of von Richthofen's Circus after the Red Knight's death, was one of these. At the beginning of the war he held a commission as leutnant in the Prussian artillery and was wounded late in December 1914. By July 1915 he had transferred to the Air Service and was sent to the Verdun front as an observer with Flying Section 205. He served in this capacity for more than a year and then was given a chance at pilot training. From this point he went into a career unequalled by any pilot on either side of the line.

In October 1916 Reinhardt was flying an old L.V.G. two-seater on the Salonika front. He spent a tour of duty against the Russians. Next he flew an Albatros C.3 stationed near Constanzo, Italy. Two months later he was back on the Western Front with Flying Section 28, but before he had located the officers' bar he was rushed off to a *Jastaschule* (school of fighting) in Germany and made an instructor. So well did he handle the obsolete fighter models there that he soon attracted the attentions of his superiors and by July 4, 1917, was back on the Western Front with Staffel 11 of the newly formed von Richthofen Jagdgeschwader No. 1. For a man who had flown only ancient vintage aircraft and obsolete school machines to suddenly find himself a member of the most famous Staffel of the Air Service was quite a promotion; but Willy Reinhardt was a very unusual person.

By the fourth of August he had scored five times, but late that afternoon he took on too many British Camels over Houthulst Fôret and was badly shot up. He was fortunate to be able to land his machine before he fainted from the loss of blood.

Reinhardt was back in action in November and made C.O. of Staffel 6 but did not add to his score until January 4, when he downed a Bristol Fighter. Again he was lucky, for after taking a pasting from the Bristol's gunner, he sprayed the Britishers from long range and managed to puncture their petrol tank. The two-seater immediately burst into flames as a spray of vaporized petrol enveloped the hapless crew.

His next two victims were also Bristols, one going down in flames, the other folding up in mid-air after losing its outer wing struts. On March 27 he sent down his tenth, an R.E.8, and thus entered Germany's ranks of *Kanone*, their ten-victory aces. He was promoted to the rank of captain on April 1 and celebrated by shooting down an S.E.5 at Martinpuich. Nine days later von Richthofen went down for his last landing.

On the day following Manfred's death a few select German war birds met to go over von Richthofen's private papers before they were sent to his parents. Among them they found one dated March 10, 1918, which read:

Should I not return, Oberleutnant Reinhardt (Staffel 11) shall become the leader of the *Geschwaders*. Signed, Manfred von Richthofen.

The Red Knight's word was law and the Imperial Air Service confirmed Reinhardt's appointment. But Reinhardt was not a von Richthofen type of leader. He did not maintain strict discipline, neither did he weed out the inferior pilots in order to keep the organization up to the von Richthofen tradition. A number of useless pilots found their way into his squadron and for a time casualties were alarmingly high. On May 21 Reinhardt's Staffel was moved down to the French front where they found Spads and Bréguets more to their liking. No less than seventy victories were scored over their first month in this area, Reinhardt destroying seven Spads in thirteen days. It had taken him seven months to destroy the same number of planes on the British front. By late June he had registered his twentieth victory, which was his last.

In that month Reinhardt and Hans Kirchstein were summoned to attend a flying meeting at Aldershof outside Berlin to make a special test of new equipment, and Reinhardt made a particular request to try out the new Friedrichshafen A.2A, a fighter expected to outclass the Fokker D.7.

For the first twenty minutes all went well and then Reinhardt tried a steep dive from a height of 2,000 feet. Observers below saw the nose tilt down, and hardly had the dive started than the upper wing tore away, the fuselage buckled amidships, and Reinhardt went over the side. The audience waited to see the parachute open, but Reinhardt's body continued on at high velocity; the parachute never opened and the second leader of the von Richthofen Circus crashed to his death.

Another little-known but high-ranking German ace who had a tragic end was Erich Lowenhardt, a star performer with the von Richthofen Circus and credited with fifty-four victories. Like Reinhardt, he died shortly before the end of the war when his Paulus parachute failed to open.

This German officer won the British esteem for his valour, dash, and compassion. He was to kill Captain Bush, the pilot who flew the F.E.2b in which I had my brush with Baron von Richthofen. I was on leave in England at the time, and it was one of the few times Bush had flown without me as his gunner-observer.

Lowenhardt was born in 1897 in Breslau and was enrolled in the Lichtfelder Cadet School when war was declared. He was immediately posted as standard-bearer to the 141st Infantry and sent to the Eastern Front, where he was wounded near Lodz before the conflict was a month old, but he remained with his battalion all through the Battle of Tannenberg and for gallantry there was promoted to leutnant.

In October he was placed in command of Germany's ski-troops that fought so valiantly in the Carpathian struggle. He won the Iron Cross First Class for gallantry and leadership, and by June of 1915 was transferred to the Austro-German Alpine Corps for service in the Dolomites and later took part in the advance through Siberia.

During the trials of this latter campaign Lowenhardt contracted a fever and was invalided home as unfit for further service. The young leutnant, however, refused to accept the decision and after five months of enforced rest managed to pass the physical requirements to enter the Imperial Air Service. His progress through the flying schools was so rapid he was sent to Jagdstaffel 10 of the von Richthofen Geschwader 1 in July of 1917.

Very little is known about his early weeks of air fighting, but his logbook shows that he took on everything. He was victorious over twelve Sopwith Camels, seven balloons, sixteen Spads, three Bristol Fighters, two Nieuports, one F.E.2d (a night-fighter), two D.H.9's, two Sopwith Pups, and an odd collection of R.E.8's, D.H.5's, Bérguets, and an S.E.5.

During the first week in November 1917 Lowenhardt had a hair-raising adventure while flying over Saint-Eloi, when he received a heavy strafing from a pair of mobile anti-aircraft guns. One shell which somehow failed to explode tore off his left wing tip, and his Albatros fell in an uncontrolled spin. When less than 50 feet from the ground he managed to regain some control, but it was almost too late; the machine hit very hard, turned two complete somersaults, and finished up a complete wreck in a hedge. To the amazement of a party of soldiers who had seen the crash, a tattered figure in a flying suit rose up from the wreckage and started to walk away. Lowenhardt was badly shaken but otherwise unhurt.

He was commanding Staffel 10 by April 1918, when it was moved down to the French front, where he reaped his harvest of Spads and Bérguets. Between June 1 and 8 no less than forty French machines fell to the pilots of Geschwader 1, and Lowenhardt became the top surviving German ace.

Shortly after the noon hour of August 10 Staffel 10 joined up with a formation from Staffel 4 for an offensive patrol. They encountered a number of S.E.5's over the town of Chaulnes. Lowenhardt gave the signal to attack and set up his own death sentence. Several machines from Staffel 11 had now joined the German force and, seeing Lowenhardt's signal, they all poured down to join in the fray. One of the newcomers, a Leutnant Wentz, roared at an S.E.5 at the very moment Lowenhardt turned to bring his guns to bear upon the same British machine. The left wheel of Wentz's Fokker tore through the right wing of Lowenhardt's fighter, and for a few harrowing seconds both planes hung locked together. Then the Fokker's wheel tore loose, both planes began to fall, and both pilots took to their parachutes.

Wentz, the unknown, landed safely, while the famous ace fell like a plummet, his unopened parachute trailing behind. And so Erich Lowenhardt died, the victim of an accident similar to the one that had taken the life of Oswald Boelcke.

Once they had trumpeted their final hour of glory during the March push, the fortunes of the Imperial German Air Force began to wane for the last time. By mid-summer their situation was very grave; the great armies of the Fatherland, which had never received true air support, had been beaten to a standstill and were tottering back toward the Rhine. The national defeat was first suffered in the skies; of that there is no question. The much-debated failure of their economy was to be felt during the last few weeks of the war, but the German Air Force had been outfought, outgunned, outgamed and outflown. For years they had selected their battleground over their own territory with the prevailing winds in their favour. Their combat problems were simple, their planning uncomplicated, but with all these obvious advantages they went down finally before the youthful daring, the Allied loyalty to its cause, and the eventual superiority of Allied aircraft. The bulk of Germany's air effort was mistakenly devoted to the single-seater circus concept, which, while theatrical in its execution, was by the same token most extravagant with the technical and personnel resources available.

Strangely enough, Hermann Goering, who was the last airman to command the von Richthofen group, an honour he never actually deserved, was to head Germany's *Luftwaffe* in World War II, and his monumental mistakes in its guidance again contributed to Germany's downfall.

True, September 1918 saw great scarcities of food and raw materials. Rubber in particular was at a premium, and in an effort to save this commodity an order was issued that when an aeroplane landed the tyres were to be removed and wooden wheels fitted for taxiing purposes. Rubber shock absorbers were replaced by springs, while the shortage of petrol resulted in the manufacture of a synthetic fuel, a mixture of benzol and crude petroleum. By this time, however, Germany had lost the war.

All in all, German pilots claimed to have shot down 6,794 Allied aircraft. Their own losses were given out as 3,713 officers and 4,798 other ranks. Of the entire German Air Service, seventy-two airmen were awarded the highest honour the Kaiser could bestow, the Order *Pour le mérite*, and thirty-two recipients gave their lives in exchange for that decoration.

Speaking of honours, it might be added here that over the same four years of warfare Great Britain awarded her Victoria Cross to only nineteen of her air heroes, and, of these, only nine were fighter pilots.

From August 1914 to September 1918 German aircraft factories produced 48,876 machines, and of this total 2,850 were turned over to the Allies under the Treaty of Versailles. Below is the inventory of military planes produced by German manufacturers during the last year of the war.

GERMAN WARPLANES OF 1918

Make	Engine	Speed m.p.h.	Purpose
A.E.G. C.4	Benz 200 h.p.	86	Ground-attack
Aviatik D.6	Benz 200 h.p.	125	Scout
Brandenburg	Mercedes 175 h.p.	109	Seaplane
D.F.W. C.5	Benz 225 h.p.	120	Bomber-fighter
D.F.W. C.37.3	Benz 225 h.p.	128	Reconnaissance
Friedrichshafen	Benz (2) 224 h.p.	92	Heavy Bomber
Fokker D.7	Mercedes 200 h.p.	135	Scout
Fokker D.8	Oberursel 140 h.p.	124	Scout
Fokker C.1	B.M.W. 185 h.p.	118	Bomber-fighter
Gotha	Mercedes (2) 260 h.p.	102	Bomber
Halberstadt	Mercedes 180 h.p.	105	Ground-attack
Pfalz D.R.1a	Siemens-Halske 160 h.p.	125	Scout
Pfalz D.12	Mercedes 200 h.p.	126	Scout
Roland D.6	Benz 185 h.p.	118	Scout
Siemens-Schuckert D.4	Siemens-Halske 200 h.p.	138	Scout
Siemens-Schuckert G.8	Mercedes (4) 260 h.p.	95	Bomber
Zeppelin Giant	Maybach (6) 200 h.p.	75	Bomber

The Royal Air Force came into being during the heat and fury that marked Germany's dramatic stand in the spring of 1918. The new Air Ministry, created on the opening day of the year, brought every concept of air defence into play. After some political manoeuvring and bitter debate General Trenchard was eventually allowed to organize a strategic command to be known as the Independent Air Force. As was the order during the Battle of Britain twenty-two years later, air fighting was not to be staged to add to the glory of the aces. Infantry ground support was more vital than spectacular conflict above the clouds. Precision bombing of important targets took priority over unpremeditated attacks on enemy fighters, whether the bombing was carried out by Handley-Pages, gorged with 250-pound missiles, or fleets of fifty Camels, strafing with 20-pound Cooper bombs.

The new Allied Generalissimo Foch brought new spirit to the Headquarters Staff and insisted on better co-operation between the artillery and the air services. It was he who discovered that the artillery batteries had become so slack concerning this ground-to-air operation that they did not erect their wireless aerials until they had been in any new position for several days. Thus, it was impossible to order any direct artillery fire, although the Art-Obs airmen were risking life and limb to stay in the air and seek out these rewarding targets.

At the same time it was found that multi-squadron defence was most important to the artillery, reconnaissance, and bombing operations, and by April 1918 the British were putting up circus formations as cover for the "working" flyers; but these escort fighters were warned to provide just that—not to seek out air fights in the hope of promotion or decorations.

It will be recalled that in 1940 the *Luftwaffe* tried to lure the few R.A.F. low-flying fighter patrols from their cover routines. I am speaking, of course, of the operations prior to the retreat from Dunkirk. The result was that Britain not only saved most of her expeditionary force but also her fighter squadrons for the eventual Battle of Britain. In 1918 the new R.A.F. staged the same tactical defence and the losses inflicted on the German infantry were, according to Ludendorff, extraordinarily high. Years later German historians complained that they were unable to provide suitable air support because they had prepared no advanced landing grounds from where their Army-co-operation machines could refuel or rearm in order to stay in the air long enough to be of any tactical value. The Allies huddled behind no such excuse; they built emergency strips as fast as they lost or regained ground.

The R.A.F. put up a supreme effort to halt the March push, and the instant fine weather prevailed, were in the air from dawn to dusk flying altogether 3,240 hours. Every pilot of No. 201 Squadron (formerly No. 1 Naval) flew their Camels in action for more than five and a half hours daily. The bomber formations were incredibly active over the enemy's rear areas and lines of communication. What fighting ensued proved most rewarding. Captain H. W. Woolett, who was flying a Camel for No. 43 Squadron, shot down six German aircraft in two patrols on one day. When the untried Portuguese troops, holding a sector in front of the Lys, broke under the German pressure, a number of low-flying Camels and S.E.5's took over the defence; German battalions were cut to ribbons by these little single-seaters which attacked savagely from barbed-wire height with machine guns and light fragmentation bombs. German historians later recorded that nothing could be done to stop these low-altitude raiders, for they maintained a form of aerial supremacy for which the Germans had no counter measures.

This year produced seven new Victoria Cross winners and hundreds of gallant epics which would fill many volumes such as this, but the amazing feat of Lieutenant Alan A. McLeod, a nineteen-year-old Canadian, perhaps best represents the heroic stature of these youngsters of the new force. McLeod, who was the youngest R.F.C. man to win the V.C., was born April 20, 1899, in the small town of Stonewall, Manitoba. His father was one of the hardy Scots who helped to conquer the Canadian wilderness, blazing the trail of Empire under the banner of the Hudson's Bay Company.

Young McLeod early took to soldiering and at fourteen joined the Fort Garry Horse for their annual summer training encampment. He was supposed to be eighteen, of course, but the town of Stonewall admits that Alan always had a persuasive manner. For two weeks he groomed horses, wore natty breeches, tunic, and a bandoleer of rifle ammunition. He did a real man's job.

He was but fifteen years old when the German Kaiser sent his armies swarming across Belgium toward Paris, and Canada eagerly threw in its lot with the Mother Country. The First Canadian Division was the pick of the Dominion; ex-Mounties, men who had fought in the Boer war, the cream of the crop from Canada's many military schools, tough men who had grown up in the Far North or in the vast timber country. There was no place for a fifteen-year-old, and so young McLeod stepped aside.

In the spring of 1916, when seventeen years old, McLeod applied for admission to the R.F.C. flying school in Toronto but was told he would have to wait a year. The following spring he passed the medical examination and donned the R.F.C. uniform. He made striking progress, and his instructors permitted him to solo after only three dual-control training flights and by the end of July he had gained his wings. Once in Britain, where he had the usual check training and advanced courses of flying, he was again held up when it was learned that he was not yet nineteen. He put in the next few months flying with a British Home Defence squadron. McLeod did about three times more flying than necessary, for he hoped by some favour of Providence to pile into a Gotha bomber and prove he was worthy of a front-line squadron.

By late November 1917 Second Lieutenant McLeod arrived at the pilots' pool outside Saint-Omer. He had set his heart on joining No. 2 Squadron, the senior outfit of the R.F.C. (No. 1 had been an airship squadron). He probably thought No. 2 would be flying the very latest aircraft, but to his chagrin discovered that No. 2 Squadron was flying—of all things—the hulking, slab-sided, sluggish Armstrong-Whitworth artillery spotter. All he was supposed to do was to take a trained observer over the line every day, fly a dreary figure-eight course between enemy targets and the British guns while his back-seat Charlie tapped out corrections for the gun-layers. He couldn't have picked a less romantic duty had he stayed with the old Fort Garry Horse. The Armstrong-Whitworth was listed as a two-seater reconnaissance-bomber, which was more of an honorary title than a legitimate evaluation of its capabilities. Actually, it was a steady air platform most suitable for the unspectacular work of the Art-Obs performers.

For the next few weeks McLeod carried out these spotting patrols with youthful integrity, but the minute the ground batteries had put their salvoes on the targets, he generally went off to add to his air time. One day he found a covey of bright-coloured Huns, and the enemy aircraft poured down on them. McLeod later insisted he immediately headed for home. His observer did what he could with his lone Lewis gun and, in fact, made the Fokker formation split up and take time to re-form. McLeod decided the enemy had become panic-stricken, so he turned the tables and roared back at the leader, firing one short burst. His observer, Lieutenant Comber, yelled, "You shot the damn thing down!"

When they returned Comber made out a routine report, adding McLeod's little side venture, but no one believed a word of it. After all, no one in his right mind went anywhere near Albatros or Fokker formations in an Armstrong-Whitworth. To insist that one actually attacked such an enemy formation was really laying it on.

Nevertheless the British balloon observers in the area confirmed the fight and victory, and overnight McLeod became something of a superman in No. 2 Squadron. "The kid actually attacks Fokkers with an old Ack-W!"

On January 14, 1918, McLeod was flying with an observer, Lieutenant Reginald Key, who had ideas similar to his. They decided to knock off a balloon, up 12 miles inside the enemy lines. They crossed over, headed for Lille, and found the great bag bobbing in the icy winter wind. The enemy anti-aircraft roared up, and they blundered through thuds of concussion,

216

but McLeod held the old artillery-spotter dead on and pressed his trigger. The kite immediately burst into flames.

As they zoomed for height and turned for their field, they were greeted by three Albatros scouts. McLeod coaxed what extra speed he had from the 120-h.p. Beardmore, and Key knew the rest was up to him. While his pilot threw the heavy old Ack-W all over the sky and got as much as 85 m.p.h. out of her, Key shot down one Albatros and discouraged the others so they were able to sneak back to their own side in safety.

"Now he's attacking kite balloons!" was the wail at Squadron 2.

McLeod next attacked and put out of action an enemy anti-aircraft battery which had been particularly offensive in their area. He did this with machine-gun fire and two small Cooper bombs.

Key was transferred to another sector where imaginative observers were badly needed, and Lieutenant A. W. Hammond, a veteran gunner who had already won the Military Cross, was posted to McLeod's back seat. Their C.O. explained that from now on they could fight as they pleased—when not on routine patrols—and over the next few days McLeon and Hammond put on a two-man air-force show that had the front ablaze. They spotted for the artillery in the morning and in the afternoon bombed anything in the German areas that moved or looked hostile. Late in the afternoon they became two-seater fighters or trench strafers. Sometimes they combined all three missions and generally came home shot to rags.

When the German spring offensive was launched in March, the Royal Flying Corps put every available aircraft into the air in an attempt to stem the advance around Bapaume; day and night they were bombing roads and batteries, machine-gunning enemy concentrations, and fighting off swarms of hostile fighters. On March 27 McLeod and Hammond were on a bombing mission and were seeking out a German battery in the Bray-sur-Somme area when a Fokker triplane appeared directly ahead. McLeod turned from his ground target, put a burst into the Fokker, and then allowed Hammond to do a good job of it with his Lewis; the triplane went down completely out of control.

This byplay attracted the attention of Leutnant Hans Kirchstein, a member of Jagdstaffel 6 of the von Richthofen Jagdgeschwader 1. Some reports say that McLeod next turned his attention to a German kite balloon which he was supposed to have attacked and destroyed before Kirchstein caught up with him. Other versions of this incident make no mention of the balloon.

When the German Staffel came down on them, McLeod and Hammond fought like tigers, the pilot throwing the lumbering old bus around like a scout, while Hammond, conserving his ammunition, took short-burst shots at every Fokker that came within range. One Fokker triplane got in a salvo that damaged McLeod's controls and for a minute the Ack-W seemed in serious trouble. Kirchstein made the most of that and came up from below with a long volley that wounded both the pilot and observer and set their fuel tank on fire.

At this point the fight seemed over; both Ack-W men were wounded and their machine was in flames; they were at 2,000 feet and looked like roasting before any sort of a landing could be made; and they were well over the enemy lines.

But McLeod was far from through. First, he swung around in the direction of his own lines and put the plane into an easy glide. Hammond kept hammering away at the swirling triplanes. Next, McLeod had to get out of his cockpit to evade the flames and take refuge outside, standing on the wing root (where the wing joins the fuselage), and as best he could putting one arm inside to hold the control stick. The flames sweeping back finally burned out the floor of Hammond's cockpit and forced the wounded observer to sit on his Scarff gun ring. But from that position he shot down a Fokker triplane.

Meanwhile McLeod had the Armstrong-Whitworth in a side-slip trying to keep the flames from eating up their fuselage. They continued down in this way until they could see their own lines. The Fokkers made one last attack and Hammond was again wounded and knocked back inside his cockpit, but he hung on to his seat supports.

McLeod was badly burned but managed to keep some control until he saw an opportunity of pancaking the burning plane near the British front lines. They hit fairly hard as the triplanes raked them for the last time. McLeod was thrown clear, but his observer was trapped in the burning fuselage. While enemy infantrymen drilled rifle and machine-gun fire at them young McLeod calmly tore the artillery machine apart and dragged out his gunner. Then crawling in and out of shell holes, he finally got him to the safety of the British trenches.

Hammond had been wounded six times, McLeod five. The bombs they had forgotten to drop exploded when flames finally consumed the wreck.

For months McLeod was in the hospital fighting for his

life. He was awarded the Victoria Cross, and Hammond received a bar to his Military Cross. When he was able, McLeod went to Buckingham Palace to receive his award from the King, and following the investiture was sent home to fully recuperate, but in his weakened state was seized with influenza then sweeping North America and died five days before the Armistice.

While the Sopwith Camel was rightfully the greatest single-seater air fighter in all history, that snub-nosed little gadfly was fortunate in that its victory record was compiled during its one-man operations. Every enemy pilot shot down by its twin guns was credited to an individual pilot, and there was never any argument or division of the statistics.

On the other hand, the Bristol Fighter might possibly claim the "aircraft destroyed" championship except for the fact that it was a two-seater. The kills scored by the gunner-observer, as explained before, were never credited to the individual in the rear seat. They were credited to the squadron's record. Because of this hard and fast rule of the British service it has been impossible to figure accurately how many enemy aircraft fell before Bristol Fighter guns. As pointed out earlier, the British were not particularly "ace" conscious, and no accurate records of aircraft destroyed were kept until well after the middle of 1915.

However, there are a number of Bristol Fighter pilot aces listed in R.F.C. records. They are all commissioned officers. The column is headed by Major Andrew E. McKeever of No. 11 Squadron who is credited with thirty enemy aircraft. McKeever came to a deplorable end after returning to Canada when an automobile he was driving skidded on an icy road on Christmas Day of 1919. A tragic finish for a man who had fought the best of the German Air Service without suffering a scratch.

The list of pilots who became Bristol Fighter aces, and their scores, runs as follows:

	Squadron	Victories
Major Andrew E. McKeever	11	30
Captain Edward McKelvie	22	29
Captain Henry G. Launchford	20	29
Captain J. D. Gurdon	22	27
Lieutenant W. McK. Thompson	20	22
Captain D. Lattimer	20	22
Major A. M. Wilkenson	48	20
Captain E. A. Beaver	20	19
Captain E. J. McLaughey	20	19

*Lieutenant Thayer Iaccaci	22	18
Captain T. P. Middleton	20	16
*Lieutenant Clive Warman	22	15
*Captain Fred Libby	48	14
*Lieutenant Paul Iaccaci	20	11

* American serving with the R. F. C.

I should explain here that Captain McKelvie has often been confused with Major McKeever of No. 11 Squadron. Their names were similar, both flew Bristol Fighters and both at one time had gunner-observers named Powell. McKeever's back-seat man was a Lieutenant L. F. Powell whereas McKelvie's gunner was a hut-mate of mine, Sergeant Edward Powell. McKelvie was an Englishman, who when last heard of was living in Wiltshire.

McKelvie was to become a very important member of our No. 22 Squadron. After a few weeks spent in learning the ropes and becoming acquainted with the front, he became very adept with the Brisfit and on June 21, 1917, engaged an Albatros D.3 on a fighter-to-fighter basis. He had no trouble outmanoeuvring and shooting down the German and from that time on decided to use the Bristol two-seater in that manner. McKelvie never claimed the distinction of originating this mode of fighting. He simply worked out more variations of two-seater attack. By July 10 he had racked up his fifth with a spectacular victory.

McKelvie had decided early that N.C.O. gunners were better-trained fighting airmen than the officer observers, because most of them were putting in many more hours than the commissioned gunners. He selected Eddie Powell of A Flight and together these two became famous.

One morning McKelvie was leading an early morning patrol when Powell spotted a two-seater Roland just below them. He gave the pilot a signal and they nosed down. The Roland was hit hard and went up in flames. Then Powell's gun began to chatter and McKelvie turned and saw five gaudy Albatros fighters diving after them. In a running fight which lasted all the way back to the British lines, McKelvie downed two and Powell shot the wings off another. The pilot was awarded the Military Cross but his gunner was not even mentioned in the daily combat report.

In August, with the help of Powell, McKelvie received a bar to his Military Cross when he led a low-bombing attack against a German airfield. Loaded to capacity with 20-pound Cooper bombs, the Brisfits of A Flight wrecked three hangars and destroyed eleven planes. On their way back they were intercepted by a formation of enemy Pfalz fighters, but the Brisfit gunners calmly took them apart, downing five in the melee.

For a time there was no stopping the McKelvie-Powell combination. Unofficially, Powell was credited with eight enemy planes and before 1917 was over he was sent back to England for a commission and pilot training.

On August 28 they scored another triple victory, McKelvie downing an Albatros and a new Pfalz scout. Powell torched an Albatros D.3. Like the rest of us they were also engaged in trench-strafing, and on one occasion Mac destroyed a kite balloon while Powell wiped out a winch crew and knocked down a Pfalz assigned to guard the *Drachen*.

This represents a typical day with a Bristol Fighter squadron. We might escort D.H. bombers to the airship sheds at Gontrode or we might hound moving transport just behind the front lines. We bombed machine-gun posts, shot up trench-mortar redoubts, attacked any formation of enemy aircraft or did photographic reconnaissance anywhere within the enemy lines. There never was a military aircraft like the Bristol Fighter.

McKelvie and Powell fought their last battle together on November 30. This was the dud-weather period during the Battle of Cambrai. I remember this episode very well, as the weather was abominable. Soon after breakfast, G.H.Q. called for a special look-see flight over an area where much activity was going on. The weather was so bad, only volunteers were considered. McKelvie and Powell were the first selected and before they were 60 feet off the ground, fog enveloped them. Cambrai was nearly 80 miles away, and the pilot had only a simple compass to guide him. As they prowled about looking for a hole in the muck, a tremendous roar sent a great gush of flame up through the fog. An ammunition dump had erupted, and in the sharp clarity of the explosion, Powell saw German infantrymen trying to subdue the flames. At least, that is what he thought he saw.

McKelvie, however, became suspicious. He was positive this was not an accident or a lucky hit by British artillery. He was confident that the dump had been exploded by intent. He went down to make sure. They were churning around at 1,000 feet, trying to make some sense of the furore below, when they were attacked by a flight of nine Albatros scouts. A burst of gunfire shot the drum off Powell's gun and more bullets tore into McKelvie's cockpit, smashing several instruments. Powell got a new drum on and opened fire on an Albatros that zoomed over their top wing; the enemy plane

221

rolled over and exploded. Another D.3 crossed McKelvie's line of flight, and the pilot blasted it out of the skies. Powell turned on a third Albatros and three German fighters were falling to the ground at the same time. All this happened within thirty seconds.

The remaining Albatros pilots drew off, re-formed, and then took up the challenge once more. McKelvie was still prowling about, trying to make certain whether the confusion below was accidental or created by intent. Later, both he and Powell were positive that the Germans were pulling out of Cambrai to a new line of defence. When McKelvie saw enemy planes roaring at them again, he nosed up, pressed his gun control, and another Albatros went up in flames and still another was harried into a crazy spin from which it had no space to recover.

By now the Bristol Fighter was stitched from rudder to propboss. A piece of metal had slashed Powell's cheek, a bullet had cut McKelvie's flying boot to ribbons, and suddenly, he was out of ammunition. There was nothing to do but call it a day. They zoomed up into the murk, lost their adversaries, and then went down, hedge-hopping all the way back to Estree Blanche.

For that performance McKelvie was awarded the Distinguished Service Order and Powell the Distinguished Conduct Medal.

McKelvie's suspicion of the German intent at Cambrai caused G.H.Q. to ask for more volunteers, and another Bristol Fighter went out into the fog, but hit the slag heaps around Lens. A third took off and was never heard from again. About noon of that day I accompanied a Lieutenant Davidson to Cambrai and we had an experience similar to that of McKelvie and Powell. We came back with further evidence that the Germans *were* pulling out of Cambrai, but neither I nor Powell were commissioned officers, and our reports were not immediately accepted. By the time G.H.Q. decided that there might be something in what we had reported, the Germans had consolidated their positions, counter-attacked, and retaken most of the ground the British had won over the previous three weeks.

As stated before, Cambrai might have been a major victory in 1917 had the observation reports of two N.C.O. gunners been accepted at their face value, but I presume greater battles have been won or lost on less.

Probably the most colourful and paradoxically the least known of the long list of Canadian aces is Major Raymond

Collishaw, credited officially with destroying sixty-eight enemy aircraft. Today he lives in healthy retirement in Canada.

The lure of adventure called early to Collishaw, who was born in Nanaimo, British Columbia, in 1892. When he was still in his teens, he served as a second mate aboard a vessel plying between Victoria and Alaska. Before he was twenty he had sailed with the ill-fated Scott Expedition to the South Pole. He was twenty-one years old and an officer on a Pacific coast steamer at the start of the war. He resigned, crossed a continent and an ocean to enlist. At first he considered the Royal Navy, but then learned of the Royal Naval Air Service, and by January of 1916 was a qualified pilot assigned to coastal-patrol duty. That August he was sent to the R.N.A.S. Third Wing, which was made up of bombers and their escorts. This organization went over to France, where Ray found himself flying a Pup scout acting as an escort to the heavier bombers. While engaged in this dreary work he knocked down his first enemy plane—a Fokker fighter over Oberndorf. That was on October 12, 1916, and on October 25 he downed two more of the same type over Luneville, for which the French awarded him the *Croix de guerre*.

Early in 1917 Collishaw was posted to No. 3 (Naval) Squadron on the Somme under the command of R. H. Mulock, another Canadian, who already had destroyed a submarine and a number of enemy aircraft. Collishaw had little luck while serving under Mulock but was later transferred to No. 10 (Naval) Squadron and sent back to the coast. Here he was promoted to flight commander and personally hand-picked four other Canadian fighters to follow him. They were Flight Sub-lieutenants Ellis Reid of Toronto, J. E. Sharman of Winnipeg, J. E. Nash of Hamilton, and M. Alexander of Montreal—all in their early twenties and keen on individual scrapping.

At this time the Sopwith triplane had started to move off the production line, and while it was not in particular favour in the R.F.C., two squadrons of the R.N.A.S., Nos. 10 and 8, were eager to have them and were the first squadrons to fly the British three-decker on active service.

Collishaw's flight decided they should adopt a distinctive marking and after some deliberation concluded that they would be outstanding if their five triplanes were painted black. They also decided to name them, Collishaw calling his *Black Maria* and the others, *Black Death, Black Prince, Black Roger,* and *Black Sheep*. Their first duty assignment was with the Home Fleet, but they saw few enemy aircraft.

However, on April 28 Collishaw caught a venturesome Roland scout out beyond Ostend and in no time sent it to its finish. He scored three more times in the first twelve days of May while patrolling the coastline. Then they were transferred to the Ypres front with the Eleventh Wing of the R.F.C.

There the black Tripes made their presence felt. Four enemy scouts went down before Collishaw's guns in five days, and the other flyers all tasted victory. On June 5 Collishaw shot down his first two-seater and on June 6 nailed three in one day for his sixteenth victim.

Disaster touched the Black Flight when on June 26 Lieutenant Nash crashed down from a mass attack by the von Richthofen Circus. Seeking revenge, Collishaw went out the next day to look for the Circus.

He found it.

He caught up with a formation of red-splashed jerries, and the all-black Tripes flashed about looking for a particular Albatros that had followed Nash to the ground. Like a black wraith, Collishaw swooped down on a green-striped ship and cut him away from the rest of the formation. They were equally matched. The German flew and fought well, but Collishaw was fighting with a spirit of vengeance in his hands and heart. They were circling high over the outskirts of Lille when the break came. The German had gained a momentary advantage from above and behind, but Collishaw went up on one wing tip, and the Albatros missed and swooped past. Collishaw pivoted on his horizontal axis and his guns spat flame.

For a second the Albatros hung on a sharp turn and then its nose snapped down and a white scarf trailed behind; the white gradually turned to black and there was a brief flicker of flame and a shattering crash on the old fortifications of Lille. When Collishaw looked around to take stock he discovered he had been carried well over the German lines, but his Black Flight was re-forming. The Germans had scattered, and three of the Circus besides his especial victim had gone down. High in the blue, 2,000 feet above the combat, a blood-red Albatros that had not come down during the fight wheeled and then flew back toward Germany.

The man in the red Albatros might not have been von Richthofen, but the man who died in the green-striped Albatros was Leutnant Allmenroeder, second highest ranking ace in Jagdstaffel 11 with his bag of thirty and reputed to be the closest friend of the Baron. It may be interesting to note that while Allmenroeder was downing Nash and the others of the

Circus were tying up the Black Flight the day before, von Richthofen had brought down the two-seater Collishaw's crowd had been escorting.

But Collishaw had no respect for any German ranking ace or neophyte. In the first twelve days of July he added twelve more to his sheet and on July 30, with his score up to thirty-seven, he was sent back to Canada for a leave of two months. By mid-November he was back again and given command of No. 13 (Naval) Squadron and on December 1 added to his score by downing two seaplanes and an L.V.G. two-seater.

When the Royal Air Force was formed in April 1918 Collishaw was given the commission of major and placed in command of No. 203 Squadron, which was flying Sop Camels. Through the next four months, while flying the 1917 Camel against the new German squadrons of Fokker D.7's and their like, he accounted for twenty more victims, ten of which were the vaunted Fokker. In that period he also scored "doubles" on seven occasions. He had the British Distinguished Service Cross, the Distinguished Service Order, the Distinguished Flying Cross, and on August 3 was given a bar to his D.S.O. He was returned to England about October 1, promoted to lieutenant colonel, and joined Billy Bishop, Andy McKeever, and other famous Canadian airmen who were laying the basic plans for a Royal Canadian Air Force, but the war ended in November and the proposed R.C.A.F. did not emerge until 1924.

Although Ray Collishaw had done more than his share, unlike most of the others, he stayed on when the war ended, taking command of an Allied air force that went to the aid of the Czarist cause under General Denikin, who was trying to oust the Bolsheviki from Russia. It is not known how many planes Ray clobbered in this doomed campaign, but the British government admitted that twenty would be a very modest figure, none of which, of course, were added to his World War I score.

When the Russian White Army collapsed in 1920 Collishaw was brought back to England, given a tropical uniform, and sent out with No. 84 Squadron to Persia, where the Bolsheviki were menacing a British protectorate. He was still flying Camels and by April 1921 was back in Mesopotamia for service against insurgent Arabs. Here he was raised to the rank of wing commander.

Collishaw stayed with the R.A.F. and was in action again in 1939 when World War II erupted. This time he was in command of a Fleet Air Arm Fighter Group that swarmed off Royal Navy aircraft carriers. He fought all through that war with great distinction—but with little publicity—and when last heard of had finally accepted honourable retirement and a country home in Nanaimo, B.C.

Whenever there is talk about fighting airmen and comparisons are made, the name of Ray Collishaw always comes up and it is very difficult to select anyone else who can match his service and exploits.

Another Royal Air Force ace who is still living is Major Donald MacLaren of Canada, who is credited with fifty-four enemy planes. I met MacLaren at a reunion of R.F.C. and R.N.A.S. pilots held in Toronto early in 1958, and he looked like a man of thirty-five. Like so many of his breed, he was disinclined to talk of the old days and much of his story presented here has been taken from a number of articles written about him by knowledgeable British writers. Actually not too much is known of his career, as he was always a very uncommunicative man, and his great record was hung up in 1918 when the air war had been greatly broadened in scope and victories came with comparative ease.

MacLaren grew up in the Peace River country of northern British Columbia and much of his early life was spent in the Arctic areas, where the MacLarens had opened a trading post in opposition to the Hudson's Bay Company. The war seemed a long way off and unimportant in the far North, but by 1916 Donald's brother Roy had joined up and the full impact of the conflict reached home. After talking it over with his father, Donald mushed out for Vancouver and eventually signed up with the R.F.C. and was trained at Camp Borden, Ontario. By the autumn of 1917 he had his wings and was on his way to England. In November he was posted to No. 46 Squadron, which was flying Camels, and he arrived at the front just in time to encounter the bad weather that marked the Battle of Cambrai period.

Instead of getting into the air-fighting action, MacLaren went on tactical operations, and it wasn't until late in February, when he was on a patrol organised expressly for air fighting, that he downed a German Pfalz. In March, between the low-down activity, he scored over another Pfalz and an old Albatros. On one afternoon he got a mixed bag of a mobile railroad gun, an Albatros two-seater, and a kite balloon. As the kite balloon floated down he was attacked by a Hannoveraner two-seater, but after a few tight Camel circuits the Hannah went down and crashed on the bank of the Péronne-Douai canal. MacLaren was awarded the Military Cross.

The rest of MacLaren's story is a repetition of what has

been written of other aces. When the Great War was two weeks from its bloody climax he had boosted his tally to fifty-four, but one afternoon, while playing rugby with a pickup team composed of pilots and mechanics, he broke a leg. He never flew a Camel again and ended the war fifth on the list of British fighting airmen.

As mentioned previously many fighter stars were consumed by some personal hate or prejudice that goaded them on to great heights. Captain G. E. H. McElroy of No. 40 Squadron, R.F.C., nurtured a hate of enemy two-seaters and ended the war with forty-six victories, more than half of which were biplane machines, the kind that were coming into prominence during the last year of the war.

McElroy, whose personality was high-lighted with a variety of backgrounds, was something of a mystery. No one seems to know whether he was born in Ireland or Canada. He is believed to have been the son of an Irish schoolmaster and born in Donnybrook, Dublin, but Canadian records claim he was born in Windsor, Ontario. The most likely version is that he was born in Ireland, taken to Canada at an early age, and then went back across the Atlantic to England sometime before the war began.

He seems to have begun his military life as a motorcycle despatch rider, linking London and Woolwich Arsenal, before he was granted a commission in the Royal Garrison Artillery. This home service did not appeal, however, and late in 1915 he applied for a transfer to the R.F.C., but wasn't accepted until February 9, 1916.

McElroy wasn't much of a pilot. A long series of crashes kept him in the hospital or on the training aerodromes—even through the scarlet period of Bloody April 1917, when anyone who could get off the ground was sent to the front. Instead, he was retained in Britain on so-called Zeppelin patrols and finally when a month passed without his logging a crash landing he was considered ready and shipped out to Bruay on August 23, 1917, to fly a Nieuport for No. 40 Squadron.

Within a week Mac came within a hair's breadth of being returned to Home Establishment by completely wrecking a new Nieuport through a faulty landing and then giving a repeat performance four hours later. However, he convinced the C.O. to keep him on but didn't blunder into a combat for nearly eight weeks. It was perhaps fortunate for him that No. 40 turned in their Nieuports and were given new S.E.5's, for from that point on Dame Fortune began to smile.

On December 28 he destroyed an L.V.G. two-seater and this latent success acted like a charm. Three days later he had a "double" as his final contribution of 1917. This came about after Mac was separated from his formation and, in searching for his comrades, ran into a flight of seven enemy scouts that were shooting a lone Camel to bits. He tore into the enemy formation, and two yellow and grey Albatros scouts went down in flames with an expenditure of less than fifty rounds.

In the new year of 1918 McElroy was on the sky-road to success, going all out for photographic or contour-fighting machines that harassed the infantry. Nevertheless he was not just a "cold-meat" expert, for the German two-seaters of this period were very capable of taking care of themselves and many a famous ace thought twice before tackling armoured L.V.G.'s, Rumplers, Halberstadts, and the most aggressive of all, the Hannoveraner. McCudden was particularly respectful of the "Flying-Whale," but McElroy shot down twelve of these biplane-tailed Hannahs before the odds of war turned against him.

On January 16 he destroyed two D.F.W.'s and sent one of the six protecting Pfalz out of control. The first two-seater fell in flames, the second plunged nose down with the observer trying to haul a dead pilot back off the controls, and the scout fluttered into a cloud with its engine smoking badly.

Two days later he caught a Hannoveraner cold with his top-wing Lewis gun, and in an effort to regain some command the German pilot so overcontrolled he finally yanked off his own wings.

McElroy was a dead shot and, like Billy Bishop, trusted his guns to only one man—himself. He sorted out his ammunition, sighted his own guns, and stood by and supervised the complete servicing of his aeroplane. This obviously paid off, for February was a red-letter month when he scored seven times in the space of two weeks, was awarded the Military Cross, and promoted to captain.

With his captaincy he was transferred to No. 24 Squadron, which necessitated a change in his fighting tactics. As a flight commander he could no longer sally forth after high-flying two-seaters. He was now expected to lead offensive patrols and take on routine fights with enemy scouts. But apparently this new responsibility had little effect on his aggressiveness and in the next five weeks he shot down thirteen scouts and one Rumpler. What spare time he had, he used up on ground-strafing expeditions. He averaged five patrols a day during the March retreat.

On March 8 Captain McElroy led his flight against a mixed formation of Fokker triplanes, Pfalz D.3's, and Albatros D.5's; at the end of the skirmish his score had risen to seventeen. A green Pfalz half rolled across his sights, and a quick burst sent it down with a serape of smoke and flame trailing behind. Mac narrowly escaped a collision with another Pfalz and turned on a black-and-white triplane and shot away its main strut; the German's wings folded back and it went down in a corkscrew spin. The next day he attacked nine German triplanes over Bohain, shot one down, and chased the others all the way back to their field. That afternoon he came upon a Halberstadt strafing a British advanced post, so he went down and killed both the pilot and observer with one short burst.

When the Germans began the great push on March 28 McElroy had rammed his score up to twenty-eight and on the first day of the attack logged eight combats. While attacking the charging German troops with Cooper bombs and machine-gun fire, three Albatros scouts came down to break up his formation. In less than five minutes two had gone down completely out of control and a third spun in with a dead pilot, but because of the speed of the retreat McElroy was credited with only one. Later in the day he downed an armoured L.V.G., which was fully confirmed.

Over the next few days he was in the air practically every moment of daylight, fighting like a man determined to win the war on his own and by the time April was a week old his score stood at thirty-eight. But this pace began to tell, and against his will Mac was ordered home for a complete rest. In his absence Germany played her final fighter card.

The new Fokker D.7, which had won out in a fighter-type competition in January against the best produced by Albatros, Pfalz, Dornier, Rumpler, Aviatik, and others, was coming off the Schwerin and Johannisthal production lines. An initial order for 400 D.7's began to reach the front-line Staffels late in April and their appearance put temporary life in the German Air Force.

This machine was an orthodox biplane with steel-tube N-struts, powered with a 160-h.p. Mercedes engine, which gave it a top speed of 120 m.p.h., using the available synthetic fuel. It was also produced with a 180-h.p. Mercedes, a 220-h.p. Mercedes, and the 185-h.p. B.M.W. (Bayerische Moteren Werke) engine. Its speed was not equal to the best Allied fighters, but it had another feature that gave it some ascendancy in that it retained a sensitive control at slow speeds, whereas most machines of this classification tended to become loggy or slack. It was its ability to climb fast from sharp dives, "hang on the prop" at slow speeds, and rake any aircraft overhead that made it an outstanding performer. With it, Tony Fokker had at last countered the tiltable Lewis gun of the S.E.5 and the Nieuport scout. But even more important the D.7 was supposed to be easy to fly. I had the questionable pleasure of flying one late in 1918 at a British fighter school and found that particular model to be rather like a Mack truck in its handling capabilities.

The Fokker D.7 was not the miracle machine so many have maintained. It was the best the Germans had produced in this class and it came at a very critical period in the Imperial Air Service's waning fortunes. Many of their great aces had passed on, and a new covey of fledglings was being rushed out to the fighter squadrons; newcomers with limited training who needed an up-to-date mount that was not too difficult to master. The D.7 fitted the requirement perfectly.

August 1918 saw a new but very short period of success when German air victories (not necessarily all Fokker D.7 victories) rose to 565 in contrast to 217 the previous April. By the autumn of 1918 practically every German fighter squadron on the Western Front was equipped with the Fokker D.7 and today the general reader has the impression that the D.7's were the chief fighter aircraft of the German Air Force. Actually the D.7 was flown for about only five months. While it did play a stellar role during the last few months of the war, it is erroneous to regard it as their premier air fighter of all times. The Albatros fighters bore the brunt of German air battles over the four long years of combat. It would be as ridiculous to state that the Sopwith Snipe was the most important British air fighter. It was a great machine, but it came too late to have made an impressive mark in the ultimate victory.

Back in England Captain McElroy heard the reports of the new German effort, but eleven weeks slipped by before he was returned to France and again he was posted to No. 40 Squadron, which witnessed the end of his eventful career. Within six weeks he had scored twelve more victories.

On July 20 he had a very narrow escape while attacking a Hannoveraner near La Bassée when a loose connecting rod of an engine in a borrowed plane finally gave way, and the severed fuel line soon smothered the machine in fire. Doing what he had been taught, he sideslipped the machine to the ground. He was only slightly burned and had a bruised knee but landed safely.

But on July 31 McElroy took off in the early morning mists and did not return. No one knows what happened, but there was one report that he had fallen near Laventie. The Germans made no claim for him and there were never the vaguest reports that might explain whether he was shot down by ground fire or finally fell a victim of some alert gunner on a Hannoveraner.

Major William G. Barker of Dauphin, Manitoba, stood sixth on the list of British Empire aces and was one of the nineteen to win the Victoria Cross. Like that of so many others who were prominent in the last year of the war, his history is vague and dim today. He destroyed fifty-three German aircraft and ended his war career in a blaze of heroism.

Again we have a cavalryman turned airman. At the outbreak of war he joined the Canadian Mounted Rifles and because of his physique, poise, and all-round soldierly manner was assigned to their "suicide section," as machine-gun teams were known in those days. In 1915 the Mounted Rifles had reached Shorncliffe, England, and by September 22 his regiment crossed the Channel to France. Once there, the C.M.R. did what most cavalry outfits did—gave up their horses and saddles and served as infantry. Barker soon applied for the R.F.C. and, like so many Canadians, was almost immediately successful. Britishers who also wanted to get out of the mud and slots were seldom so fortunate.

Barker first served as an aerial gunner in the back seat of a B.E.2c at No. 9 Squadron. While there, he won his first victory during the battle of Neuve-Chapelle in March 1916. By April 2 he was granted a commission and went to London to change his uniform. When he returned as a Second Lieutenant on April 7 he was assigned to No. 4 Squadron on the Somme. He was still in the back seat of a B.E.2c, however. Late in 1916 he was sent to England for pilot training and by January 1917 was back with No. 15 Squadron as a pilot and took over a job as a flight commander. He was probably one of the best trained Canadian airmen of his era. His many tours in these reconnaissance squadrons had taught him practically everything. He had flown for more than eighteen months on a very busy front and was certainly due for a rest.

His respite turned out to be more flight training—on the Sopwith Camel. The change from the B.E. and R.E.8, which he had flown all that time, was a revelation to him and he couldn't wait to return to France and pay back the Hun for all the rough trips they had given him.

No. 28 Squadron was just forming in England and by October 2 they flew over and landed at Saint-Omer. Barker was now a captain—a flight commander—and soon after settling

231

down he was ordered to take his A flight over the line to attack German troops who were moving up the Ypres-Menin road. This resulted in a mad foray in which the Camel flight was attacked by a Staffel of Albatros scouts. Barker knocked down two. Other pilots scored singles, but they lost two of their flight mates.

No. 28 Squadron was next shipped down to the Italian front to bolster the situation against the Austrians, where Barker fought like a madman, attacking enemy planes, bombing enemy redoubts, and doing his best to put a brake on the enemy retreat. In a short time he had graduated from a flight commander and was given command of No. 66 Squadron, also on the Italian front. Here he downed the famous Captain Linke Crawford, an Austrian who had claimed twenty-seven victories. This was an epic fight but ended with the Austrian spinning to his finish smack in the middle of his own aerodrome. By this time Barker had all the medals the appreciative Italian government could bestow and practically all those available in the British Empire. During the latter part of his term in Italy he commanded a mixed squadron of Camels and Bristol Fighters and with these worked out a plan of attack that drove the Austrian Air Force out of the skies.

Barker was finally relieved of his strenuous post early in September 1918 and appointed to command a fighting school in England, but before taking over he requested a short tour of duty on the Western Front to learn the latest tactics. He was temporarily assigned to No. 201 Squadron, which was flying the new Sopwith Snipe, the eventual replacement for the Camel. In the short time it was in the fighting area the Snipe proved itself to be the most satisfactory and efficient fighting scout turned out by the Allies. Barker was delighted with it and after a short stay on the front he set out to return to England.

The date was October 27 and he was supposed to fly direct to Hounslow, England, but instead he climbed to 20,000 feet and took on a German two-seater. He manoeuvred long enough to break it up in mid-air, but during this fight a Fokker triplane soared above him and the next thing he knew he felt an explosive bullet pierce his right thigh. He turned on the Fokker, however, and in a minute or so caused it to crash on fire. While he watched the Hun Tripe fall away a force of sixty Fokkers—a complete German Circus—closed in on him. Thousands of bullets streamed down on him from every direction and the new Snipe was riddled, and another enemy slug pierced his left thigh.

But Barker refused to capitulate and kept the Snipe turning and firing. Two Fokker D.7's crashed. Still he hung on but eventually fainted from loss of blood, and the Snipe went down in a falling-leaf pattern until he revived. He took over again and went into his fighting circle once more and found the Fokkers were still attacking. He related sometime later that he had given up all hope but decided to fight it out and take as many as possible with him.

Another Fokker burst into flames and spun out of action. With a little opening Barker attempted to guide the Snipe through the enemy formation but found his stick-arm would not function. Another jerry bullet had shattered his elbow. He tried to switch over to the left arm but fainted again. When he came out of it once more he saw the Snipe was heading for another Fokker, so he pressed the trigger and the Red Devil went down minus a set of wings.

The Staffel made one last try to get this invulnerable flyer, and in the exchange Barker's fuel tank was shot out, but he managed to switch to his reserve container and make for his own lines. How he got there he did not know but fortunately fought his way to a British rear area, where the Snipe bounced over a series of shell holes and finally nosed over on her back. A group of Scottish Highlanders rushed out of their trenches and rescued him. The only injury he received in the crash was a broken nose.

Barker lay unconscious for days in the hospital at Rouen. When he finally regained consciousness he was told that he had accounted for six German planes, downing four officially and two more listed as probably out of control. He was also told that he had won the Victoria Cross.

The war ended soon after and while medical science did all it could for him, it could never alleviate the ache of his shattered bones. He limped about for years, trying to recover but was never free of almost unendurable pain. He was posted to the new Royal Canadian Air Force after the war, where he tried to make himself useful—but there was always the pain. On March 12, 1930, he died in an air crash at Uplands Field outside Ottawa. There seemed to be no reason for the crash, and the best that can be said is that it ended Billy Barker's long agony.

Two Australian pilots who served with the R.F.C. and R.A.F. deserve mention. They are Captain R. King, who won the D.S.O. and the new Distinguished Flying Cross, and Lieutenant L. T. E. Taplin, who downed twelve German airmen while serving with No. 1 Squadron of the Australian Flying Corps in Palestine and a Camel squadron in France.

The Australians did not receive the publicity given the Canadian air fighters but for sheer reckless daring were without equal. Their Nos. 2 and 4 Squadrons made thrilling records with their continual attacks against enemy airfields. Captain King, who was a most unobtrusive man, was the leader in these dangerous exploits. No. 4 Squadron flew Sopwith Camels and throughout 1918 King was in the middle of every tactical operation the Camels were given to do. His personal bag of enemy planes included seven vaunted Fokker D.7's, six L.V.G.'s, three kite balloons, an odd Pfalz, D.F.W.'s and a Rumpler C.5 His favourite trick was to take off just as the night mists were gathering and then suddenly appear over German fields as the mechanics were putting their war birds to bed. The crazy Camels would unload their bombs on hangars gorged with aircraft. On August 16 King led no less than sixty Camels—everyone wanted to do one of these wild shows —against an enemy field at Haubourdin. When they left there was nothing worth salvaging; they even bombed out a lone searchlight standard and fired the petrol dump.

By September King's squadron was given the new Sopwith Snipe and with that machine had a field day. When they were ordered to stay on the ground by the terms of the Armistice, they ignored the order and went hangar-strafing just the same.

Lieutenant Taplin transferred to the R.F.C. in the summer of 1917. His No. 1 Squadron located "somewhere in Palestine" was equipped with B.E.12a's and most of his time was taken up with routine reconnaissance, photography, and the odd spot of desert bombing. Once, while doing a special reconnaissance show over the Nablus hills, his camera went haywire, so he held the stick between his knees, took the camera from its mounting, and calmly repaired the fault. While he was thus engaged an Albatros D.3 suddenly appeared and added to his troubles by putting four bullets through the bellows of the camera. Turning on the German, Taplin opened fire, but after one burst his gun jammed and the Albatros nosed down for safety. The Australian then cleared the gun and went after the German and poured twenty rounds into him; the Albatros spun 12,000 feet and piled up in the desert. Taplin then went on with his camera problems.

After several other such exploits Taplin was marked for better things and was next trained on Sopwith Camels at Castle Bromwich, England. Eventually he went out to France with the Australian No. 4 Squadron, where he concentrated on the new German Pfalz fighter.

On July 26 he had a brush with death on his own aerodrome. While he was taking off on a bombing raid his undercarriage hit a bump and the axle snapped. Fortunately he had forgotten to fasten his safety belt and when one of his 40-pound bombs exploded it threw him clear of the wrecked Camel. But he was still not entirely out of danger, for, ignited by the phosphorus bomb, his ammunition belts and Very signal cartridges exploded and he had to lie flat on the ground for five minutes to avoid being shot by his own machine-gun bullets.

Taplin was soon in the air again and ended his twelve-Hun record on September 5, 1918. Something of a Camel circus had been arranged to do a special offensive patrol, and Taplin was selected to lead one flight. The idea was good but was unluckily timed with the return of a larger group of Fokker D.7's. There was a mix-up of signals and half the Camel force dived for home, but Taplin's crew either missed the signal or decided that a few Camels were equal to a couple dozen Fokkers.

They were wrong. Taplin downed three of them before he was badly wounded and had to land in German territory. However, the Armistice soon intervened and freed him from a German hospital, from where he was returned to Australia. Nothing has been heard of him since.

To conclude this portion of Britain's effort through 1918 without some reference to the Independent Air Force would be a slur on the memory of Major General Sir Hugh Trenchard, the Father of the Royal Air Force. This splendid soldier, who was born in 1873, first served in India with the Royal Scots Fusiliers. He was wounded in the Boer War and did not get back to his mother country until 1912. The Royal Flying Corps was then in its infancy, but Major Trenchard had foresight enough to realize that this flying service would eventually displace the cavalry. When he requested a transfer he was told, "Sorry, Major, but aren't you too old for flying? You must be forty. Besides, to get into the R.F.C. you must have a pilot's ticket and pass a Central Flying School examination."

Trenchard looked up T. O. M. Sopwith, who had a flying service of sorts, and within ten days had flown solo, passed his C.F.S. test, and wangled a Royal Aero Club certificate. He had beaten the age limit by seven hours!

A few days after the opening of the Great War Trenchard was appointed head of a new military wing and by August 1915 was Colonel Trenchard, commander of the Royal Flying Corps in France.

He was a great and wise leader, but his views were contrary to those of the gravel-crushers and he was often in trouble with the Red Tabs at Whitehall. As we explained, he had little time for the air aces. He was the first to propose the theory of a strategic air programme and his war of words with his superiors and the politicians eventually undermined his position and he found it wise to resign his post and return to Britain.

The full details of this service quarrel have never been fully explained, but it is generally agreed that Trenchard wanted to use the R.F.C. as a complete strategic weapon, whereas the military insisted that his planes and pilots support front-line activities, where their efforts could be seen and appreciated by the infantrymen.

Soon after his arrival in London Trenchard evidently found a few sympathetic ears.

"Just what is it you want to do, Boom?" someone inquired.

"I want a free and independent service of at least sixty squadrons of my own choice," he eventually told Parliament. "The war can drag out indefinitely if we continue to hurl our weight against the German Army in the field. It can be won quickly by striking at the heart of that army through a relentless attack on its sources of supply. I agree, the bombing of Germany was a luxury when we did not have sufficient aircraft to do the work required by the Army. Now, the bombing of Germany is a necessity."

After long debate "Boom" Trenchard finally won and on May 20, 1918, he returned to France to organise the Independent Air Force. When the force actually came into being on June 1, 1918, it was composed of only four squadrons, not sixty as he had planned. However, with Nos. 55 (D.H.4's), 99 (D.H.9's), 100 (F.E.2b's), and 216 (Handley-Page bombers) he began what may have been the series of strategic thrusts that brought the German nation to capitulation.

He started his hammer blows on that fateful June day and never stopped sending out his bombers until the Armistice was signed. Over the first month the above handful of machines raided constantly in a strategic area 136 miles removed from their base in Nancy. That meant flying 272 miles, fighting there and back. Even the old F.E.2b, painted black for night flying, had no dread of long-distance raids. They

236

went out night after night and the history of No. 100 Squadron shows as much daring, heroism, and devotion to duty as any work in military annals. The Fees and D.H.4's were festooned with extra fuel tanks, so that their usual three-and-a-quarter-hour range was extended to five and a half hours. The new two-engined Handley-Pages, of course, could stay in the air eight hours.

Colonel Billy Mitchell, commander of the U.S. Air Force, was most enthusiastic about Trenchard's bomber ideas and soon offered his help. "We have no American bombardment squadrons ready," he said, "but we can supply escorts for your bombers. It will be a wonderful opportunity."

In that short but sincere appreciation Billy Mitchell laid the foundation for America's great Strategic Air Command of today.

But the French would have no part of Trenchard's Independent Air Force. Their bomber crews were very tired. They were too busy complying with the *matériel* and training requests of their new ally—the United States. They had too many duties to perform.

Colonel Mitchell sensed that the French were using his handful of pursuit squadrons in extravagant support of the French Army and immediately saw why Trenchard had refused to have a hand in such wasteful operations. Mitchell decided his available fighters would be better employed supporting Trenchard's Independent Air Force so long as he had no bombers of his own to escort. From that time on Mitchell and Trenchard were sincere friends.

Late in June Trenchard put on his first big raid. By now No. 104 Squadron, flying D.H.4's, had been added to his meagre strength. They attacked a tremendous German dump at Fère-en-Tardenois from an altitude of 500 feet, while high above them British and American fighters battled with the enemy defence Staffels. That raid was an epic of the war. Almost a hundred bombers swept over the secluded target and twelve went down in flames. The British and American fighters, however, destroyed twenty enemy scouts with a loss of only six.

"Boom" worked the men of his five-squadron force hard, but they appreciated his leadership and willingly volunteered for raid after raid. This was a pilot's force of Britons, Canadians, and Americans who had sought out this Trenchard group because they too believed in his strategic theory. If a man got in who did not belong he was quietly moved out. When a daring spirit flamed in a regular bomber outfit he was invited to join the I.A.F. Through the latter part of 1918 the Independent Air Force was the most envied of all flying groups because, as they said, it was an answer to a good pilot's prayer.

In the next few weeks the I.A.F. carried out 709 major air raids. These were divided as follows: 374 on larger German cities, 209 on important German airfields, and 126 on important military objectives. They destroyed 156 German planes in air combat and lost 111 bombers to the enemy defences. They started out with five squadrons and never could boast of more than ten. There are not many survivors left today and unfortunately no one has as yet written a worthy account of the Independent Air Force.

Eventually an ominous demand was noted throughout the force. Everyone realised by now that the German people had to feel the full impact of the war. "Let's bomb Berlin!" was heard again and again.

Trenchard rushed to Britain to needle the British aircraft manufacturers. He knew that Handley-Page and Vickers machines capable of bombing Berlin had been on their drawing boards for some time. If they realised he had the men willing and able to fly there, they might get a dozen or so off the assembly line.

It was not to be. Handley-Page did get one flight of their four-engined V-1500 bombers to No. 166 Squadron, being formed at Bircham Newton. It would have carried thirty 250-pound bombs and a crew of four. It could have reached Berlin from any field in eastern Britain. The Vickers Vimy bomber, another machine designed with Berlin in mind, wasn't quite ready, but when it was it became the first aircraft to fly the Atlantic, under the hands of Alcock and Brown in 1919.

All the whispers along the grapevine must have reached Berlin. Germany must have known that there was no stopping Trenchard's Independent Air Force. They must have known that Trenchard planned to bomb Berlin with three Handley-Page V-1500 bombers on November 20. The Germans must have known, for they gave up on November 11, and "Boom" Trenchard was deprived of his greatest hour.

Below is the list of warplanes designed and produced for the Royal Air Force during the last year of the war. Only a few went into full production. Many were especially designed for the proposed push against Berlin, a plan that never went into action. Had the Germans learned what aerial bombing was really like they might not have supported Adolf Hitler and brought on World War II.

Make	Engine	Speed m.p.h.	Purpose
D.H.9a	Liberty 400 h.p.	110	Reconnaissance-bomber
D.H.9a	Rolls-Royce 450 h.p.	117	Reconnaissance-bomber
D.H.10a	Liberty (2) 400 h.p.	128	Night Bomber
Armstrong-Whitworth	R.A.F. 90 h.p.	85	Trainer
A.W. Armadillo	A.B.C. 320 h.p.	140	Fighter
A.W. Ara	A.B.C. 320 h.p.	150	Fighter
Austin Greyhound	A.B.C. 320 h.p.	130	Two-seater Fighter
Avro 530	Hisso 200 h.p.	128	Two-seater Fighter
Avro Manchester	Siddeley Puma 300 h.p.	125	Photo-reconnaissance
Avro Pike	B.H.P. (2) 230 h.p.	?	Long-range Bomber
Avro Spider	Bentley 180 h.p.	124	Fighter
B.A.T. Bantam	A.B.C. 200 h.p.	138	Fighter
B.A.T. Basilisk	A.B.C. 300 h.p.	162	Fighter
B.A.T. Baboon	A.B.C. 170 h.p.	90	Trainer
Beardmore W.B.1	B.H.P. (2) 230 h.p.	91	Two-place Bomber
Beardmore W.B.2	Beardmore 515 h.p.	120	Two-seater Fighter
Beardmore W.B.3	Le Rhone 80 h.p.	103	Ship-deck Scout
Beardmore W.B.4	Hisso 200 h.p.	110	Ship-deck Scout
Beardmore W.B.5	Hisso 200 h.p.	112	Flight-deck Fighter
Beardmore W.B.6	Rolls-Royce 350 h.p.	102	Torpedo Carrier
Blackburn	Rolls-Royce (2) 250 h.p.	101	Long-range Bomber
Blackburn Baby	Clerget 130 h.p.	101	Seaplane-fighter
Blackburn S.P.	Rolls-Royce (2) 250 h.p.	105	Seaplane-bomber
Blackburn	Rolls-Royce (2) 350 h.p.	92	Torpedo Carrier
Boulton & Paul	Bentley 236 h.p.	125	Fighter-scout
Boulton & Paul	A.B.C. (2) 300 h.p.	124	Fighter-bomber
Bristol F.1	Sunbeam 200 h.p.	138	Fighter-reconnaissance
Bristol M.R.1	Sunbeam 200 h.p.	110	All-metal Fighter

Make	Engine	Speed m.p.h.	Purpose
Bristol Braemar	Liberty (4) 400 h.p.	125	Triplane Bomber
Fairey F.16	Sunbeam 260 h.p.	93	Seaplane Bomber
Fairey F.127	Rolls-Royce 190 h.p.	103	Seaplane
Fairey 3B	Sunbeam 260 h.p.	97	Sea Bomber
Fairey 3C	Rolls-Royce 375 h.p.	104	Naval Reconnaissance
Gosport	A.B.C. 50 h.p.	65	Flying-boat
Gosport	Rolls-Royce 280 h.p.	91	Patrol-boat
Grahame-White	Sunbeam (3) 270 h.p.	105	Day Bomber
Martinsyde F.4	Rolls-Royce 275 h.p.	145	Fighter
Nieuport Nighthawk	A.B.C. 320 h.p.	151	Fighter-scout
Handley-Page	Rolls-Royce (4) 375 h.p.	103	Night Bomber
Parnel Panther	Bentley 230 h.p.	122	Ship Reconnaissance
Phoenix Cork	Rolls-Royce (2) 360 h.p.	106	Flying-boat
Short N.2B	Sunbeam 275 h.p.	90	Seaplane-bomber
Short Cromarty	Rolls-Royce (2) 700 h.p.	101	Seaplane-bomber
Short F.3	Rolls-Royce (2) 400 h.p.	85	Anti-submarine Boat
Sopwith Snipe	Bentley 230 h.p.	121	Fighter
Sopwith Dolphin	Hisso 200 h.p.	121	Fighter-scout
Sopwith Salamander	Bentley 230 h.p.	125	Ground Fighter
Sopwith Hippo	Clerget 200 h.p.	115	Two-seater Fighter
Supermarine Baby	Hisso 150 h.p.	117	One-seater Flying-boat
Supermarine AD	Hisso 200 h.p.	90	Flying-boat
Vickers FB.16H	Hisso 300 h.p.	147	Fighter
Vickers Vampire	Bentley 200 h.p.	121	Pusher-fighter
Vickers Vimy	Hisso (2) 200 h.p.	90	Night Bomber
Vickers Vimy	Rolls-Royce (2) 375 h.p.	103	Night Bomber
Westland Wagtail	A.B.C. 170 h.p.	125	Altitude Fighter
Westland N.16	Bentley 150 h.p.	108	Seaplane-scout

To imply that the French did no bombing throughout 1918 would be most unjust. They did, but it was tactical bombing, not the long-range, around-the-clock strategic attack devised by General Trenchard. Their efforts through the early spring were aimed at the enemy railheads and front-area communications centres. On January 29 Captain Vuillemin and Sub-lieutenant Lecreux, flying a Bréguet, staged a daring attack on the munitions siding at Thiaucourt. At only forty feet above the ground the pilot strafed with his gun while Lecreux released their bombs, completely wiping out the whole station.

Through February French bombers dropped 460 tons of high explosive but suffered heavy losses trying to get back. On the fifth, fourteen Bréguets attacked the Mauser factory again and on the return trip eleven of the bombers were destroyed.

With the March push French squadrons were also placed on low-level attacks and important reconnaissance and photography patrols. During this terrible period French fighters downed 127 enemy planes against a loss of ninety-one of their own machines. The heaviest casualties occurred among the reconnaissance groups, but the scouts also suffered disastrously. When it was feared the famous Storks would be decimated, René Fonck was transferred from Escadrille S.103 and quickly put new life in Les Cigognes by downing a new Pfalz on March 17. It was his thirtieth victory. Nungesser scored twice on the opening of the ground attack but was wounded on March 28 during a fight with five Albatros scouts, the first of thirteen wounds he received in 1918. Madon was also making a name for himself by raising his score to twenty-five with a double victory on March 9.

The French had acquired manufacturing rights for the new Italian Caproni bomber and the first of these dreadnoughts appeared on the Western Front in April of 1918. Why this plane was adopted is somewhat of a mystery, since the French had been very successful in producing bombers that fitted their particular needs. However, they were soon being flown on raids against nearby railway centres and ammunition dumps.

Their Naval Air service was prominent this month, accounting for nineteen enemy planes, three balloons, and five U-boats. On April 18 Sub-lieutenant Rossai and two companions sighted two submarines on the surface. Once it was determined that they were enemy craft, Rossai attacked both deep-sea raiders, but the U-boat gunners answered with heavy machine-gun fire and one of the naval aircraft fell in flames. Rossai immediately drove the German gunners down their hatchways and then attacked with light bombs. One submarine went down like a stone but during this attack the other opened fire again and a large shell chunk almost severed

Rossai's left arm at the shoulder. He turned away, sought a quiet section of water, where he put his machine down, and awaited help for nearly two hours before being picked up by a French destroyer.

A French seaplane was fired on by the German submarine U.29 over the Straits of Gibraltar on May 11. The seaplane pilot scored with a light bomb and damaged the U-boat's diving gear. Realizing the advantage he held, the French pilot signalled the sub commander to head his vessel toward the French shore. This amazing patrol continued for some time with the air pilot dropping bombs or firing his machine gun whenever the German appeared to be making any move to escape. It is probably the only instance of an aircraft capturing a submarine single-handed.

Another freak of war was registered between May 14 and 17 when French bombers dropped 110 tons of bombs on enemy dumps. During this spree a night formation involving eight Bréguet bombers arrived over an artillery-shell dump at Bois de Champion and, nosing down in single file, scored direct hits on the main storage sheds. That same night the Dutch Meteorological Institute reported a "local earthquake" between 9.46 and 9.50 p.m. This was later traced to the Bois de Champion area, and the French put up one bombing claim that could not be denied.

The French had a very hard time throughout June. The von Richthofen Jagdgeschwader 1 had been moved down to the Verdun front and they had a taste of what the British suffered in Bloody April of 1917. So great was the toll, the Royal Air Force was called in to their aid. On June 1 a formation of Gothas attacked Paris and while one Gotha was shot down by a combined attack of Spads and a Bréguet, five defence planes flamed down. In another attack on June 27 a similar formation of Gothas lost one machine as the result of a direct hit by an anti-aircraft battery outside Compiègne, but the Gotha gunnery was superb, and four more defence aircraft were lost.

Through the early summer French bomber losses were abnormally high, which perhaps explains why General Trenchard's long-range plans were not considered with enthusiasm. One group alone had eighty-one pilots and observers killed and thirty-seven bombers destroyed in three weeks. When fifteen Bréguets of B.117 crossed the enemy lines on June 27 they were met by forty-eight enemy scouts; twelve of the fifteen were shot down, and the three survivors were raked with fire when they landed on their own field; this killed one pilot and two observers. This particular escadrille was ill-starred, for in thirteen weeks it lost forty-five machines and 116 men, the highest casualty list ever recorded in a like period by any World War I squadron.

The day after those twelve bombers were lost B.117 scored something of a revenge—at least from the tactical point of view. Learning that the Germans were massing troops for an attack near Cutry, they sent ten bombers off to halt them. Five tons of bombs rained down on these unfortunates, and then the observers raked what was left with their machine guns. In less than an hour the ground around Cutry was scarlet with human devastation.

French fighter squadrons were also having a very bad time and great names were continually being written on the roll of honour. One ranking ace, Captain Derode, made an attack on four Fokker D.7's, sending down one to a fiery finish—his seventh victim. A short time later he came upon a Halberstadt two-seater and proceeded to stalk it, but in the meantime two Pfalz stalked him and he crashed with three bullets in his head without ever seeing his attackers.

Another seven-victory pilot, Jean Marty, in diving to the aid of a companion, collided with an Albatros and both machines fell in flames. Pierre Rosseau, who had flown constantly for ten months and had six official kills, was sent to Britain to lecture on aerial fighting. With Lieutenant Pierran he left France to fly to Hounslow but while making a final turn for their landing a control jammed and they fell in the peaceful English countryside and were crushed beyond recognition in the wreckage.

But the high-ranking aces continued to add to their scores and through September and October the French *L'Aviation Militaire* was swarming over enemy territory. The Germans had the Fokker D.7 and the new Pfalz, but the French would not be denied. Nungesser closed his war record by destroying four balloons in less than twenty minutes but shortly after that received his seventeenth wound, which made him unfit for further military service.

By now the Allied aces were scoring easy victories. Coiffard brought his tally to thirty when he destroyed five balloons in two days. He downed two more on September 14 and three on the 15th. René Fonck obtained his second six-in-one day record when he demolished three D.7's, two Halberstadts, and a D.F.W. An unfortunate argument arose concerning the D.F.W., since it was also claimed by a Lieutenant De Sevin, one of Fonck's companions. However, the French officials decided in favour of Fonck. During the last three months of the war Fonck is said to have used an improved version of Guynemer's 37-mm. Spad cannon and claimed sixteen enemy aircraft with the tricky weapon.

In the last few days of the war German pilots took several of the leading French aces with them to Valhalla. On September 20 Boyeau, who then ranked fifth, fell before the guns of some unknown shortly after he had watched his thirty-fifth plane flutter to its end. France's leading balloon-strafer, Coiffard, also fell in flames from the firing of some ground machine gunner.

When the white flags of surrender fluttered the French Air Service had a strength of 6,000 first-line aircraft, 6,417 pilots, 1,682 observers, and a ground personnel of 80,000 officers and men. Their losses were far in excess of any other belligerent and represented over fifty-eight per cent of their total effective strength. In all, 5,353 pilots and observers made the great sacrifice and 3,085 received wounds in action.

There were 162 Frenchmen who could be considered aces. Of these, thirty-two lost their lives while an additional forty-seven were wounded. All in all the French Air Service accounted for 2,962 enemy aircraft and 347 observation balloons. Their bombers delivered a record of 6,460 tons of bombs and this branch of their service produced five aces and claimed the destruction of ninety-one aeroplanes and six kite balloons. A worthy record for the pilots and gunners of those old bombers. Below is presented the full complement of military aircraft designed and produced for the French Air Service in 1918. As in the case of the British many of these were only prototypes, and the war ended before they could be put into service production.

FRENCH WARPLANES OF 1918

Make	Engine	Speed m.p.h.	Purpose
Bréguet 16BN.2	Renault 450 h.p.	110	Bomber
Bréguet 17C.2	Renault 450 h.p.	126	Bomber-fighter
Bréguet 14H	Renault 300 h.p.	90	Sea Patrol
Caudron R.11	Hisso (2) 200 h.p.	116	Bomber
Caudron C.23-BN.2	Canton-Unne (2) 250 h.p.	90	Bomber
De Marcay C.	Hisso 300 h.p.	162	Fighter
Farman F.13B	Liberty 400 h.p.	115	Bomber
Farman F.50-BN.2	Lorraine (2) 275 h.p.	90	Bomber
Farman F.50P	Lorraine (2) 275 h.p.	93	Bomber
Farman F.60	Salmson (2) 260 h.p.	68	Bomber
Hanriot 3C.2	Salmson 230 h.p.	120	Fighter

Hanriot 5C.2	Salmson 270 h.p.	122	Fighter
Letord 9BN.2	Liberty (2) 400 h.p.	90	Bomber
Nieuport 28C.1	Mono-Gnome 160 h.p.	115	Fighter
Nieuport 31C.1	Hisso 300 h.p.	128	Fighter
Nieuport 39C.1	Lorraine 350 h.p.	142	Fighter
Salmson 7A.2	Salmson 230 h.p.	118	Reconnaissance
S.E.A. 4C.2*	Lorraine 350 h.p.	128	Fighter
Spad 17CA	Hisso 300 h.p.	138	Fighter
Spad 18CA.1-2	Hisso 300 h.p.	130	Reconnaissance
Spad 11	Hisso 220 h.p.	120	Reconnaissance
Spad 22	Hisso 300 h.p.	142	Fighter
Voisin Triplane	Hisso (4) 220 h.p.	110	Bomber
Voisin 10 BN.2	Renault 280 h.p.	115	Bomber
Voisin 12BN.2	Hisso (4) 220 h.p.	91	Bomber
Voisin 13BN.2	Hisso (4) 220 h.p.	91	Bomber

* Societe d'Etudes Aeronautiques, Aubervillers, Seine.

Although Raoul Lufbery and the rest of the Lafayette Escadrille had transferred to the new American Aviation Service there were still a number of American volunteers fighting with various French squadrons and two of them, Frank Baylies and David E. Putnam, deserve more than passing mention in this portion of the book, for they both had splendid records.

Lieutenant Frank Baylies from New Bedford, Massachusetts, was a typical American boy of his day. His early schooling was spent at Brown Preparatory School in Providence, but instead of continuing on to college he returned home and entered his father's business. The Baylieses represented the upper middle class of those days, and Frank was fortunate in having access to an automobile. He learned to drive while in his early teens and showed considerable interest in mechanics. A quiet and unassuming personality, he became a very skilled motorist while driving for his father.

World War I had been on about two years when Frank, like so many others of his class, developed definite ideas concerning the right and wrong of the conflict and, since his sympathies were with the Allies, decided to do something about it. At that time the idea of becoming a flyer did not enter his mind; instead he joined the volunteer group of the American Field Service and was sent overseas to drive an ambulance. Many other American airmen found their way into the French and British services through this renowned organization which again aided the French and British forces in World War II and is still in existence.

Baylies served on the Verdun and Argonne sectors for more than a year, continually bringing out French wounded under fire with total disregard for his personal safety. The French government awarded him a special citation and shortly after that he applied for a transfer to the French Aviation Service and was accepted immediately and sent to the Avord school, where he graduated with high honours and was assigned to serve with the illustrious Storks Escadrille.

Nevertheless Baylies did not immediately set the front afire. He took his time, was prudent in his attacks, and spent hours figuring out the various problems that came up in the varying phases of aerial combat. It was not until February 19, 1918, that he made his first kill and another month passed before he repeated it. The latter part of April he was getting the feel of the requirements, and two more Fokkers blazed down.

Throughout May he fought almost daily and seven German fighters fell before his guns. On June 2 his twelfth official sky success was written into the records. Baylies may have accounted for more than twenty victories in this period, but several were scored so far behind the line it was impossible to gather the necessary evidence for confirmation. Throughout 1918 both the French and British were demanding complete information on all requests for victory records. As was to be expected many young impetuous flyers were prone to exaggerate reports, and officials responsible for these credits had to insist on more definite details of the action before the claims were acknowledged. Only planes seen to fall in flames or actually crash on the ground were considered. The action had to be witnessed and sworn to by at least two other members of the flight. Confirmation would be completely accepted only after a further report had been received from balloon observers or agents planted inside the enemy lines. As a result it often took weeks to fully confirm a victory.

Of course many planes were shot down during action above the clouds, in which case it was impossible to state that the victim had been seen to crash on the ground. And again an Allied pilot might engage an enemy machine, fire a number of bursts into it and kill the pilot, but the plane might go on flying unguided for some time, or until the fuel supply had been exhausted, and the victor would never know of his success. As a matter of fact the writer knows of one instance where a British R.E.8, flying an artillery-spotting mission, was attacked by a Fokker. The first burst must have killed both the pilot and the observer, but the stolid old bus continued on, heading for home with a dead man's hand on the stick. The remarkable climax of this particular case came when the artillery machine, flying on unguided by human hand, eventually ran out of fuel, simply dropped its nose, went into a normal glide, and landed without further damage in a ploughed field only 400 yards from its home airfield. When the mechanics and others ran over to investigate they were amazed to find both occupants stiff in death.

In this instance a German pilot scored a victory but never knew it and probably did not even enter a combat report on the incident.

It can readily be seen then that Baylies may have had many more victories, since he was the type who, once he started a fight, usually attempted to finish it no matter how far across the enemy line the combat took him. This quality in Baylies's fighting spirit was the cause of his death. On June 17 he was flying a two-ship patrol late in the afternoon with his closest friend, Lieutenant Edwin C. Parsons. Baylies's Spad was a particularly fast mount and he got far ahead of Parsons in his anxiety to get at a formation of Fokker triplanes. Probably believing Parsons was near at hand, Baylies attacked immediately, and before Parsons could get close enough to help, another triplane snapped out of a cloud above and latched on Baylies's tail. The first enemy burst caught the Spad cold and it went over on its back, dragging a long plume of smoke. Parsons saw it gliding into the enemy area but was unable to escort it for any distance, since the Fokkers turned to attack him and he only just managed to get safely into his own lines.

A few days later a German pilot roared across the Storks' field and dropped a message which stated that Baylies had been killed and had been buried with full military honours.

It has generally been conceded that Baylies might have become the leading American ace, with a record comparable to that of any British or French flyer, had he been more cautious and devoted more time to planned strategy as did his squadron leader, René Fonck. But with each succeeding week Baylies became more impetuous and his earlier quiet unassuming character was discarded, so much so that one French journalist stated that, "Baylies will either be shot down early in his career or he will accumulate an unbelievable number of victories."

It is quite possible that the change in Baylies's character occurred during his service with the American Field Service. There he saw the cruelty of war, what happened to infantrymen trapped in the trenches. At a very impressionable age he was brought face to face with the dead, dying, and wounded, and it is quite understandable why this lad, who had as yet

247

not reached his twentieth birthday, would brood on the grim effect of shot and shell and eventually volunteer for the flying service.

Another volunteer who flew the Spad was David Putnam of Brookline, Massachusetts. This young man is almost unknown today but had he lived he might have become not only American's ace of aces but a personality as fabulous as that of Charles A. Lindbergh. Dave Putnam had everything that makes a national hero; he was young, handsome, modest, skilled, and exemplified what we would set up as the all-American Boy. He died in action on September 12, 1918, having scored more victories than any other American in any service except Raoul Lufbery.

Lieutenant David Putnam was a direct descendant of Israel Putnam of Revolutionary War fame and probably one of the most splendid examples of American youth to volunteer and make the great sacrifice. He was tall, slim, athletic and above all knew how to smile. (We have produced too many scowling heroes.) He enjoyed robust health, was adventurous by temperament, and his flying was always daring. His courage contributed to his end.

As did many New Englanders, Putnam wished to serve the minute he could absorb the details of the war. He could not wait for the politicians and early in 1917 volunteered to serve with the French. He was quickly accepted on his personal appearance alone and was soon being trained at the famous French school at Avord. He was one of the few natural flyers. Everything came easy to him. He had good hands, a keen sense of balance, and his faith in himself overcame all the usual training-school dangers. The *Cigognes* heard of David and made a quick bid for him the minute he was breveted a pilot.

"Just give me a few days to figure out the front," he requested when he arrived at the group headquarters.

Within a couple of days David Putnam had the *Croix de guerre* for knocking down three enemy machines. Within a month he was an ace and had gained his commission.

Putnam loved to fly. He would volunteer for anything and felt hurt if left out of any daring enterprise. He had an appealing manner, the gentlemanly approach, and few people could deny him any request. As a result he racked up an ungodly number of flying hours every week. He would sooner fly than eat.

On looking back on his record, it is surprising that he never became an outstanding hero in the eyes of the American public. There is, of course, one possible explanation. He was serving with the French when the United States had its own Air Service in the field. The publicity at home was concentrated on the American heroes in the American Services. This was the hectic summer of 1918 and all too long the British and French air heroes had held the stage. Now it was time to tell of America's part in the war. David Putnam was just another frantic youth "who couldn't wait," and their stories had been told over and over.

On June 9 Putnam won his ninth victory and on the following day made history when he downed five enemy planes between sunup and sunset. The news roared along the front until the French officials interposed and explained that while they did not question Lieutenant Putnam's report, they could credit him with only three; it seems two were scored so far over the line that there were no other Allied airmen in the vicinity to confirm the results.

But Putnam made no complaints. He simply stated that he had destroyed five enemy planes in one day and that if they could not be confirmed for the records, he was perfectly sure in his own mind that five had gone down—and that was all that mattered.

"You can't shoot them all down in your own backyard," he had laughed. He had actually shot down four during one flight!

Dave Putnam lost his life while fighting five more German machines. He probably was still trying to register a five-in-one day exploit. He was twenty-one years of age when he died and had been credited with twelve victories without receiving a scratch. Between June 9 and September 12, 1918, this splendid gentleman from Brookline had become America's ace of aces.

On that fatal day, when every pursuit pilot in the A.E.F. was watching the French air combat reports, Dave went into the air on a noonday patrol. He had an unnamed companion with him and they encountered a Fokker patrol of eight planes. The two quickly broke this up, and three Fokkers scurried away. Putnam charged into the five-ship formation but apparently was hit almost immediately as he fell away out of control, spiralled down, and burst into flames.

David Putnam lived and died a gallant gentleman. He added a very glorious page to our war history. He belonged in the first rank of our aces and should be better known and revered.

7

AMERICA'S GREAT
CONTRIBUTION

1918

☐ The United States financial contribution to the Allied effort in World War I was $35,000,000,000; 75,280 of her men were killed in action, 201,847 were wounded, and 8,668 prisoners and missing. All this was her basic investment over the eighteen months that passed between the declaration of war in April 1917 and the Armistice of November 1918. Her great subscription in courage, heroism, and personal sacrifice can never be computed.

It is my intention to present the simple factual story of America's effort in this concluding chapter and to refrain from making comparisons or evaluations of any kind. There was honour and glory enough for all.

The U.S. Aviation Service put up a splendid effort during the seven months it shared the Allied cause but was never able to fulfil the chauvinistic promises of the politicians and armchair military leaders. No air force could have done that. In addition, U.S. pilots and observers were hamstrung by their lack of equipment, delays in service organization, and the failure of their manufacturers to deliver one truly American military plane.

America, which had given the world the first successful heavier-than-air machine, the Wright biplane, a few years later abandoned the science and its creators. When war was declared in 1917 America had not even begun to create a military air arm. Although her experts and military observers overseas had watched the progress of the war in the air for nearly three years, nothing had been done to form an air force or develop one aircraft or engine.

An experimental squadron had been established to provide "air support" for General Pershing's Mexican Border campaign in 1916 but this proved to be a pathetic fiasco. Of the eight biplanes collected for this foray not one was able to cross the 10,000-12,000-foot mountains guarding Casas Grandes, Mexico. Only four actually completed the short flight from American territory to their proposed base in "enemy" country.

The American aircraft industry, which had promised to deliver 22,000 planes during 1917, was totally unequal to the task. In March of that year there were only twelve companies capable of producing aeroplanes and their total production during 1916, when war must have seemed inevitable, was less than 400 planes of all types, and only by a great stretch of the imagination could any of them be considered true military aircraft. By January 1918 production had been stepped up to 700 engines and 800 aircraft, 700 of which were primary trainers. Not one combat plane had been put together, but no one seemed to be disturbed.

By February 21 the War Department announced with great fanfare that the first American-built planes were on their way to the front in France. Actually one British-designed D.H.4 (by now practically obsolete) had been shipped from Dayton but did not leave the Hoboken docks until March 15. The merchant vessel carrying it across was torpedoed off the Azores and as a result the first American-built D.H.4 did not take off from French soil until May 17—thirteen months after the formal declaration of war.

After a searching Congressional investigation, aircraft-production plans were revised and resulted in marked improvement. The main problem was to shift from the production of Curtiss "Jennies" to combat aircraft, the military machines in this case being the early 1917 de Havilland two-seater day bomber—the D.H.4. This was the original Flaming Coffin, a grim title earned because of its reputation for catching fire in the air at the most inopportune moment. It also had an unhappy arrangement of seats widely divided by the petrol tanks, making cockpit cooperation most difficult. However, the "Four" had been a wonderful contribution to the Allied air effort, since it could operate at very high altitude and evade many of the enemy fighters and actually completed a splendid percentage of its missions. By early 1918 it was being replaced by the D.H.9, powered with the Beardmore-

Halford or the Siddeley Puma engine, but more important the two cockpits were placed close together similar to the successful arrangement of the Bristol Fighter.

U.S. engine production from July 1917 to the end of the war totalled approximately 32,000, of which half were the new Liberty engines, a quarter were Curtiss OX-5's used on contemporary trainers, and the rest a mixed inventory of Hispano-Suizas and Le Rhones.

Of the almost 6,300 planes delivered to the American Air Service in France only 1,200 D.H.4's came from the United States. Almost 4,500 were purchased from the French, and most of these were training planes. Put in a more definite manner, the actual strength of U.S. aviation in the Zone of Advance on November 11 was 1,005 military planes; 325 of these were American-built D.H.4's, the rest were foreign-built such as Spads, Salmsons, and Nieuports. Of the 740 planes with active-service squadrons at the front only 196 were D.H.4's. During their seven months of combat on the Western Front American pilots flew foreign planes most of the time, and since France and Great Britain naturally kept their best aircraft for themselves, Americans usually found themselves flying outmoded types. In other words, American aviation industry had contributed practically nothing to their valiant efforts.

Fortunately the great home pool of manpower was more than ready and willing to be trained. The stirring stories of Allied aces had created a romantic appeal for the American youth and once the legal channels were opened he swarmed in with enthusiasm. In April 1917 the Aviation Section of the Signal Corps, as America's air arm was then known, consisted of a handful of 1,200 officers and men and three flying fields. In nineteen months this nucleus was expanded more than one hundred and fifty times. A commission headed by General Benjamin D. Foulois was sent up to Canada to find out how military aviators were produced and by the time he got back some 18,000 Americans had volunteered for flight training and before the war was over more than 10,000 of them had made it.

The U.S. had plenty of training machines but few completed airfields from which to fly them. In the spring of 1917, shortly after we had entered the war, a reciprocal agreement was made between the British and Americans whereby the R.F.C. trained ten U.S. squadrons in Canada during the summer and autumn of that year. In return the U.S. provided three fields in Texas for the training of both R.F.C. and U.S. airmen throughout the winter months.

Eventually twenty-six first-class flying schools were established in this country and sixteen more in Europe. At the primary schools in Texas flight cadets could earn their "wings" in about eight weeks, but they were not pilots in the front-line sense of the word since they had flown only Curtiss "Jennies" or some similar school craft. They were later shipped overseas, where they gained advanced training with the French or British and eventually had final check-outs on their own fields under their own instructors. Many American mechanics were also trained at British factories and schools.

The American Air Service came into being when U.S. aviation was transferred from the Signal Corps to two agencies under the Secretary of War, as the Bureau of Aircraft Production and the Division of Military Aeronautics. At first no one was appointed to head up this unusual combination, but on August 27, 1918, President Wilson appointed the former head of Anaconda Copper, John D. Ryan, as Director of the Air Service and Second Assistant Secretary of War.

There were five U.S. aviation officers in Europe when we declared war; three were attending French flying schools, one was an assistant military attaché in London, the fifth, Major William Mitchell, was an air observer in Spain. Mitchell soon made his way to the Western Front, where he studied the air war and talked to General Trenchard. On his own initiative and with some French guidance he drew up a plan for the organisation of an American air force for service in Europe. Later he presented to General Pershing a proposal for an air service composed of two distinct forces; one to consist of a number of squadrons attached to the ground armies and under the control of ground commanders; the second force to be made up of large aeronautical groups trained for "strategic" operations against enemy aircraft and enemy material stored a great distance from the front line. He suggested that the bombardment and pursuit formations of this force would have an independent mission and would be used to carry the war well into the enemy's country.

Again we note the influence of the foremost prophet of air power of his time, Major General Hugh M. Trenchard.

General Pershing appointed a board of officers, including Mitchell, to recommend the composition and organisation of the Air Service, A.E.F. This board began with the assumption that *a decision in the air must be sought and obtained before a decision on the ground can be reached,* disclosing the incipient rash of Pentagonese. The board therefore recommended a strategic force of thirty bomber groups and thirty fighter groups and a second force of a size based on the strength of the ground forces to which it would be attached. In this we see that America's orginal concept was to create a strategic air force.

Unfortunately General Pershing did not accept the board's recommendations. He insisted on units trained and equipped for Army-co-operation missions. While later programmes included bombardment and pursuit squadrons, permission never was granted to establish an American strategic bombardment force.

All these good intentions were later tempered by the type and numbers of aircraft available rather than by any programme of tactical doctrine. Perhaps American manufacturers were bewildered or impressed by the emphasis the British and French were now placing on strategic bombing; whereas the popular concept was to get as many fighter squadrons and pilots as possible to the front in order to show what was being accomplished by American airmen. They were also told that the American ground forces would require supporting air units if they were to do their part on the Western Front. A third priority was for bombers and long-range fighters for a strategic air force. By the time we were in a position to turn out production-line equipment the war had ended.

In the summer of 1917 the U.S. set up an Air Service headquarters in Paris with a stack of plans but no planes. A field-artillery officer, Brigadier General William L. Kenly, was Chief of Air Service; Major Raynal C. Bolling served as Assistant Chief in charge of supply and Colonel Mitchell became Air Commander, Zone of Advance. In November of the same year General Foulois arrived in France with a ready-made Headquarters Staff of 112 officers and 300 enlisted men. After looking over the general situation, Foulois replaced Kenly as Chief of Air Service, A.E.F. This provided service difficulties and complicated all attempts at organisation. There were jealousies and friction. Air and ground officers were frequently at loggerheads, and Mitchell and Bolling seldom could agree on their departmental responsibilities.

As a result, Pershing regarded the new Air Service with some contempt and in May 1918 appointed his old classmate, Brigadier General Mason M. Patrick, Chief of Air Service. Mitchell was subordinated to Foulois, who had been placed in charge of aviation at the front with the title of Chief of Air Service, First Army. Mitchell ignored this and cut through red tape whenever possible. Foulois finally recommended that Mitchell be given the combat command and requested to be appointed Assistant Chief of Air Service under General Patrick. This change occurred in August 1918 and paved the way for Mitchell to become what he had yearned for—America's air combat commander.

From this point on the Air Service expanded rapidly and additional combat commands were organized as new American armies came into the field. In October Colonel Frank P. Lahm became Chief of Air Service, Second Army, and Mitchell, newly promoted to brigadier general, became Chief of Air Service, Army Group. The establishment of Air Service, Third Army, just before the Armistice completed the air organization at the front up to November 11, 1918.

The development of the U.S. Air Service in the field followed the accepted pattern with a few American innovations tossed in. Most of the flyers and mechanics available by late 1917 and early 1918 had been trained in Europe. It had been claimed that certain Allies wanted these Americans to reinforce their own battle-weary squadrons and it is a fact that a few U.S. flyers were either loaned out or "attached" to the French or British for actual combat experience. This was an interim measure and probably gave aid and support to all concerned.

The 1st Aero Squadron of Mexican-border history arrived in France under the command of Major Ralph Royce on September 3, 1917, and had the honour of being the first American squadron to reach Europe. After training at French schools, No. 1 received French planes and further training as an observation squadron. Other U.S. squadrons arriving in France during the autumn and winter followed a similar pattern of training in preparation for their eventual transfer to a sector allotted to the American ground forces.

The Allied High Command then decided that American units should gradually concentrate in the Toul area toward the eastern end of the 350-mile front stretching from the Channel to Switzerland. This area in eastern France had been comparatively quiet since the first year of the war and was believed to be a good sector for blooding the new American army.

With the arrival of No. 95 Pursuit Squadron in February 1918 the American air build-up began. No. 94 joined it on March 5, but while both pursuit squadrons had been provided with Nieuport scouts the planes had not been fitted with machine guns. When guns were made available it was discovered that none of the pilots of No. 95 Squadron had been given any form of machine-gun training. Thus, the honour of being the first American-trained pursuit squadron to fight on the front went to No. 94. This famous hat-in-the-ring outfit, later commanded by Captain Edward V. Rickenbacker, began its operations on April 3. On April 14 Lieutenants Alan F. Winslow and Douglas Campbell shot down the squadron's first (two) German planes. Now reasonably adept with their automatic weapons, No. 95 returned from the French training school by April 25 and these two outfits were subsequently formed into the First Pursuit Group.

Meanwhile No. 1 Aero Squadron, flying Spad two-seaters, had arrived in the Toul sector and on April 15 performed its first reconnaissance mission over the enemy lines. One whole year had passed since the declaration of war on Germany. Two more observation squadrons arrived before the end of May and these three were formed into the 1st Corps Observation Group, under French tactical control.

The first day-bombardment squadron to see action was No. 96, which had been equipped with French Bréguets and operated with American divisions near Toul. By the middle of June representative units of all four elements, pursuit, observation, day-bombardment, and balloon companies of the U.S. Air Service, had gone into action around Toul. At the end of July American ground and air units were moved up to the vicinity of Château-Thierry at the tip of the great salient the Germans had driven into the French lines. The American First Pursuit Group and 1st Corps Observation Group with some French units were organized into the First Brigade under Mitchell and given responsibility for a portion of the battle area. There the Americans found conditions quite different from those encountered on the Toul sector. They were sadly outmatched, outnumbered, and outfought by the Fokkers that had been moved from the rough-tough British front, and the First Brigade found itself on the defensive for a dreadful five weeks, until the German attack was stopped and thrown back. The First Brigade paid a heavy toll in attempting to provide observation information and tactical defence. The Château-Thierry campaign was a bitter awakening but it stiffened the American forces for the final attack that was to come.

The history of the American infantry through the St. Mihiel and the Meuse-Argonne campaigns has been told many times and rightly so. American troops upheld their finest traditions and shed their share of blood toward the eventual triumph. But it must be added that the U.S. Air Service of that time also played a valuable role with what they had in the time available. This is no place to attempt any form of comparison with the efforts of any of the other Allies. The Americans had their own front, their own problems, their own leadership, and their own methods of seeking the desired decisions.

By November 11 General Mitchell had forty-five combat squadrons under his command at the front. In these were 767 pilots, 481 observers and 23 aerial gunners. Two of these units, the British-trained No. 17 and No. 148 Pursuit Squadrons, had just rejoined the U.S. forces after serving with the R.A.F. on the British front since June 1918. In Italy Captain Fiorello H. La Guardia led a detachment of eighteen bomber pilots against the Austrians in June 1918 and all in all sixty-five American pilots flying Caproni bombers saw action on the Italian front.

The 740 American planes in squadrons at the front at the Armistice constituted a little more than ten per cent of the total aircraft strength of the Allies. The Air Service carried out 150 separate bombing attacks during which it delivered about 138 tons of bombs and penetrated as far as 160 miles behind the German lines. American losses in combat were 298 planes and 48 balloons, including 57 planes piloted by officers flying with the British, French, and Italians. All told, 237 American airmen were killed in action and many of these lives might have been saved had suitable parachutes been available.

American air fighters had confirmed claims of 781 enemy machines and 73 balloons. Seventy-one airmen qualified as "aces" and this select group destroyed 450 planes and 50 balloons.

The true history of America's contribution to World War I is told best through the individual stories of her heroes. Above all, they brought a new triumphant spirit to the war-weary. While we had encountered some of the American dash in the early months of the war with members of the Lafayette Escadrille and those who volunteered to serve with the Royal Flying Corps, we had not as yet been exposed to the mass effect of the Yankee spirit which was unleashed once an American force began to operate on the Western Front.

At first it engulfed us like a wave of collegiate rowdyism but gradually congealed to a definite measure of service enthusiasm. Charged with healthy confidence, ignited by the volatile publicity they had read, and probably believed, concerning themselves, they swarmed into the various war areas like triumphant athletes. They were alive with interest in the war, amazingly ignorant of its facts and figures but voracious for data and details whenever they cornered anyone who had served time over the line or could provide information about fighting in the air. In spite of this sophomoric enthusiasm they seemed much older and more mature than the British. Compared to the French, they were gigantic figures and even more voluble than their new Gallic comrades.

As in the World War that followed almost a quarter of a century later these Americans were flush with money, provided with expensive but most impractical uniforms and were overly generous in their social contacts with any of their new Allies, regardless of rank or service. They had no idea of the breadth of the front, how long the war had been in progress, or the fuel range of a Spad or Nieuport.

But these vociferous young gods were good for us. They brought new life and a new language to the war. They revolutionized our furlough programmes and many of our regimental social codes. Most certainly they widened our ideas of taproom and men's bar behaviour. We who had been out there since the early days nurtured new hopes of military co-operation—for these were airmen who thought much as we did. Tyros they were, but they were willing to listen and they gave warm promise of a brighter future. I for one sensed that at last we had been joined by trustworthy comrades who would willingly share our war skies and generously co-operate in any military undertaking.

For the first time in that war I was right.

Of this valiant if rowdy company I always think of Lieutenant Frank Luke as the standard-bearer. Luke is little known or revered today but he was the epitome of the brave, brash, undisciplined two-fisted Yank, so dear to the pulp-thriller school of literature.

This savage unreasoning air fighter from Phoenix, Arizona, was the first American airman to win the Congressional Medal of Honour, and was the only one to be awarded that decoration during the course of the war. Seven others were thus honoured but only after their records had been considered by Congressional boards years after the close of hostilities. Luke was also awarded the Distinguished Service Cross but he did not live to wear either medal and had he returned from his last patrol he would have been court-martialed—for taking off on the flight!

Luke lived but a few weeks on the Western Front but in that space of time set a mark no other airman of any nation has even approached; yet if every newspaper in this country were to publish his photograph today only a handful of readers would recognize him.

Few people will believe the figures of his meteoric career, but for the record they are offered here.

259

Luke took off on combat missions over a period of nine days, logging less than thirty hours of air time, but when he was through he was America's leading air ace at that time. As a result of ten combat patrols, flying a 120-h.p. Spad biplane, he destroyed fifteen enemy observations balloons and shot down four German planes. Some records insist Luke had downed five German planes, but his official record of nineteen enemy aircraft in thirty hours of flying should be good enough for anyone.

He was the Peck's Bad Boy of the Air, for he deliberately broke every rule, evaded every code, disdained all laws of military discipline, and died in a savage, unreasonable scuffle in a graveyard against a platoon of German infantry, when he might have honourably surrendered and lived out the last six weeks of the war in a prison camp.

It may be argued that Second Lieutenant Frank Luke failed to act with intelligence. But what is intelligence in a war? Luke was only twenty when he fired his last round of ammunition—too young to use any of the defences of perspective. He had wanted no part of the war and since his sister Eva, who was a Red Cross nurse, had taunted him to join up, he decided to run his sector of it his own way. He was definitely the Mickey Mannock type; instead of posed gallantries he used the tactics and brutality of the dock walloper, the knee-in-the-gut attack of the bar brawler, the everything-goes code of the gutter bully. Had he ever encountered a captured airman he in all probability would have dismembered him with his bare hands.

There was nothing personal in his animosity. He didn't hate the enemy; he simply resented the situation in which he found himself. Military life was absurd and it had deprived him of the sunshine and simplicities of his native Arizona. In France he was given a new Spad, posted to No. 27 Pursuit Squadron, and expected to live up to the traditions established by men such as Quentin Roosevelt, Raoul Lufbery, Jerry Vasconcelles, Harold Hartney, Malcolm Gunn, James Miller, and all the paragons of the Lafayette Escadrille. But Luke displayed no awe or respect and after two unfortunate preliminary patrols was grounded for a month to teach him that rookie airmen were expected to stay in formation, to practise teamwork, and, above all, obey the orders of their superiors.

At the front everything was new, each day a flipped page in an unfamiliar book, and he had no friends. Few in his own outfit remember him, so short was his stretch of glory, and the only flying companion he attracted was Lieutenant Joseph Wehner, who was under suspicion because of his name. The two social outcasts became firm friends as long as each lived, which was just a few short weeks. Captain Eddie Ricken- backer topped Luke's sum of victories, but Rickenbacker had six more weeks of air action ahead of him when Luke wasted his meteoric life in a graveyard at Murvaux on the Meuse.

Frank Luke was born in Phoenix, Arizona, May 19, 1897. His mother was from Brooklyn and his father an immigrant from Dalhausen, Germany, who had moved to Arizona in 1880. There were nine tow-headed youngsters in the Luke family, but Frank, Senior, managed somehow to keep them all in food and clothing, and most of the boys and girls had advanced educations. Frank, however, after finishing high school went to work in the New Cornelia copper workings in Ajo, where the heavy toil added to his athletic physique until he was 170 pounds of bone and rawhide. He was tall, lithe, and hawk-featured and without a spot of humour in his mas- sive frame. Sparing of speech, he hated the wind of words; to him deep thinking was a tedious detour and only action paid its way.

After a summer of wandering through the hills and along the mountain streams of Arizona he returned home to find his family in a ferment of patriotism. His sister Eva, who was a trained nurse, was in the Red Cross; his oldest brother Edwin had enlisted in the artillery and was working for a commis- sion. Frank hated the idea of military restraint, but Eva showed him the error of this thinking and so on September 25 he went to Tucson and enlisted in the Signal Corps. He easily passed the physical examination, but one wonders if he real- ized he had signed up for flying. He passed out from a Texas ground school in November 1917 and went to Rockwell Field, San Diego, where he successfully completed his prelim- inary flying course. What few letters he wrote were addressed to Eva, who had always been his confidante. His Arizona background glowed through each line, the big cities were strange and uncomfortable, the people unaccountable in their habits and custom. When he went overseas after gaining his commission on January 23 he was utterly bewildered.

His first station abroad was the Third Aviation Instruction Centre at Issoudun, where he learned to fly more-advanced types. Here he displayed his natural skill and was soon tick- eted for single-seater pursuit work. He learned to fly Spads and tricky Nieuport scouts and much of his instruction was devoted to formation flying, acrobatics, and aerial gunnery. He proved to be a first-class pilot and an even better shot, two skills seldom found in any single pilot in those days.

By the end of May he was a finished flyer and was next

shipped to Cazaux, a pilot-pool area where replacements were sent out to the combat units. While waiting, the pilots were kept occupied with routine ferry work, delivering new machines to front-line squadrons, replacing those damaged or destroyed in action. So Luke flew Spads, Salmsons, Nieuports, anything that could get off the ground. He didn't appreciate it, but the extra flying time was adding materially to his touch and skill. He continued to bellow and eventually he bellowed loud enough, for long before his turn he was posted to Major Harold Hartney's No. 27 Aero Squadron of the First Pursuit Group located at Saintes in the old Aisne-Marne salient. The First Pursuit needed plenty of good pilots, for the toll was heavy and the few hardy souls left were doing two and three shows a day. A few weeks before they all had been eager replacements, but too many patrols, too many Huns in the sun, too many extra missions had taken all the glory out of war.

The Saintes field was the typical conglomerate mess of slatternly buildings, decayed canvas hangars, and yawning shacks. The accommodations were grouped in unruly disorder around an L-shaped patch of uneven turf. There were portable power plants set up on White trucks, cookhouses with crooked tin chimneys, storehouses, and mud. There was always plenty of mud, even in late July.

Luke dropped off the back of a truck and walked into what looked like the administration shack. He had expected to report immediately to Major Hartney, but Hartney was engaged.

"I know . . . I know," Hartney was saying to a ramrod-stiff figure in front of him. "I believe you, Joe, but these tin-horn Intelligence gaffers keep hounding me, too."

Joe was a slim lean-cut pilot wearing an unusually clean overall and standing stiffly to attention. He had a pale oblong face, a shock of raven-black hair parted in the middle, and deep-set brown eyes.

Many years later Colonel Hartney explained this interview to me over a drink in a New York hotel bar.

"Luke walked in just as I was reassuring Joe Wehner that he had nothing to worry about. Because of his name some over-anxious Intelligence operator had been hounding the boy and he was not happy about it. A funny thing, as he walked out he and Luke exchanged just a hint of a grin. I didn't know it then but in that brief encounter was born one of the greatest fighting teams the U.S. Air Service was to inscribe on its records."

The rest went something like this.

"Second Lieutenant Luke reporting, sir."

"Nice to have you, Luke. Your logbook, please."

"That guy who just went out . . . He's in trouble?"

Hartney nodded. "Just the wrong sort of name, that's all. A real guy, actually."

Luke continued boldly: "My father was born in Germany. That make any difference?"

"Not to me. This is all I'm interested in." Hartney thumbed the pages of Luke's logbook. "Looks like you can be ready for a balloon-line show any day."

"You just assign me a ship."

"You can go tomorrow, but remember we fly a tight formation up here. This is the real war. The fun is over from now on. You survive the first two weeks and you're well over the hill. Otherwise you'll probably spin in quick."

"Not me."

Hartney looked up and sensed he had trouble. Luke offered no respect, no sirring or deference to experience. He seemed to be saying, "Don't kid me. I'm not afraid of any bogeyman."

"Stay in formation," Hartney said and tossed the logbook back. "See the mess sergeant and he'll assign you quarters. We live rough here, but it's home."

The next afternoon Hartney took a small formation of Spads up to the line. Luke and another fledgling were included, but they were tucked safely away inside the element of experienced airmen who were ordered to protect the wide-eyed innocents. For the first time Frank Luke saw the fester and scar that was war. Below were battered towns, miles of infantry slots, and a huddled world pockmarked with shellfire. Most rookies would have been content to sit out a few missions and learn the area, but no sooner had they reached their own balloon lines than Luke flipped out of place and went hunting on his own. What took place after that has never been recorded officially, but Luke turned up safely a few minutes after the rest of the flight had sideslipped back into their field.

"What happened to you?" Hartney barked when Luke walked into the operations shack.

Without batting an eye Luke said, "I had engine trouble."

"Engine trouble? But you stayed out longer than the rest of us. What sort of a line is that?"

Luke did not bother to explain, and Hartney had to accept the fact that whatever had happened, the kid had stayed out his full patrol time—and found his way back.

Two days later Luke was again assigned to a routine familiarizing patrol under another leader and again he disappeared the minute they reached the front line. This time the war caught up with him. He was set upon by a Hun he had not seen. There was a jangle of metal, the scream of torn plating, and the rupture of engine parts. He was lucky and was able to dive for his own field. The impact of the attack and his good fortune gave him some distorted idea that he had not simply escaped but that he might have shot down a German aeroplane. He honestly believed this.

When Hartney demanded an explanation, while eyeing the shot-up Spad, Luke snarled back, "So I broke formation. Nothing ever happens in formation, so I went off and got me a Hun!"

"You did? Where?"

Luke had no idea. He couldn't have identified Paris, Saint-Quentin, Verdun, or Mt. Saint-Eloi, but he insisted he had destroyed a German plane. Only Hartney and Joe Wehner believed him.

Unfortunately for Luke, Hartney was promoted the next day and given command of the new First Pursuit Group. Captain Alfred A. Grant took over No. 27, and the squadron moved up to the Verdun front and settled down at Rembercourt. Luke and Grant were immediately at loggerheads. Luke was ordered to help make the new camp shipshape and was put in charge of erecting new hangars, grading roads, and acting as squadron engineer officer. The records disclose that following his August 16 patrol, when he claimed an enemy aircraft, he did not fly again until September 12.

On the evening of September 11, two months before the Armistice, the pilots of Luke's squadron were discussing the difficulties of balloon strafing. Captain Jerry Vasconcelles, one of the few aces of the group, wanted no part of them. He said that a million bad things could happen to a man when he attacked a Jerry balloon. Someone else said it cost about $100,000 to equip and put up a kite balloon—and no wonder they have special five-ship fighter formations to defend them.

Luke took it all in and later confided to Wehner that he was going to get a balloon. Joe repeated the remark and there was considerable doubt that Luke had the courage to tackle a tied-down Y.M.C.A. hut, but after lunch the next day he "borrowed" a Spad and went out for his first balloon over the town of Marieulles, which was now a battered clutter of debris. It was a typical Luke show from start to finish.

Actually he first tied in with a formation that was heading for the line but over Lavigneville he spotted three Hun biplanes and gave chase. For no particular reason the enemy

264

craft sped east and disappeared in the mists over Metz. Turning back toward his own lines, Luke then spotted a jerry gasbag. He pulled the Spad up on her tail and climbed until the kite was a mere speck against the pockmarks below. He forced his head forward until the eyepiece of his Aldis sight brought in the full details of the bloated bag. His guns coughed as he saw the observer outlined in the basket rigging.

But to his consternation, nothing happened!

He pulled out hard, went into a loop, and came through again to trigger another long burst. The ground fire eased off because of the danger of hitting their own observers. One of them, a Leutnant Willi Klemm, who had received his commission only the day before, was experiencing his first enemy air attack.

Luke's guns jammed after the second burst, so he swung off to one side and applied immediate action until one of the Vickers responded. Below him, the Germans almost had the big bag down into its pit but with one final desperate attack Frank banked over sharply and pounded the shapeless bundle. This final burst ignited her and she flopped in a dismal heap on top of the winch. Willi Klemm had been hit under the heart and was dead before he could be untangled from the rigging.

Accepting the inevitable, Captain Grant said to Luke two days later, "Corps is going nuts about a Jerry *Drachen* up over Buzy. It's all yours. I suggest you take one man with you. . . ."

"I'll take Joe Wehner."

Luke and Wehner took off with the regular formation but dropped out over Buzy. Wehner immediately kited for altitude and moved to get into the sun. This time Luke's first burst torched the bag immediately, but Wehner was really in trouble with eight Jerry planes that had drawn the defence assignment. From below Luke had difficulty identifying Joe's Spad. Either the light was bad or he lacked the experience and was still airblind. Then his guns jammed, and Wehner had to fight off the eight Fokkers while Luke eased out and cleared the gun stoppages. By that time the Fokkers had flown away to "protect" another bag further north.

Together Joe and Frank found and rejoined their original formation, patrolling between Abancourt and Boigneville. During this tour Luke spotted another bag and peeled off after it. The balloon observer replied boldly with several bursts from a light machine gun, but since Luke continued to roar in he finally took to the parachute that hung in its leather cone on the outside of the basket. Luke, however, finished this second bag and when he returned his bullet-pocked plane was more than enough to convince everyone in No. 27 that he had really been in action again.

"Why didn't you get that observer?" someone asked. "He sure pooped off a lot of stuff at you."

"Hell!" Luke growled. "The poor guy was helpless."

The "poor guy" was Sergeant Muenchoff of No. 14 Balloon Company, who still relates how he did his best to shoot down Luke. His signaller, a Corporal Gasser, had jumped when Luke made his first pass at the bag. Luke could have riddled them both but in this instance he made no attempt to fire on the helpless men.

Two offensive patrols—three balloons!

The next day, September 12, Luke and Wehner took off after another balloon over Boigneville. This time they were provided with incendiary ammunition but instead of making a concerted attack they separated and when it was over Luke had downed two more balloons and Wehner had destroyed a balloon and two planes!

Wehner nailed his bag with about 100 rounds of ammo, but five defence ships pounced on him. He evaded them over Chambley when a flight of French Spads joined in the fray. Next, remembering a *Drachen* he had once spotted over Bois d'Hingry, he swept off in that direction but as he approached the wood he found the bag in flames and concluded that Luke had fired it. By the time he was well overhead he spotted a design of ack-ack puffs and sensed that Luke was probably in trouble.

Above Rourois a Spad came charging out of the smoke, its nose well down for speed and safety. It was Luke roaring away with seven Albatros biplanes tacked on his tail. Wehner tore in and nailed one before the Jerries realised there was anyone else in the fight. The Albatros fell out of formation, sideslipped, and spun in. Next he spotted another pecking at Luke's tail, so he pooped off at him and a second Jerry took the long last dive. With that, Joe took a position on Luke's tail and they both streaked for the American lines, the remaining Albatros fighters following them until they were eventually held off by a curtain of accurate ack-ack fire.

Late that afternoon when the evening shadows were creeping across the field Luke went out again. Just north of Verdun he found another balloon which he boldly attacked and successfully destroyed. He was again battered by anti-aircraft fire and frantic bursts of machine-gun hosing, but he crossed the line safely, became lost in the semi-darkness, and around 9.30 p.m. landed in a French wheatfield near Angers. When he returned to his squadron confirmation was already on file in the office, but another Spad was on the "unserviceable" list.

The next day Joe and Frank prowled the enemy balloon line, but the big bags were being hauled down before they could get in a clean burst. Late the same day they obtained special permission to try another early evening show when they hoped to catch the Jerries just as they were presumed to be taking their last look at the opposing trenches. Luke, who had devised the plan, called Major Hartney at Group Headquarters for special permission, saying they had three particular balloons in mind.

"We'll take the first at 7.10," Luke explained, "the second at 7.20, and the third at 7.30 . . . right on the nose."

Hartney ordered a special ground crew out and turned up himself to see this unbelievable exhibition.

The first balloon went up with a scarlet bloom right on the dot . . . 7.10; on the second Luke was one minute late turning up the wick. By 7.30 every man in the observation party was growing impatient.

7.31 . . . 7.32 . . . 7.33 . . . 7.34 . . .

Hartney was chain-smoking and hardly noticed Colonel Billy Mitchell drive in to witness this fantastic show.

7.36 . . . and the third rosy-red glow came up as though someone had raised a monstrous stove lid.

Hartney then had the field lined with signal rockets to help Luke and Wehner in, and before the two pilots landed Mitchell was working on an idea to provide night-landing facilities that would make it safer for the balloon boys who wanted to fly around the clock.

On September seventeenth Luke and Wehner were confined to the ground with a combination of bad weather and mechanical troubles but on the eighteenth all hell broke loose again when Luke and Wehner left their field and headed for Saint-Mihiel, where two balloons were reported to be up and operating.

This time Luke took the highest bag first and it required but a short snarling volley. The big sausage fluttered, opened the draught and went down dragging a scarlet choker. The ack-ack guns roared at him as he levelled off and went for the second *Drachen*, which obliged with a curling pillar of black smoke and a gush of crimson flame. (Available German reports from the statements of Leutnants Finster and Heicke of 112 Balloon Company say, "that crazy Spad pilot came down to about 70 feet from the ground to get that balloon.")

But where was Wehner? Luke had thought Joe would take the second bag and thus split the hate, but pulling out from his attack and climbing again, he saw Joe leading a very neat formation of Fokker D.7's. Realizing Joe was in trouble, he went to the rescue, blasted smack into the centre of the Jerry formation, and it scattered to the four winds. But four D.7's returned and two picked on Wehner and two concentrated on Luke. Luke charged head on at a D.7 with both guns roaring until the Jerry folded and spun in. Next he felt his ship recoil under the battering of a second Hun, so he went into a tight climbing turn and caught the Fokker pilot cold and hammered him into a death dive. Realizing he had no business air-warring at this ridiculous altitude so far over the line, Luke concentrated on getting some height and once more looked for Wehner.

Joe was nowhere to be seen, and Luke decided he had eased off for the American line, so he turned too and over Verdun came upon a lumbering old Halberstadt observation plane being harried by a flight of French *Cigognes* Spads. Since he had altitude now, he sneaked in ahead of his French pals and torched the jerry observation ship right before their eyes.

In that blistering ten minutes Luke had destroyed two observation balloons, two fighter aircraft, and one two-place observation ship. At that point Luke's fuel gave out and he had to switch over to his emergency tank, which provided a ten-minute supply of *essence*, enough to get him to a friendly emergency field, where he dropped down below Verdun, borrowed a motorcycle, and tore up the road for No. 27 Squadron, hoping to find Joe and get further details of their scrap from him.

No one on the field had the courage to tell him, and he didn't realize that Joe had not come back until he went out on the line and looked for his plane.

It didn't matter now that Frank Luke was America's leading ace, that he had a total of fourteen victories—four planes and ten balloons—whereas Rickenbacker had only nine confirmations at this point. None of it mattered. All Luke could think of was an official report which now read: "One of our machines is missing." He didn't touch a meal for the rest of the day, just sat around the mess lounge staring into space. He didn't fly on the nineteenth and still sat brooding, and by nightfall Hartney decided to send him off to Paris for a furlough and a change.

They typed out his orders, filled out a leave warrant, and made sure America's leading ace had enough money. Dull-eyed, silent and morose, Luke allowed them to pack his bag, button him into his cleanest jacket, and Hartney himself drove him to the nearest railroad station. That was September 19. On the afternoon of September 25, less than a week later, Luke had returned from Paris still silent and morose. Everyone stared at him in amazement and Hartney roared over from the First Pursuit Headquarters. When asked what he was doing back so early, Luke said, "There wasn't anything to do."

The gayest wartime city in the world had nothing to offer. The wine, women, and song prescription was just words from a wheezy old ballad. It seems Luke had a new plan—to get balloons—and he wondered if Hartney wouldn't okay the idea of having a special balloon-flight use an old advanced field closer to the line. Hartney was dubious about who else would volunteer for such crazy work, but eventually Luke had his way and plans were made for Jerry Vasconcelles to take a flight up there.

But on the twenty-sixth, while plans were being made to move up the advance flight, Luke took young Lieutenant Ivan Roberts of South Lee, Massachusetts, on a dual show. Luke went after a balloon, but they ran into five Fokkers. One went down after a short burst from Luke's guns, but when he looked around for Roberts, the youngster was nowhere to be seen. The Yank balloon observers reported they had seen Roberts crash inside the German lines, but that was all that was ever heard of him.

Once more Luke went into surly seclusion and the next day left the field without permission and drew a scathing reprimand from Captain Grant. Obstinate and sulky, Luke again took off on an unauthorized flight and torched a partially-inflated balloon resting on its bed near Banthenville. This time he had to go down to within 30 feet of the ground to make his kill and when he pulled out he skimmed through a wicked anti-aircraft barrage and headed for the French *Cigognes* field, where he spent the night. He returned to Rembercourt the next day, and when Captain Grant asked him where he had spent the night all he would say was, "Over at the *Cigognes*." And when Captain Grant bellowed his wrath, Luke added, "Oh, and I got another balloon near Banthenville."

Then Grant really ripped into Luke and grounded him until further notice. Luke saluted, rushed out, slammed the door, and headed straight for the Spad.

"She needs petrol and oil, Lieutenant," his mechanic argued.

"I'll fill her up at Vasconcelles' flight up the line. Swing that prop!"

Grant sensed what was happening and shouted to his adjutant, "Tell Vasconcelles to put Luke under open arrest and ship him back by sidecar. I'll send up another pilot to fly his ship back."

"Then what?" the adjutant said with a shielded grin.

Grant frowned. "First, I'm recommending him for the Distinguished Service Cross and then, by God, I'm going to courtmartial him!"

Luke landed at the Verdun strip and Vasconcelles started out from his dugout office to give him the bad news, but fortunately Major Hartney circled the field and came in for a landing, so Jerry wisely withheld Captain Grant's order.

Luke charged up to Hartney: "Major, there's three more balloons up beyond Verdun. I can get all three if you let me go now."

Hartney glanced at his watch. "Too early. The sun will go at 5.22, and you can take off then—not before!"

By 5.20 Luke had his Spad refuelled and was starting the engine.

Hartney bellowed, "Shut off that Hisso, Luke. I said 5.22!"

Later Hartney said, "That's the last I remember of him, sitting in his Spad laughing at me while I bawled him out. I guess it was the only time I saw him really laugh."

At 5.22 Luke was in the air again, heading for the American Balloon H.Q. in Souilly. He banked over wildly and flipped a note to a group of waving observers. It read:

Watch those three Hun balloons along the Meuse.

Luke

He climbed away and headed for Dun on the far bank of the ancient river. His guns raked the first kite and it exploded as he hung in a half roll. Then he cleared and headed for Brière Farm, where another lazy sausage lolled in the evening twilight. He started down with it dead in his sights—and then suddenly he gasped from a sharp blow below his ribs. He looked around and saw a formation of Hun fighters moving into position above him. A hornet trail of tracers was smacking into his tail assembly, so he nosed down hard and headed for the cover of the ground smoke.

This was a new Luke. He was concentrating on protective cover. The Huns veered off, figuring he had piled up below, but instead he had remembered the Brière Farm balloon. This time he stitched it with short, uneven bursts of sizzling incendiary ammunition. It went up in oily smoke.

Frank lugged on his stick, but the Spad bucked in a new

270

and unruly manner as he swung for Milly, where the third balloon was hanging. The ground observers saw the Spad flutter and hesitate. He finally blundered on toward the bulbous target but the ack-ack fire was a flaming curtain by now. His Spad staggered on, picked up the bag, and again two streams of fiery incendiary laced its sides.

His third for the day and the last of his wild career went up in smoke and flames.

This time Luke made no pretence of scrambling for altitude or cover. Maybe he was too tired to drag the stick back. Instead of making a 180-degree turn and heading for his field, he seemed to fly toward the village of Murvaux, huddling on the north bank of the Meuse.

Why? No one knows. The collected records disclose that the outraged Hisso roared on and Luke fluttered over the village until he sensed that enemy troops were crowding the main street. He nosed down uncertainly, opened his guns again, and drove them to cover.

What happened then? There are several versions from the villagers of Murvaux, but we do know for certain that Luke continued on until he almost hit the spire of the village church. He circled it once, sideslipped, and landed in the meadow that made a grassy carpet all the way up to the churchyard wall. He sat there until his prop zig-zagged to a stop, then drew his automatic, thumbed the safety catch, climbed out, and groped his way to a tiny brook, cupped his hands in the water to quench his thirst or perhaps bathe a wound. All that took place.

Next he staggered back to his Spad but realised the enemy were approaching, for they were firing snapshots at his craft, so he climbed the old stone wall and was seen stumbling among the ancient headstones until he found a broad-beamed mausoleum, where he made his stand. German voices ordered his surrender, but he answered with automatic fire. Perhaps he had no idea what they were saying. They deployed and some men in field grey fired at him again and he returned the hate with telling effect. More harsh voices, more Mauser shots, but Luke had only one clip of ammunition and he finally went down among the gravestones. He was carried to the street and someone brought a farm cart, and the villagers wanted to lay straw in the bottom, but the German commander refused. He was quickly buried nearby.

That was the ironic end of Frank Luke and today he is almost forgotten, although there is a Luke Field in Hawaii and an athletic stadium erected to his memory in Phoenix.

Few people have any idea who Frank Luke was or what he did to merit such memorials. He was just the Balloon Buster from Arizona . . . for a few days.

Captain Eddie Rickenbacker, who was the complete antithesis of Frank Luke, also provided an unbelievable victory record that was totted up in a race against time. Unlike the Arizona Balloon Buster, Rickenbacker was the most humble of America's long list of fighting valiants. Had he served in any other branch but the Aviation Corps he probably would not have gathered even a modest citation. It took a warplane and many enemy Fokkers to put him in the history books.

Rickenbacker disdained the role of the swashbuckling hero. While he shot down twenty-six enemy planes in less than two months of front-line action, he provided no extravagant highlights on which to write his history. Today he is top man and chief brains of the great Eastern Air Lines and, other than Donald MacLaren of Canada, is possibly the only World War I hero who made good in postwar aviation. All too many aces came home to wind up on the discard heap or get themselves killed in pitiful air crashes. Too many hadn't the courage to face up to the facts of a peacetime world. Too many stumbled about trying to live up to their logbooks. In many respects Rickenbacker resembled a few of the more mature British airmen who, with little verve or showy display, ran up remarkable scores and performed amazing deeds of glory.

Unlike most Aviation Corps performers of that day Rick was an unassuming man with a limited education, having had to leave school and go to work early in life. With little more than a grammar-school diploma Rickenbacker sensed the automobile was coming into prominence and he managed to attain a post every American boy, even today, regards as "something real keen"—that of an automobile test driver. Before he could vote he had become so proficient he was selected as a racing driver for a noted automotive company and actually drove the famous Indianapolis-500 three times. Prudent but fearless, Rickenbacker never won a major race but he was a most competent driver.

At the outbreak of the war in 1914 he was in Britain conferring with the Sunbeam Motor Company about representing them on American race tracks. At the time the Sunbeam was one of the most efficient all-round machines anywhere in the world and had done exceedingly well in the famous Vanderbilt Cup event at Sheepshead Bay. Unfortunately the Sunbeam company had to convert its interests into the aviation-engine field, and the prospective deal fell through. Nevertheless during the short stay Rick had seen and caught the thrill of the war. He had encountered some of the glamour of the Royal Flying Corps.

When the United States entered the conflict Rickenbacker had the idea of forming a special flying squadron of American racing drivers. He took his plan to Washington, where it was ridiculed and discarded. While there, however, he was approached by the upper brass of the day to become General Pershing's chauffeur.

By early January 1918 Rickenbacker deserted the Commander in Chief and "worked" an aviation-service commission and took some instruction at Tours, where he was given five and a half hours of dual control before going solo. He learned fast because of his experience as an auto racer. He could judge speed and distance and had an inherent knack of timing. But he was also a very good mechanic, a quality that almost kept him from flying, since it was decided he would make a good engineer officer and was sent to Issoudun —an important air base and replacement depot for men and machines.

He went through the motions of an acting engineer officer but he also got in considerable time on many types of planes. Today he would be called a test pilot. Nevertheless Rick hated normal aerobatics and the required school manoeuvres and had to make himself spin and roll the trainer types available.

He became bored with the work of an engineer officer, for he wished to get up to the front. To force the issue he faked an illness, had himself placed in the hospital for two weeks, and then pointed out, "You see, I am not indispensable after all. Now will you let me join a fighting unit?"

There was no argument, so he was sent to the aerial gunnery school at Cazeau, where he was entrusted with planes fitted with machine guns and boxes of ammunition. He put in weeks doggedly practising on ground and towed targets.

Early in March he was posted to the untried No. 94 Pursuit Squadron located at Villeneuve, headed by the famous Raoul Lufbery. Another month went by and both Nos. 94 and 95 were equipped with a few aircraft and with that hope they moved on up into the Toul sector. From Toul, Rickenbacker made his first flight over the line accompanied by Raoul Lufbery; they were flying French Nieuport scouts, but nothing much happened except Rick saw some enemy balloons in the air and caught the first pungent whiff of anti-aircraft.

But it was at this point where his comparative maturity came in. Unlike the youngsters, he had no immediate desire to roar over the lines and get himself a bag of Huns. He quietly assayed the situation and came to the conclusion that he had learned very little in flying school. He sensed that his flying was not easy, smooth, and instinctive. His maturity told him that in an air battle his mind would be fully occupied matching wits and manoeuvre for manoeuvre with the opposition without having to concentrate on the process of performing tight turns, loops, and chandelles.

As a matter of fact Rickenbacker was never considered a stunt flyer and his victories came as the result of careful planning. Once he spotted his quarry he worked to set up the safest and most satisfactory fighting conditions. The programme took longer but in the end the precautions paid off. If he made a mistake he returned to his field and flew through the manoeuvre again and again until he had solved the problem.

Six weeks of front-line flying passed before Rickenbacker scored his first victory. Another month went by before he was successful again. Up to that point he was just another war pilot with little of what was known as colour and the least spectacular performer in No. 94, but his first victory gave some hint of what was to come. Here surprise and anticipation of the enemy's moves played a big part.

Flying with James Norman Hall, Rick encountered an Albatros over Pont-à-Mousson. He let Hall go up into the sun and then went headlong at the German fighter. Hall took his turn, making the jerry swing right. Rick anticipated the move and was exactly where he should be and nailed the Albatros cold. The more-experienced Hall continued on around and moved in smartly to cover Rickenbacker's tail.

Rick wasn't so happy about his second triumph. He took off with Reid Chambers, but the two became separated in the clouds. Patrolling Toul, Commercy, and Nancy at 20,000 feet he came upon three Albatros fighters and stalked them, hoping they would cross into the Allied area, but the German ack-ack pointed him out, so he had to attack over the woods at Mont Sec. He was so anxious he went in too fast and when he pulled out after shooting down one of the Albatroses he lost a lot of upper-wing covering and only just made his own lines.

Rick's third victim provided unexpected drama. Along with Reid Chambers he agreed to take a newcomer, a Lieutenant Kurtz, over the line to let him see what war-flying was like. Kurtz was slated to become an armament specialist.

Over the line they encountered three Albatros scouts, which attacked first. The Nieuports evaded them, turned the tables, and chased them into Germany. Over Thiaucourt Rick met one making a climbing turn and firing wildly; with a quick half turn he got on his tail and shot him down. On the way home Kurtz apparently fainted in the air and crashed in flames.

Timing played a great part in Rickenbacker's fourth kill. Taking off with Doug Campbell, he met two Albatros two-seaters, which were accompanied by four Pfalz fighters at 18,000 feet over Mars-la-Tour. Rick and Campbell had 2,000 feet on the enemy planes but they withdrew into the sun until the Huns were within the Allied lines. Once they started their dive attack, the Albatroses turned for home. The Pfalz ships stayed over the two-seaters and escorted them back to Thiaucourt. While the two Americans stayed aloft wondering what the next move would be, the Pfalz planes made a turn indicating they were leaving the observation two-seaters. Campbell took a chance on the bait planes, but Rickenbacker watched the jerry fighters.

Both sides played their strategy back and forth until one Albatros was moved off, obviously for bait. In an instant both Rick and Campbell struck and the Albatros went down; it all happened so fast the Pfalz had no time to retaliate. Later Rickenbacker was given full credit for the kill, although Campbell had fired a few rounds.

On May 30, 1918, Rick became an ace. Two flights of six Nieuports had gone out to help escort in a long-distance bomber formation of British two-seaters which had been out on a raid, and Rick asked to go along as a free lance. As the Nieuports were approaching the de Havilland bombers, they were suddenly attacked from below, and one went down obviously out of control. Rick noticed the two Albatros planes which were causing the trouble, so he moved in fast to intercept. He shot down one and then went into a very un-Rickenbacker pell-mell attack and later drove off an Albatros that was annoying Jimmy Meissner, who was floundering home with the fabric ripped off his top wing.

Shortly after this, No. 94 turned in their dainty Nieuports for the more rugged French Spad.

By now his superiors recognised that Rickenbacker was a very dependable officer and he was promoted to flight commander. When he was later given full command of No. 94 he retained his rank of captain and was not made a major, the rank usually bestowed when one is given such a command. One wonders whether his lack of a college education was the reason for this slight. There was class distinction in the U.S. Air Service as well as in the British R.F.C.

Shortly after scoring his fifth victory, Rickenbacker caught a severe cold which resulted in a serious ear condition which kept him on the ground most of the time until September 14, a period of more than fifteen weeks. Those who were acquainted with his condition believed he would not fly again.

By June 27 the First Pursuit Group was gathered together at a field twenty-five miles south of Château-Thierry. Rick tried to get into action, but after leading his flight several times, he had to go to Paris for more treatment, as his fever had increased. While there, he learned of the Spad depot outside the city and during convalescence managed to study these new planes. Eventually he was well enough to fly one back to their new field.

During the Saint-Mihiel drive in September Rickenbacker got back into his stride; the weather was bad but on the twelfth Rick and Reid Chambers went over on a personal strafing expedition and obtained some very important information on the progress of the battle. While thus absorbed, they were assaulted by a number of planes in a flying circus. By stunting like mad to escape, they somehow cut off one Fokker, and with a very short blast Eddie shot it down.

Later in September he got his ninth and tenth victims on one patrol. He was flying alone near Etain and spotted two Halberstadt two-seaters. He was about to go in when he caught sight of a flight of five Fokkers above them, so he quickly changed his position, went up into the sun, nosed over, and caught a Fokker cold. Instead of zooming out to clear, he continued on through the Fokker formation. Evidently they were carrying out a camera patrol, for they never left their course and Rick's first burst put the leader in flames, although the rear gunner battered the American's Spad ferociously.

On September 26 Rick had a very grim experience. His flight was ordered to attack some balloons that were spotting for the opening of the Argonne drive. He had Cook, Chambers, Taylor, Coolidge, and Palmer with him. He planned for three Spads to take one of two balloons up between Brabant and Dun. His flight men got the two balloons before Rick could fire a shot, so he went after another he remembered seeing in the vicinity of Damvillers. But it wasn't his day for balloons. When he got there some other Yank had torched it, so he slipped into some murk to try trapping some unsuspecting Hun and to his amazement found himself flying wing tip to wing tip with an enemy Fokker. They each made turns, exchanged shots, and finally Rick scored with a long burst that raked the Fokker's fuselage. Almost immediately Rick's Hisso engine began pounding and vibrating badly. He watched the Hun go down in flames and then had to give his attention to his own aircraft. He cut his power and headed for his own lines.

The First Pursuit Group got ten balloons that morning—and Rickenbacker got a Fokker.

The war went on in this way for him; he did nothing spectacular and because most of his action was carefully planned, many of his "kills" came after long periods of crafty strategy and cautious planning. He made few mistakes, for he realised that in those war skies the first could be the last. If a wing was shot off or the control system damaged one simply had to sit it out. At best, if the plane caught fire, the coolest pilots could maintain a long sideslip to keep the flames away from the cockpit long enough to make a crash landing. Not many were that lucky.

Rickenbacker returned from the war a great hero but a very humble man. The spirituality he had gained in World War I skies stood him in good stead thirty-four years later when he was bobbing about in a rubber raft for twenty-one harrowing days in the wide Pacific.

Like so many others, Rickenbacker found peacetime a very difficult period. He was America's ace of aces. He had a string of reputable decorations (although it took twelve years for an appreciative Congress to award him the Medal of Honour) and a social status many notches above what he had known.

What does a man do when his war-hero world topples about him? Rickenbacker took it calmly and went back into the automobile business. Wise money available decided to capitalise on his name and background. A company was set up to manufacture what was called the Rickenbacker car and on its radiator shell it carried the old No. 94 Squadron's insignia—the hat-in-the-ring-trade-mark. It was a good car but it was produced at the wrong time, and Rickenbacker found himself head of a bankrupt company.

He joined Tony Fokker, who had invented the machine-gun interrupter gear that gave Germany a temporary lead in the air war late in 1915. Fokker was trying to get started in aviation in the United States and some of his early transports helped give America the lead in the field.

Whatever contribution Rickenbacker made was immediately recognized in the industry and he was soon taken into the infant Eastern Air Lines. That company is a great monument to America's greatest air hero—still a very humble man.

As Benjamin Franklin once said, "After crosses and losses, men grow humbler and wiser."

In contrast to both Frank Luke and Eddie Rickenbacker was Captain Elliott White Springs, who returned from the Western Front with a dozen confirmed victories, many decorations, and a reputation for hilarity that has no equal in American military aviation. I am fortunate to include Elliott among my friends and am sure he will not resent this presentation of his gay, happy-go-lucky career. Would there were more like Elliott White Springs, for the duty of fighting for one's country would be greatly lightened.

Springs's history during World War I reads like something concocted by Thorne Smith. Things happened to Elliott that were later presented by air-story writers as out-and-out fiction. He was one of the few who fought the war with joy in his heart and utter contempt for the enemy. He wrote much of his air-war life in a series of riotous novels that to many of us were equal to anything penned by the late F. Scott Fitzgerald. For years the Elliott White Springs version of front-line flying was the basic idea of every Hollywood air-war epic. Pulp writers wantonly lifted his plots, characters, and hilarious situations and offered them as original; but Springs only laughed and turned out more.

By the time he was through with the war-time airman's history and had settled down to his father's cotton-mill business most of us felt we had been cruelly defrauded in that we had not served under him.

Someday some keen-sighted publisher will reissue all of Springs's air-war stories. I personally recommend *Above the Bright Blue Sky*, *Nocturne Militaire*, *Contact*, and *War Birds and Lady Birds*. If that should ever happen the whole free world will learn to laugh again.

Springs was the only son of a wealthy Southern cotton-mill owner and up to the outbreak of the war probably looked forward to a long life of complacency and ease. Instead, he quit Princeton to join America's newly formed Air Service. From the start he was a combination playboy, daredevil, and gay-hearted character who seemed destined for an early grave.

All he learned in primary schools about radio, bombing, and the theory of flight was unlearned once he was sent to England, where his particular group discovered one of the great maxims of military service. They had been shipped overseas in a great hurry, but no arrangements for their care and feeding had been made. For days they wandered about

278

the streets of London minus uniforms, identity papers, or any evidence of rank. This was the lost squadron of the U.S. Air Service. No one had ever heard of them. No one had any idea where they came from, and there was nothing definite as to where they were going.

When things became really bad Springs wired home for money and enough was sent so he could put up his group in hotel luxury. Once bedded down, he next went to the British and explained the situation and it must have been quite a bill of goods, for the Royal Flying Corps provided housing and food. They were also given air training and living quarters at Oxford, where they gratefully joined the formal classes the British were providing for their own trainees.

Hair-raising tales of these next few weeks have been related a hundred times wherever old-time aviators gather. Springs and his friends seem to have set up a new standard of cadetship and thoughtfully provided instruction in subjects somewhat incongruous to those usually expected in the flying services. It was great fun until at last the greater part of them were taught to fly and sent off to join various British or American squadrons. It should be explained that by this time Uncle Sam experienced a reversal of interest and soon demanded that perfidious Albion give up these all-American volunteers.

Throughout this sizzling period Springs was the leader in all the frantic goings on that kept staid old Oxford rocking. He learned to fly every available type and his stunting displays at the advanced schools are still spoken of in sepulchral tones whenever British war pilots meet. A series of sensational crashes made up part of the story and by rights Springs should have been killed a dozen times, but he seemed to lead a charmed life.

However, although his life on the ground and in the flying schools might be considered unusually gay, Springs totted up so much flying time that he came under the notice of Major Billy Bishop, the Canadian ace, who immediately selected him to join his newly organized No. 85 Squadron in the R.A.F. Two other Princetonians, Lawrence Calahan and John Grider, went with Springs. It is now generally known that Grider was the "unknown" hero of Springs's air-war book, *War Birds —The Diary of an Unknown Aviator*.

Bishop's No. 85 Squadron went to France on May 22, 1918, and occupied a field a few miles below Dunkirk, which was close enough to the line to be very uncomfortable most of the time. The pilots and mechanics spent most of their nights in dugouts evading bombs dropped by night-flying jerry airmen and during the day were continually engaged in extra-patrol work against low-flying reconnaissance planes.

Springs received considerable instruction under Bishop and scored his first triumph on June 5. Three more fell before his S.E.5 guns and then on June 27 he himself was shot down and only just managed to get into his own lines. He cracked up badly and went to a nearby hospital, where he spent some time recovering.

When he was ready to return to action he was told to report to No. 148 Squadron of the American Air Service. The order was something of a shock, for by now he was quite at home with the R.A.F. and had practically forgotten he had been sent overseas by the United States. He liked the R.A.F. and felt, as did many others, he owed them a debt for the training they had provided, but the order stood. He was equipped with a high stiff-collared uniform and given a Sopwith Camel, instead of the ragtime garments he and his pals had devised for uniforms and the beloved S.E.5a.

But the transfer had some compensations, for he was promoted to captain, made a flight commander, and the outfit was made up of many other Americans who had trained and served with the R.A.F.

Springs took up his new role with his old-time zest and was soon back in the air battling the Boche. While leading his flight on August 3, he knocked down his fifth enemy plane and became an ace. Eventually his squadron, No. 148, became as famous as Rickenbacker's No. 94 and ranked second to them in the number of victories scored; No. 94 had been in action from April, however, whereas No. 148 did not begin operations until late in July.

Today, the man who was probably one of the wildest and happiest characters on the Western Front, who overcame bureaucratic inefficiency and a great hurdle of departmental ineptitude, is one of the country's leading businessmen. He has taken over his father's mills and built them up to one of the largest textile businesses in the South. Notwithstanding the years, his name still sparkles brightly when World War I airmen gather and talk over the highlights of their youth.

Elliott White Springs was undoubtedly one of the gayest of the winged clan.

Another living American ace long since forgotten is George A. Vaughn, Jr., one of the many students from Princeton who volunteered and served with distinction. This group also included the famed Hoby Baker, Jesse Creech, and Lansing Holden. Vaughn ended the war with thirteen confirmed victories, seven of which were won while serving with No. 84 Squadron of the Royal Air Force.

After some primary ground training at Princeton Vaughn was sent to England, where he came under the tutelage of many experienced British instructors and in May 1918 was assigned to No. 84 Squadron, which was holding down the Amiens sector, and for three very busy months he flew with seasoned veterans. His ship was the famed S.E.5 and because of the squadron's insistence on tight formation flying and a general taboo on freelance excursions, he learned a great deal and was soon marked as one of the most dependable and experienced fighters in the squadron.

Since teamwork was the rule in the old R.A.F. Vaughn absorbed every skill employed and learned to fly his plane under all war conditions, particularly in crowded combat. The man who can stunt and grandstand over his own field is often chilled stiff with fear if he is suddenly attacked from behind by an enemy Fokker. Vaughn was exceptionally skilled in air-battle manoeuvres.

Once he was attacked by an enemy Pfalz which poured in a wicked round of fire that riddled his tail. Recovering quickly from his surprise, Vaughn zoomed up hard and the Boche went on through in a continuation of his dive. Vaughn then heeled over and went after him and rapped home two short bursts that exploded the Pfalz's fuel tank. This occurred on his second trip over the lines.

On his third Vaughn went on a balloon-busting show and succeeded in destroying one, sending it down in flames. Pulling away from that success, he met an enemy two-seater over Méricourt which was patrolling at 500 feet. George roared through a storm of enemy ground fire, emptied a drum of ammunition, and the two-seater plunged to a shattering finish in a back area. On a later occasion he found another biplane over Villers-Carbonel and chased it into the ground, where it smashed and burned.

With seven victories to his credit Vaughn was then transferred to the newly formed No. 17 Squadron of the American Air Force and had to switch from S.E.5's to Sopwith Camels. The S.E.5 was faster, but the Camel was much more manoeuvrable and once Vaughn and his flying mates became fully acquainted with the darting little Sopwith they soon realized they could outfight any German mount.

The Camel, a small and very chunky biplane, was powered with a Le Rhone or Clerget rotary engine which provided much of the manoeuvrability. The rotary engine had its cylinders set in a circular ring about a master crankshaft, and the engine itself actually rotated about this central point, and so the heavy engine whirling about its master crankshaft provided a strong pull or torque in the direction of rotation. Because the Camel was so small, stub-winged, and short in the body it whipped over startlingly fast on right-hand turns. By employing this feature in fighting manoeuvres, Camel pilots were able to outfly most of their adversaries. They simply right-hand-turned them to death, as the saying goes.

In a few short weeks Vaughn had mastered the Sopwith and added six more kills to his total.

At one time when he was leading an upper-level flight fifteen Fokkers snapped down on a lower-level flight of five Camels below. He caught one Fokker and sent it down out of control. Zooming out of that action, he came out just above another; a short burst and that one went down with a wing off, and by this time the sky was swirling with single-seaters and criss-crossing tracer fire. Two Fokkers stormed at Vaughn, so he wisely went into a spin as the enemy machines tried to nail the corkscrewing target. He held this manoeuvre until he could see details of the barbed-wire entanglements below and then pulled out. One Fokker tried a long burst, but Vaughn evaded him and then tried to zip up his engine.

Nothing happened and he thought he was out of petrol.

Then just as he was gliding down into no-man's-land, he remembered the Camel had a small reserve fuel tank, so he quickly switched over to that and the engine picked up instantly. On the way back to his field he suddenly sensed that his back was wet and cold and concluded he had been wounded; the muscles of his back felt stiff, his coat and shirt dripping wet—it must be blood. He recalled that wounded men often have no idea they have been hit until sometime after, so he twisted back and forth and decided it must be only a flesh wound, since he could feel no damage to any of his bone structure.

He grinned to himself, realizing it meant a spell in the hospital and probably a month's leave in London, which he felt he could well use.

He landed safely and confided to his mechanic that he thought he had been wounded by a bullet grazing his back. The mechanic inspected, sniffed at the sodden portion of Vaughn's coat, and then examined the Camel, at which he let out a hilarious howl. The "blood" was nothing more than petrol that had sprayed out of a corner of the tank through a series of bullet holes while the plane was spinning down and had drenched Vaughn's flying clothes.

Instead of a trip to London he received a new Camel and

was recommended for the Distinguished Service Cross for his gallant attempt to save the Camel flight below with his timely attack on the Fokkers. He lost one of his mates, but the remaining three were credited with two more kills.

He lived out the war, returned to his home in Brooklyn, and was for many years connected with various aeronautical projects. He ranks next to Rickenbacker among the surviving aces of World War I.

To only a few people will the name of David Stinton Ingalls mean anything in connection with that war. A small group may remember him as a member of the Ohio legislature at one time. In 1929 President Hoover appointed him Assistant Secretary of the Navy for Aviation, and while holding that post, he actually flight-tested every new plane accepted by the Navy and even did a tour of duty aboard the giant dirigible *Akron*.

During World War I David Ingalls was said to be the youngest American ace. He certainly was the youngest Assistant Secretary of the Navy in U.S. history. But more important, and a fact generally unknown in America, David Ingalls was the only American naval ace in World War I.

Ingalls was born in Cleveland, January 28, 1898. In the autumn of 1916 he entered Yale, where he was a hockey and football star. When the United States declared war Dave enlisted in the Yale aviation unit, which had been organized by F. Trubee Davison, later Assistant Secretary of War for Aviation. This unit was later taken over and trained by a naval squadron.

In the middle of 1918 Ingalls was in France but had nothing to do. There were no U.S. naval or aircraft squadrons available. After a few days of messing around what was called a bomber squadron, Ingalls discovered the British 213 (naval) Squadron and managed to become attached to that group.

Either the British liked Ingalls or Ingalls liked the British, but whatever, he seemed to enjoy flying the Sopwith Camel and was soon in action. His first brush with a flight of Fokkers was almost his last. However, he remembered the Camel ritual "right-turn 'em to death" and was able to scamper out of that difficulty. Two days later he knocked down his first Hun. Coming upon a two-seater well behind the line, he gave chase and, risking the fire of the German gunner, he went in and sent down the Hannah.

A few days later he ran into another two-seater, this time a Rumpler near La Panne, but the observer was a wily character who held his fire, used short snap bursts, and generally gave Dave a hot time. When Dave went in he overshot; again the Rumpler gunner lashed him with tracer and regulation ammo. This went on for some minutes, and Ingalls wondered how it would end. Finally he feinted an attack from the left and the German pilot swung his plane around to meet it. With that, Ingalls half rolled and came out with both guns blazing. One short, careful burst rang the bell and the two-seater fell in flames.

The fight had taken him far over the enemy lines, and when he turned for his field the German ack-ack gave him a sizzling time, so he nosed down and risked the ground machine-gun fire rather than the heavier stuff. No sooner had he reached tree-top level than his rotary engine faltered. He caught a pungent stench of petrol and judged he had petrol-tank trouble, so quickly switched over to the reserve supply; the still-twirling engine caught again and with a prayer of thanks Ingalls finally roared across the enemy trenches and landed on his own field.

This fight gave him a lot of confidence and he was named a regular and booked for all important patrols. The Germans had a well-known air base at the Belgian town of Varsenne, where bombers and protective fighters flew to harass the British with night raids. It was decided that the Fifth Group of the R.A.F. should blast this German force off the map. The Americans No. 17 Squadron was part of this group and their Camels were loaded with 20-pound Cooper bombs and ammunition and given a part in this destruction programme. Ingalls's No. 213 Squadron was ordered to destroy the machine shops. The heavy bombing was to be done by the British D.H.9's.

The raid was one of the bomber epics of the war. It was a beautiful day with just enough cloud to afford cover for individual operations. When the D.H.9 bombers went down the Camels stayed with them and then they split up to complete their part of the operation.

Ingalls went in very low to make sure his 20-pounders would find their mark. The enemy was not asleep and they were all greeted with a storm of machine-gun and heavier ack-ack fire, but the Nines had hit hard and the camouflaged hangars were soon ablaze. When Dave was all set to deliver his eggs he happened to glance up and saw he was directly below a flight of D.H.9's and had to swerve fast to avoid their salvo of high explosive. He lost his initial chance to rake the machine shops which had been set up in the rear of the hangars, so he fluttered back and forth across the field, shooting up anything that moved until the air was clear for him to get rid of his Coopers.

Finally, realizing that practically everyone else had gone home, Ingalls went back over the burning hangars and deposited his bombs on the portable machine shops. On the way out he spotted a machine-gun pit that had escaped the onslaught, so he roared through the smoke and flame and blasted at the gun crew. When he was satisfied there was no more opposition there he zoomed into a low cloud bank and started for home. Another Camel appeared from nowhere and Dave discovered that his British C.O. had come back to find out what was keeping him, a gesture Ingalls especially appreciated.

A few minutes later as they roared along the Belgian coast an enemy two-seater popped out of the clouds over Ostend. Both Camel pilots went after it. Ingalls was closest and got in the first burst, but the German slithered into a cloud bank. Ingalls went in after it and they both came out on the other side and all Dave had to do was press his triggers; the Hun went down trailing a long smoke scarf.

The British were so pleased with this young American they made him a flight commander in No. 213 Squadron. To celebrate this promotion he took his flight over to do a balloon show. When they went over there were three up in the area but all three were burned before they came back. Ingalls got one, although his Camel was badly riddled, and he only just got back to his field.

There was plenty of bomber-escort work to do, and since he was a flight leader, Ingalls was expected to stay up front and command the operation, but one noon he spotted four Fokker D.7's sauntering about over the German lines. He went in fast and found the Fokker leader trying the old head-on attack to see if the young American would give ground. Dave didn't and they nearly collided, but his bold action was enough to drive off the D.7's.

On another bomber-escort show Ingalls saw a D.H.9 in trouble as the result of anti-aircraft fire. Two Fokkers moved in to pick off the straggler, but Dave was too fast for them. He swung around to the rear and caught one Fokker cold. The other was so intent getting his sights lined up he never saw what was happening all around him. But, again, Dave was too anxious and overshot his target. With that the Fokker came to life, half rolled, went into a tight spin, and ducked home.

But Dave still had the D.H. to worry about, so he sat over its tail with the idea of escorting it back across the line. Three new Fokkers saw this byplay and Dave had to fight a defensive action with the enemy pilots snapping at his tail like infuriated terriers. However, the D.H.9 crew got back safely and were very grateful for the protection.

A short time after that Ingalls accounted for another Fokker during a melee in which No. 213 Squadron downed three enemy planes.

He finished out this tour of duty with the British, doing considerable ground strafing and low bombing, and on October 1, 1918, was sent to England, first to be decorated with the Distinguished Flying Cross by King George V and then to organise a squadron of U.S. Navy pilots. While this was under way he was awarded the United States Distinguished Service Medal.

The Armistice was signed before this new naval squadron could be organised and he ended the war with a record of five planes and one enemy balloon in six weeks of front-line flying, most of which had been devoted to bomber escort, ground attack, low tactical bombing, and contour fighting.

David S. Ingalls was a very worthy addition to any air service.

America's highest award, the Congressional Medal of Honour, was bestowed but eight times to airmen of World War I. As I mentioned, Luke was the only airman so honoured while the war was in progress, and it took more than twelve years of official consideration before Eddie Rickenbacker was given his.

For years most aviation writers were under the impression that Luke and Rickenbacker were the only Americans so honoured, but there were six others.

First Lieutenant Harold E. Goettler and Second Lieutenant Erwin R. Bleckley both were awarded the C.M.H. for a heroic action connected with the famed Lost Battalion. They were members of No. 50 Aero Squadron, and their feat has been ignored by most historians for nearly forty years.

It will be remembered that the 307th Battalion of the U.S. 153rd Brigade had been cut off on the heights of the Bois de la Naza after an advance. The 307th was commanded by Major Charles S. Whittlesey of the 77th Division.

From October second to the seventh the battalion held a ravine against heavy odds and for a time were in great trouble. Several attempts were made to support them by air, and during this tactical operation Goettler and Bleckley made a particularly heroic effort on October 6, which cost them their lives. Because of this gallant show the 307th managed to hold on another twenty-four hours and were eventually able to break out with 252 survivors of their original 679 battalion members.

These awards were not announced until 1922, four years after the close of hostilities.

The Marine Corps came into the Congressional Medal of Honour list when on October 8, 1918, Second Lieutenant Ralph Talbot and Gunnery Sergeant Robert Guy Robinson displayed a heroism that won the fullest appreciation of those who knew of their exceptional courage.

Both Talbot and Robinson were part of the First Marine Aviation Force on duty in France. On the date in question their plane, working with No. 218 Squadron of the R.A.F. on a raid over Pitthem, Belgium, was driven out of its formation by twelve enemy scouts. Motor trouble seems to have been the cause of their failure to maintain position, and in the fight that followed Talbot shot down one enemy plane. His gunner was badly wounded in an elbow and then his gun jammed. Talbot manoeuvred to give Robinson a chance to clear the gun stoppage, and they returned to the fight.

Robinson was then shot in the hip and stomach and when he collapsed Lieutenant Talbot attacked the nearest enemy scout with his front gun and shot it down. Following this, he nosed down out of the fray, crossed the enemy lines at less than 50 feet, and finally landed near an advanced dressing station, where he left Robinson, who unfortunately died later in the day.

For this fight and gallant stand both Talbot and Robinson received the Congressional Medal of Honour.

Two U.S. Navy men also received the C.M.H. Ensign Charles Hazeltine Hamman of Baltimore, Maryland, was awarded the medal for extraordinary heroism while flying a seaplane on a war patrol on August 21, 1918. With three other U.S. Navy planes in the Mediterranean area Hamman attacked a superior force of Austrian land planes. During this engagement Ensign George M. Ludlow was shot down and fell into the water 5 miles off Pola. Hamman immediately went to his aid and landed on the water alongside the disabled machine, from where he took Ludlow aboard. It was a very tricky effort to get his overloaded seaplane off again, but he succeeded although the Austrians tried to shoot them up throughout the whole operation. Ensigns Hamman and Ludlow finally reached their base at Porto Corsini.

The Congressional Medal of Honour was also won by Chief Machinist's Mate Francis Edward Ormsbee, Junior, of Providence, Rhode Island, on September 25, 1918, but he did not have to leave his own country to win his way into that gallant company. He was attached to the Naval Air Station at Pensacola, Florida, at the time. While flying with Ensign J. A. Jova, Ormsbee saw a plane go into a tail spin and crash about three-quarters of a mile from where they were flying. Pointing it out to his pilot, Ormsbee next made plans for giving immediate aid. Jova landed their aircraft on the rough waters and his observer-mechanic dove over the side and swam to the wreckage. Most of the plane was well under water but Ormsbee succeeded in partly extracting the gunner so that the man's head was at least out of water and held him in that position until a speeding crash boat arrived. He then made a number of desperate attempts to rescue the pilot, diving into the tangled wreckage with complete disregard for his own life, but it was too late. The pilot had been under the water too long and nothing could be done for him.

To conclude this chapter about American air heroes of World War I we bring in a Brooklyn boy, Major James Meissner. Jimmy, as he was affectionately known to practically everyone in the service, is credited with eight enemy aircraft and when the war was over went into business in Birmingham, Alabama. He also organized the National Guard Air Squadron for the state of Alabama and became its commanding officer.

Meissner left Cornell in his junior year to join up and made his first flight over the line with No. 94 Pursuit Squadron under the guidance of Raoul Lufbery on April 9, 1918. Twice during that month Jimmy escaped death by a narrow margin. On that first flight he made a frantic dive to escape enemy attack over Verdun. Congratulating himself on his close shave, he sensed a disturbing shock; his Nieuport seemed to have collided with something in the air. Glancing over the machine, he discovered that the fabric along the upper wing had been torn away by the suction of the air passing over the airfoil. This often happened with the French scout. Meissner forgot all about the enemy pursuers and tried to regain control. Tracer bullets caught up with him and he knew he was in for a bad time, but fortunately Rickenbacker came to his rescue, driving off the Fokkers while Jimmy gradually pulled the Nieuport out of its dive. He maintained partial control for the rest of the way in and was able to land on his own field with no further trouble.

Two weeks later the same accident happened and again it was Rickenbacker who intervened and saved him from the

288

Fokkers. There was a great sense of relief when No. 94 Pursuit Squadron discarded the Nieuport for the sturdier Spad.

On June 7, 1918, Meissner won his fifth victory and was awarded his captaincy. In October he was given command of No. 147 Squadron with the rank of major. This is an interesting point since Rickenbacker, who was given command of No. 94, never rose higher than a captain.

LIST OF ALLIED
AND ENEMY ACES
WORLD WAR I

U.S. ACES OF WORLD WAR I

Name	Rank	Squad-ron	Vic-tories	Home
Edward V. Ricken-backer	Captain	94	26	Columbus, Ohio
Frank Luke, Junior	Second Lieut.	27	19	Phoenix, Ariz.
Raoul G. Lufbery	Major	94	17	Wallingford, Conn.
George A. Vaughn	Major	17	13	Brooklyn, N.Y.
Field E. Kindley	Captain	148	12	Gravette, Ark.
Elliott W. Springs	Captain	148	12	Lancaster, S.C.
Reed G. Landis	Captain	25	10	Washington, D.C.
Jacques M. Swaab	Captain	22	10	New York, N.Y.
Paul F. Baer	Lieutenant	103	9	Fort Wayne, Ind.
Thomas G. Cassady	Captain	28	9	Spencer, Ind.
Chester E. Wright	Lieutenant	93	9	Cambridge, Mass.
James D. Beane	Lieutenant	22	8	Concord, Mass.
Henry R. Clay, Junior	Lieutenant	148	8	Fort Worth, Texas
Hamilton Coolidge	Captain	94	8	Boston, Mass.
Jesse O. Creech	Lieutenant	148	8	Washington, D.C.
William P. Erwin	Lieutenant	1	8	New York, N.Y.
Lloyd A. Hamilton	Lieutenant	17	8	Burlington, Vt.
Frank O'D. Hunter	Lieutenant	103	8	Savannah, Ga.
Clinton Jones	Second Lieut.	22	8	San Francisco, Calif.
James A. Meissner	Major	94	8	Brooklyn, N.Y.
Joseph F. Wehner	Lieutenant	27	8	Boston, Mass.
Wilbur W. White	Lieutenant	147	8	New York, N.Y.
Charles J. Biddle	Major	13	7	Andalusia, Pa.

Name	Rank	Squadron	Victories	Home
Howard Burdick	Lieutenant	17	7	Brooklyn, N.Y.
Reid M. Chambers	Major	94	7	Memphis, Tenn.
Harvey W. Cook	Captain	94	7	Toledo, Ohio
Lansing C. Holden	Lieutenant	95	7	New York, N.Y.
John Huffer	Major	103	7	Paris, France
De Freest G. Larner	Captain	103	7	Washington, D.C.
Wendel A. Robertson	Lieutenant	139	7	Fort Smith, Ark.
Leslie J. Rummel	Lieutenant	147	7	Newark, N.J.
Karl J. Schoen	Lieutenant	139	7	Indianapolis, Ind.
Sumner Sewall	Captain	95	7	Bath, Me.
William H. Stovall	Lieutenant	13	7	Stovall, Miss.
Jerry C. Vasconcelles	Captain	27	6	Denver, Colo.
B. V. Baucom	Lieutenant	1	6	Milford, Texas
Arthur R. Brooks	Captain	139	6	Framingham, Mass.
Douglas Campbell	Captain	94	6	Mt. Hamilton, Calif.
Edward P. Curtiss	Captain	95	6	Rochester, N.Y.
Arthur E. Esterbrook	Lieutenant	1	6	Port Flagler, Wash.
Murray K. Guthrie	Lieutenant	13	6	Mobile, Ala.
James Norman Hall	Captain	94	6	Colfax, Iowa
Leonard C. Hammond	Captain	91	6	San Francisco, Calif.
Harold E. Hartney	Lieut. Col.	27	6	New York, N.Y.
Frank K. Hayes	Lieutenant	13	6	Chicago, Ill.
Donald Hudson	Lieutenant	27	6	New York, N.Y.
Howard C. Knotts	Second Lieut.	17	6	Carlinsville, Ill.
James A. Keating	Major	R.A.F.	6	New York, N.Y.
Robert O. Lindsay	Lieutenant	139	6	Maderson, N.C.
John K. McArthur	Second Lieut.	27	6	Buffalo, N.Y.
Ralph A. O'Neil	Lieutenant	147	6	Nogales, Ariz.
William T. Ponder	Lieutenant	103	6	Mangum, Okla.
Kenneth L. Porter	Second Lieut.	147	6	Dowagiac, Mich.
Martinus Stenseth	Captain	28	6	Twin Valley, Minn.
Edgar G. Tobin	Captain	103	6	San Antonio, Texas
Remington D. Vernam	Lieutenant	22	6	New York, N.Y.
William T. Badham	Lieutenant	91	5	Birmingham, Ala.
Herbert L. Baer	Lieut.	R.A.F.	5	Fort Wayne, Ind.
Clayton Bissell	Captain	148	5	Kane, Pa.
Harold R. Buckley	Captain	95	5	Agawam, Mass.
Lawrence R. Calahan	Lieutenant	148	5	Chicago, Ill.
Everett R. Cook	Captain	91	5	San Francisco, Calif.
George W. Furlow	Lieutenant	103	5	Rochester, Minn.

Name	Rank	Squadron	Victories	Home
Harold H. George	Lieutenant	139	5	Niagara Falls, N.Y.
Charles G. Gray	Captain	213	5	Chicago, Ill.
Edward M. Haight	Lieutenant	139	5	New York, N.Y.
James A. Healy	Captain	147	5	Jersey City, N.J.
David S. Ingalls	Ensign	R.A.F.	5	Cleveland, Ohio
James Knowles	Lieutenant	95	5	Cambridge, Mass.
Frederick E. Luff	Lieutenant	25	5	Cleveland, Ohio
Zenos R. Miller	Lieutenant	27	5	?
J. Sidney Owens	Second Lieut.	139	5	Baltimore, Md.
David McK. Peterson	Captain	94	5	Honesdale, Pa.
Orville A. Ralston	Lieutenant	148	5	Lincoln, Neb.
John J. Seerley	Lieutenant	13	5	Chicago, Ill.
Victor H. Strahm	Major	91	5	Evanston, Ill.
Francis M. Simonds	Lieutenant	147	5	New York, N.Y.
William Thaw	Lieut. Col.	103	5	Pittsburgh, Pa.
Robert M. Todd	Lieutenant	17	5	Cincinnati, Ohio
Rodney D. Williams	Lieutenant	17	5	Everett, Mass.

LIST OF U.S. ACES WHO SERVED WITH R.A.F.

(Who did not transfer to U.S. Service.)

Name	Rank	Victories
Warren Gillette	Captain	20
John W. Malone	Captain	20
Alan Wilkenson	Captain	19
Stanley Rosevar	Lieutenant	18
Frank L. Hale	Captain	18
Thayer Iaccaci	Lieutenant	18
Oren J. Rose	Captain	16
Howard Kolburg	Lieutenant	16
Clive Warman	Lieutenant	15
Fred Libby	Lieutenant	14
Paul Iaccaci	Lieutenant	11
Lancelot L. Richardson	Lieutenant	10
Dean I. Lamb	Lieutenant	8
D. M. Longton	Lieutenant	7
Frank A. Robertson	Lieutenant	6
William Pace	Lieutenant	5
Alexander Matthews	Lieutenant	5
Frederick Westing	Lieutenant	5
W. D. Tipton	Captain	5
Francis Magoun	Lieutenant	5

LIST OF U.S. ACES WHO SERVED WITH THE FRENCH

(Who did not transfer to U.S. Service.)

Name	Rank	Victories
Frank Baylies	Sergeant	12
David Putnam	Lieutenant	12
Edwin C. Parsons	Lieutenant	8
James J. Connelly	Lieutenant	8

BRITISH ACES OF WORLD WAR I

(With Twenty or More Victories)

Name	Victories	Squadron
Major Edward Mannock (B)	73	74
Colonel William Bishop (C)	72	85
Major Raymond Collishaw (C)	68	203
Major James B. McCudden (B)	58	56
Captain Donald MacLaren (C)	54	46
Major William G. Barker (C)	53	66
Major Phillip F. Fullard (B)	53	1
Captain W. A. Proctor (SA)	52	84
Captain Robert A. Little (NZ)	47	203
Captain G. E. H. McElroy (C)	46	40
Captain Albert Ball (B)	43	56
Captain T. Larkin (B)	41	
Captain Ira T. Jones (B)	40	74
Major Roderic Dallas (NZ)	39	40
Captain John Gilmore (NZ)	37	65
Captain W. G. Claxton (C)	37	41
Captain Henry W. Wollett (B)	35	43
Captain Frank Quigley (C)	34	70
Captain Frank R. McCall (C)	34	41
Major Albert D. Carter (C)	31	19
Captain J. L. M. White (C)	31	65
Captain W. L. Jordan (B)	31	203
Captain H. Hazel (A)	31	1
Captain B. M. Frew (B)	30	45
Captain Cedric E. Howell (B)	30	45
Major Andrew E. McKeever (C)	30	11
Captain Kinkead (B)	30	201
Captain Henry G. Launchford (B)	29	20
Captain Edward McKelvie (B)	29	22
Captain Brunwin-Hales (B)	27	56
Captain G. D. Gurden (B)	27	22

Name	Victories	Squadron
Captain James A. Slater (B)	26	64
Captain John Leacraft (B)	25	19
Captain John Andrews (B)	24	209
Captain Shields (C)	24	41
Captain Francis McCubbin (B)	23	46
Captain Henry Burden (C)	22	56
Lieutenant W. McK. Thompson (B)	22	20
Captain A. J. Cooper (B)	22	24
Captain K. C. Patrick (I)	22	23
Captain D. Lattimer (B)	22	20
Captain E. R. Tempest (B)	22	64
Lieutenant C. J. Venter (B)	22	29
Captain P. J. Clayson (B)	21	1
Captain A. H. Cobby (A)	21	4
Captain C. E. Thompson (C)	21	46
Captain Cecil King (B)	20	43
Captain F. C. Falkenburg (B)	20	84
Captain Whistler (B)	20	80
Captain Harrison (B)	20	
Major Gilbert Green (B)	20	
Lieutenant John J. Malone (American)	20	
Major A. M. Wilkenson (B)	20	48

A—Australian; B—British; C—Canadian; NZ—New
Zealander; I—Irish; SA—South African

FRENCH ACES OF WORLD WAR I
(With Twenty or More Victories)

Name	Victories
Captain René Fonck	73
Captain Georges Guynemer	53
Lieutenant Charles Nungesser	45
Lieutenant George Madon	41
Lieutenant Maurice Boyeau	35
Sub-lieutenant Coeffard	34
Lieutenant Bourgade	28
Captain Armand Pinsard	27
Lieutenant Guerin	23
Lieutenant Dorme	23
Lieutenant Haegelin	22
Sergeant Marinovitch	21
Captain Heurteaux	21
Lieutenant Deullin	20

ITALIAN ACES OF WORLD WAR I

(With Twenty or More Victories)

Name	Victories
Major Francesco Baracca	34
Lieutenant Silvio Scaroni	26
Lieutenant Col. Pier Ruggero Piccio	24
Lieutenant Flavio Baracchini	21
Captain Fulco di Calabria Ruffo	20

BELGIAN ACES OF WORLD WAR I

(With Twenty or More Victories)

Name	Victories
Captain Willy Coppens	34

AUSTRIAN ACES OF WORLD WAR I

(With Twenty or More Victories)

Name	Victories
Captain Brunowsky	34
Captain Link Crawford	27
Lieutenant Arrigi	26
Lieutenant Fiala	23

GERMAN ACES OF WORLD WAR I

(With Twenty or More Victories)

Name	Victories
Rittmeister Manfred von Richthofen	80
Oberleutnant Ernst Udet	62
Oberleutnant Erich Lowenhardt	56
Leutnant Werner Voss	48
Leutnant Fritz Rumey	45
Hauptmann Bruno Loerzer	45
Hauptmann Rudolf Berthold	44
Leutnant Paul Beaumer	43
Leutnant Josef Jacobs	43
Hauptmann Oswald Boelcke	40
Leutnant Franz Buchner	40
Oberleutnant Lothar von Richthofen	40
Leutnant Karl Menckhoff	39
Leutnant Heinrich Gontermann	39
Leutnant Karl Bolle	36
Leutnant Max Muller	36
Leutnant Julius Buckler	35

Name	Victories
Leutnant Gustav Doerr	35
Hauptmann Edward von Schleich	35
Leutnant Joseph Veltjens	34
Leutnant Otto Koennecke	33
Oberleutnant Kurt Wolff	33
Leutnant Heinrich Bongarth	33
Leutnant Hermann Frommherz	33
Leutnant Emil Thuy	32
Leutnant Paul Billik	31
Oberleutnant Harald Auffarth	30
Leutnant Karl Allmenroader	30
Leutnant Karl Degleow	30
Leutnant Heinrich Kroll	30
Leutnant Josef Mai	30
Leutnant Ulrich Neckel	30
Leutnant Karl Schaefer	30
Leutnant Walter von Bulow	28
Leutnant Walter Blume	28
Oberleutnant Fritz Roth	28
Oberleutnant Otto Bernert	27
Vizefeldwebel Otto Fruhner	27
Leutnant Hans Kirchstein	27
Leutnant Karl Thom	27
Hauptmann Adolph von Tutscheck	27
Leutnant Kurt Wusthoff	27
Oberleutnant Oscar von Boenigk	26
Oberleutnant Eduard Dostler	26
Leutnant Arthur Laumann	26
Leutnant O. von Beaulieu-Marconney	25
Oberleutnant Robert Greim	25
Leutnant Georg von Hantelmann	25
Leutnant Max Nather	25
Leutnant Fritz Puetter	25
Leutnant Erwin Bohme	24
Leutnant Hermann Becker	23
Leutnant Georg Nyer	22
Oberleutnant Hermann Goering	22
Leutnant Hans Klein	22
Leutnant Hans Pippart	22
Leutnant Werner Preuss	22
Vizefeldwebel Karl Schlegel	22
Leutnant Rudolf Windisch	22
Leutnant Hans Adam	21

Name	Victories
Leutnant Fritz Friedrichs	21
Leutnant Fritz Hohn	21
Vizefeldwebel Friedrich Altemeir	20
Oberleutnant Hans Bethge	20
Leutnant Rudolf von Eschwege	20
Leutnant Walter Goettsch	20
Leutnant Friedrich Noltenius	20
Hauptmann Wilhelm Reinhardt	20

CONCLUSION

☐ Throughout these pages I have tried to present the overall picture of the air conflict of the First World War, but my readers will have noted that I have devoted much space to the air duels and victory scores of the aces. This was not my original intent, but I must confess that these individual combats gripped my imagination and interest far more than any other feature of the campaign.

I have been influenced also by years of correspondence with the public who read my earlier magazine articles and serials on air-war combat. Over the years I have been approached for every conceivable scrap of information concerning the air fighters of World War I; what kind of uniforms they wore, the colour of their eyes, the details of the machines they flew, and the microscopic features of their every battle.

The inquiries were seldom about the Handley-Page bomber, the Spad two-seater, or the type of air camera or bombsight we used. The interest was only in aces and single-seater aircraft. In fact, I have never been able to sell a feature article on an air-gunner, the Bristol Fighter, or the epic flight of Lieutenants Goettler and Bleckley over the trapped lost battalion, for which they won the Congressional Medal of Honour.

This continued interest in the air combat of World War I has puzzled many writers, editors, and publishers. There was a period prior to World War II when my mail brought in an average of five hundred letters a month from enthusiasts all over the world. The reason—so I was told—is that young or old can grasp the meaning, the activity, the equipment, and the scope of battle in that campaign. They are positive they could fly a Spad or an S.E.5; they certainly could load and fire a Vickers or a Lewis gun, and the war front of 1914-18 is more familiar to them than any other.

"Your war in the air was as simple in its conduct as anything in the Arthurian period," my readers have told me. "We understand it and can picture ourselves playing an important part. When World War II opened up with its multi-cannon fighters, its super-speed high-altitude bombers, and complex radio-radar communications, it took the personal touch out of air action. Pilots and air-crews no longer were individuals. They were simply skilled operators of very intricate equipment. No, World War I saw the first and the last of the true air fighter."

All well and good, but in spite of capitalizing on the reader's "participation," and as one who spent the greater part of his air-war with a two-seater squadron, I must admit the individual performer of the scout squadrons (especially in the French and American services) was overpublicized. He undoubtedly played an important role in the war, but not so important as his many Boswells would have us believe. This was not entirely his fault, since the strict rules of tactical aviation had not been fully outlined. As pointed out, the air forces were not employed in true tactical operations until the spring of 1918.

For many years I have been concerned over the disparity in claims and credits of the aces of all nations. Overzealous historians and writers of popular aviation features usually contrive to add to the scores of their favourites. Either that, or they resort to the old plaint that their hero should have been credited with many more, but unfortunately most of his fights took place so far over the enemy line it was impossible to get the required confirmation.

Even the British, who were most conservative in their claims, later admitted that several of their top-scoring aces had been credited erroneously with victories to which they were not entitled. I refer to the records of Ball and Mannock in particular.

The official scores of some American aces shortly after the close of World War I appear to be less than those appearing in records of more recent issue. It has been explained that over the years further investigation has been made and incomplete confirmations have been fully documented. However, it is noted that no ace's score has been lessened by these investigations.

Today I find names in the ace lists that were never mentioned in the early 1920s. I have never noted that a name has been deleted from the list.

In the light of my own experience I wonder how these records can be kept with any degree of accuracy. I have seen all kinds of air fights involving all types of machines on both sides of the line. In most cases I would hesitate to declare who shot down whom. Werner Voss provides a striking example. It will be remembered that Voss had been cut off by a flight of S.E.5's led by Major Jimmy McCudden. Practically every pilot in the flight must have fired at least one burst at the gallant German. I was in a Bristol Fighter flight on the fringe of this particular battle, and several of our gunners fired at Voss; but when it was all over the victory was credited to Lieutenant Rhys-Davids. Why? True, Rhys-Davids followed Voss down and fired the last burst at him, but Werner may have been killed some minutes before. Was the victory awarded the youngster because he was very popular in the squadron or because he followed Voss down? Or did they, as was done so many times, cut cards to see who would be given credit for the kill?

How can one tell how many planes he shoots down in a dogfight? There isn't time to make sure that each one either catches fire or is seen to crash. There isn't time for members of the flight to look on your handiwork and confirm your claims. At best it must be some sort of gentleman's agreement by which any reputable member of the flight has his claims fully substantiated by those who were in the air at the same time.

I recall one hectic afternoon when I positively shot down three German two-seaters. My pilot swore he had seen all three plunge down entirely out of control, but at the same time we were well over the line and one of our aircraft had to land in enemy territory. During all this fighting our flight commander was making a game try to pick up the crew. My pilot also joined in this quest, which was unsuccessful. When all this finally wound up and we made our way back to our own lines, no one remembered seeing my three planes go down and later on I had great difficulty in convincing our flight commander that I had actually engaged that many machines. I was credited finally with one—and commended for going down with him in his unsuccessful attempt to rescue two very popular members of our squadron.

301

As Laurence La Tourette Driggs points out, many victories never were confirmed and many confirmed victories were erroneous. Unquestionably many aces have never appeared on any list. Captain Carleton Clement, my flight commander, was one of this unlucky band. To my knowledge Clement must have downed a full dozen of the enemy, but his name does not appear on any ace list anywhere.

The list of aces included in this volume is the most authentic that can be offered under the circumstances. At best, it is simply a record of the men who fought with such courage and skill in the first war in the air. But, as can be appreciated, a man who is credited with fifty victories is no better, no greater, no more courageous than one who has scored ten. Air fighting was geared to certain temperaments; whereas the stoic duty demanded of pilots and observers of the artillery and bomber squadrons was something else again. He who was a great success at one might have been a complete dud at the other. Major William Barker was one of the few who starred in all types of air activity.

The most successful fighter, regardless of his score, was the one who carried out his patrol obligations to the letter, day after day. If he scored often and yet lost pilots and machines of his own flight, his worth was questionable. The headstrong and unpredictable, like Ball, Luke, Guynemer, Rhys-Davids, Nungesser, Immelmann and Navarre, to name but a few, provided whirlwind copy for the war news, but considering the theories of General Trenchard, they seldom carried their weight or earned their pay. This may seem a harsh appraisal of well-known war heroes, but it bears considerable merit in the long view.

It must be admitted that single-seater pilots were not always cruising around hoping to find a sitting duck. Generally speaking, the lone eagle had a fairly cushy time. He could attack or ignore the opposition, depending on how bloodthirsty he felt that day. There was no one to question his mood or his degree of courage. Who knows, on the day he did not score he might have spent his time flipping in and out of handy clouds or taking pains to avoid enemy formations.

But if a scout pilot is a member of a flight or element detailed to do a specific job, there is no backing out. He stays in formation, plays his part in the team, and distributes his allotment of fragmentation bombs and machine-gun ammunition.

These low-down sorties were fifty times more hazardous than a man-to-man combat at 15,000 feet. First you risked the ground fire, both ack-ack and machine gun. You had to know how to fly a tight formation or you set up dangerous collision conditions. You found yourself in real trouble if you became entangled with a balloon cable or the prop-wash from a machine directly ahead. Becoming involved with prop-wash was very dangerous. One minute you were secure in your proper formation position, the next you were spiralling down with not enough room to pull out.

Dozens of scout pilots went to their finish in this manner.

Carrying out a bomber or photography escort job and doing it right could dredge up a hundred ways of getting yourself in the casualty lists. Again, you were expected to be there on time. You were expected to stay in your protective position, come what may. You were not supposed to be sucked out of the play by the appearance of a piece of Hun bait, all set up to add to your score. One had to put on a reversal of thinking. Rather we had to compute how many planes we brought back over the months, than the number we thought we had shot down.

As stated before, the observation or photography patrol was a two-way proposition. The bomber could go to his target, clobber it for a fare-thee-well, and then be shot down—but he would have fulfilled his mission. The observation pilot must fight to his pin point, get his pictures or information—and still get back. In other words a successful observation show is one that is most colourless. Nothing much has happened! If it *does* get back it owes much to the escort, and if the escorting fighter has been true to his trust, he has simply stayed on the observation plane's tail and taken some of the hate intended for it. That is the only way these missions could be carried to a successful conclusion. Cutting out to shoot down enemy planes but leaving the observation aircraft to its evident fate is poor arithmetic.

If I were asked to name an airman for any roll of honour or reward for invaluable service I would select first Major Kenneth P. Littauer, commanding officer of the U.S. No. 88 Observation Squadron, as my representative of the men who efficiently and faithfully served.

Because of his daring, devotion to duty, and his ability to establish a productive organization he eventually became Chief of the Air Service of the Third U.S. Corps, a promotion and responsibility that was well earned.

Yet, outside of the literary circles of New York City, who has heard of Major Kenneth P. Littauer?

Littauer was first of all a great Corps pilot who could take a trained observer anywhere and bring him back with the information headquarters wanted. When you have written that of a man you can add no more. Littauer was awarded the

French *Croix de guerre* with two palms and the Belgian Chevalier Order of Leopold. America gave him the Distinguished Service Cross. He had served in observation squadrons since early in 1916 when he joined the French Air Service. He flew anything on any type of mission and so far as is known never suffered a scratch.

When the United States entered the war Ken immediately offered his services to his country, although he knew full well he would have to handle untrained men, fly second-best machines, and serve under unimaginative commanders only a few weeks removed from some U.S. cavalry depot. While he was never included with the "ace" glamour lads, Littauer can be bracketed with Major Jimmy McCudden, who also fought in practically every type of squadron and served with brilliant efficiency wherever he was assigned. It was the McCuddens, Littauers, and Barkers who won this first war in the air.

Their kind we shall never know again.

GLOSSARY

Terms In Popular Use By Aviators Of World War I

Ace—Originally a French term first used in 1915 for any fighter pilot who had destroyed five enemy machines. It was later adopted by the U.S. Air Service but not by the British.

Ack-Ack—Front-line expression for anti-aircraft. The letter *a* was pronounced "ack" by signallers to avoid mistakes in transmission. Thus, *a-a* was pronounced ack-ack.

Aerodrome—The original name for any field used for flying. The term was used by the French and British throughout World War I.

Archie—A derisive term for anti-aircraft fire originated by the British.

Art-Obs—Vernacular for artillery-observation.

Aviate—A professional expression for flying: "Let's aviate!"

Balloon—An inflated gasbag used for various military purposes. A kite balloon was tethered by a steel cable to any desired height. It carried a basket below in which two observers stood and watched for enemy movements in the areas behind the trench lines. A system of barrage balloons was used in Great Britain for the defence of London. These were flown linked together by steel cables from which dangled other lengths of loose cable to form a curtain around the city. The idea was to entangle attacking enemy aircraft.

Barrel—Rolling the aircraft over and over in the air—like a barrel.

Besseneau hangar—A canvas-covered shelter large enough to accommodate a flight of six aircraft. It could be taken down or assembled in about three hours.

Biplace—A two-seater aircraft.

Biplane—An aircraft with two sets of wings, one above the other. A triplane has three. A quadruplane four. (There were such machines.)

Blériot—Generic term applied to all early monoplanes after Louis Blériot, who first flew the English Channel in a monoplane of his own design in 1909.

Breeze up—One has a breeze up when he is frightened. A gust up means one is practically scared to death.

Brevet—Originally referred to a commissioned rank in which an officer is given a higher grade than that for which he receives pay. Later it was taken to mean that a student had received his wings and commission at the same time. Thus "brevet" was often understood to mean a man had won his wings.

Brisfit—A term of affection for the Bristol Fighter.

Brolly—A British phrase for an umbrella. During the war it was applied to the parachute by balloon observers. "I went over the side and took to my brolly!"

Bung off!—Trench parlance meaning to get going, clear out, mooch, vamoose, or simply get-the-hell-out-of-here!

Caudron—A French biplane manufactured by the René Caudron Company.

Ceiling—the limit of an aircraft's altitude. When it won't fly any higher, it has obtained its ceiling.

Centre section—A small airfoil set above the fuselage to which the outer wings are bolted.

Chandelle—To go into a corkscrew climb. Often talked about but seldom performed.

Chasse—French for "chaser." All scouts were supposed to be chaser aircraft designed to chase the enemy. Americans later changed this to "pursuit."

Contact—In starting an engine the pilot warns the mechanic when the ignition switch is on by shouting "Contact!" The mechanic then uses caution when he swings or turns the propeller.

Contour chaser—An aircraft specially designed for contour fighting. It is generally armoured below, carries light bombs or grenades, and in some instances has two machine guns set at a downward angle to fire into enemy trenches.

Contour fighting—Engaging enemy troops and defences low down. The pilot follows the contour of the terrain and makes the most of the cover afforded.

Coupez—To "cut" or switch off the ignition after landing. Many of these French terms were adopted by American pilots early in the war because they often had French mechanics to service their planes.

Dawn patrol—The first scheduled duty flight of the day. Usually the least active, since the Germans were notoriously late risers.

Dogfight—A wild aerial mêlée in which dozens of aircraft participate and fight at very close quarters. As a result more planes were lost in mid-air crashes than by the exchange of gunfire. There have been no true dogfights since World War I.

Drachen—The German word for kite balloon.

Dual-control—When a student is flying with an instructor he is said to be under dual-control. When he flies alone he is flying solo.

Dud—Anything that doesn't work. A shell that doesn't explode is a dud. A pilot who can't stay in formation is a dud. Any plane that doesn't fly correctly is a dud.

Dump—Any area used for storing military supplies.

Elevator—The horizontal control surface set on the tail plane to control the up-and-down direction of the nose of the aircraft. Also known as flippers or horizontal controls.

Empennage—The complete tail assembly of an aircraft. It includes the fin, rudder, tail plane, and elevators.

Epaulette—The shoulder strap of a military tunic, jacket, or blouse on which a man's rank or regimental insignia is affixed.

Escadrille—French term for aero squadron.

Essence—French term for gasoline. The British called gasoline petrol, since it was a product of petroleum. Americans called it "juice" or "sauce."

Fee—Familiar term for British F.E.2b pusher plane.

Feldwebel—In the German service a warrant officer. A special rank between noncommissioned and commissioned officers. All the responsibility without the pay.

Flechettes—Small steel darts dropped from an aircraft on massed troops.

Flight—A unit of six planes. A squadron was generally composed of three flights—A, B, and C.

Flight Sergeant—Chief N.C.O. responsible for all mechanics and the aircraft servicing in a flight.

Fourragère—A braided cord decoration worn by members of a military regiment or squadron after the organization has been awarded that honour. Sometimes called an aiguillette.

Free lance—A pilot who elects to fly lone patrols after his regular missions have been completed.

Funk hole—Any handy shelter used to avoid enemy fire—or to evade unpleasant duty.

G.S.—General service. Anything belonging to the British military forces. There were G.S. jackets and G.S. wagons. The British variation of G.I.—general issue.

Glide angle—The shallowest angle a plane will glide in safety after the engine has been switched off.

Gravel crushers—Slang expression for the infantry.

Ground strips—Coloured cloths laid out on the ground by the infantry for signalling purposes. White strips were used at airfields to warn incoming aircraft of certain ground conditions or other emergencies.

Hauptmann—A German aviation rank equivalent to a captain.

Haversack—A bag of heavy web or canvas fitted with a shoulder strap and used by British soldiers for personal gear and rations. Comparable to the French musette bag.

Hisso—Simplification of Hispano-Suiza, a well-known Spanish-French aircraft engine. It was a V-type water-cooled power plant.

Hoik—To pull up sharply from level flight. To zoom.

Hun—A term of contempt for German soldiers or airmen, used chiefly by the British. It was also used in British flying schools derisively for heavy-handed students who broke up more than their share of training aircraft.

Immelmann Turn—A sharp manœuvre in which a plane changes direction by zooming up, turning on its side so that controls are reversed (the rudder becomes the elevator, etc.) and the elevators whip the machine around very fast. Incorrectly credited to Max Immelmann. It was in general use as a stunt or exhibition manœuvre before the outbreak of World War I.

Incidence—The angle at which the wings are set to the line of flight. The angle of incidence determines the aircraft's ability to climb or produce lift.

Jagdgeschwader—A German fighter command. Generally five squadrons.

Jagdstaffel—A fighter squadron. Generally ten aircraft.

Jastaschule—School of air fighting.

Joy rags—Your best uniform reserved for furlough or special occasions.

Joystick—Slang for control column. There is one view that the original control stick which replaced the early wheel control was invented by an Englishman named Joyce. Thus the phrase may have originated as Joyce-stick.

Kanone—German phrase for a fighter pilot who had destroyed ten enemy aircraft.

Keel surface—All aircraft surface seen when viewing the plane from either side.

King post—The short lever above or below a movable surface to which the control cable is attached.

Kiwi—Royal Flying Corps vernacular for any non-flying officer. It alludes to the flightless bird of New Zealand called a kiwi.

Lager—Enemy prison-camp area.

Landing lights—In World War I night landings had to be made with the aid of primitive flares set out along the available landing strip. They were usually discarded oil drums filled with oil-saturated rags which were lighted when a friendly plane signalled its return.

Landing wires—All wires or cable supporting the plane when it lands or stands on the ground. Flying wires take over the support of the plane in the air.

Leading edge—The front edge of a wing or airfoil. The edge that strikes the air first. The rear edge is known as the trailing edge.

Liberty engine—A 12-cylinder water-cooled engine developed in the United States after the declaration of war against Germany in 1917.

Logbook—History of an air pilot's training and war flights.

London Gazette—The official journal of the British government. All commissions, decorations, and awards are gazetted or announced officially in its columns. For instance: "He was gazetted a major."

Longerons—The main structural members running the length of the body or fuselage.

Main spar—Chief structural member of a wing to which all ribs and bracings are attached.

Melinite—A French picric powder about two and a half times as powerful as ordinary gunpowder.

Monocoque—A type of fuselage or aeroplane body in which the main loads in the structure are taken by the skin covering.

Nacelle—A body that encloses either the crew or the engine.

Office—Vernacular of the professional. He always calls his cockpit "the office."

Oleo—The shock-absorbing portion of an undercarriage leg.

Pancaking—Landing the aeroplane slowly so that it drops hard and flat—like a pancake.

Performance—The flying characteristics of an aircraft such as its speed, rate of climb, and seiling.

Pilot tube—An air-inlet tube set outside the cockpit but connected to the air-speed indicator, the pressure from which actuates a diaphragm and indicator needle.

Pocket—There is no such thing as an air pocket. Aircraft in flight may experience violent upward or downward lurches, but these are caused by turbulent air, rising or falling. There are no holes or vacuum spaces in the atmosphere.

Prototype—The first machine of a new type to be built.

Quirk—British slang term for a very new and very unskilled flight student.

Radial engine—An aviation engine with its cylinders arranged radially around a master crankshaft. The cylinders are stationary and the crankshaft revolves.

Rigger—One employed in assembling or servicing the body of the aircraft. A fitter took care of the engine.

Rotary engine—An aviation engine in which the cylinders are set radially around its crankshaft, but in this case all cylinders and the engine shell revolve around the crankshaft.

Sausage—A conical tube of fabric flown over an airfield to indicate the direction of the wind. It was also used to deride the German kite balloons—known as sausage balloons.

Scarffring—A machine-gun mounting used on most Allied two-seaters. It was invented by Warrant Officer Scarff of the Royal Naval Air Service.

Slip stream—The zone of disturbed air noted behind a whirling propeller.

Tarmac—Permanent artificial paving made of tar and macadam. Generally laid down in front of British overseas hangars.

Tractor aeroplane—A machine in which the propeller or propellers are mounted in front of the main support planes.

Zoom—A sudden change of direction upwards.

INDEX

A.B.C. engine, 180
Abeele, 35, 96, 123
Aces, 54
Aces, American, 291, 292, 293
Aces with 20 or more victories:
     Austrian, 296; Belgian,
     296; British, 293, 294;
     French, 295; German,
     297; Italian, 296
A.E.F. (American Expedition-
     ary Force), 249
Aero Club of France, 19, 23
A.G.O., 17
Air cannon, 133, 190, 244
Air gunners, 149
Akron, 283
Albatros, 28, 42, 46, 52, 53,
     226, 266; *D.1:* 105, 113,
     119; *D.2:* 119; *D.3:* 150,
     160, 190, 234; *D.5:* 228
Aldershof Field, 210
Allied Air Training Plan, 176
Allmenroeder, Leutnant Karl,
     152, 155, 203, 224
American Field Service, 132,
     245, 247
American Volunteers, 132
Andreae, Flight Lieutenant F.
     G., 70

Archie, 29, 108, 134
Argus, H.M.S., 17
Armistice, 17, 219, 234, 236,
     258
Armstrong-Whitworth, 216, 218
Arsiad gun gear, 60
Auger, Captain Alfred, 100,
     195
Australian Flying Corps, 234
Australian records, 201
Austrian Air Force, 232
Aviatik, 19, 25, 34, 37, 49, 53,
     95, 101, 119, 135-36
Avord Flying Field, 248
Avro, 21, 27, 70

Babbington, Flight Commander,
     27
Baker, Hoby, 280
Baldarmus, Leutnant Hartmut,
     152
Balkan War, 16
Ball, Albert, 52, 122, 126, 130,
     152-55, 172, 201, 204, 300,
     302
Balsley, H. Clyde, 137
Baraca, Major Francesco, 98
Barker, Major William G., 13-
     15, 231-33, 302, 304

Battle of Britain, 213
Battle of Somme, 114, 126, 129
Battle Squadrons, German (Special Bomber Force), *No. 1*: 37; *No. 3*: 167; *No. 4*: 168; *No. 5*: 168; *No. 6*: 168
Baylies, Sergeant Frank, 245-48
B.E.2c, 22, 66, 81, 91-93, 95, 121, 152, 204; *B.E.8*, 22; *B.E.12a*, 234
B.H.P. engine, 180
Belgium, 21, 95, 98, 168, 193, 215
Ben-My-Chree, H.M.S., 93
Bentley B.R.I., 13
Benz, 17
Bernard-Thierry, Captain, 90
Bettington, Major A. V., 60
Bishop, Major William A., 51, 124-26, 153, 158, 170-76, 279
Black Flight, 223
Bleckley, Lieutenant Erwin R., 286, 299
Blériot, 22, 100
Bloody April, 118, 143, 148, 152, 156, 166, 227
Boelke (Boelcke), Frederick, 87, 88; Hauptmann Oswald, 52, 58, 88-92, 105-09, 112, 114, 115, 118, 137, 158, 162, 177, 211; Wilhelm, 87-91, 112
Bohme, Erwin, 115
Bois de Champion dump, 242
Bolling, Major Raynal C., 255
Bourne, Corporal Walter, 153, 172-75
Boyeau, Lieutenant Maurice, 195, 244
Bozon-Verduraz, Lieutenant, 192-93
Breguet, 30, 167, 242-44, 257
Briggs, Commander, 27
Bristol Bullet, 21
Bristol Fighter, 83, 152, 180, 206, 219, 231, 253, 299; aces, 219

Bristol Scout, 25, 96
Brocard, Major, 100, 192
Brock bullet, 63, 82
Brown, Lieutenant A. Whitten, 238
Brown, Captain Roy, 201, 202
Buckingham bullet, 63
Bulow, Walter von, 93
Bureau of Aircraft Production, 254
Burgess Flying School, 132
Bush, Captain, 158-62, 210

Calahan, Lieutenant Lawrence R., 279
Cambrai, 115, 121, 130, 153, 197, 221, 226
Campbell, Lieutenant Douglas, 257, 275
Canadian Mounted Rifles, 231
Caproni, 241, 258
Caudron, 20
Chambers, Major Reid, 274, 276
Chapman, Sergeant Victor, 134, 182
Château-Thierry, 206, 257, 276
Chatkoff, Herman, 185
Chevalier Order of Leopold, 304
Churchill, Winston Spencer, 27, 172, 176
Claims, German, 212
Clemenceau, Premier Georges, 198
Clement, Captain Carleton, 159, 302
Collishaw, Major Raymond, 223-26
Congressional Medal of Honor, 259, 277, 286, 288, 299
Constantinesco, George, 61, 65
Cooper bombs, 198, 213, 217, 220, 284
Coppens, Willy, 52, 98
Courtney, Squadron Commander I. T., 70, 71
Cowdin, Elliot C., 51, 134, 182
Crawford, Captain Linke, 232

Creech, Jesse, 280
Croix de guerre, 183, 185, 223, 248, 304
Cross of Hohenzollern, 208
Cross of St. George, 189
Crowe, Captain, 154
Curtis, Fraser, 132-33
Curtiss, Jenny, 181, 253, 254; plant, 181; OX5 engine, 253

D.F.W., 17, 228
Davison, F. Trubee, 283
Dean, Adjutant General H. T., 184
D.H.2: 97, 112-16, 121-22, 129-30, 152, 164; *D.H.4:* 62, 237, 253; *D.H.9:* 236, 252, 285
De Laage de Meux, Lieutenant, 134, 138, 190
Demoiselle monoplane, 44
Deniken, General, 225
Deperdussin monoplane, 94
Deullin, Captain, 100, 192
Diary of an Unknown Aviator, 279
Dibovsky, Lieutenant Colonel V. V., 60
Dietrichs, Fritz, 42
Distinguished Conduct Medal (British), 150, 202
Distinguished Flying Cross (British), 202, 225, 286
Distinguished Service Cross (British), 202, 225
Distinguished Service Cross (American), 259, 269, 283, 304
Distinguished Service Medal (American), 285
Distinguished Service Order (British), 84, 129-30, 153, 173, 222, 225
Division of Military Aeronautics, 254
Dorme, Lieutenant René, 100, 119, 142, 190

Dostler, Oberleutnant Edward, 165
Douai, 58, 90, 91, 107, 112, 114, 121, 157, 159
Doumer, Captain René, 189
Dover, 21, 37
Dugan, Lieutenant William, 186
Dunkirk, 69
Düsseldorf, 26

Eagle of Lille, 109
Eastern Air Lines, 272
Eindekker, 105, 108
Estrée-Blanche, 222
Euler (L.V.G.), 17
Explosive bullet, 14, 182

Farman aircraft: Horace, biplane, 67; Longhorn, 22; Maurice, biplane, 24; Shorthorn, 21, 22, 38, 80
Farman, Henri, 91
F.E.2b (Fee), 64, 106, 109, 121, 122, 150, 159, 169, 204, 211, 236
First Canadian Division, 215
First Corps Observation Group, 257
Flaming Coffin, 252
Fleet Air Arm, 225
Flying Circus, 14, 83
Flying Fury, 124, 165
Foch, Marshal Ferdinand, 214
Fokker aeroplanes, 130, 249; *D.5:* 191; *D.7:* 206, 225, 229, 230, 232, 233, 235, 243, 268, 285; *E.1:* 55-59, 90, 105; triplane, 166-67, 201, 228, 232
Fokker, Anthony, 55-59, 87, 91, 119, 229, 277
Fokker fixed gun, 105, 108
Fokker Fodder, 55
Fonck, Captain René, 190, 194-95, 243
Fort Garry Horse, 216
Foulois General Benjamin D., 253-55

French Air Service, 19, 37, 195, 244-45

French Foreign Legion, 132, 137, 184

French Naval Air Service, 187, 241

Friedrichshafen *A.2A*, 210

Furious, H.M.S., 60

Garros, Roland, 42-55, 59, 66-70, 80, 105

Gaskell, Lieutenant Penn, 33

Gastin, Captain Paul, 189

Genet, Edmond, 184

George V, King, 79, 172, 286

German Air Force, 17, 29, 148, 152, 154-55, 164, 169, 199, 205, 212

Giallet, Sub-lieutenant, 188

Gibbons, Floyd, 158

Gilbert, Eugene, 46-51

Goering, Oberleutnant Hermann, 52, 116-19, 163, 165, 199, 212

Goettler, Lieutenant Harold E., 286, 299

Gontermann, Leutnant Heinrich, 166-67

Gordon-Kidd, Lieutenant A. L., 128

Gotha, 95, 167-69, 198, 242

Gower, Lieutenant W. C., 169

Grahame-White, Flight Commander Claude, 70

Grange, Flight Lieutenant E. R., 170

Grant, Captain Alfred A., 206, 264-65, 269

Grant-Dalton, Captain S., 129

Graves, Major C., 170

Grey, Charles G., 32

Grey, Commander Spenser, 26, 73, 74, 79

Grider, Lieutenant John, 279

Gros, Dr. Edmund, 133

Guillemin, General, 186-87

Gunn, Lieutenant Malcolm, 260

Guynemer, Captain Georges, 51, 67, 98-102, 119, 139-42, 190-95, 201

Haig, General Sir Douglas, 198

Halberstadt, 105, 119, 120, 141, 165, 228, 229, 243, 268, 276

Hales bomb, 121

Hall, Lieutenant Bert, 134, 182

Hall, Captain James Norman, 184

Hammond, Lieutenant A. W., 216-19

Handley-Page, 180, 213, 237-38, 299

Hannoveraner, 178, 181, 228, 230

Hartney, Colonel Harold E., 262-64, 267-70

Harvey-Kelley, Lieutenant H. D., 19, 22

Hauss, Marechal des Logis, 190

Hawker, Major George Lanoe, 52, 94-97, 116

Heinecke parachute, 164, 206

Heinemann, Rudolph, 109

Henderson, Brigadier General Sir David, 21

Hesler, Leutnant von, 93

Heurteaux, Captain Albert, 51, 98, 142, 190, 192

Hindenburg line, 148

Hirschauer, General, 133

Hispano-Suiza engine, 142, 253

Hispano-Suiza one-pounder air cannon, 67

Hitler, Adolph, 238

Hoeppner, Air Commander von, 168

Holden, Lansing, 280

Holland, 26

Home Establishment, 14, 227

Hoover, Herbert, 283

Hotchkiss machine gun, 24, 49-51, 53, 65, 166

Hounslow aerodrome, 14, 232, 243

Houthulst Foret, 96, 143, 209

Hudson's Bay Company, 215, 226

Huskinson, Flight Lieutenant B. L., 70

Immelmann, Max, 52, 59, 90, 91, 105, 108-12, 302

Incendiary bomb, 26

Independent Air Force, 213, 237, 238

Indianapolis-500 Race, 272

Ingalls, Ensign David S., 283-86

Iron Cross, 29, 87, 89, 91, 117, 164, 210

Issoudun, 261, 273

Italian Air Service, 98

Italian Front, 232

Jagdgeschwader *1:* 209, 242

Jagdgeschwader *3:* 165

Jagdstaffel *2:* 112, 114

Jagdstaffel *26:* 164

Jane's *All the World's Aircraft,* 181

Kanone, 54, 197, 209

Kenley, General William L., 255

Key, Lieutenant Reginald, 216-17

King, Captain R., 233-34

Kirchstein, Hans, 210, 217-18

Kite balloons, 29

Klemm, Leutnant Willi, 265

Kluck, von, 28

Krupps, 19, 29, 188

Kurtz, Lieutenant, 274-75

Lafayette Escadrille. *See* Squadrons

La Guardia, Captain Fiorello H., 258

Lahm, Colonel Frank P., 256

Leckie, Captain Robert, 79

Leefe-Robinson, Lieutenant W., 79-83

Leffers, Leutnant Gustave, 124

Legion of Honour, 38, 53, 79, 102, 139, 186

Le Prieur rocket, 65, 130

Le Rhone engine, 41

Letord bomber, 188

Lewis, Captain Cecil, 154

Lewis machine gun, 16, 35, 60-61, 95, 100, 123, 300

Liberty engine, 180, 253

Lindbergh, Charles A., 248

Linnarz, Hauptmann Carl, 72-76

Littauer, Major Kenneth P., 303

Loening fighter, 180

Loerzer, Hauptmann Bruno, 52, 117-19, 163-64

Lost Battalion, 286

Loughead, 181

Lowenhardt, Oberleutnant Erich, 199, 211

Lufbery Circle, 83

Lufbery, Raoul, 46, 137-39, 181, 183, 186, 245, 248, 260, 273, 288

Luftwaffe, 116, 212, 214

Luke, Lieutenant Frank, 158, 259-72, 286, 302

L.V.G., 90, 102, 130, 140, 167, 190, 208, 227-28

Lyautey, General, 186

MacLaren, Major Donald, 226, 272

McConnell, Sergeant James R., 134, 182-83

McCudden, Major James B., 24, 51, 123-26, 165, 173, 177-78, 228, 301, 304

McElroy, Captain G. E. H., 227-31

McKeever, Major Andrew E., 51, 219-22

McLeod, Lieutenant Alan A., 215-19

Madon, Lieutenant Georges, 38, 39, 189-90, 195, 241

Mannock, Major Edward C., 125-26, 157-58, 171, 300

March Push, 197, 206

Marechal, Lieutenant Pierre Antoine, 66, 144

Marix, Flight Lieutenant R. L. G., 26-27

Martin bomber, 181

Martinsyde, 34

Martinsyde Elephant, 128

Mathy, Commander Heinrich, 84-85

Maubeuge, 22, 29, 33

Mauser factory, 241

Maxim gun, 50, 65

May, Lieutenant W. R., 201-03

Maybach engine, 73, 76

Meates, Lieutenant B. C., 70

Médaille Militaire, 38, 101, 141, 188

Meintjes, Captain, 154

Meissner, Major James A., 275, 288-89

Melinite bomb, 95

Mercedes engine, 17, 115, 119

Meynard, Captain, 39

Military Cross, 28, 122, 129, 173, 219, 221, 226, 228

Military Medal, 150, 186

Miller, Captain A. M., 127-28

Miller, Captain James E., 260

Mills, Sub-lieutenant, 74-76

Mitchell, General William, 200, 237, 254-58, 267

Morane Bullet, 41, 44, 53, 59, 80

Morane Parasol, 21, 35-36, 47, 73-75

Morse, Thomas, Scout, 180

Mottershead, Sergeant Thomas, 169

Muenchoff, Sergeant, 266

Mulock, Lieutenant R. H., 73-74, 223

National Guard Air Squadron, 288

Navarre, Lieutenant Jean, 139-40, 302

Nieuport Scouts, 19, 50, 66, 100, 119, 122, 132, 137, 138, 170, 230, 253

Nungesser (Nungessor), Captain Charles, 98, 140-42, 190, 195, 241, 243, 302

Oberursel engine, 56, 93, 109

P.B.O. (Poor Bloody Observers), 125, 150

Packard, 181

Parabellum gun, 34, 53, 56, 77, 91, 93, 95, 118

Paris, 80, 90, 184, 203, 215, 255, 268, 276

Parsons, Lieutenant Edwin C., 183, 247

Patrick, Brigadier General Mason M., 255

Paulus parachute, 164, 210

Pershing, General John J., 252, 254-55, 273

Pfalz, 221, 226, 241, 243, 275, 281

Pilots' pool, 216

Pinsard, Armand, 39, 46-48, 66-67, 190, 195

Poison gas, 30

Pomeroy bullet, 64, 82

Pom-pom (gun), 64

Pour le mérite, 107, 114, 164, 166, 205, 212

Powell, Sergeant L. F., 220-22

Prince, Sergeant Norman, 51, 132-39, 181, 182

Putnam, Lieutenant David E., 245, 248-49

Pyott, Captain J. V., 79, 85

R.E.2 (Reconnaissance Experimental), 21; *R.E.5:* 94; *R.E.8:* 203, 211, 231, 246

Red Knight of Germany, 158

Rees, Major L.M.B., 129

Reinhardt, Hauptmann Wilhelm, 208, 210

Reinhold, Oberleutnant, 166, 190

Rhodes-Moorhouse, Lieutenant W. B., 24, 30-32

Rhys-Davids, Lieutenant Albert, 165, 301

Richthofen, Oberleutnant Lothar von, 152, 155, 162, 203, 205

Richthofen, Baron Manfred F. von, 51, 65, 113-16, 151, 155-59, 162, 163, 170, 200-04, 209

Rickenbacker, Captain Edward Vernon, 51, 158, 257, 261, 268, 272-78, 286, 288-89

Robinson, Sergeant Robert Guy, 287

Rockwell, Sergeant Kiffin Yates, 134-37, 181-82

Roland, 123, 130

Rolls Royce, 180

Roosevelt, Lieutenant Quentin, 260

Rosher, Flight-Lieutenant, 70

Royal Aero Club, 235

Royal Aircraft Factory, 22

Royal Air Force, 16, 198, 200, 213-14, 225, 238

Royal Army Medical Corps., 125

Royal Canadian Air Force, 225, 234

Royal Engineers, 126

Royal Flying Corps, 16, 20, 29, 60, 63, 69, 150, 201

Royal Garrison Artillery, 227

Royal Naval Air Service, 26, 37, 60, 64, 70, 73, 133, 223

Royce, Major Ralph, 256

R.T.S. bullet, 64

Rumpler, 17-19, 25, 33, 46, 93, 96, 118, 190, 191, 228, 284

Ryan, John D., 254

Salmond, General W. G. H., 198

Salmson biplane, 253, 262

Samson, Wing Commander C. R., 26

Santos-Dumont, Alberto, 43, 44

Scarff-Dibovsky gear, 60

Scarff mounting, 218

Schaeffer, Leutnant Karl, 152

Schutte-Lanz airships, 18, 80

Scott Expedition, 223

Scottish troops, 15, 233

S.E.5: 142, 152-53, 157 189, 230, 280, 300

Sherwood Foresters, 122

Short seaplane, 93

Signal Corps, 16, 253

Sopwith aircraft: Baby Seaplane, 93; Camel, 61, 142, 153, 157, 201-02, 205, 207, 231, 280, 283; Pup, 59-60, 223; 1½-Strutter, 59, 113, 121; Snipe, 13, 208, 230, 232, 233; Tabloid, 26; Triplane, 120, 157, 223

Sopwith-Kauper gear, 60, 65

Sopwith, T. O. M., 235

Soubiran, Captain Robert, 186

Sowrey, Lieutenant Frederick, 79, 84

Spad, 67, 141-42, 189-90, 192, 244, 247, 253, 260, 262, 300

Spandau gun, 14, 65

Sportsmen's Battalion, 72

Springs, Captain Elliott White, 278-80

Squadrons: Australia
  No. 1: 234
  No. 2: 234

Squadrons (Escadrilles):
  France
  Américaine, 133, 135
  Lafayette, 137-38, 182, 184-85, 245, 258
  No. 3 S, 141. See also Storks
  No. 11 C., 185
  No. 23 M.S., 46, 145
  No. 24 F., 185
  No. 25 F., 187
  No. 46 C., 187
  No. 68: 142
  No. 83: 142

No. 101 V.B., 133
No. 102 V.B., 187
No. 103 S., 142, 241
No. 108 V.B., 133
No. 113 V.B., 133
No. 218 M.S., 39
Squadrons (Sections): Germany
No. 28: 208
No. 62: 91
No. 205: 208
Squadrons (Staffels). Germany
No. 4: 206, 211
No. 5: 118, 166
No. 6: 165, 209, 218
No. 10: 165, 211
No. 11: 152, 162, 206, 209, 211, 224
No. 15: 166, 190
Squadrons: Great Britain
No. 2: 21, 216-17
No. 3: 21, 22, 25, 29, 51, 60
No. 4: 21, 60, 121, 231
No. 5: 21, 25
No. 6: 34, 94
No. 8: 60
No. 9: 60, 231
No. 11: 122
No. 13: 60, 122
No. 15: 231
No. 20: 122, 169
No. 22: 149, 150, 220
No. 24: 96, 97, 115-16, 149, 170, 228
No. 25: 109, 122
No. 27: 128
No. 28: 231
No. 29: 203
No. 32: 129
No. 39: 80, 82
No. 40: 157, 227
No. 43: 214
No. 46: 60
No. 48: 61, 83
No. 54: 60
No. 55: 61, 236
No. 56: 61, 153, 165, 173, 178
No. 60: 127, 130, 153, 170, 172, 178

No. 66: 60, 232
No. 84: 225, 281
No. 85: 279
No. 99: 236
No. 100: 237
No. 104: 236
No. 166: 238
No. 201: 13, 214, 232
No. 203: 225
No. 209: 201
No. 213: 284
No. 216: 236
No. 218: 287
No. 1 (Naval), 70, 73, 79, 121
No. 3 (Naval), 223
No. 8 (Naval), 170
No. 10 (Naval), 223
No. 13 (Naval), 225
Squadrons: United States
No. 1 Aero, 256
No. 50 Aero, 286
No. 1 Aviation Brigade, 256
No. 96 Day Bombardment, 257
No. 88 Observation, 303
No. 17 Pursuit, 281, 284
No. 27 Pursuit, 206, 262, 264, 268
No. 94 Pursuit, 256, 274, 277, 280, 288
No. 95 Pursuit, 256, 273
No. 103 Pursuit, 186
No. 148 Pursuit, 258, 280
No. 1 Pursuit Group, 186, 256, 262, 277
No. 3 Pursuit Group 186
Standard Aircraft Corporation, 180
Strange, Lieutenant Colonel A. G., 32-35
Strategic Air Command, 237
Storks, 39, 98, 100, 189, 194, 246
Sunbeam Motors, 180, 272

Talbot, Lieutenant Ralph, 190
Tanks, 15, 199

Taplin, Lieutenant L. T. E., 233-35

Taube planes, 17

Tempelhof Field, 17

Tempest, Lieutenant L. W. J., 79, 85

Tennant, Captain J. E., 121

Thaw, Lieutenant Colonel William, 134, 182, 186

Thenault, Captain Georges, 134-35, 184

Toul, 257, 274

Tracer bullets, 62

Trenchard, General Hugh, 106, 120, 129, 171, 198, 200, 235-38, 242, 254

U-boats, 242

Udet, Oberleutnant Ernst, 52, 199, 205-08

United States Aviation Service, 139, 185-86, 200, 237, 246, 251, 255, 257, 260, 276, 279

United States Contribution (men and money), 251

United States Marines, 287

United States Navy, 179

United States War Department, 252

Vanderbilt Cup, 272

Vasconcelles, Captain Jerry, 260, 264, 269-70

Vaughn, Major George A., Jr., 280-82

Vedrines, Jules, 46, 100

Verdun, 107, 113, 136, 143, 209, 246, 268

Very signal flare, 83

Vickers company, 60-61

Vickers Gunbus, 106, 113

Vickers machine gun, 13, 61, 300

Vickers Vimy bomber, 238

Victoria Cross, 15, 24, 79-81, 96, 129, 155, 171, 173, 176, 215, 219, 231, 233

Vieux Charles, 190, 192, 194

Voisin, 16, 23, 93, 106-07, 132, 133, 143

Vosges, 132, 134, 144, 183

Voss, Leutnant Werner, 151, 165, 301

Vought, 181

Waller, Corporal J. H., 52, 110, 111

Warneford, Flight Lieutenant R. A. J., 52, 72, 74-80

War planes: Great Britain, 23-24, 87, 130-31, 178-79, 238-40; France, 20, 103, 145, 195, 244-45; Germany, 17-18, 94, 120, 169, 213

Wehner, Lieutenant Joseph, 260, 262-66

Wilhelm, Kaiser, 88, 107

Wilson, Lieutenant J. P., 74-76

Wilson, Woodrow, 184, 254

Wolff, Oberleutnant Kurt, 152, 165, 167

Woodward, Benjamin, 185

Woolwich Arsenal, 81, 227

Wright biplane, 16, 251

Wright Brothers, 43

Ypres, 30, 71

Zeppelin casualties, 83

Zeppelin, Count Ferdinand von, 17

Zeppelin Giant, 168

Zeppelin raids, 18, 26, 29, 63, 66, 69, 71-74, 79, 81-83, 85-86

Zeppelins: *L. 21:* 84; *L. 31:* 84, 85; *L. 32:* 84; *L. 33:* 84; *LZ. 37:* 77-78; *LZ. 38:* 73, 76; *SL. 11:* 84

Zinn, Frederick W., 185

Zone of Advance, 253